TRANSFORMATION BY FIRE

AMERIND STUDIES IN ANTHROPOLOGY

SERIES EDITOR **JOHN WARE**

Transformation by Fire

The Archaeology of Cremation in Cultural Context

Edited by **Ian Kuijt**, **Colin P. Quinn**, and **Gabriel Cooney**

THE UNIVERSITY OF
ARIZONA PRESS

TUCSON

The University of Arizona Press
www.uapress.arizona.edu

We respectfully acknowledge the University of Arizona is on the land and
territories of Indigenous peoples. Today, Arizona is home to twenty-two federally
recognized tribes, with Tucson being home to the O'odham and the Yaqui. The
university strives to build sustainable relationships with sovereign Native Nations
and Indigenous communities through education offerings, partnerships, and
community service.

ISBN-13: 978-0-8165-3114-1 (cloth)
ISBN-13: 978-0-8165-5548-2 (paper)
ISBN-13: 978-0-8165-9870-0 (ebook)

Cover designed by Miriam Warren
Cover illustration from *The Cremation of Sam McGee*, written by Robert W.
Service and illustrated by Ted Harrison. Used by permission of Kids Can Press
Ltd., Toronto. Illustrations © 1986 Ted Harrison.

Library of Congress Cataloging-in-Publication Data
Transformation by fire : the archaeology of cremation in cultural context / edited
by Ian Kuijt, Colin P. Quinn, and Gabriel Cooney.
     pages cm — (Amerind studies in anthropology)
   Includes bibliographical references and index.
   ISBN 978-0-8165-3114-1 (cloth : alkaline paper)
   1. Human remains (Archaeology) 2. Cremation—Social aspects—History—
To 1500. 3. Funeral rites and ceremonies—History—To 1500. 4. Social
archaeology. 5. Ethnoarchaeology. 6. Ethnology. I. Kuijt, Ian. II. Quinn,
Colin P. III. Cooney, Gabriel.
   CC79.5.H85T73 2014
   393'.2—dc23

2014000130

Printed in the United States of America
♾ This paper meets the requirements of ANSI/NISO Z39.48-1992
(Permanence of Paper).

CONTENTS

ACKNOWLEDGMENTS

Surprisingly little research has explored the archaeological context of cremation in the Old and New Worlds. Recognizing this gap, over the years we have discussed the need for a broader comparative discussion of cremation. This book is a first step in this process. It emerged from a larger session at the Society for American Archaeology's annual conference held in Sacramento, California, in April 2011. We are very grateful to John O'Shea, Museum of Anthropology, University of Michigan, for taking on the role of discussant in the session. O'Shea's comments and support helped to steer the subsequent development and publication of the volume.

After review, the session was selected for the Amerind Foundation award for the best conference session at the Sacramento SAA conference. This led to a professional workshop seminar with the participants at the Amerind Foundation, Dragoon, Arizona, in November 2011. The purpose of the seminar was to assist with the development of the original conference session and to synthesize the results as a volume in the Amerind Studies in Anthropology Series, published by the University of Arizona Press. We greatly appreciate the understanding of colleagues who contributed to the original session but could not be included in the volume due to the need for an international and geographical balance. The opportunity to use the Amerind seminar facilities and the hospitality of the Amerind Foundation were critical in shaping the content and approach of the volume. The setting and time for discussion allowed us to tease out points of complementarity between different contributors, as well as to identify issues that needed more discussion and elaboration. We are very grateful to John A. Ware, executive director of the Amerind Foundation, and Barbara Henson, seminar house coordinator, as well as all the staff at the Foundation for all their support and assistance during the seminar and in facilitating the travel arrangements of the participants.

As executive director, John has been a constant source of support and encouragement for the project since the initial involvement of the foundation. He also proved a vital link in our discussions with the University of Arizona Press. At the University of Arizona Press, Allyson Carter, editor in chief, and Scott De Herrera, editorial assistant, were both patient and extremely helpful in getting the volume over the line. We are very pleased to acknowledge our gratitude to them, to Kathryn Conrad, director of the UA Press, and to Sally Bennett Boyington and Amanda Krause for their sharp eyes and clear minds in copyediting and revisions. Our thanks also to Brendan O'Brien for undertaking the onerous task of compiling the index for the volume.

The development and publication were supported by several institutions. Ian Kuijt would like to acknowledge the Office of the Dean of Arts and Letters, University of Notre Dame, for travel and funding support to co-organize the original conference session, as well as logistical support from the Department of Anthropology, University of Notre Dame. Colin Quinn would like to thank the University of Michigan Rackham Graduate School for financial support to co-organize the original session, as well as support from the faculty, students, and staff of the University of Michigan Museum of Anthropological Archaeology and Collaborative Archaeology Workgroup. Gabriel Cooney is pleased to acknowledge the support of the College of Arts and Celtic Studies, University College Dublin, in assisting with the costs of travel and co-organizing the SAA conference session and is grateful to his colleagues in the UCD School of Archaeology for support and advice.

We would also like to warmly thank Ted Harrison, the Canadian artist, for permission to reproduce his painting, *The Cremation of Sam McGee*.

Finally and most importantly, our thanks as editors have to go to our colleagues who contributed to the volume. The background and development of the volume outlined above created a collaborative context, with contributors actively involved not just through their individual contributions but also in shaping the overall direction and tone of the book. The editors and the volume itself greatly benefited from their active involvement. We are also appreciative of their patience with editorial demands and deadlines!

TRANSFORMATION BY FIRE

Introduction

Contextualizing Cremations

Colin P. Quinn, Ian Kuijt, and Gabriel Cooney

> There are strange things done in the midnight sun
> By the men who moil for gold;
> The Arctic trails have their secret tales
> That would make your blood run cold;
> The Northern Lights have seen queer sights,
> But the queerest they ever did see
> Was that night on the marge of Lake Lebarge
> I cremated Sam McGee.
> —R. W. Service, "The Cremation of Sam McGee"

Cremation is an important, widespread, and often overlooked means of dealing with death, the body, and the social world. On a material level, cremation provides a means of fragmenting the body and creating a new form of human remains. But cremations also serve as venues where concepts of person and body, individual and community, and life and death are challenged, negotiated, and constructed. The highly sensory experience of witnessing the physical transformation of the body creates a social context in which the ephemeral nature of identities and social constructs is laid bare. Written in 1907, the Robert Service poem "The Cremation of Sam McGee" engages the reader to confront the sensory realities and emotional tensions of cremation. Service's poetic narrative plays on the contrast between hot and cold as well as the potential discomfort and fear of witnessing the transformation of the familiar human form to bare bones and ash, both of which were situated in the world of the Victorian and Edwardian British Empire, where inhumation was the dominant mortuary rite. Service uses humor to tap into the visceral discomfort of people in the Western world with the transformation of the body in cremations. This poem underscores the sights and smells, the social rights and obligations, and the perspectives of life and death that are all present when fire and the body are combined. The emotional tensions and spiritual challenges experienced by the characters in the poem parallel the intellectual tensions and evidentiary complexities posed by the archaeological study of cremation. In introducing the reader to the topic of cremation in this chapter, we frame our discussion around Service's poem and follow Sam's journey, through places and spaces and from life to death and life again, throughout this chapter.

What Is Cremation?

On a Christmas Day we were mushing our way over the Dawson trail.
Talk of your cold! through the parka's fold it stabbed like a driven nail.
If our eyes we'd close, then the lashes froze till sometimes we couldn't see;
    It wasn't much fun, but the only one to whimper was Sam McGee.

And that very night, as we lay packed tight in our robes beneath the snow,
And the dogs were fed, and the stars o'erhead were dancing heel and toe,
    He turned to me, and "Cap," says he, "I'll cash in this trip, I guess;
    And if I do, I'm asking that you won't refuse my last request."

Well, he seemed so low that I couldn't say no; then he says with
a sort of moan:
"It's the cursèd cold, and it's got right hold, till I'm chilled clean through
to the bone.
Yet 'tain't being dead—it's my awful dread of the icy grave that pains;
So I want you to swear that, foul or fair, you'll cremate my last remains."
            —R. W. Service, "The Cremation of Sam McGee"

Defining cremation is not easy or straightforward. As an authoritative source, *The Encyclopedia of Cremation* (edited by Davies and Mates) represents an ambitious interdisciplinary collaborative project designed to integrate a broad account of the nature of cremation across time through many different societies (Davies and Mates 2005:xvii). In light of its length of nearly five hundred pages, therefore, the fact that there is no entry for *cremation* itself is surprising. In fact, the editors do not provide an explicit definition of cremation in the introduction, instead framing their discussion around basic principles: "In cremation, fire combines with death not simply as some mechanical technique of corpse combustion, even though at certain times and in certain cultures that industrial image may predominate, but also as a value-laden and socially grounded means of coping with death and reflecting upon the meaning of life" (Davies and Mates 2005:xvii).

Echoing this, we believe that the complexities within cremations, as material remains and social practices with deep histories and global extents, preclude a restrictive definition of *cremation*. In this volume we start with a simple premise: *cremation is the combination of fire and the body*. As can be seen throughout the volume, this broad categorization subsumes an incredible amount of variability in material remains, practice, and meaning. As researchers begin to understand such variability and the range of practices, purposes, and meanings of cremation, we gain a clearer insight into cremation as a social process.

It is important to keep in mind that cremation is linked with, yet distinct from, other funerary practices (see Williams, chap. 5, this volume). Archaeologists must develop and employ analytical and theoretical techniques that study both the specific unique aspects of cremation and the larger context of mortuary practices within which cremation is one of many possible choices. While the study of cremation has deep roots within mortuary archaeology (e.g., Beck 2005; Binford 1971:25; O'Shea 1995; Parker Pearson 1982; Rakita and Buikstra 2005), surprisingly little research has considered the coexistence of cremation and inhumation, the comingling of burnt and unburnt bone, and the factors and processes that blur the distinction between cremation and inhumation. At the same time, cremations pose a unique set of social, economic, and archaeological circumstances that necessitate theorization that is distinct from other ways of treating the body (see Oestigaard 1999; T. Sørensen 2009; Sørensen and Bille 2008; Williams 2008a).

The complexities of cremations, and the diverse contexts in which cremations are found, make clear and restrictive definitions of cremation extremely difficult (see Quinn et al., chap. 1, this volume). *Cremation* refers to both an archaeological phenomenon (burnt human remains recovered from archaeological contexts) and a social process (a range of practices from death to deposition). As a social process, cremation can refer only to the act of burning the corpse (McKinley 1997:130) or to the wider range of practices and movements involving burning, the living, and the dead (see Downes 1999; Cerezo-Román, chap. 8, and Goldstein and Meyers, chap. 11, this volume). In its wider application, the cremation process involves multiple nodes of activity (i.e., locations where mortuary acts take place) and pathways of the body (i.e., routes of movement of the body from death to entry into the archaeological record). This approach allows researchers to consider different stages of the process, including the roles of different rituals, actors, and participants; the diverse purposes or place of participants within these rituals; and how these actions are likely to be materialized differently in the archaeological record. The reasons why people chose to cremate, how people were selected to be cremated, and who organized the cremation are all key, and largely unexplored and undertheorized, topics.

Cremation in a Global Context

Cremation has a long history in human culture and was employed in a range of geographic and cultural contexts (see Kroeber 1927) (figure I.1, table I.1). One of the earliest dated cremations (circa 30,000 BP) comes from Lake Mungo in Australia (Bowler et al. 1970). Recent work has identified evidence of cremation in Paleo-Indian North America (Potter et al. 2011). Other examples of cremation from around the world spanning the past ten thousand years include Mesoamerica (e.g., Duncan et al. 2008), the Pacific Islands (Scott et al. 2010), and China (Fengming 2005), to name just a few.

Because of prevailing ideologies of the afterlife in Western societies, however, cremation was rarely practiced in Europe and North America in the historical periods prior to the mid-nineteenth century. From the mid-nineteenth century on, there has been a movement in Western societies, against a complex background of social change, to establish cremation as a legal and socially acceptable mortuary practice (Davies and Mates 2005:xviii–xix). In many areas of the world, the expanded adoption of cremation was encouraged as a social reform to improve public health (e.g., Rosen 2004; Davies and Mates 2005:xix). Over the course of the twentieth century, changing mores, increasing tolerance by different religions, and in many cases a favorable cost differential when compared to inhumation facilitated the broader acceptance and adoption of cremation.

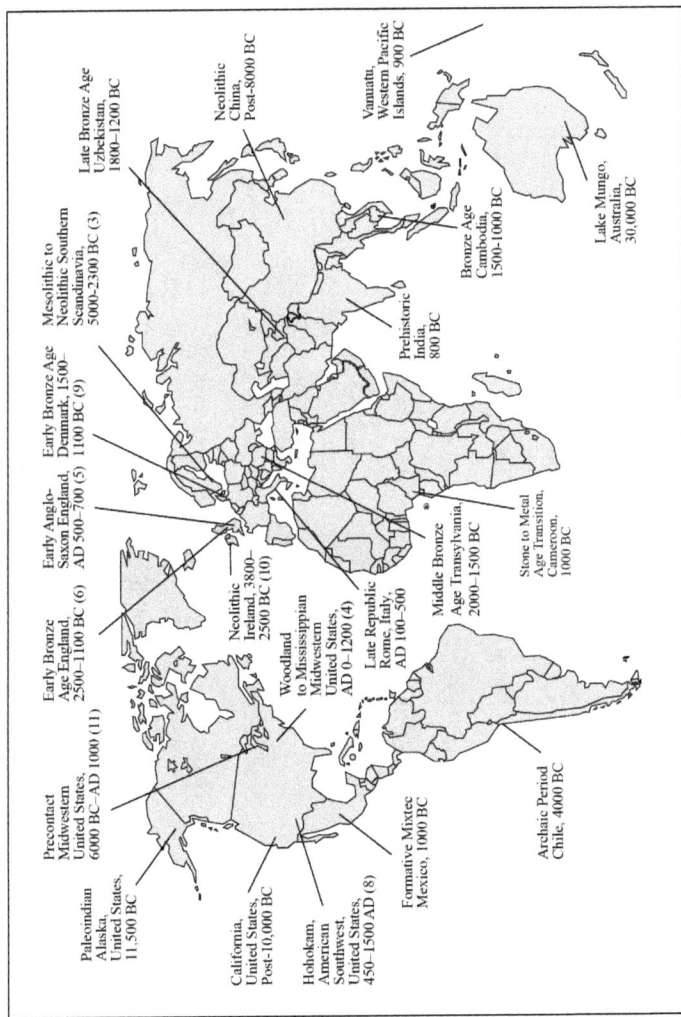

Figure I.1. Select examples of the cultural and temporal contexts of cremation in the Old and New World. Case studies in this volume are indicated by chapter number in parentheses, and additional detail is provided in table I.1. Note that this listing is not comprehensive and is largely focused on prehistoric rather than contemporary case studies.

Labels on the map:

Neolithic China, Post-8000 BC

Vanuatu, Western Pacific Islands, 900 BC

Late Bronze Age Uzbekistan, 1800–1200 BC

Neolithic Southern Scandinavia, 5000–2300 BC (3)

Early Bronze Age Denmark, 1500–1100 BC (9)

Early Anglo-Saxon England, AD 500–700 (5)

Early Bronze Age England, 2500–1100 BC (11)

Mesolithic to Neolithic

Bronze Age Cambodia, 1500–1000 BC

Lake Mungo, Australia, 30,000 BC

Prehistoric India, 800 BC

Neolithic Ireland, 3800–2500 BC (10)

Woodland to Mississippian Midwestern United States, AD 0–1200 (4)

Late Republic Rome, Italy, AD 100–500

Middle Bronze Age Transylvania, 2000–1500 BC

Stone to Metal Age Transition, Cameroon, 1000 BC

Precontact Midwestern United States, 6000 BC–AD 1000 (11)

Paleoindian Alaska, United States, 11,500 BC

California, United States, Post-10,000 BC

Hohokam, American Southwest, United States, 450–1500 AD (8)

Formative Mixtec Mexico, 1000 BC

Archaic Period Chile, 4000 BC

Table I.1. Select Old and New World examples of the cultural and temporal contexts of cremation

Location	Cultural context	Period	Source
England	Early Anglo-Saxon	AD 500–700	Williams, chap. 5, this volume
Italy	Late Republic Rome	AD 100–500	Adkins and Adkins 1999
India	Prehistory	800 BC	Peregrine and Ember 2001
Vanuatu, Pacific Islands	Prehistory	900 BC	Scott et al. 2010
Cameroon	Stone to Metal Age transition	1000 BC	Lavachery 2001
Cambodia	Bronze Age	1500–1000 BC	Higham 2009
Denmark	Early Bronze Age	1500–1100 BC	Sørensen, chap. 9, this volume
Uzbekistan	Late Bronze Age	1800–1200 BC	Kuzmina 2008
England	Early Bronze Age	2500–1100 BC	Brück, chap. 6, this volume
Romania	Middle Bronze Age	2000–1500 BC	Boroffka 1994
Ireland	Neolithic	3800–2500 BC	Cooney, chap. 10, this volume
Southern Scandinavia	Mesolithic to Neolithic	5000–2300 BC	Larsson and Nilsson Stutz, chap. 3, this volume
China	Neolithic	8000 BC	Fengming 2005
Australia	Lake Mungo	30,000 BC	Bowler et al. 1970

Old World

Table I.1. (continued)

	Location	Cultural context	Period	Source
New World	Arizona, United States	Hohokam	AD 450–1500	Cerezo-Román, chap. 8, this volume
	Midwestern United States	Middle Woodland to Mississippian	AD 0–1200	Schurr and Cook, chap. 4, this volume
	Mexico	Formative Mixtec	1000 BC	Duncan et al. 2008
	Chile	Archaic	4000 BC	Santoro et al. 2005
	Midwestern United States	Precontact	6000 BC–AD 1000 AD	Goldstein and Meyers, chap. 11, this volume
	California, United States	Prehistory	Post-10,000 BC	Duke 2006
	Alaska, United States	Paleo-Indian	11,500 BC	Potter et al. 2011

Note: The locations of these case studies are noted in figure I.1. This listing is not comprehensive and is largely focused on prehistoric rather than contemporary use of cremation.

The recent shift away from inhumation toward cremation in mortuary practice in the United States is borne out in the statistics compiled by the National Funeral Directors Association (2013) demonstrating that in 2010 cremation approached 40 percent and estimating that by 2025 cremation will have risen to over 50 percent. Changes in modern mortuary practices have been surprisingly rapid and broad. As recently as 1970, the cremation rate in Canada was less than 6 percent and in the United States less than 5 percent. Increased selection of cremation by people can also be seen in the United Kingdom and other Anglophone countries such as Australia and New Zealand.

Cremation is a choice made against a complex cultural, ethnic, and religious backdrop. As a result, there is heterogeneity in the nature of cremation across space. For example, there were significant differences in the cremation rate in the United States (42 percent) and Canada (almost 60 percent) in 2011 (Cremation Society of Great Britain 2013). Even though the traditional Roman Catholic discouragement of cremation, based on a strong theological interest in the dead, has softened (Davies and Mates 2005:109), there are lower rates of cremation in countries with a strong Catholic tradition, such as Poland, Italy, and Ireland. This can be contrasted with higher rates in countries where the attitude of many Protestant churches in seeing a sharp division between life and death in theological terms has facilitated the growth of cremation. There is also dramatic variation even within the same countries. For example, in Nevada nearly 70 percent of the population is cremated after death, while in Mississippi the figure is less than 12 percent (National Funeral Directors Association 2013).

In many non-Western societies, cremation represents a continuity of traditional religious practice. For example, Hinduism, Sikhism, and Buddhism specify the use of cremation to assist the liberation of the spirit for its transmigratory journey. Other religions, however, including Islam and the Eastern Orthodox and Oriental Orthodox churches, specifically oppose cremation as incompatible with religious beliefs. Judaism has a varied attitude toward cremation, with Orthodox Jews opposing it on religious terms and a secular reaction to its use because of links with the Holocaust (see Pursell in Davies and Mates 2005:284–86).

There is both a contrast and a tension between the relatively recent post-nineteenth-century adoption of cremation in the Western world, with formal and legal institutionalization, and the traditional, long-established use of cremation in other parts of the world, which tends to be more locally and loosely regulated. This contrast is starkly seen in the cremation process itself and in the deposition of the cremated remains afterward. The "modern" cremation in Western societies occurs in a crematory or cremator that is housed within a crematorium. The crematorium may be situated in a funeral home or cemetery. The cremator is a furnace designed to efficiently burn the corpse, which is placed in a chamber known as a retort (Mates in Davies and Mates 2005:146–51).

The following description of the appropriate ritual that is followed in Ireland captures the general character of modern cremation practice: "Similar to burials it is usual to hold an appropriate service in your local church or place of worship. The coffin is then removed to a chapel in the crematorium where a short committal service takes place (similar to that at the graveside). At the end of the service the coffin is moved into the committal room (behind curtains) and the mourners leave. The coffin is taken to the crematorium. The body and coffin are cremated on the same day as the service" (Citizens Information 2013). After incineration the white dry bone fragments are taken out of the retort and pulverized in a cremulator to produce ashes. These are placed in a container and given to the next of kin.

In contrast with this very controlled process led by professional undertakers, traditional cremation practices depend on the active involvement and engagement of the mourners, particularly the family of the deceased. This can be illustrated with reference to different traditions of practice. In many cases the participants are required to clean and purify themselves. It is a Hindu tradition that a close member of the family begins the cremation process by putting the first fire to the body. In India and Nepal, cremation takes place on public open-air pyres, or *ghats*, located close to sacred rivers such as the Ganges. Nevertheless, in the holy city of Banaras, or Varanasi, on the Ganges there is now an electric crematorium (Parry 1994). In Balinese Hinduism, often cited as an example of the complexities of cremation practice, cremation takes place on auspicious days decided on at the village level, and it is families that cremate the dead. Corpses, disarticulated bone, or symbols of such bone are conveyed in procession from the home to the cemetery, where women place the remains in effigial or simple pyres. Offerings are placed with the dead. After the cremation the remains are carefully raked to assist cooling, and the bone fragments are then collected by the women of the family for the next stage in the funerary rituals (Hobart et al. 1996). In the Buddhist rite in Japan, family and friends acting in pairs pick up bone fragments from the pyre with chopsticks and place them in an urn (Kretschmer in Davies and Mates 2005:281–83). Although there is variation in practice, in traditional contexts of cremation the mourners are not just passive observers; rather, they are agents of cremation. While in some contexts guided by ritual practitioners, they are integral to the successful and proper transformation of the dead body. Interestingly, Western and non-Western forms of cremation come together where traditional practice takes place in a Western country, as in the case of Hindu cremations in Britain (Firth in Davies and Mates 2005:238–40).

The contrast between the Western mode of cremation and a more diverse range of traditional practices can also be seen in the deposition and disposal of ashes or bone fragments: the cremated remains. Placement of cremated remains in cemeteries is still a common practice in North America and Europe (e.g., T. Sørensen 2011), and the scarcity of space, particularly in urban cemeteries, has long been one of the factors behind the promotion of cremation. However, the practice of scattering ashes in a location chosen by the deceased is becoming increasingly common. The move away from interment in consecrated ground could be seen as an indicator of increasing secularization of cremation as a mortuary rite. This is supported by the variety of ways in which ashes may be retained in memory of the deceased. Thomas Lynch (2000:91) has noted that cremated remains may be "cast into bookends or paper weights or duck decoys. They can be recycled as memorial kitty litter, sprinkled on our rose bushes, mixed with our oil paints to add texture to fresh masterpieces!" By contrast, the deposition of cremated remains in traditional religious practice is often seen as an essential element in the spiritual journey of the deceased. Not surprisingly, the deposition of cremated remains often takes place in locations regarded as sacred or as portals to the other world, such as rivers, the sea, or a temple.

Cremations in Temporal, Spatial, and Social Contexts

> And every day that quiet clay seemed to heavy and heavier grow;
> And on I went, though the dogs were spent and the grub was getting low;
> The trail was bad, and I felt half mad, but I swore I would not give in;
> And I'd often sing to the hateful thing, and it hearkened with a grin.
>
> Till I came to the marge of Lake Lebarge, and a derelict there lay;
> It was jammed in the ice, but I saw in a trice it was called the "Alice May."
> And I looked at it, and I thought a bit, and I looked at my frozen chum;
> Then "Here," said I, with a sudden cry, "is my cre-ma-tor-eum."
> —R. W. Service, "The Cremation of Sam McGee"

Cremation is a process, rather than a distinct and discrete event. The activities before and after the burning of the body, which are often poorly understood, also define the cremation process. Returning to the place of cremation or the place of dispersal or interment and the reuse of remains, tombs, and graves extend social actions and the materialization of mortuary practices, generating specific histories, ancestors, and references to the past (Bradley 2002a; Helms 1998; Williams 1997; Sørensen, chap. 9, this volume). There is also considerable variation in the tempo of cremation practices. The journey from life to death to burning and deposition can take days or even years (Downes 1999). Monitoring the variability in the tempo of cremation, within and between cultural contexts, is one of the most important avenues for understanding cremation as a social context. At longer time scales, cremation practices are often repeated and modified over generations. By breaking down these larger blocks of time and examining how the participants and practices of cremation change or stay the same, archaeologists can reconstruct the dynamic roles of cremation within a society (see Quinn and Kuijt 2013).

Cremations are made up of a complex suite of activities that take place at multiple physical locations. At least in terms of the human body, these locations start at the place of death and include where fire and the body combine. The activities performed at locations along the rest of the body's journey, however, are highly variable, both within and between cultural contexts. Each place and pathway would have included different participants and observers, from immediate family

Table I.2. General and specific reasons why people might cremate their dead

Nature of explanatory framework	Explanation/meaning/causal mechanism/purpose	Citation
Functional	Disease control, transport (portability/partability), space saver, cleanliness(?), odor(?), accident	T. Lynch 2000; Oestigaard 1999; Cerezo-Román, chap. 8, this volume
Social roles	High status, low status, gender, age class, outcast, cultural identity	Scott et al. 2010; Brück, chap. 6, and Cooney, chap. 10, this volume
Social process	Destroying identity, creating identity, transformation, ancestor creation/veneration, communal integration, destroying the past	Sørensen and Bille 2008; Larsson and Nilsson Stutz, chap. 3, Williams, chap. 5, Cerezo-Román, chap. 8, Cooney, chap. 10, and Schurr, chap. 13, this volume
Other	Deliberately vague	Sørensen, chap. 9, this volume

members to entire communities. As such, cremation offers several opportunities for integrating multiscalar social units, such as the family, the broader household, sodalities, and the entire community. The multiple spatial scales of cremation require archaeological approaches that are also multiscalar. These approaches include focusing on small-scale archaeological features, such as pyres (e.g., Buikstra and Goldstein 1973; Wilkins 2008) and burial locations (e.g., M. O'Sullivan 2005), through sites (e.g., Cerezo-Román, chap. 8, Schurr and Cook, chap. 4, and Williams, chap. 5, this volume) and larger regional (e.g., O'Shea 1995; Brück, chap. 6, Cooney, chap. 10, and Sørensen, chap. 9, this volume) and macro-regional landscapes (e.g., Goldstein and Meyers, chap. 11, and Larsson and Nilsson Stutz, chap. 3, this volume).

Why do some people cremate their dead, why do others bury them, and why do some people alternate between the two over time or indeed do both at the same time? This is a surprisingly complicated question. To facilitate thinking about this issue, it is useful to separate the reasons why people cremate from the act itself. There are many possible reasons why people might cremate their dead (table I.2). Because of the diversity in reasons why people cremate, no singular explanation for why people cremate across the globe can be invoked. Linking social meaning to particular instances of cremation requires a detailed understanding of the specific context and culture.

Recasting Cremation: Material Considerations

> Some planks I tore from the cabin floor, and I lit the boiler fire;
> Some coal I found that was lying around, and I heaped the fuel higher;
> The flames just soared, and the furnace roared—such a blaze you seldom see;
> And I burrowed a hole in the glowing coal, and I stuffed in Sam McGee.
>
> Then I made a hike, for I didn't like to hear him sizzle so;
> And the heavens scowled, and the huskies howled,
> and the wind began to blow.
> It was icy cold, but the hot sweat rolled down my cheeks,
> and I don't know why;
> And the greasy smoke in an inky cloak went streaking down the sky.
> —R. W. Service, "The Cremation of Sam McGee"

Burning of the body is a destructive act. Despite the fiery physical context of cremation, however, all information about the body does not go up in flames. There is no question that cremation makes research much more complicated. Researchers are required to commit more time to complete relatively straightforward bioarchaeological tasks, such as identifying the age, sex, height, and health of the dead. Similar to the study of inhumation, reconstructing the pathways of cremation requires sophisticated methodological analyses (e.g., McKinley 1997; Schmidt and Symes 2008), as well as the development of theoretical approaches (e.g., Williams 2008a). The methodological challenges notwithstanding (see Schurr, chap. 12, this volume), the range of information available to archaeologists studying cremations has the potential to be similar to that gained from the analysis of inhumations and other types of mortuary treatments.

The fiery transformation of the body encourages archaeologists to confront the sensory aspects of cremation: the heat, the flames, the sounds, and the smells. While in the case of Sam McGee this was a frightening experience for the narrator, cremations would have evoked different responses in other individuals and social contexts. In all contexts, however, the rituals associated with cremation would have been significant events within the lives of participants and the wider communities. Therefore, cremation, like many other instances of ritual performance, would have provided opportunities for people to establish, challenge, inflate, or undermine identities and social conventions.

Because only a portion of the actions and locations of cremation is materialized in the archaeological record, many aspects of these practices are likely to remain unknown. This is further complicated by the occasions when cremated remains are not buried. Practices such as spreading the remains or placing them in water, which have the potential to render large segments of a population (if not the entire population) archaeologically invisible, pose challenges to interpretation by researchers. The social moment of the wake, the temporary hosting of the body in a specific social setting such as the home to commemorate and say goodbye to the dead, is traditionally an important stage along the pathway in which the body travels. It is also, however, likely to be materially invisible or materially equivalent to other social events such as feasting among the living.

For archaeologists, it is dangerous to assume that cremation, by virtue of often materializing additional nodes of activity (namely, pyre locations), necessarily allowed for longer and differential interactions between the living and the dead than inhumation. In all mortuary rituals, the body travels along a range of pathways that have little or no material manifestation. Even many stages and movements associated with cremation will leave no material traces. At the same time, however, archaeologists can and should take advantage of the materialization when it occurs and should seek new and innovative means to trace the pathways of cremated skeletal remains with new methods.

Engaging with Cremation: Agenda of This Volume

Collectively, the chapters in this book illustrate that the study of cremation needs to be recast as the study of the dynamic social contexts associated with death, movement of the body, and final deposition of burnt human remains. This framework provides the foundation for linking patterns and variability in the archaeological record to past social action. From this framework, chapters in this volume generally focus on two aspects of cremation: (1) the distinction between cremation and noncremation practices (primarily inhumation); and (2) the distinction among cremation practices.

The authors contributing to this volume consider several key dimensions of cremations. First, both archaeological and ethnographic studies illustrate that there is significant diversity in how cremation is practiced. For example, Schurr and Cook (chap. 4) describe Middle Woodland tomb cremations at the Yokem site that were subsequently set on fire. This type of practice produces burnt human remains but does not have other features that are often associated with cremation processes such as a pyre and the collecting and transport of burnt remains. In contrast, Cerezo-Román's documentation of Hohokam mortuary practices through ethnohistoric and archaeological evidence (chap. 8) reflects a very different set of archaeological signatures that include separate locations for burning and deposition. What kind of diversity exists in cremation through time and space? Second, as many authors have noted, cremation changes what constitutes "the body." How do different comparative case studies help us understand this process? Third, cremation changes the relationship between the living and the dead, often through the process of remaking the body. How are concepts of individual, personhood, and community reinforced, challenged, and remade through cremation? Finally, cremation is a multistage process that creates multiple nodes of activity (increasing the stages and actions associated with the funerary ritual while extending the transition from death to burial) that may be archaeologically visible. How does this process compare to inhumation, and how are we to understand the similarities and differences of these rituals?

These key topics are addressed through Old and New World case studies. After an introduction to core issues within archaeological studies of mortuary practices in general and cremation specifically, the book focuses on two broader themes. First, several authors consider the co-occurrence of cremation and other types of mortuary treatment, such as inhumation, and attempt to understand the patterned variability between these different body treatments. Traditionally, inhumation and cremation have been posed as representing diametrically opposed worldviews. The case studies in this book, however, demonstrate that they can be found together, even within the same community. Such a perspective on cremations necessitates more nuanced social interpretations on why some people were cremated and some were not. Second, at a different scale of inquiry, several authors consider variability within cremation practices themselves and explore what this means in terms of chronology, social roles, gender, age, ancestors, social networks, community organization, legitimization, and a suite of other social processes. Because cremations have been so understudied by archaeologists interested in social narratives of the past, research into the significance of patterned variability of cremation practices is almost nonexistent in the literature. In fact, few researchers have taken steps to recognize variability within cremation practices at all. The case studies in this volume demonstrate the interpretive potential of examining cremation as a heterogeneous set of practices.

These chapters highlight that a lot of information can be retrieved from cremations—information that archaeologists have long thought had "gone up in the flames" of the funerary pyre. The study of mortuary practices, as idealized and intentioned ritual actions, can inform our understanding of the past in ways that are both different from and complementary to other forms of research into the past (including the archaeology of nonmortuary contexts, oral histories, and ethnographic comparisons). Understanding why some people chose to cremate their loved ones in the past can provide important information about social networks, worldviews, cultural identities, and belief systems that enriches our knowledge of our shared human past. This enrichment provides a deeper understanding of the nuanced cultural processes that were eventually materialized in the ground.

As the diversity of chapters in this volume demonstrates, the factors that distinguish cremation from other practices or represent different types of cremation practices are not necessarily universal. As with any historically contingent social practice, cremation is contextually specific. Consequently, we do not believe that there is a single reason why people cremated their dead. In this volume, the authors approach the meaning of cremation grounded in their case studies and examine cremation with a broader purpose connected to a view of life and death, as well as the social way of dealing with the body.

Through the presentation of case studies, this volume demonstrates the large quantity and diversity of information we can obtain by studying cremations, illustrates how collaborative research can be conducted in a way that is sensitive toward human remains and descent communities (and how this reflects multiple voices from multiple stakeholders), and aims toward socially responsible research. In their chapter, Nilsson Stutz and Thomas (chap. 2) explore the balancing of socially responsible and culturally conscious research with human remains. Through this chapter, in combination with the case studies, they explore the problems and potentials of research with human remains and the contrasting social and cultural contexts of studying cremated materials in the Old and New Worlds. This chapter highlights the need for archaeologists to engage with multiple stakeholders and to do so in contextually specific ways. In some cases, this means that studying cremations is not feasible, but in other cases (and, we hope, the majority of cases around the globe), it may be possible to incorporate multiple communities and perform research on human remains that is socially conscious and contributes significantly to our understanding of the specific history of a region or community as well as the human past. Although this book is not envisioned as an exhaustive treatment of the ethical considerations of studying human remains, to varying degrees all of the authors in this edited volume engage with this topic, particularly in the archaeological contexts that most warrant it. Instead of an explicit ethical discussion, this book is intended to serve as an example of how to learn about the past through the study of human remains in a socially conscious manner.

Just the Spark

I do not know how long in the snow I wrestled with grisly fear;
But the stars came out and they danced about ere again I ventured near;
I was sick with dread, but I bravely said: "I'll just take a peep inside.
I guess he's cooked, and it's time I looked"; . . . then the door I opened wide.

And there sat Sam, looking cool and calm, in the heart of the furnace roar;
And he wore a smile you could see a mile, and he said:
"Please close that door.
It's fine in here, but I greatly fear you'll let in the cold and storm—
Since I left Plumtree, down in Tennessee, it's the first time I've been warm."
—R. W. Service, "The Cremation of Sam McGee"

In the final chapter of this volume, Cerezo-Román and Williams (chap. 13) put forth a call toward an archaeology of cremation: one that is multiscalar, multivocal, and global. The authors, in part aided by several days of discussion at a symposium at the Amerind Foundation, propose multiple avenues for future research in the archaeology of cremation. These avenues range from research design to integrating the study of modern cremation into archaeological frameworks. The chapter by Cerezo-Román and Williams both reconnects with concepts, such as rites of passage, that have long been associated with cremations and explores innovative social theoretical concepts, such as cremated remains as mnemonic and emotive substances that had a complex and dynamic relationship among the living. Cerezo-Román and Williams argue for a historical approach to cremations, one embedded within specific histories (cultural and disciplinary), but also a comparative approach to cremation that promotes dialogues, collaboration, and a global perspective on one, distinctive way of treating the body.

Many elements of the social process of cremation, such as the transformation, destruction, or construction of the body (Brück, chap. 6, this volume; Oestigaard 1999; Williams 2001 and chap. 5, this volume) as well as fragmentation (Cerezo-Román, chap. 8, and Larsson and Nilsson Stutz, chap. 3, this volume), can also be associated with inhumation or noncremation secondary mortuary practices. Noncremation mortuary practices also involve multiple steps, movements, and extended opportunities for interaction between the living and the dead, although the presence of these actions is poorly understood in contexts of primary inhumation. The theoretical approaches to cremation that emphasize movement, social action, and transformation underscore the need to consider, and provide testable models for, the archaeological footprint of funerary practices in low-visibility contexts. As such, a detailed study of cremation, within the context of the full range of mortuary practices, can significantly enhance theoretical approaches to mortuary archaeology as well as the broader study of all rites of passage.

The focus on North American and European contexts in this volume reflects not only the research areas of the authors but also the state of global research in cremation studies. Cremation is common across the globe, although research into the social significance of cremation is almost nonexistent in the archaeological literature outside of these contexts. We are hopeful that with increased recognition of cremation both archaeologically and as a social phenomenon, archaeologists in other parts of the world will take a more critical look at cremation. The information that can be gained, and how it will augment our perspectives of cremation, is limited only by a lack of research.

In this volume, many of these underlying issues of cremation, social theory, and archaeological methodology are raised but not resolved. The goal of this volume, however, is not resolution. Rather, the volume should serve as the spark that promotes and aids efforts toward this end. By situating cremations within a context of ritual performance, mourning and celebrating the dead, and bringing together the living, the chapters in this volume go beyond discussions of static material remains of the past and advance a richer understanding of the dynamic social processes involved in cremation rituals, the methods scholars can employ to learn about the past, and how the use of cremation helps us understand the social and ritual lifeways of the past. This more comprehensive understanding of cremation requires cross-cultural comparative perspectives, an approach that is at the core of anthropological archaeology as well as this volume. Our hope is that the dialogues started here will allow for an increasingly detailed and nuanced perspective on cremation as a social context.

PART I

Fire and the Body

Reframing Perspectives on Cremation

Perspectives—Complexities of Terminologies and Intellectual Frameworks in Cremation Studies

*Colin P. Quinn, Lynne Goldstein,
Gabriel Cooney, and Ian Kuijt*

The study of cremation does not have a single standardized vocabulary. There are many differences, some large and most small, in how archaeologists from across the globe label and describe the social processes and archaeological manifestations of fire and the body. At the Amerind workshop that produced this volume, contributors were asked whether they wanted to create a single set of terms to be employed across the diverse case studies in this book. The answer, perhaps unsurprisingly, was "no." At first glance this decision might come across as sloppiness or as a group of scholars unwilling to critique, evaluate, and possibly change the terms they have used to discuss cremation. It is true that changing terms and definitions would require a series of complex addendums to past research and to connect with previous literature on mortuary and cremation archaeology. At a deeper level, however, this decision reflected the participants' view that complex terminologies can serve as a tool for fostering dialogue across disciplines and intellectual frameworks. In this brief chapter, we want to highlight some of the reasons why a standard terminology is impossible at this time. Instead of asking whether there *should* be a standard glossary for cremation studies, we would like to use a few examples to explore the potential benefits of the terminological complexities that exist in cremation studies.

Factors in Complex Terminologies

There are many reasons for the terminological complexity when discussing cremations, but we would like to draw special attention to four: (1) cremation is not only an archaeological phenomenon (many stakeholders must be considered); (2) there are diversities in intellectual frameworks within archaeology; (3) cremation is a complex and diverse social process that produces material remains; and (4) the presence of cremation as a mortuary practice is heterogeneous over time and space.

Many Stakeholders

Cremation plays a part in modern treatments after death, and it has a major role in society today (see Quinn et al., introduction to this volume). It is a process that many people are familiar with, either from knowing people who have been cremated after death or from the many references to cremation in literature, movies, and other media. Cremation has been discussed by cultural anthropologists, historians, forensic anthropologists, theologians, funeral directors, and poets, just to name a few. To expect succinct, commonly accepted, and restrictive definitions of cremation terminology in this context is wishful thinking. The best example of this may be the *Encyclopedia of Cremation* (Davies and Mates 2005), in which variable vocabularies of cremation from multiple stakeholders in a global context exhibit why a single, reasonable terminology is not possible.

Diverse Intellectual Frameworks

Within archaeology, cremation has been studied through multiple intellectual traditions, each with its own history, sets of questions, and approaches to data. In particular, geo-disciplinary histories have shaped archaeological discourse in distinct and parallel dimensions (see Trigger 2006). The development of European archaeology (closely associated with history) and North American archaeology (closely associated with anthropology) has contributed to many of these differences. The limited degree of cross-Atlantic transfer and sharing of ideas and approaches to cremations, as well as challenges associated with research in multiple languages (Kristiansen 2001), has led to the establishment of different conventions.

A Complex Social Process

Another source of variability in cremation vocabulary is the incredible diversity of the social practice and material remains of cremations themselves (see Larsson and Nilsson Stutz, chap. 3, and Cooney, chap. 10, this volume). In many cases, bodies follow different pathways through the cremation process and enter the archaeological record in different ways. Sometimes the body is cremated, while in other contexts only defleshed bones are burned. Sometimes all of the bones are collected; other times, only portions. Sometimes they are then buried; other times they are not. Sometimes objects are burned with the body; other times they are placed with the body only after the cremation. As the case studies in this volume illustrate, there is no "standard form" of cremations and with it, no standard vocabulary to discuss them.

A Heterogeneous Phenomenon

In the past, cremation practices were unevenly distributed across time and space. Researchers who work in areas and times where cremations are more prominent have engaged with cremation terminology differently than researchers in contexts where cremations are rare, undervalued, and often overlooked. In many places, cremations are seen as devoid of information, leading to a lack of systematic study, collection, or curation of cremated remains (see Goldstein and Meyers, chap. 11, this volume). The abundance of European archaeological contexts where cremation is the most common form of mortuary treatment has spurred archaeologists working in Europe to find both methodological and theoretical ways of accessing social information in cremations. This has also resulted in more sophisticated modeling, terminology, and attempts to unpack multiple dimensions of information from cremations. In contexts where the study of human remains has more political and ethical challenges, there have been fewer studies and less of an emphasis has been placed on the social implications of cremation (see Nilsson Stutz and Thomas, chap. 2, this volume).

Advantages of Multiple Terminologies

It is clear that currently there is no set terminology for cremation studies. It is also clear that creating such a set of terms would be potentially misleading, potentially undesirable, and not easy. So what, if anything, is gained by having multiple terminologies of cremation? We believe that understanding the discrepancies in terms, definitions, and uses can actually inform our understanding of cremation as a complex process of transformation, negotiation, fragmentation, and integration. Here some examples are discussed of how comparing the variable terms used across different intellectual frameworks can inform the larger study of cremation as a social process.

Bodies

The material remains of burnt bodies are described in many ways. Terms such as *cremated remains, cremains,* and *ashes* are often used interchangeably to describe the remains of burnt bodies. The term *ashes* is particularly complicated. It reflects the material output of modern techniques of cremation (see Quinn et al., introduction to this volume). It also does not adequately reflect most non-Western and past cremation practices where relatively large and recognizable fragments of human bone are preserved after the completion of the cremation. The use of the term *ashes* may have contributed to the preconceived notion that no bioarchaeological or social information can be recovered from cremations. However, the term *ashes* does a better job than *cremains* or *cremated remains* of invoking the dynamic process of fiery transformation from a recognizable individual into a set of material remains that are no longer recognizable as a single person—a process that is integral to the social processes of making and unmaking identities, negotiating new relationships, and characterizing the link between life and death that can be seen in all of the case studies in this volume.

Archaeological deposits with different quantities of bone can be an important source of information about treatments and conceptualizations of the body (see Brück, chap. 6, Cerezo-Román, chap. 8, and Cooney, chap. 10, this volume). The term *token* has been used to describe burials with low bone weights (see McKinley 1997). However, there are questions as to the specific formation processes that lead to variations in bone weight and the implications for conceptualizations of identity, gender, and personhood (Brück, chap. 6, and Cerezo-Román, chap. 8, this volume). They could reflect loss over generations of curation, a change in what represents an individual, or the potential deposition of a single individual in multiple locations. The use of *token* as a descriptive term might unnecessarily prescribe specific social meanings to an archaeological phenomenon. This is not problematic when those meanings are appropriate, but it may become problematic when applied in different cultural contexts. As several authors in this volume demonstrate, challenging the baggage that comes with terminologies associated with cremation can reveal new insights into the social processes of cremation.

Schurr and Cook (chap. 4, this volume) use the terms *accidental cremation* and *incidental cremation* to describe bones burned in situ in a tomb rather than on a pyre. One of the possible scenarios posed by the authors is that the burning was not part of the original funerary practice. Instead, the burning of bodies may have taken place generations later, by a different community. This challenges traditional perspectives that mortuary rites were fully conducted by the community from which the dead came. In this way, this form of fire and the body is not part of the coherent mortuary program of the treatment of bodies, but it is part of the ritual action of the later community. Complications in describing these phenomena remain, however, as the burning of these mortuary structures and the bodies inside are likely deliberate actions for which terms like *accidental* or *incidental* may not fully account. This case does highlight the need to consider the full range of peoples and practices that produced the material mortuary record.

Goods

The terms used to describe artifacts found with cremated remains have significance. For example, the term *pyre goods* has been employed to describe artifacts that were cremated along with the body on a pyre (see McKinley 1997; Williams 2008a). This is in contrast to *grave goods* which were placed in association with the human remains in graves only after cremation. Distinguishing pyre goods from grave goods has provided a line of evidence that has been employed within several archaeological studies to understand the multistage process of cremation and different social factors associated with different steps in the mortuary rite (e.g., Polfer 2000). In archaeological terms, it is very difficult to distinguish between material culture items burned during cremation with the body and those burned in a separate context only to be later reunited with the body in the grave (see Sørensen, chap. 9, and Brück, chap. 6, this volume).

Special terms for ceramics—in particular, *urns*—are often linked with cremations. The link between cremation and ceramic production as fiery technologies (Larsson and Nilsson Stutz, chap. 3, this volume) and the link between bodies and pots as vessels (skins) (Williams, chap. 5, this volume) are made because ceramics are commonly found with buried cremated remains, and often as containers for these remains. Terms like *urn*, which is often more associated with burial deposits than living deposits, can reference specialized ceramics for the dead. In many cases, however, this may obscure the links between domestic and mortuary contexts and uses. Some containers holding cremated remains may have originally been used in domestic contexts or are of a form that is common outside of graves. The presence or absence of similar ceramics in noncremation contexts is important for understanding how people conceptualized the practice of cremation, life, and death. The link to wider material culture, beyond grave assemblages, is a necessary part of mortuary archaeology—it is not something that can be studied without any reference to or awareness of the social contexts of the living. Cremation, as a process of movement and transformation, creates opportunities for bodies to pass through a series of social contexts prior to burial, and terminology associated with ceramics provides a reminder of those links.

Places

There are many terms used to describe the places and spaces associated with cremation. The place of burning of the body is described alternatively within this volume as a *crematorium, pyre,* or *primary cremation*. When compared, *crematorium* and *pyre* appear to be terms of scale, with pyres being suggestive of small-scale and infrequent burning and crematoria as an almost industrial area. These terms, however, have not been standardized and often refer to the same features regardless of scale. Linking these terms to the issue of scale might make them more useful in typifying cremation social practice.

The term *primary cremation*, as used by Cerezo-Román (chap. 8, this volume), references the place of burning, while *secondary cremation* is used to describe contexts where burnt remains are deposited following the burning, collection, and transport of the body. While these particular terms may be problematic given the common use of *primary* and *secondary* to describe full inhumation burials and all burials of disarticulated human remains, respectively (e.g., J. Brown 2010; Hertz 1960 [1907]; Kuijt 1996; Å. Larsson 2003; O'Shea 1984, 1988, 1995), there is an important distinction to be made between human remains found at places of burning and those found separate from burning. This distinction, often unrecognized, can reveal important social information, such as what parts of the body may be most important for representing the individual, or who does and does not get to be moved from pyre to grave. Further complicating the issue is the use of *primary* to describe the first burials in cemeteries, often the central burial in a tomb (see Brück, chap. 6, this volume), and *secondary* to describe more peripheral or subsequent burials. While the use of *primary* and *secondary* in these contexts may overly complicate contexts where multiple mortuary treatments (including inhumation and cremation) are employed, these terms highlight the diachronic nature of mortuary context formation, a fact that is often overlooked in mortuary studies (see Quinn and Kuijt 2013).

Goldstein and Meyers (chap. 11, this volume) discuss the complexity associated with *accretional mounds*, *crypts*, and *charnel houses*, which are commonly used in the literature of the eastern United States. As they highlight, there is often real significance in both the archaeological pattern and social processes that lead to their formation. Add to this other terms for tombs used elsewhere (such as *court tombs* and *passage tombs* in Ireland [see Cooney, chap. 10, this volume]), as well as terms like *ossuary*, *burial*, and *grave*, and there are clearly a lot of terms used to describe the final resting places of cremation deposits. While *mounds* is one of the most widely used terms in European archaeology, the dichotomous split between *accretional mounds* and *mounds* is not common in European literature and might prove useful in European cases.

Moving Forward

The discussion of the potential advantages of multivocality in the terminologies of cremation studies should not be taken as a license for terminological sloppiness (see Whitley 2002 for a discussion of the perils of terminological sloppiness for *ancestors*). Rather, it is a call for archaeologists who study cremation to be self-aware of the terms they choose to use or avoid, even if not agreeing with the use of terms by others. Variable terminologies, which are often contextually specific, are both a hindrance to, and a vital part of, cross-cultural cremation studies. Attention and careful consideration should accompany the terminological choices authors make, with recognition of the potential for new methodological and theoretical insights that arise from interdisciplinary and interregional research.

Whether a restrictive, common, and shared cremation terminology *should* exist remains unclear. The fact that we do not employ a single terminology throughout this volume should not be taken as attesting that such a venture is not worthwhile. As the examples above illustrate, however, we believe that there can also be advantages in the multivocality of terminologies associated with cremation. Archaeologists must be aware of terminological variability across cremation studies when attempting cross-cultural comparisons. As such, researchers must make efforts to explicitly define the terms used to describe social processes and archaeological features so that comparisons may be made. Being able to draw upon the global variability and diverse terminologies will open up new methodological and theoretical research avenues in specific cultural contexts. Ultimately, cremation terminologies, whether standardized or multivocal, remain tools to be used to articulate and explain patterns and variability in social and archaeological contexts. Employing different tools to recognize and characterize the variability within terms and the processes and features they aim to describe will continue to be an important part of the ongoing development of cremation studies.

PART II

Connecting Treatments of the Body
Cremation and Inhumation as Social Practices

Perspectives—Socially Responsible and Culturally Conscious Approaches to Cremations in the New and Old World

Liv Nilsson Stutz and David Hurst Thomas

This is a conversation about the highly contested topic of death. Across cultures and time, people are affected by death in ways that engage them both emotionally and spiritually. The way in which we deal with the death of a loved one may be very variable from one individual to the next, and from one culture to another, but it is always deeply personal. This emotional and personal dimension is important for archaeologists, who have the privilege of studying the remains of mortuary practices in the past. We must understand why the study of death and the dead may be controversial.

This may surprise some European archaeologists, who often analyze mortuary remains as part of their fundamental research. But the study of mortuary remains in North America can be quite controversial and contested, requiring a socially responsible and culturally conscious approach. Conversely, many North American archaeologists probably wonder about the ease with which European archaeology books are illustrated with images of human remains, as well as the unproblematic role mortuary archaeology plays in the research on the deep and recent past. Reflecting many of these complexities, researchers working in North America and in Europe, two academic contexts with rich archaeological traditions and histories, often have very different experiences and views about the ethical dimensions of the excavation and study of human remains and past mortuary practices. For archaeologists working across national borders and cultural boundaries, it is not unusual to experience how cultural sensitivities and experiences collide, and therefore we need to find ways to engage with and mediate between these different perspectives.

Perhaps the most immediate reason to engage with different cultural sensitivities is that archaeology does not just deal with the past: it is conducted in the dynamic cultural, economic, and increasingly global context of today's world. Combined with other local traditions and beliefs, archaeology helps to create a historical past that allows people to situate themselves in the world they live in today. Archaeologists need to acknowledge and understand different cultural and historical sensitivities in order to engage with and help descent communities, researchers, and the general public understand our pasts. This goal, however, is complicated, as even the most reflective and sensitive archaeologist on some level is a product of, or reflects, the ethics and approaches of his or her Old or New World agendas. Agendas, values, and cultural approaches to the past and death vary, and we need to maintain an open-minded attitude as we intersect with the people who hold to these.

While archaeology is deeply rooted in the local and reflects the deep personal history of people, it is also a global discipline. While human (pre)history can be best understood by taking into account the immediate context of lived experience in the past, our reflection is not limited to the immediate context with which we work. Humanity shares some fundamental experience, and this enables us to reach an understanding across cultural divides and to learn from other cultures. To fully understand an archaeological context, we need to understand the local and regional setting. To more fully understand the past, however, we also must draw on our colleagues and other stakeholders for insights into regions and time periods other than our own. Thus, it is important that Old and New World archaeologists working with cremation, which is very sophisticated both technologically and eschatologically, exchange insights and experiences. At its best, archaeologists strive to understand something fundamentally human. Therefore, excluding the rich North American prehistory from this exchange of ideas would be unfortunate. At the same time, however, as we incorporate the North American past in this exchange of ideas, we must take care to proceed in a way that is sensitive to the regional histories and experiences of people and respects members of present communities who have a stake in the past we help create.

Bringing together archaeologists from North America and Europe comingles multiple perceptions about what it means to be a socially responsible archaeologist. This brief essay seeks to explore and contextualize some of these differences. It is our hope that through this discussion we will learn from one another.

A North American Context

To appreciate contemporary attitudes of stakeholding communities toward the study of human remains (cremated and otherwise), we must first understand the relationship between mortuary archaeology and the larger mainstream narratives that have dominated North American history.

Several chapters in this volume discuss the role of cremation in Native American societies. Cremation clearly has a complex and extensive history extending well back into the deep American past, when many American Indian societies cremated their dead in a way that vividly distinguished cremation from other mortuary practices.

That said, contemporary Native American stakeholders do not differentiate cremation from other mortuary practices. Rather, there is a virtually universal concern among American Indian communities regarding the sanctity and respectful treatment of their ancestors' human remains, period. Whether cremation was involved does not seem to matter. In contrast, European stakeholders and descent communities appear to have very different attitudes toward cremation.

These fundamental differences in perception, of course, reflect the inescapably disparate histories of archaeological inquiry on opposite shores of the Atlantic Ocean. Archaeology in Europe evolved as an intellectual pursuit of the dominant majority where, in effect, Europeans felt they were studying their own ancestors. By stark contrast, archaeology in America historically evolved as a distinctly colonial enterprise with the dominant society perceiving and studying Indian people as "the other." It is impossible to overstate the extent to which this imperialistic legacy continues to color the perceptions of archaeological practice in North America (T. Bray 2001; Fine Dare 2002; Mihesuah 2000; D. Thomas 2000).

The colonial agenda was firmly established by Christopher Columbus in 1492. When the Admiral of the Ocean Sea waded onto a Caribbean island called Guanahani, he formally took possession of this New

World, declaring that its riches belonged to Spain and local inhabitants would henceforth be Spanish subjects. Columbus changed the name of Guanahani to "San Salvador" (to honor the Holy Savior who had protected him during his perilous voyage), and he coined the term *los Indios* for the indigenous people who lived there (broadening the geographical subcontinent of India to all of Asia east of the Indus River). This invented word, "Indian," still carries enormous colonial implications. As conqueror, he first claimed "undiscovered" land and then renamed the spoils of the new "discovery" into his own tongue. Columbus understood the power of naming in establishing the underlying control of lands, overwriting indigenous people and histories, and establishing the protocols to ensure that American colonialism would play out by European rules.

Three centuries later, Thomas Jefferson (the third president of the United States and their first scientific archaeologist) reaffirmed these same basic principles with the Lewis and Clark expedition across the trans-Mississippian West (D. Thomas 2006). As military naturalists, Lewis and Clark effectively imposed the new American order by renaming the plants, the animals, the rivers, and the mountains they encountered. The Corps of Discovery also collected and curated the territorial resources, returning home with the material proof of their conquest—including botanical, faunal, and mineralogical samples and a breathtaking array of Native American artifacts. Many of the specimens ended up in Jefferson's home at Monticello (Virginia), where the president proudly displayed mastodon bones and other fossils along one wall and prized Indian relics adorned another. Jefferson also excavated a burial mound near his property, earning him the title of "father of scientific archaeology in America." In effect, Monticello had become the nation's first natural history museum—clearly reflecting Jefferson's view of American Indian people as belonging to the larger American heritage, not terribly unlike mastodons and glaciers. This is how the intellectual study of American Indian people—and their human remains—became an instrument of the state.

In the 1860s, the U.S. surgeon general ordered his medics to collect the Indian dead from western battlefields, then ship the remains to the major natural history museums of the Eastern Seaboard—all in the service of state-sanctioned science. A brisk trade in human skeletons ensued, as these museums followed President Jefferson's lead by amassing huge collections of relics and the bones of *los Indios*. Such "skull libraries" had become vital tools through which to understand human racial history. Franz Boas, almost universally hailed as the father of American anthropology, helped lead the charge. In British Columbia, Canada, he secretly assembled an impressive collection of skulls and skeletons, at one point instructing a photographer to distract the Indians so he could dig up a burial ground near Victoria. At the going rate of five dollars per skull and twenty dollars for a complete Indian skeleton, Boas hoped to turn a tidy profit. In the summer of 1888, Boas wrote his wife, "It is most unpleasant work to steal bones from a grave, but what is the use, somebody has to do it" (quoted in D. Thomas 2000:59). Seven years later, Franz Boas was hired as the curator of anthropology at the American Museum of Natural History. Seen in this light, it is not surprising that archaeology has been perceived as an oppressive practice that without permission has taken the right to define the histories and the bodies of Native Americans.

Over a hundred years later, this familiar scenario played out again in July 1996, when a nearly complete skeleton washed out of the riverbank near Kennewick, Washington (Burke et al. 2008). A local archaeologist claimed the 9,300-year-old bones for science, and following long-established scientific protocols, he named the find "Kennewick Man." But the rules had changed, and Americanist archaeologists found themselves meshed in an evolved ethical and legal landscape (Ousley et al. 2005).

In 1990, the U.S. Congress passed and President George H. W. Bush signed into law the landmark legislation called the Native American Graves Protection and Repatriation Act (NAGPRA). This was a significant triumph for Indian people, moving cultural resources law away from the area of preservation and into the field of human rights legislation. Beyond protecting Indian graves on federal and tribal lands, NAGPRA also required that museums in America consult with appropriate Native American tribes regarding the repatriation of certain human skeletal remains, funerary objects, sacred objects, and items of cultural patrimony.

With the 1990 passage of NAGPRA, science lost its monopoly on the deep American past. For the first time, Native American people became bona fide stakeholders in the national narrative, and they demanded to be heard. Shortly after the discovery of "Kennewick Man," the Umatilla tribe claimed the skeleton as their own and insisted on the right to bury their dead. They also objected to the scientist's imposed name and coined their own term *Oyt.pa.ma.na.tit.tite* for "The Ancient One." The twin powers to name and possess continue to reflect the disparities among divergent histories (Burke et al. 2008).

Contemporary archaeological attitudes and practice now differ sharply from the biological determinism of Jefferson and the grave robbing by Boas. But it is hardly surprising that many Native Americans still associate the practice of archaeology with robbing their ancestral graves. That said, there are encouraging new directions emerging that promise to engage with human mortuary populations in a more respectful and productive fashion. For one thing, so-called indigenous (or collaborative) archaeology is already redefining the relationships between stakeholding, descendant communities and traditional archaeological inquiry (Colwell-Chanthaphonh and Ferguson 2007; Killion 2007). With an emphasis on open communication, multiple voices, personal involvement, discussion of ethics, and a sharing of authority and interpretation, many indigenous communities are today engaging in archaeological inquiry to understand their own heritage (Silliman 2008:3). To cite but one example, Dorothy Lippert is a Choctaw woman who earned a Ph.D. in biological anthropology (with a specialty in human osteology). She observes that just a decade ago, only a handful of Native American scholars held doctorates in archaeology—starkly reflecting a past in which American archaeology was "something that is done to Native people by outsiders" (Lippert 2013:292–93). Today, the number of Native Americans directly involved in, and in control of, their archaeology and history is vastly greater.

Lippert sees archaeology as "a humanistic endeavor, one in which we come to know and respect people of the past in the same way we should people of the present day." In her own studies of health and medical theory, Lippert turns to archaeology to understand more deeply the experiences of those who lived and died centuries ago. "I could never quite see my research as the simple practice of collecting data; rather

I felt myself to be engaged in communication with the ancient ones. Their cold, white bones used my breath and mind to tell this world their long forgotten story. Through the practice of this science, I became their voice." This attitude toward the past and its people is characteristic of many contemporary archaeologists—regardless of whether they are descended immediately from the people they study.

Similar sentiments arose from a very different brand of collaborative archaeology practiced at the African Burial Ground in New York City. Although most Americans think of slavery as confined to the cotton-based plantations of the Old South, the truth is that slavery was deeply ingrained in northern economies as well. This forgotten past reemerged in 1991, when the remains of 427 enslaved Africans were discovered beneath a parking lot two blocks north of the New York City Hall. For more than half its history, slavery had been an integral part of New York City, and descendant communities embraced the opportunity to tell this story, empowered by mortuary archaeology.

The very existence of the African Burial Ground in colonial New York raised the issue of false historical representation. Michael Blakey (trained as a biological anthropologist and formerly a professor at Howard University, the nation's premier black research university) organized a research team of anthropologists, historians, geneticists, and other scientists—prominently including African American and African scholars who shared many of the descendant community's concerns. "Following partly from the African-American tradition of 'scholar activism,'" Blakey (2013:342–43) writes, "it is important for a community to be empowered to evaluate its own past, for better or worse. . . . [W]orking with the remains of the dead also means having an impact on living communities that are affiliated with the dead."

Both examples underscore the changing trajectory of mortuary archaeology in North America. More and more, various stakeholders and descendant communities are becoming involved in collaborative bioarchaeological investigations, transcending to some extent the colonial context and perceived legacy of government-sponsored grave robbing (Baadsgaard et al. 2011:18–19). Nevertheless, the role of cremation within the North American past remains inextricably immersed in the larger context of mortuary archaeology and the respectful treatment of human remains.

A European Context

In Europe, archaeology generally has a very different history from North American archaeology. This is not necessarily a less problematic one. As in North America, the history of the discipline influences the attitudes of archaeologists toward different stakeholders today. In Europe, archaeology has always been dominated by the majority population; they have been both the subjects of study and its practitioners. In a way, it can be said that archaeologists perceive that they are studying their own ancestors. From a North American perspective this may sound very sympathetic, but it has not always been completely unproblematic. As European archaeology established itself increasingly as an academic discipline in the nineteenth century, it soon became associated with nationalist projects. The deep past revealed by archaeology was viewed as the roots of contemporary nation-states, and it was drawn upon to establish and define nations' origin, history, character, and even destiny. The practice was mainstream in nineteenth-century and early twentieth-century Europe. While most of these efforts were clearly patriotic and viewed as highlighting the importance of individual nations, they were not all as extreme as the most notorious example of Nazi Germany's use of prehistory to construct the myth of the superior Germanic people and the Third Reich (Arnold 1990; Arnold and Hassmann 1995; Eickhoff 2005; Halle 2005). This experience, however, continues to be a reminder for contemporary archaeologists to view with caution all claims to the past by an exclusive and excluding group of people.

Since the Second World War, European archaeologists have become increasingly aware of the relationship between archaeology and politics in general, and archaeology and nationalism in particular. The growing field of history of archaeology and archaeological thought has critically examined this relationship on a worldwide scale (see Atkinson et al. 1996; Diaz-Andreu and Champion 1996; Gathercole and Lowenthal 1990; Kohl and Fawcett 1995; Kohl et al. 2007), and over the years archaeologists have distanced themselves and the discipline from exclusive claims to the past. The past, it is now often argued, belongs to all of humanity, not to any particular group. This idea also finds support in the much older ideology of public museums and cultural heritage as belonging to mankind, as well as the rationale that underlies UNESCO World Heritage projects.

In Europe today, the voices that claim exclusive right to the prehistoric past are often found on the extreme right and generally have very little interest in contemporary archaeological interpretations. For example, in Scandinavia the extreme right underground scene often uses Viking symbolism, and the more polished nationalist political parties have attempted to use cultural politics, including funding for archaeology, to protect the national culture from the perceived dangers of multiculturalism. Most archaeologists openly resist this deployment of the past in xenophobic discourse, and their experience of claims to culture leads them to a radically different conclusion than that of their American colleagues. The idea that one group of people could claim the right to material remains of the past and their interpretation because of a perceived connection (real or imagined) to these remains has become anathema to the critical examination of the discipline and its past.

But then, of course, there are also groups that identify themselves as indigenous to Europe yet are not part of the majority culture. An example is the Sámi of northern Scandinavia. In the nineteenth century, they too saw their graves plundered and the human remains ending up in medical collections, and their material culture collected for ethnographic research (Schanche 2002; Sellevold 2002; Zachrisson 2002, 2004). It is worth pointing out here that while archaeology in America is a part of the larger field of anthropology, it is a separate discipline in Scandinavia. The collection of human remains from Sámi graves was conducted mostly for research in the medical field. Archaeologists at the time simply did not show a lot of interest in the archaeological heritage of the Sámi. Omission can, of course, also be a strategy of domination. Of note is the fact that the archaeology of the Sámi world remains underplayed in museum collections and national curricula even today.

Recently, a rather different set of claims to culture has been voiced by neo-pagan groups in the United Kingdom. These claimants view themselves as descendants of the prehistoric populations of the British Isles and as custodians of their religious traditions. On these grounds they have put forward claims for repatriation and reburial of prehistoric human remains (see Blain and Wallis 2004, 2006; Sayer 2010:119–24; Wallis and Blain 2006). One can debate the relevance of their claims, but we should also note that the discourse and arguments, based on right to culture and right to difference, are very similar to what we see among indigenous peoples in North America and elsewhere (Nilsson Stutz 2008a).

The differences in the history of archaeological practice also translate into differences in attitudes toward excavation and exhibition of archaeological artifacts and human remains. Overall, this has not been considered controversial in Europe, something that surprises many North American archaeologists. The reasons for this are complex and varying but are probably linked to the role that archaeology has had within European culture as a public enterprise. In the eyes of the European public, uncovered human remains reflect their own ancestors and past. Museums, still today, tend to implicitly but systematically represent the prehistory of a territory that is very recently defined and corresponds to the contemporary nation-state, disregarding variation through time. This is not necessarily a political or ideological choice but simply the result of national responsibilities to protect and curate the archaeological remains from within a nation's contemporary borders. Even if curators, exhibition producers, and archaeologists understand the difference, these exhibitions are likely to be perceived by many visitors as reproducing the idea of a long-term history of the nation, of their past, and of their people. This shifts the dynamic of exhibition and the relationship to the remains on display. Instead of seeing "the other," the viewers see "themselves." The more widespread cultural acceptance of exhibiting human remains may also be linked to a view that overall tends to value museums, academia, and science. That being said, there have also been calls for reburial of human remains among majority populations, and these claims may grow stronger in the future as people's relationship to the past shifts.

These observations are all relevant when we consider the impact and status of cremations in the archaeological record and in communication with the public. Until the twentieth century, inhumation was the dominant mortuary practice in Europe. But even if cremation was not practiced extensively in the majority population, there is no indication that the practice was looked down upon or rejected. Cremations could be viewed as "different" or "other," yet these remains and the people they represent were often held in high esteem, especially when the archaeological period is viewed as having been important to national identity construction. For example, in Scandinavia where the Bronze Age and the Viking Age (both periods with a high prevalence of cremation in the archaeological record) have been central to the construction of identity, cremation has been viewed as a practice of the ancestors. And while it may have been considered as different, it has also been framed within the glorifying nationalist narrative. The relative invisibility of cremation in museum displays is probably due to their fragmented nature. Their size and fragmentation make them difficult to study and more challenging to link to a visual message and display to the public. In the past this may have led them to be less visible in exhibitions; the remains of a cremation are less visually striking compared to a well-preserved skeleton that can represent an individual from the past. It is thus by virtue of their humble character, rather than their "otherness," that cremations have sometimes been overlooked in the grand narratives created both through archaeological publications and through engagement with the public in museums. Moreover, typical museum visitors and traditional archaeologists alike have tended to be more interested in the artifacts that accompanied the dead than in the human remains.

As contemporary North American archaeology has moved toward an active inclusion of voices that were not previously represented, a similar move can be seen in Europe. In Sweden we see an emerging Sámi archaeology that has developed along with other revitalization efforts in the Sámi community (Ojjala 2009; Viklund et al. 2011). Another movement driven by the archaeological community is to intentionally deconstruct the nationalist notion of archaeology by including immigrant communities in the practice of archaeology and to actively identify connections between these people and past experiences that transcend national borders (Burström and Rönnby 2006; Svanberg and Wahlgren 2007; see also Burström 1999; Holtorf 2009). These efforts, it could be argued, would not be possible in a climate that claims exclusive rights to the remains of the past for descendants.

Concluding Thoughts

All archaeologists work in cultural, political, and social contexts that influence our attitudes and experiences. But North American and European archaeologists tend to have quite different experiences and views about the ethical dimensions of the study of human remains and past mortuary practices. These different contexts require sensitivity to different cultural cases, and above all else, the need to find ways to engage with and mediate between these different perspectives. As seen in our discussion of Old and New World contexts, discourse in one geographical and political situation is not always immediately transferable to another. By learning from others, however, we deepen our understanding of the complexity of the issue at hand. Collectively, this essay and book do not tell people what to believe about their past. Our purpose is more humble in scope and reach: help develop a richer understanding of the past from the material traces people have left for us.

3

Reconcilable Differences

Cremation, Fragmentation, and Inhumation in Mesolithic and Neolithic Sweden

Åsa M. Larsson and Liv Nilsson Stutz

[A]uthority is verified by appearing natural because on the one hand it incorporates the evident processes of biology and on the other it corresponds to deeply felt emotions. Ideology feeds on the horror of death by first emphasising it then replacing it by itself.
—M. Bloch, "Death, Women and Power"

Cremation is not one but many mortuary practices, connected in our minds through the common medium of fire. When discussing cremation in archaeology, we tend to view the practice as radically different from inhumation. This is partly due to the fact that in Europe the introduction of Christianity in contrast to pagan religions is often traced archaeologically through the appearance of inhumations. But this dichotomy in mortuary practices (burnt/unburnt) may not have been as straightforward in the past as contemporary practitioners and later scholars would portray it, and it is now being readdressed in a more nuanced fashion (see Å. Larsson 2009a; Williams 2002a, 2011a, and chap. 5, this volume). Despite this current reexamination of the categories, however, the dichotomy between burnt and unburnt still has had a profound impact on the way European archaeologists have approached ancient mortuary practices. The division between cremation and inhumation remains central to how we categorize mortuary practices in the archaeological record. In any given period, one is often assumed to be the "norm," and any appearance of the other tends to be viewed as exceptional, signaling individuals that for one reason or another were singled out for special treatment (i.e., dangerous, holy, unnatural death, outcast, stranger, etc.).

In Scandinavian archaeology there has been a long-standing consensus that cremation burials were introduced during the early Bronze Age as part of a new religious and social structure (Kaliff 1997). This paradigm has been so strong that even when cremated human bones were found in Stone Age contexts, they were often interpreted as intrusive and belonging to younger periods. The unfortunate consequence of this perception has been that these remains were not taken into consideration when reconstructing the mortuary practices at sites. Thus, the research process itself has continued to reproduce a dichotomy that probably failed to capture the complexity of past practices. Recently, at least since the method of ^{14}C-dating burnt bones was developed in the late 1990s, there has been increasing evidence that cremation was part of mortuary practices as early as the Mesolithic. The accumulating evidence invites us to rethink both our understanding of the mortuary practices in these prehistoric periods and our archaeological categories.

In this chapter we argue that in the case of mortuary rituals of the Scandinavian Stone Age, it is not the presence or absence of fire that was of principal importance. Instead, we propose that the focus was on the destruction of flesh and the fragmentation of the bodies of the dead: whether through fire or defleshing by some other means (through human agency or natural processes). The active production of bones as a response to the challenge that the death of a member of the community poses to the living is well documented in many parts of the world and in many different societies, ranging from hunter-gatherers to monarchies (Århem 1988; Bloch 1982; Helms 1998; Huntington and Metcalf 1979; Kan 1989; Parker Pearson 1982; Wiessner and Tumu 1998). Possible examples of this are also discussed in several chapters in this volume (e.g., Cerezo-Román, chap. 8; Cooney, chap. 10; Goldstein and Meyers, chap. 11; and Schurr and Cook, chap. 4). Usually, defleshing is a stage of secondary mortuary practices (sometimes called burials in multiple episodes). These forms of burial practices include several stages of deposition, with a primary deposition and subsequent interactions with the remains with the objective of extracting bones for redeposition in another location. The time between the primary deposition and the subsequent intervention can range from a few months to decades. Following a ritual structure in several stages described in a classic study by Robert Hertz (1960 [1907]), the first funeral is often associated with a period of grief and lament over the person who has died by close family and friends. The second event is usually more organized and involves a greater community, such as the extended family, affines, and allies and often marks a transition for the mourners out of an active period of grief, and for the dead a transition from a liminal stage to become fully incorporated into the afterlife, or the collective of ancestors. The focus is now less on the person and more on the cultural ideals a member of society should aspire to (Bloch 1982; Håkansson 1998; Kan 1989).

The secondary mortuary event often includes a collective of all the individuals who have passed away in the intermediate period. The ceremony, therefore, becomes a very powerful manifestation of community solidarity and strength in the face of loss. The body is one of the most powerful metaphors that humans use to think about the world, since our perceptions and experiences are channeled through the body and its senses (Lakoff and Johnson 1999; Varela et al. 1991). Loss of flesh becomes a metaphor of the ephemeral status of individuality. This metaphor derives its power from the fact that the decay of the soft tissues of the body is, both by smell and by sight, something that causes deep discomfort in humans. Mortuary rituals often seem to enhance and revel in that which is seen as revolting, frightening, and dangerous, such as putrefied flesh, uncontrolled sexuality, and filth, to create a powerful image of that which is ultimately defeated at the end of the ceremony (Bloch 1982, 1988). The positive is by default articulated as the opposite of the negative. We can understand this as antistructure: elements that by the power of the transgressions simultaneously clarify and reinforce the cultural structure once the period of liminality has come to an end (e.g., Douglas 1966; Turner 1972 [1964]).

In this chapter we address how deeper attention paid to the coexistence of cremation and inhumation—along with other practices of body manipulation—at several Mesolithic and Neolithic sites in Sweden challenges our preconception of burnt and unburnt as opposite categories. These cases highlight that the practices associated with cremation and inhumation should not be viewed as incompatible; instead, they can be part of a single coherent program of mortuary practices that simultaneously handle the dead body and make sense of death. The aim of cremation is not necessarily so much about hiding or circumventing decay and decomposition or necessarily "freeing the soul." Rather, the process seems to be aimed at highlighting the symbolic difference between flesh (decay) and bones (constant). We believe that this focus on "producing bones" allows us to see the strategies of inhumation and cremation as complementary rather than opposing. The perspective also invites us to reflect on what role these bones thus extracted played in the society of the living.

Cultural/Archaeological Context

The archaeological cultures discussed here both involve hunter-gatherers, although they are separated in both time and, to a degree, geography. The classic Late Mesolithic of southern Scandinavia, with burial sites like Skateholm and Vedbæk-Bøgebakken, dates to the fifth and sixth millennia BC (L. Larsson 1988; Nilsson Stutz 2003). These groups are understood as hunters and gatherers and predate any Neolithic presence in Scandinavia. The Pitted Ware culture along the southeastern Swedish coast and the islands in the Baltic is dated to circa 3300–2300 BC (Å. Larsson 2009a) and is technically defined as Neolithic. However, while the Pitted Ware culture is part of a Neolithic sequence of cultures that followed the introduction of domesticated plants and animals in the area, the people of the culture relied mainly on marine seal hunting and fishing, as evidenced by both the osteological material and diet analyses made on human bones (Fornander 2011). The Mesolithic sites have a stronger inland hunting component with deer, wild boar, and so forth—animals that also can be found, though to a lesser degree, in the Pitted Ware sites. Both groups have domesticated dogs.

Mesolithic cemeteries are found on several sites around the Baltic Sea, like Skateholm and Tågerup in southern Sweden, Vedbæk in Denmark, Zvejnieki in Latvia, Tamula in Estonia, Oleni Ostrov in Karelia, Dudka in Poland, and so forth (for more examples, see Zvelebil 2008:38–41). They are the earliest examples of formal disposal areas for the dead in the region and are often viewed as an indication of increased social complexity and new forms of resource management among these hunters and gatherers. For the Pitted Ware culture, burials are mainly known from the island of Gotland, where the conditions for preservation in the lime-rich soil are optimal for preservation. For both groups, the burials are well preserved and seem to conform to what we have come to expect from people with a small-scale hunter-gatherer way of life: individual inhumations with personalized burial gifts and variation in the position of the body, including sitting and perhaps even standing burials (but the evidence for this unique position that has been recognized only in Oleni Ostrov has been questioned; see Jacobs 1995); burials with several individuals deposited together, spectacular deposits of animal remains (such as deer antler); and even dog burials.

While the observed variation is often interpreted as "complex"—simply because deciphering a clear pattern for the variation is difficult (for a discussion, see Nilsson Stutz 2003:180–92)—the repeated inhumations in large concentrations are viewed as straightforward by many Westerners today because the phenomenon seems familiar. We argue here that this first impression led archaeologists to overstate the similarities with our own mortuary practices. A closer look at the actual archaeological record, however, suggests that a lot more is going on than meets the eye. As we start to see beyond the inhumations and focus on what the remains at the sites can tell us about the practices that were taking place here, a new kind of complexity emerges, one that escapes the previously established norm.

The Mesolithic

Let us first look at two sites with concentrations of Mesolithic burials in southern Scandinavia. Skateholm in southern Sweden, with its two consecutively used cemeteries and a total of eighty-five burials, is known for the well-preserved inhumations and the variation in the grave goods and position of the body that we have come to expect from the Mesolithic around the Baltic (figure 3.1). In these burials the human remains are often associated with deposits like fish bone concentrations (often interpreted as food) and modified or nonmodified animal remains (including beads made from teeth of different animal species, deer antler, and isolated animal bones, such as, for example, a vertebra of a porpoise). Several dogs are buried in the Skateholm cemeteries, sometimes independently with grave goods (the best-known example is a dog buried with an ornate antler axe) and other times placed with a human—perhaps as a companion. In Vedbæk-Bøgebakken a similar pattern of inhumations with quite elaborate deposits of faunal remains

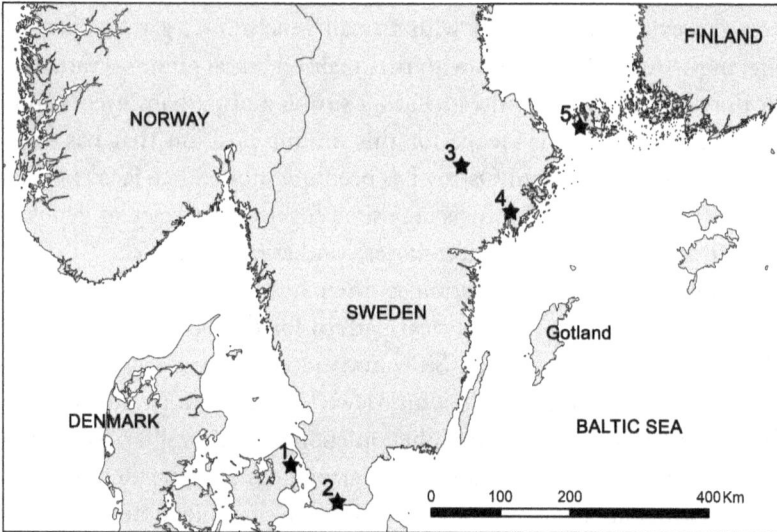

Figure 3.1. Map of southern Scandinavia with the main sites mentioned in this chapter: 1. Vedbæk-Bøgebakken, 2. Skateholm, 3. Bollbacken, 4. Korsnäs, 5. Jettböle. During the third millennium BC, because of higher sea levels, Bollbacken was situated on the shore of a deep bay of the Baltic Sea.

dominate. Here eighteen burials containing twenty-two individuals have been excavated. Again we find depositions of deer antler placed in burials, but there are also large amounts of perforated shells and the incorporation of other faunal elements such as the wing of a swan deposited with a small child.

At both sites, however, cremations as well as inhumations are found. Three cremations were found in Skateholm. At the older site Skateholm 2, one cremation was found. Grave XVIII contained the burned remains of one individual (Persson and Persson 1988:97–98). At Skateholm 1, which follows Skateholm 2 chronologically, two cremations were identified. Grave 11 is described as a complex deposit described by Lars Larsson as burnt human bone associated with a series of seven small pits identified as postholes (see Nilsson Stutz 2003:app. 38). Additional burnt human bone was found in the overlying layers, perhaps indicating that some kind of activity resulted in secondary disturbance. The human bone was mixed with animal bone (Persson and Persson 1984:18–19). In grave 20 a few burnt human bones were encountered in a round and shallow (0.1 meter) feature (L. Larsson 1982:13). All the bones were identified as skull fragments (Persson and Persson 1984:28). In addition to these cremated human remains, traces of fire were associated with three other graves in Skateholm I (graves 23, 26, and 60).

While there are no cremations at the Vedbæk-Bøgebakken site per se, several Late Mesolithic cremations were found in the larger Vedbæk fjord context (for a good overview and an interesting discussion of this material, see Brinch Petersen and Meiklejohn 2003). At Vedbæk Boldbaner, a Mesolithic cremation was identified in 1946 in a site that also contained an inhumation (Mathissen 1946; see also Brinch Petersen et al. 1976; Brinch Petersen and Meiklejohn 2003). At the time, the discovery was met with some skepticism, but with an increased number of finds of burnt human bone in Mesolithic contexts, this interpretation has gained general acceptance. At Gøngehusvej 7, the remains of a settlement were found along with several inhumations of adults, children, and a dog, and these were associated with two features containing the remains of cremated bones. One of the features, N, contained the remains of at least five individuals. The remains were deposited along with charcoal and burnt artifacts (Brinch Petersen and Meiklejohn 2003:488–89). The osteological study suggests that some of the bones were burned dry, while others appear to have been burned in a fresh state. One bone—a mandible—had a cut mark (Brinch Petersen and Meiklejohn 2003:489). The other cremation consisted of the burnt remains of one individual placed in a pit on top of a wooden plate along with pieces of burnt and unburnt flint. On top of this deposit were the intact remains of a roe deer faun (Brinch Petersen and Meiklejohn 2003:489).

Isolated burnt human remains have also been identified at several other Mesolithic sites, including Stationsvej 17–19, Maglemosegaard, and Møllegabet I (Brinch Petersen and Meiklejohn 2003:490–91). So, while our image of Mesolithic burial practices is not dominated by cremation, the archaeological record clearly confirms that cremation co-occurred with inhumation. This is supported by evidence from the European continent, where cremation has been identified in Mesolithic contexts in Gotland (Lindqvist and Possnert 1999), Holland (Arts and Hoogland 1987; Verlinde 1974), Poland (Marciniak 1993), Belgium (Cauwe 2001), France (Ducrocq 1999), and Greece (Cullen 1995).

In Skateholm there is also one clear case of postdepositional removal of specific bones from a burial (grave 28 in Skateholm 1). The analysis has shown that this intervention was premeditated and planned at the time of burial (Nilsson Stutz 2003:310–12, 2008b). The removal of select bones from a primary inhumation burial has been interpreted as an example of bone extraction—a production of bone through the well-known and controllable natural processes of decomposition (Nilsson Stutz 2003:346–48, 2008b:173–74). This burial further indicates that while the processes of decomposition may be hidden by the inhumation of a fresh cadaver, the knowledge about them was so good that this kind of intervention could be staged with minimal disturbance to the rest of the grave.

Grave 13 at Skateholm provides an important counterexample of the perceived dominating pattern of inhumation. Here an incomplete and partially disarticulated human body was placed in a burial pit, probably in a container of some kind (Nilsson Stutz 2003:249–50, 2008b:174–75). The reason for this is difficult to ascertain. The deceased could have been guilty of some kind of transgression and punishment was meted out on the dead body. Alternatively, the body could have been damaged during or after death and a container was used to shield the living from the state of the incomplete body, providing a burial as close to the norm as possible (Nilsson Stutz 2003:249–50, 348–49, 2008b:174–75, 2010:37). Of course, the incomplete state of the skeleton could also mean that this is another example of intentional removal of body parts, as with grave 28.

These examples clearly challenge the norm of primary inhumation at the sites and invite us to think about cremations in a new way. In a previous study (Nilsson Stutz 2003), one of us argues that respect for the integrity of the body was a fundamental component of the ritual production of death in Skateholm. The focus was on the preservation of the integrity of the body, at least until the soft tissues disappeared through the natural processes of decomposition (Nilsson Stutz 2003:349–54). Evidence of practices that did not conform to this was seen as deviations from the norm. But there may also have been something else going on that earlier analysis overlooked. The discrete traces of body manipulations after decomposition, such as the premedited removal of bones from the grave (Skateholm, grave 28), at times combined with the processing of fresh bodies (Skateholm, grave 13), may reflect a more general pattern of body processing in which cremation was also used as a means to transform the body.

Finally, the patterns of preservation and disturbance of the graves provide additional clues for our understanding of Mesolithic perception of the dead body. At Skateholm and Vedbæk-Bøgebakken, the concentration of burials is high and the number of disturbances by later burials is relatively low. To manage this, care must have been taken not to interfere with the older graves. This suggests that the places of the dead were known and perhaps also marked. Disturbances do occur, but they do not appear to have motivated any action of correction or reparation. In fact, in the few cases where disturbance appears, the damage to the older burials is rather massive. The contrast to the care taken in removing isolated bones with minimal disturbance in grave 28 in Skateholm could not be greater. Decomposition of the soft tissue of the buried individual was transformative in a way that the identity of the dead was affected. The bones—once disarticulated through the natural decomposition processes—had been transformed and lost their immediate connection to the individual (Nilsson Stutz 2003:349–54, 2008b).

There has been a renewed interest in Mesolithic mortuary practices in light of recent finds of deposited human skulls at Kanaljorden, Motala, in central Sweden. Similarly, Nicolas Cauwe's and Amy Gray Jones's work on several sites in Belgium (Cauwe 1998, 2001), France, and the Netherlands (Gray Jones 2010, 2011) with disarticulated human remains sometimes co-occurring with inhumations illustrates the fallacy of conceiving of Mesolithic mortuary practices as being dominated by inhumations. We are now seeing that the mortuary practices—especially what people did with the dead bodies—may have been much more complex and variable than we initially thought. By looking beyond inhumation we find evidence for a wider range of mortuary practices, including cremation, retrieval of bones and defleshing, and other intense processing practices of the human bodies. The mortuary evidence of the Mesolithic is understandably limited. While these cemeteries are extensive, they cannot have been the final resting place of a majority of the prehistoric population in the region. It is difficult to tell, however, whether there were other similar burial grounds that are now gone or whether these graves represent more of an exception than a rule.

It is important to remember that our understanding of early hunter-gatherer mortuary practices is based primarily on modern preconceptions and a few lucky finds. It is also important to realize that even this material shows a lot of evidence of extensive treatment and handling of dead bodies, through defleshing, cremation, and/or removal and manipulation of bones after the process of decomposition was advanced or even complete. These cases deserve to be taken fully into account, not relegated to "exceptions" without some serious investigation first. As we show below, there are other contexts in which these variations can be seen as interdependent, rather than as contradictions. While being an integral part of a different cultural context, this Mesolithic "prelude" can thus serve as a background to think about how we archaeologically create norm and difference and how we understand the use of fire in mortuary practices.

The Neolithic: Pitted Ware Culture

Southern Scandinavia entered the Neolithic phase circa 4000 BC, when agriculture and domesticated livestock were introduced in association with the Funnel Beaker culture, all the way up to the Dala River (Daläl-ven) (Hallgren 2008). The Pitted Ware culture first appeared around 3300 BC along the east coast of southern Sweden. It does not, therefore, reflect an unbroken continuation of the "Mesolithic," hunter-gathering way of life. Rather, it developed out of a gradual "de-Neolithization" in eastern and southern Sweden at around the time the megalithic passage tombs were constructed. Whereas Funnel Beaker communities in western and southern Sweden readily adopted the megalithic traditions found in large parts of Europe at the time, Funnel Beaker groups in eastern Sweden instead strengthened their preexisting networks north and east across the Baltic Sea. Both the material culture (stone tools and pottery decoration) and ceremonial traditions (zoomorphic imagery in stone and clay) show increasing influence from these northern and eastern areas. The economy gradually lost traits of agriculture and animal husbandry; instead, hunting and gathering, especially of marine mammals, became the dominant way of life. The reason for this is hotly debated—climate, ideological crisis, and migration have all been suggested (Å. Larsson 2009a:chap. 3)—and it is beyond the scope and aim of this article.

Around 3000 BC, Pitted Ware culture was present from Gästrikland in the north to eastern Skåne in the south, including the large islands of Öland, Gotland, and Åland. The settlements are fairly easy to find, thanks to their large quantities of pottery sherds, often with the emblematic large pit impressions (Å. Larsson 2009a). On the island of Gotland, several large cemeteries have been discovered. As with the Mesolithic cemeteries, these graves contain the bodies of adults (both men and women) and children, mostly placed on their backs and accompanied by tools, hunting equipment, and jewelry. Fitting with what we have come to expect from hunter-gatherers, these burials are understood to represent the norm of Pitted Ware mortuary traditions (Malmer 2002). The lack of similar cemeteries and burials on the mainland was explained as being due to the more acidic soil conditions.

The Pitted Ware burial traditions of the mainland and Gotland are not straightforward. Several burials from these cemeteries, which were initially interpreted as disturbed by plowing or other human activities, contain remains of one or several individuals apparently deposited in a package or bundle of some kind. This illustrates that they were at least partly defleshed at the time. A few inhumation burials have missing skulls, which cannot be explained in any other way than deliberate removal (Andersson 2004; Å. Larsson 2009b). Similar complex practices of removal and redeposition have been identified at the Jettböle site on the island of Åland, where human bones were found scattered across a large area but also concentrated in an assemblage containing bones from at least thirteen individuals: adults, adolescents, and children. DNA analysis has shown that both men and women are represented. The concentration also had dog and seal bones. The human bones had been subjected to heat and had cut marks, raising the possibility of cannibalism. This may be the case, but the remains fit better with patterns associated with secondary treatment and cleansing of the bones—possibly with some ritual consumption involved (Götherström et al. 2002; Å. Larsson 2009b; Nuñez 1990).

One of the few mainland sites with good preservation of unburnt bones is Korsnäs, south of Stockholm. Here, five burials were discovered during the original excavation, and recent excavations have found additional human remains (Fornander 2011; Olsson et al. 1994). Human bones were found scattered in the culture layer. One of the most interesting features was a dark, greasy layer with large amounts of fish bones, which also contained a single human lower jaw, as well as the skull of a dog (without the lower jaw). One of the eye sockets contained a clay pearl, packed in fish bones, showing that it had been decarnated when it was deposited.

These sites all seem to indicate the practices of secondary removal/ redepositing of bones, of combining several individuals, and sometimes of depositing several species. At Jettböle there was some evidence of fire being part of the mortuary treatment. But are there any cases of proper cremations associated with the Pitted Ware culture?

The Cremated Remains at Bollbacken

The most prominent example of cremation practices has been found at the settlement of Bollbacken in Västmanland, central Sweden (Artursson 1996) (figure 3.2). The site comprises four houses marked by postholes and one with a different construction: a ditch surrounding a plank-built wall. It was separated from the rest of the settlement by a semicircular row of posts. In the ditch and inside the small house was a modest amount of cremated, mainly human, bones. Ditch houses of this type have been found at a few places in Sweden during this period and are associated with burnt and unburnt human bones (Å. Larsson 2003). At Bollbacken, only cremated bones were found, whether human or animal. As is the case at most mainland sites in central Sweden, unburnt bones do not survive in naturally acidic soil, so unburnt human remains theoretically could have once been present at Bollbacken as well.

Within the separated area and close to the house were several pits containing cremated human and animal bones, mainly dog but also seal. The pits varied in size, appearance, and the amount of bone found in them. One was a large feature with fire-cracked stones interpreted as a cooking pit, a definition that became somewhat problematic for the archaeologists when it was discovered to have remains from at least one adult and one child. A small pit (1106) was packed with bones from at least four individuals (three adults and one adolescent), as well as an

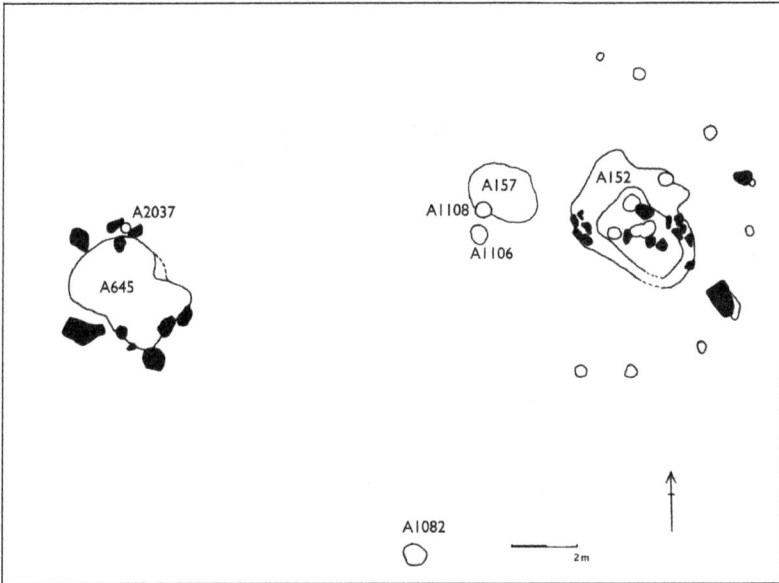

Figure 3.2. Mortuary area at Bollbacken settlement site. Black shapes are stones. Numbered features contained cremated human bones. A152 was a ditch surrounding a plank-built wall of a small house, which was demarcated from the rest of the site by a semicircular row of posts. Some pits (A1108, A1082, A2037) contained only a few fragments; others (A645, A1106) had remains from several individuals, as well as bones from dog and seal. The bones in the ditch were few and heavily fragmented.

almost complete dog. Still others contained no more than a few human bones altogether (Artursson 1996; Å. Larsson 2009a:320) (figure 3.3).

When the human bones from the different features were compared, an interesting pattern emerged. The "cooking pit" was especially rich in cranial elements, while the mortuary house contained a high percentage of bones from hands and feet (phalanges, tarsals, and carpals)—small but durable bones that tend to be left behind when remains are disinterred and moved from one place to another. Pit 1106 contained the remains of four individuals, and it is interesting to note that all parts of the skeleton were amply represented. Interestingly, two large fragments of a mandible (lower jawbone) could be perfectly refitted, but there was no evidence of the other three jawbones—in fact, they seemed to be missing. Because of their dense structure, jawbones are usually well

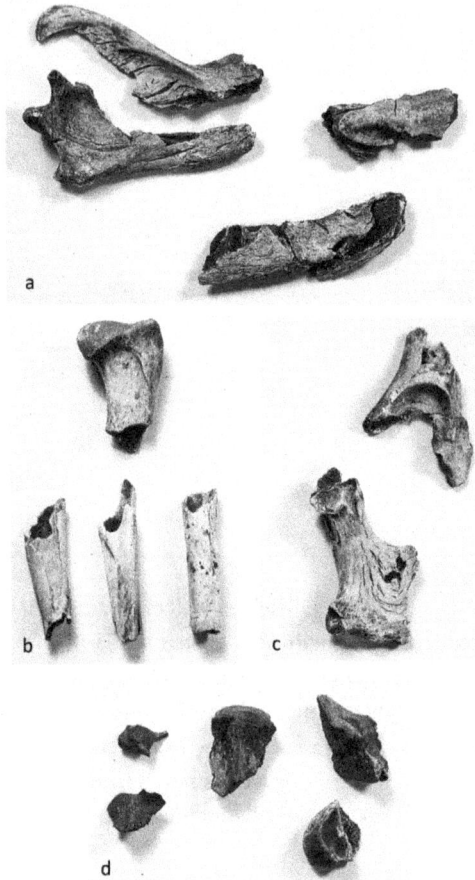

Figure 3.3. In the small pit of 1106, cremains of at least four individuals were found. There was also the almost-complete remains of a cremated dog. The animal must have been placed on the pyre soon after death, as the bones show the fracturing and cracks typical of a fleshed body. There are elliptical cracks on the pelvic bone (*c*) as well as the jawbone (*a*), which also shows deforming; curved fractures on the shafts of the long bones (*b*); and blue-black vertebra (*d*), as they were protected the longest from incineration. In contrast, many of the human bones showed little or no similar evidence of being cremated fleshed. (Photos by Åsa M. Larsson.)

preserved and easy to identify osteologically. The lack of the other three mandibles indicates further manipulation of the human remains. The assemblage does not contain all the bones from the four individuals, as the total weight of the cremated human and dog materials is only 2.5 kilograms. The absence of the jawbones was just the most compelling example that indicates some body parts must have been removed on purpose, before or after cremation.

The excavator suggested that the house with the ditch could have been used for excarnation, where bodies were kept until they were de-fleshed before being cremated (Artursson 1996), but whether this hypothesis can be evaluated is unclear. Researchers (e.g., Buikstra and Swegle 1989; Dehaan 2008; Hummel and Schutkowski 1986; McKinley 1989; Schultz et al. 2008; Shipman et al. 1984; Symes et al. 2008) have studied the effect of heat on bone in various stages, from fleshed to defleshed to dry. The results have not been conclusive, yet the more substantive analyses generally agree that the cracks and fractures that appear on cremated bones vary depending on whether soft tissue was, or was not, present during the firing. Apart from the muscles and fat surrounding the bones, soft tissue contains organic materials such as proteins and fat. A defleshed bone that is still fresh ("green") there-fore reacts somewhat differently compared to a dry bone (Buikstra and Swegle 1989).

The difference in how bones crack and fracture is a matter of de-gree more than an absolute marker. Compact long bones normally sur-rounded by lots of soft tissue, such as the upper and lower extremities, get deep checkered cracks, both laterally and longitudinally. More spe-cifically, where the shaft (diaphysis) meets the end (epiphysis) of the bone the cracks will become curved and elliptical. Curved fractures are also found on other bones such as skull bones and hip bones. They are produced when the outer surface dries out and shrinks more rapidly than the inner surface and causes tension in the bone. This tension is more marked in fresh bones that still contain a high percentage of water and organic material. The presence of soft tissue, especially body fat, will also cause great heat on the surface of the bone, whereas a de-fleshed bone will have a more even calcination process during firing. Defleshed bones that are still fresh tend to get fewer cracks, especially of the curved kind, and are calcinated more evenly, without the blackened patches often produced on bones that were cremated with flesh still on the bone. Still, the temperature variation, where the fire reaches the surface immediately on defleshed as compared to fleshed bones, can result in an exfoliated surface. Bones that are even drier when burned will have few fractures, and mainly along the length of the bone rather than across it (Å. Larsson 2009a:302–7).

These gradual differences make it difficult to evaluate the state of the body at the time of a cremation with absolute certainty. For example, the presence of multiple deep lateral cracks and deep checking, curved fractures, and uneven coloring is a strong indication that the body was fleshed when cremated. The lack of these distinguishing marks, however, is not necessarily proof that the body was defleshed. The nature of the pyre and the time spent on the pyre would influence the result. Also, to get a full picture of the state of the body, any archaeological evaluation should ideally be on bones from the entire skeletal remains of a single individual. To make a judgment on a single bone would be extremely tentative.

At Bollbacken there is the added difficulty that the pits containing more than a few bones also tend to have remains from more than one individual. The feature with the largest deposit of bones, which were also the best preserved, had remains from at least four individuals. Of these, three were adult and one was an adolescent. An in-depth analysis of the bones in this pit provides some interesting results (Å. Larsson 2009a:308). Many of the bones were well preserved, with large pieces of diaphyses, epiphyses, and skull bones. Many showed clear evidence of having been cremated when still fresh and most probably also fleshed. Many of the upper and lower arm and leg bones, however, did not have these telltale signs. They were completely calcinated and had little or no variation in color, very few fractures and cracks, and no curved cracks. In contrast, other bones from the same pit had blue-black interiors, deep checking, and elliptical fractures.

Most interesting were two examples of the occipital bone from the back of the skull of two different individuals. In contrast to other human bone, the human cranium is special and different when cremated. Not only is it a sphere containing organic substance in the form of the brain, but the human skull bones are peculiar in that they consist of two rather thick plates of compact bone separated by spongy bone (diploë). If the

skull is cremated when still fleshed and attached to the body, the resulting pressure will be intense, often causing the skull bones to delaminate
and peel away (Pope and Smith 2004). The occipital bone at the back
of the head is quite thick and will often develop deep checking on the
exterior, curved fractures and is often not fully calcinated, with a blue-
black core. This was clearly observed on several pieces of occipital bone
from pit 1106. There was, however, one almost intact occipital bone,
completely calcinated and with only a few cracks and fractures and no
checking of the surface.

The bones in pit 1106 were tightly packed and that, as well as the
preservation, suggests that they were deposited at the same time and
had probably not been handled extensively before deposition. The most
plausible scenario is that the bones came from simultaneous cremations.
The state of the bones suggests that not all the bodies were in the same
state when placed on the pyre. One of the adults and the adolescent
were probably still fleshed, but one adult was probably defleshed and
partly dried. The third may have been partly defleshed, but it is difficult
to say for certain. There is possible evidence of scraping and cutting
on two bones. The defleshing seems to have been mostly the work of
natural biological processes. This all suggests that the mortuary house
may have been used as a storage place of the dead until a communal
mortuary ceremony took place but that it was not an excarnation house
per se, as bodies did not have to be completely defleshed before they
were burned.

Destroying Bodies, Making Bones

Excavations on Pitted Ware sites often yield scattered cremated human
bones. Traditionally, these finds were interpreted as partial remains of
destroyed Iron Age burials or were simply ignored by archaeologists, as
they represent a difficult category to deal with. These cremated remains,
however, can no longer be ignored, and archaeologists need to acknowledge the variation of practices that created the archaeological record.
Likewise, the past few decades of excavations and publications of Mesolithic burials have shown that mortuary practices were much more
varied than we previously understood, especially in the treatment of
bodies. Fire appears to have been one of the means used to manipulate

bodies and flesh. But should it always be seen as inherently different from other forms of manipulations, such as defleshing by natural processes or human agency?

In some cultural contexts, cremation is symbolically and physically enacted in opposition to inhumation. The burning of witches in Europe and the nonburning of holy men in India are two examples. In the case of the burning of witches, incineration was meant to destroy a potentially dangerous individual and to punish even in the afterlife, as the body would not be able to rise on Judgment Day. In the latter case, Hindu holy men are in effect already dead, their worldly possessions and preoccupations abandoned, all family ties and obligations severed. The body that remains after death is, therefore, in effect earth already, and the soul does not need to be released through fire (Kaliff and Oestigaard 2004). It thus seems clear to us that cremation and inhumation can be constructed as opposing categories of treatments of the body. This should not, however, be something that should be taken for granted (see also discussions in Brück, chap. 6, Goldstein and Meyers, chap. 11, and Williams, chap. 5, this volume). We instead argue that in the case of both the Pitted Ware and the Mesolithic case studies, the use of fire reflects a complementary rather than contrasting strategy. In both cases, perhaps especially for the Pitted Ware culture, it does not seem as if fire was used to differentiate between the dead. Rather, the use or nonuse of fire can be interpreted as alternative and complementary means to reach the same end: the destruction of individual bodies and the creation of bones (e.g., Cerezo-Román, chap. 8, and Cooney, chap. 10, this volume). In the Pitted Ware culture, the bones seem to have been alternately mixed and dispersed to turn them into a durable representation of the community, a community where the living may represent different factions, desires, and goals but beneath it all share a common core: possibly fragmented but always connected.

The focus on the removal of soft tissue, be it by decomposition or fire or both, is the classic strategy of defining a positive by focusing on the negative (Bloch 1982). Many mortuary practices and ceremonies revel in decomposition, decay, filth, chaos, pollution, promiscuity, and dangers as a way of highlighting the positive aspects of society: purity, order, continuity, fertility, and safety. Rituals can be charged with emotion and meaning, or they can be comforting repetitions of actions and movements that suggest to the participants that all is under control (Bell 1997:81). Mortuary rituals are unusually charged, as they draw upon very strong personal emotions, whether grief for the lost or fear of death by the living. The physical act of handling the body, the sights and smells, sounds and touch, all come together to bring back memories of other such events (Chesson 1999; Kan 1989; Sørensen, chap. 9, this volume).

Several different cultures and societies have elaborated the burial process to the extent that some anthropologists identify it as secondary mortuary practices. In these cases, a death is followed by an almost immediate outpouring of grief by the living, focused on the dead person. The body is then disposed of in a temporary manner, which might mean anything from a burial in the ground to being placed in a jar or on the porch. This is followed by an intermediate period, which can last from weeks to decades according to cultural prescriptions. During this time the dead and, by extension, the mourners are in a state of limbo. The dead individual is finally put to rest in a second ceremony, and this usually involves a much larger community—such as affines, allies, and the extended kin group. The intermediate period accomplishes two things: it lets the bereaved organize the resources needed for a greater gathering and it lets the immediate grief subside. The secondary ceremony is less about loss and more about the triumph of the community over the impermanence of nature (Bloch 1982; Chesson 1999; Kan 1989; Wiessner and Tumu 1998).

Rituals receive much of their potency through the very fact that people act them out. Physically doing something incorporates—literally speaking—those actions in the person and blends the immaterial ideology with the realm of the natural world. Sights and smells trigger memories, and shared experience can be one of the most potent psychological forces affecting human beings. During secondary burials, sadness is transformed into joy, loss into gain, the personal into the communal. All of this is tied up in the natural process of decay and loss of flesh that occurs after death. That decay is no longer a loss of the living but the revelation of the ancestral unity that guarantees the continuation of life and fertility, both of the group and of nature in general.

To conclude, in our material from the Neolithic and the Mesolithic there are examples of defleshing, removal of body parts, bundling, mixing, fragmentation of bodies, and dispersal. We suggest that in contexts where there is evidence of extensive postmortem treatment of bodies and body parts, the use of fire can potentially be seen not as a wholly other form of mortuary practice but as an alternative method of removing soft tissue. Ascertaining whether the variation in method was due to locally held traditions or simply seasonal expediency in a temperate climate where the ground was frozen for parts of the year is currently impossible. That is not to say that the use of fire did not have important connotations for the living. The experience of heat on the skin, smoke stinging the eyes, smells filling the noses, and the play of flames across the bodies of loved ones must have been deeply affecting (see also Sørensen, chap. 9, this volume). Fire allows the process of defleshing to be both speeded up and seemingly controlled by human agency. The result is hard, anonymous, durable bones that can be easily divided, transported, mixed, and deposited. Perhaps the fairly mobile marine hunter-gatherers brought the bones of their ancestors to each new place to ensure prosperity and luck in hunting; this could explain the scattered human bones often found on Pitted Ware sites.

Acknowledgments

Åsa Larsson received a contribution from the Berit Wallenberg Foundation for the preparation of the paper presented at the Fire and the Body session at SAA 2011 and also for travel to the Amerind Foundation so that both authors could participate at the workshop. For this we are very grateful.

4

The Temporal and Cultural Contexts of the Enigmatic Cremations from the Yokem Site, Illinois, USA

Mark R. Schurr and Della Collins Cook

The region around the confluence of the Mississippi and Illinois Rivers in the North American midcontinent has long been an important research area for exploring many aspects of human mortuary behavior over time. For much of prehistory, the region had a relatively high habitation density. Over many millennia, its inhabitants buried their dead in ever-changing ways. Through much of prehistory, burials were placed in highly visible locations—either in cemeteries on bluff tops, or in artificial mounds that stood out as prominent landmarks on the river floodplains. The visibility of these cemeteries, and the sometimes spectacular burial artifacts that they produced, attracted the attention of the first American archaeologists, and these burial sites became the research interests of every generation thereafter. A long and complex archaeological sequence of human burial practices is documented with almost two centuries of an equally rich set of archaeological records.

Formal cemeteries were first established during the Middle Archaic circa 4000 BC when the largely sedentary Helton phase people created cemeteries on bluff tops overlooking the Illinois River (Buikstra et al. 1987; Charles and Buikstra 1983). The typical Archaic cemetery was composed of large facilities that contained many individuals, but with little evidence for the spatial segregation of bodies and few artifacts directly associated with individuals (see Goldstein and Meyers, chap. 11, this volume). They provide little or no evidence for social ranking, although bluff-top Archaic cemeteries seem to have been restricted to the most productive members of society, as there is some evidence that the very old or disabled were buried in habitation areas at lower elevations (Buikstra 1981). The placement of cemeteries at intervals along the bluff tops has been interpreted as evidence that lineages acting as corporate groups placed their cemeteries in highly visible locations to signal their ownership of specific territories (Buikstra et al. 1987; Charles and Buikstra 1983). Over time, later groups reused these locales for their own distinctive mortuary programs, especially during the Middle Woodland, when large and complex Hopewellian mounds were built over and behind the Archaic cemeteries, followed in turn by the less complex mounded cemeteries of the Late Woodland. Some sites were also used as cemeteries by Middle Mississippians, the last prehistoric culture of the region. The long-term use and reuse of specific landscape features is a distinctive feature of the region's prehistoric burial sites. At some times (during the Late Archaic and Late Woodland), some people were cremated as fire was employed as part of the mortuary ritual. In addition, during the Middle Mississippian period, some burials placed on the floors of wooden structures were incidentally cremated when the structures were burned.

Description of the Yokem Site

Yokem is an example of a burial site where cremation was used in different ways at different times. It is a bluff-top cemetery located above the Mississippi River valley (figure 4.1) with archaeological remains that show many similarities between coeval sites in the lower Illinois Valley. Fewer bluff-top burial sites are known from the Mississippi River valley compared to the lower Illinois, especially ones that span long periods of time. More attention has been paid to Middle Mississippian cemeteries in the Mississippi Valley because the archaeology of the great Middle Mississippian site of Cahokia has been the predominant research focus, leading to more exploration of late prehistoric sites south of the Illinois-Mississippi confluence. There were strong cultural connections between the peoples of the Illinois and Mississippi River valleys from the Middle Woodland period onward, and the Yokem site is an unusual example of a well-excavated bluff-top site broadly similar to the multiperiod mound groups of the lower Illinois Valley. Gregory Perino conducted excavations at the site after the largest mound, Mound 3, which he considered "the most perfect mound remaining in Illinois" (Perino 1967:149), was looted by artifact dealers in 1966. Perino led subsequent investigations of the site and mapped nine mounds and other

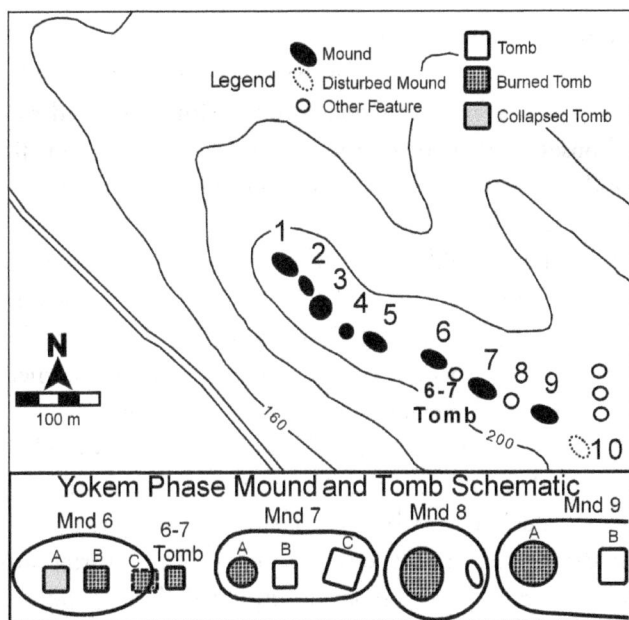

Figure 4.1. Map of the Yokem site.

structures in the area (figure 4.1). The nine mounds were linearly placed along a bluff-top ridge overlooking the Mississippi River floodplain. Excavations showed that the mounds represented three different time periods with differing mortuary practices in each period. Four mounds (6 through 9) contained tombs made of stacked limestone slabs (described in more detail below). Perino initially attributed them to the Middle Woodland period (Perino 1967, 1971) but later placed them in the early Late Woodland (Perino 2006a) Yokem phase. Mounds 4 and 5 and the lower part of Mound 3 contained late Late Woodland (Jersey Bluff phase) burials. Mounds 1 and 2 and the upper part of Mound 3 contained charnel houses and burials made by an "acculturated Mississippian–Late Woodland group" (Perino 2006a:348). The charnel houses are a different type of mortuary structure than the tombs used earlier. The tombs functioned as crypts, which are small boxlike structures that are used to hold human remains (J. A. Brown 1979; see also Goldstein and Meyers, chap. 11, this volume). They could be unlined pits or lined with materials such as logs, bark, and stone. No burial processing or rituals were performed in crypts, because they were small. Charnel houses are aboveground structures that were constructed like houses of the era (with walls made of wooden poles with a thatched roof). The charnel houses were used for the storage, processing, and display of bodies and bones and may have also been the site of rituals where the living interacted with the dead.

The best-known publication about the site (Perino 1971) describes the remains of a looted Middle Mississippian charnel house on Mound 3 and another largely undamaged one within Mound 2. Both charnel houses had been burned. Perino speculated that the charnel houses could have been accidentally ignited by lightning strikes (Perino 1971:183), and the charred burials found inside them would therefore have been incidentally cremated. However, it is also possible that such structures were deliberately burned as part of a closing ritual (Goldstein 1980; Goldstein and Meyers, chap. 11, this volume). Perino attributed both structures to a "Mississippian acculturated" Late Woodland group that was in conflict with contemporary Mississippians. Thus, the last unnamed phase represented a local Late Woodland group that adopted some burial practices of Middle Mississippian chiefdoms that evolved in the region as the site of Cahokia (Milner 1998; Pauketat 1994) developed to the south near the Mississippi-Missouri confluence.

The Yokem Cremation Features

The recent publication of a compilation of many of Perino's previously unpublished site reports (Farnsworth and Wiant 2006) has made more information about the mortuary features at the Yokem site accessible, including detailed descriptions of Mounds 4 through 9 and their contents. We focus on the burial features in Mounds 6–9 and an additional "subfloor stone structure" between Mounds 6 and 7 attributed by Perino to the Yokem phase of the middle Late Woodland period (between about AD 600 and 900). Mound 6 contained two limestone slab tombs (Tombs 6A and 6B) that were roofed with logs and a log-lined tomb (Tomb 6C). Tomb 6A apparently had been deliberately destroyed by collapsing the walls before the mound was built. Tomb 6B was roofed with logs. The logs had been burned, charring the burials inside. The walls of the tomb then either fell in or collapsed before the tomb was buried in the mound. Tomb 6C was a log-lined tomb, apparently similar to Hopewellian log crib tombs (Charles 1992), that was burned and then partially covered by the mound. Artifacts within the stone and log tombs led Perino to believe they were contemporary. Mound 7 also contained three tombs. All were composed of limestone slabs and were probably roofed with wood. Tomb 7A was burned. Tombs 7B and 7C had not been burned. The "subfloor stone structure" between Mounds 6 and 7 was similar to the burned limestone tombs in Mounds 6 and 7 but was placed between the mounds and covered with less soil. Mound 8 contained a more diverse array of burial features, including a limestone slab tomb similar to those in the other mounds. The southern end of the log roof of the tomb had been burned. The other burial features consisted of a grave covered with limestone slabs supported by timbers (which were not burned) and several intrusive Jersey Bluff burials that postdated the Yokem phase burials (see below). Mound 9 also contained three limestone slab tombs. The roof of Tomb 9A had been partially burned, Tomb 9B was not burned, and Tomb 9C was not excavated because of time constraints at the end of the field season.

As summarized in table 4.1, the portion of the site containing Mounds 6–9 included ten limestone slab tombs, one log tomb, a limestone slab–covered grave, and some intrusive burials from the later Jersey Bluff phase (in Mound 8). Five of the tombs (four of limestone and one of wood) had been burned prior to mound construction, and the stone walls of one tomb (Tomb 6A) appear to have been deliberately collapsed before the tomb was covered with mound fill. Burning or collapsing of the tombs was more frequent in the mounds closer to the bluff edge.

Because of the partially burnt tomb in Mound 8, which he interpreted as evidence that the tomb was deliberately extinguished before it burned completely, Perino believed that the burnt tombs had caught fire accidentally. Perino's scenario indicates that the burnt burials at the site would be accidental or incidental cremations. Perino's interpretation of the mounds, however, was mainly concerned with dating and associating the mounds with specific archaeological phases based on the types of artifacts found in them. He did not consider or explain why so many of the tombs came to be accidentally damaged by fire, why one of them was collapsed prior to being mantled within the mound,

Table 4.1. Attributes of the Yokem phase tombs

Tomb	Floor area (m²)	Material	Shape	Door	Burned	Artifacts	Comments
9C	—	Limestone	—	—	—		Not excavated, also subsurface like 6–7
9B	3.25	Limestone	Rectangular	No	No	Yokem points	
9A	5.13	Limestone	Round	Yes	Yes	Yokem points, pipe similar to 7A, LW boatstone point similar to 7C, spikes similar to 6B	
8A	4.73	Limestone	Rectangular with rounded end	No	Yes		
8 grave	—	Limestone	Limestone-slab covered	—	No		
7C	6.27	Limestone	Square with rounded corners	Yes	No	Mica fragments and obsidian lamellar blade, jars, points	
7B	4.55	Limestone	Square with rounded corners	Yes	No		

Table 4.1. (continued)

Tomb	Floor area (m²)	Material	Shape	Door	Burned	Artifacts	Comments
7A	4.23	Limestone	Rectangular	No	Yes		Soil filtered in to protect burials on the side from charring, so it was burned late
6–7	0.65	Limestone	Rectangular	No	Yes		
6C	3.47	Wood	Rectangular	No	Yes		Subsurface partially covered by mound
6B	4.71	Limestone	Square with rounded corners?	No	Yes		
6A	4.71	Limestone	Square with rounded corners	No	No		Walls collapsed

or the broader significance or meaning of the role of fire in the Yokem mortuary program. The social meanings of prehistoric burials in eastern North America have often relied on ethnographic analogies. For example, late prehistoric and early historic period ossuary burials from Ontario have been interpreted as products of the Huron "Feast of the Dead" (Kidd 1953), and late prehistoric Middle Mississippian charnel houses are inferred to have been structures similar to those described by members of the DeSoto expedition (Kay and Sabo 2006). Even Middle Woodland burial practices and iconography of two millennia ago have been interpreted ethnographically (Carr and Case 2005; Hall 1979). Interpreting the meaning of prehistoric cremations in eastern North America is more difficult and less constrained because cremation does not appear to have been practiced during the historic period in eastern North America and there are no ethnographic parallels or analogies that can be used. The lack of historically recorded cremations also complicates the association of prehistoric cremation sites with living Native American tribal groups because it is difficult to show cultural continuity when distinctive activities such as cremation were not part of the mortuary repertoire historically or today (for a contrasting situation in southwestern North America, see Cerezo-Román, chap. 8, this volume).

The question of exactly how fire was employed in the mortuary rituals at the Yokem site therefore merits detailed consideration. We use the burnt tomb crematory between Mounds 6 and 7 (referred to as the "Mound 6–7 tomb") to explore the role of fire and cremation at the site by examining the chronological and cultural positions of the feature. We first place the tomb chronologically by using several different lines of evidence, and we then examine how fire (and cremation) was employed through time in the region to generate explanations about why the Mound 6–7 tomb was burned.

The Mound 6–7 Tomb

The Mound 6–7 tomb was constructed of limestone slabs to create a wall about 0.6 meters tall that protruded just a few centimeters above the original ground surface (a "subfloor tomb," in Perino's nomenclature). The structure was rectangular in shape and almost square (1.5 by 1.7 meters). The tomb was roofed with logs that were in turn covered by limestone slabs. The logs were burned, producing an intense fire that charred the burials within. The tomb contained ten adults, two children, and one infant (thirteen burials in all). A total of 8.2 kilograms of bone was recovered, with 27 percent unburned, 57 percent smoked or charred, and 15 percent calcined by weight. Most of the burials can therefore be described as partial cremations. The bones were smoked and burned but not completely calcined. A large amount of fuel is required to consume a body (Barber 1990), so complete thermal reduction was apparently not the goal. The remains show no evidence for soft-tissue protection of joint surfaces or of deep versus superficial features, indicating that the burials were completely defleshed before being burned. We believe that the bodies were probably placed in the tomb while still fleshed and that they were defleshed by exposure in the tomb over time, but that is not certain, because only the mounds were excavated, and we cannot exclude the possibility of body-processing (defleshing) areas elsewhere. The defleshed bones were then cremated when the wood on top of the tomb was burned. Although at least one experiment to determine how fleshed, green, and dry bones react differentially to heating suggests that dry bones do not calcine (Buikstra and Swegle 1989), a more recent study produced calcination in both weathered and prehistoric bones upon heating (Bennett 1999), and partial calcination does not rule out the cremation of even long-defleshed bones. There is no evidence of cut marks or other signs of manual defleshing or body manipulation (see Larsson and Nilsson Stutz, chap. 3, this volume) and the features appear to have been sealed after burning and not disturbed (except for occasional episodes of looting during the historic period).

The bones were burned so that those near the walls of the tomb were less burned than those nearer the center. In many cases, long bones show differential burning along their length. The burning patterns of the bones and extensive oxidation of the soil within the tomb suggest that the tomb was covered with wood, either to form a roof or as fuel, and that the wood was then burned, partially cremating the defleshed bones in the tomb. The unburnt bones around the periphery of the tomb were partially protected by the walls when most of the fuel collapsed inward toward the center of the tomb.

To determine the chronological and cultural position of the Mound 6–7 tomb, we examined five different lines of evidence: position in the site, form of the burial feature, associated artifacts, radiocarbon dates, and human stable carbon-isotope ratios.

Position in the site

Perino's (2006a) chronology for the site grouped the mounds into three primary periods (figure 4.1). The age of each group of mounds largely correlated with the group's distance from the bluff edge, with the earliest mounds being found farthest from the bluff edge. Mounds 6–9 dated to the middle Late Woodland period (Yokem phase). Yokem phase refuse pit features were found below Mounds 4 and 5, showing that domestic activities occurred at the site around the same time that Mounds 6–9 were built and that Mounds 4 and 5 stratigraphically postdated the Yokem phase. Mounds 4, 5, and the lower part of Mound 3 were built during the late Late Woodland Jersey Bluff phase, which also intruded a few burials into Mound 8. Mounds 1 and 2 and the upper part of Mound 3 were constructed by acculturated "Mississippian–Late Woodland" peoples who built and burned two charnel houses (one each on top of Mounds 2 and 3). Like the Yokem phase burnt tombs, the burials in the Mississippian charnel houses were partially charred incidental cremations.

Perino concluded, based on the horizontal "stratigraphy," that the mounds with the limestone tombs (Mounds 6–9) were built first. Mounds 6–9 consisted of a linear arrangement of two to three tombs in each mound, some of which were burned, and all of which were eventually buried (figure 4.1). Perino did not consider the construction sequence within these mounds and treated them as a single chronological unit. Several construction sequences are possible. For example, did construction perhaps begin with Mound 9 and then progress toward the bluff edge in sequence? Or were mounds with multiple tombs (6, 7, and 9) begun simultaneously with a single tomb and then elongated as additional tombs were added over time? Were Mound 8 (with its single tomb and unique slab-covered burial) and the 6–7 tomb built later after the other mounds were completed, or were they built simultaneously with the others? Examination of the morphology of individual tombs might help answer these questions.

Table 4.1 summarizes the main characteristics of the eleven tombs. All but one were made of stacked limestone slabs. All but one were square or rectangular, and half of those had rounded corners. A slight minority (n=3) possessed a doorway or small passageway. A slight majority were burnt (n=6), and one was apparently deliberately collapsed. The average floor area was 4.17 square meters, ranging from 0.65 to 6.27 square meters. The 6–7 tomb is unusual because it is the smallest in the group. In many ways it appears to be a smaller version of the tomb in Mound 8 that was covered, in turn, with a smaller amount of soil to create a "knoll" instead of a mound. In Perino's terminology, a knoll is a small, naturally raised area on the landscape. His use of the term *knoll* for the slight topographic elevation covering the 6–7 tomb indicates that he was not sure whether it was a natural knoll or an artificial mound prior to excavation. The mound covering the 6–7 tomb was very low and less prominent than the other mounds at the site.

Each mound contained both burnt and unburnt tombs, except for Mound 8, which contained a single burnt tomb. However, Mound 8 did contain a single inhumation burial covered with limestone slabs that could date to the Yokem phase. In the mounds with burnt and unburnt tombs, the tombs farthest from the bluff edge are the least likely to have been burned, except for Mound 6, where the tomb closest to the bluff edge was not burned but was collapsed instead. One possible interpretation of this sequence is that the location of each mound was established with the tomb farthest from the bluff edge. Tombs were then added sequentially to fill in toward the bluff edge until the last tomb in the mound was burned and then covered to create the mound. The exception would be Mound 6, presumably the last one constructed, where the two tombs farthest from the bluff edge were burned and the one closest to the bluff edge was destroyed when people collapsed it.

Form of the burial feature

The differences between Middle and Late Woodland burial mounds are well understood (Charles 1992). The log tomb (Tomb 6C in Mound 6) is reminiscent of the rectangular or square log cribs that formed the tombs of Middle Woodland mounds. Similar early Late Woodland log tombs, including burnt ones, were found at the Pete Klunk mound site (Perino 1973a). The stone tombs are generally similar to log ones as well, except that some of them had rounded corners and doorways. However, the architecture of the mounds covering them is very different.

Middle Woodland log tombs were often placed on elaborately prepared surfaces, flanked by ramps that contained burials, and covered with a final earth mantle to create a large conical mound whose size is proportional to the tomb. The mounds at Yokem were low, relatively simple constructions without prepared floors and ramps.

The late Late Woodland Jersey Bluff phase mounds are typical of the Late Woodland period. During the Late Woodland period, burials were placed on the ground surface of knolls or ridges and then covered with earth to raise the height of the knoll or ridge. In the lower Illinois Valley, a simple tomb or crematory might be created on the new surface and then sealed with earth. In some cases, the crematory appears to have been used for deliberate cremation, but in other cases, the burials appear to have been burned accidentally, producing indirect cremations (Perino 1973a). Late Woodland mounds can have multiple stages to produce a low, elliptical mound whose size is largely determined by the number of burials it contains.

The structure of the Yokem phase mounds is consistent with their chronological position in the middle Late Woodland because they possess elements characteristic of each period but are identical to neither. They retain the Middle Woodland characteristic of a tomb for multiple individuals but lack other, more complex elements of the preceding Hopewell period such as surface preparation and ramps. Their low elliptical shape is characteristic of the Late Woodland. Interments, however, are placed only in limestone tombs built on the original ground surface or set into it, in contrast to Late Woodland mounds, in which burials are made throughout the mound fill. The mounds essentially consist of aboveground cemeteries formed when fleshed inhumations were placed on the surface and covered with soil. The mounds were thus produced accretionally as burials were added over time.

Associated artifacts

The types of artifacts found within and around the tombs were one of the primary reasons why Perino defined the Yokem phase as a middle Late Woodland phase. Pottery vessels from the habitation features under Mounds 4 and 5 and associated with the tombs of Mounds 6–9 are cord-marked, grit-tempered pots with rounded bottoms and sometimes have peaked rims. They are characteristic of a widespread ceramic horizon that is well recognized in the Mississippi-Illinois confluence region under a variety of names including the Yokem phase (Perino 2006a) or horizon (Morgan 1985), the Fall Creek phase in the Sny bottoms below the site (O'Gorman and Hassan 2000), and the Adams variant or tradition (Green and Nolan 2000). There is a general consensus that ceramics of this type were manufactured between about AD 600 and 800.

Other artifacts associated with the tombs include small notched points that are thought to be early examples of true arrowheads (in contrast to the dart points in use during the preceding Middle Woodland period and the unnotched triangular arrow points of the late Late Woodland onward), stone elbow pipes (known to postdate the monitor-style pipes of the Middle Woodland and predate the unstemmed bowls that became common during the later Late Woodland), a Late Woodland style of "boatstone," and "residual" Hopewell artifacts. The residual artifacts are items such as mica fragments and an obsidian lamellar blade. Mica and obsidian were frequently used in Middle Woodland mortuary rituals, often in great abundance. Lamellar blades, often of exotic materials such as obsidian or high-quality imported cherts, were produced almost exclusively during the Middle Woodland. The presence of a few of these items at Yokem indicates that such exotic artifacts still played a role in Yokem phase burial practices, but their relative rarity at the site is not characteristic of the Middle Woodland period. The Yokem artifacts could have been heirlooms, in contrast to the Middle Woodland, when these types of items were manufactured or obtained from their source areas many kilometers away. The artifact associations are consistent with mound architecture, retaining some elements of Hopewell practices but in simpler form.

Chemical Approaches

There is a long history of chemical and scientific investigations of burnt bone, beginning with alchemists, followed by chemists who discovered pyrrole and other aromatic amines (Anderson 1996). Although there have been many studies of the physical properties of burnt bones (e.g., Brain 1993; Hanson and Cain 2007; McCutcheon 1992; McKinley 1994a; Reinhard and Fink 1994; Schmidt and Symes 2008; see Schurr, chap. 12, this volume for a brief overview of the topic), the chemistry of cremated bone has been underexploited. We use several chemical approaches to examine the chronological and cultural contexts of the Yokem 6–7 tomb. One is the well-known technique of radiocarbon dating, a commonly used method for dating many different forms of carbon, especially from carbonized or burnt items. Radiocarbon can be used to date bones that contain organic carbon, as shown by blackening, where the black residue represents the charred remains of bone collagen and lipids (the organic fraction of the bone). Radiocarbon dating has even been applied to calcined bones by dating the very small amounts of inorganic carbonate retained (Lanting et al. 2001). We used conventional radiocarbon dating to date the organic fraction of burnt bone from the 6–7 tomb and compare the bone date with conventional radiocarbon dates and accelerator mass spectrometry (AMS) dates that were obtained from wood charcoal. We also use stable carbon-isotope ratios of carbonized bones from the 6–7 tomb as a cross-check on the radiocarbon date and as a way of placing the burials within a regional context that reflects substantial variations in human stable carbon isotopes over time.

Stable carbon isotopes

Numerous studies (e.g., Bender et al. 1981; Buikstra et al. 1994; Greenlee 1990; Lynott et al. 1986; Schwarcz et al. 1985; Stothers and Bechtel 1987) have shown how human stable carbon-isotope ratios increased over time after maize entered the diet in prehistoric eastern North America. The ratio of the two stable isotopes of carbon (carbon-13 [or ^{13}C] and carbon-12 [or ^{12}C]) in organic materials with natural isotopic abundances is usually expressed with the well-known "δ" value scale in units of per mil (‰). Prior to the appearance of maize, human stable carbon-isotope ratios in the study area average around -20.5‰ (Buikstra et al. 1994; Rose 2008; Schoeber 1998), reflecting a terrestrial diet in an ecosystem where plants fix carbon using the C3 photosynthetic pathway. Maize, an imported tropical cultigen, fixes carbon using the C4 pathway that produces tissues enriched in ^{13}C. In contrast to modern terrestrial C3 plants, which produce $\delta^{13}C$ values ranging between -31‰ and -23‰, modern plants such as maize using the C4 pathway range from -15‰ to -11‰ (O'Leary 1988). Prehistoric stable carbon-isotope ratios of plants were slightly higher than those of modern ones because the burning of fossil fuels has introduced a large amount of carbon dioxide depleted in ^{13}C into the atmosphere (Friedli et al. 1986). Carbonized prehistoric maize from eastern North America possessed δ^{13}C values around -9 to -10‰ (Schoeninger and Schurr 1994; Tieszen and Fagre 1993). As maize entered the diet during the Late Woodland period after about AD 500, human bone collagen δ^{13}C values increased over time from a low value of around -20.5‰ to averages around -11‰ by AD 1200. Human δ^{13}C values are therefore roughly correlated with time between about AD 600 and 1200, with bone collagen from later burials producing less negative δ^{13}C values than earlier ones.

As is the case for radiocarbon dating, stable isotope analysis can be used on the preserved organics retained in charred bones. Studies of modern bone samples heated under controlled conditions (Schurr et al. 2008) have shown that the chemistry of organic matter in bone is largely controlled by temperature, not by heating time. The nitrogen content of whole bone, expressed as %N by weight, is a good measure of protein preservation. Analyses of the nitrogen content of bones heated under controlled conditions show that partly cremated bone can contain significant amounts of organic matter. The organic portion of bones heated below 200°C is largely unaltered. Bones heated between 200°C and 350°C retain substantial amounts of thermally altered organic matter, with the degree of thermal alteration and the loss of organic matter largely correlated with heating temperature. Bones heated between 350°C and 450°C retain only traces of heavily altered organics, and heating above 450°C leads to the complete loss of organics (calcined bone). Although the organic content of bone declines with heating, controlled heating experiments show that stable carbon-isotope ratios are not altered by heating (Schurr and Hayes 2008). The organic carbon from charred bone can therefore produce reliable δ^{13}C values and radiocarbon dates.

Organic material extracted from ten bones from the 6–7 tomb produced an average δ^{13}C value of -21.3‰, a value characteristic of non-maize diets in the region. The Yokem individuals consumed no or a negligible amount of maize, and their diets are consistent with a temporal placement in the earlier half of the Late Woodland period. When the δ^{13}C values are arranged by their mean radiocarbon date and compared to those of other sites in the region (table 4.2), the radiocarbon date and

Table 4.2. Human stable carbon-isotope ratios for Middle Woodland to Mississippian sites

Site	Mean radiocarbon age (AD)	$\delta^{13}C$ (‰)	Std. dev.
Lawrence Gay	150	-20.8	0.4
Joe Gay	150	-20.6	0.3
Pete Klunk	175	-20.6	
Gibson	175	-21.0	
Knight	250	-21.0	1.0
Knight	400	-19.7	2.5
Yokem 6–7 Tomb	610	-21.3	0.6
Joe Gay	650	-19.5	1.9
Koster Mounds	700	-18.0	
Joe Gay	750	-19.1	4.5
Schild	870	-19.7	1.2
Schild Knoll A	960	-15.1	3.0
Helton Mound 47	995	-17.5	
Yokem	1000	-15.6	3.2
Ledders	1005	-17.0	
Schild Knoll B	1060	-13.0	1.2
Dickson Mounds	1175	-12.6	
Orendorf	1200	-9.2	
Kane Mounds	1200	-11.2	
East St. Louis Stone Quarry	1275	-11.0	
Florence Street	1275	-11.2	
Range	1275	-11.4	
Corbin Mounds	1275	-12.1	
Hill Prairie	1275	-14.6	
Yokem	1290	-14.6	2.1

the stable isotope ratios are consistent with regional temporal patterns for maize consumption. The isotopic evidence for little or no maize consumption during the Yokem phase is consistent with botanical assemblages from Yokem phase habitation sites, which have produced indigenous domesticates that were in use before the appearance of maize but no maize remains (Simon 2000).

Radiocarbon dates

Perino (2006a:387; see also Crane and Griffin 1972) obtained radiocarbon dates on wood charcoal from four of the Yokem phase tombs (table 4.3). These were reported among the last radiocarbon dates to be produced by the University of Michigan radiocarbon lab. When compared with recently obtained radiocarbon dates, the precision of the Michigan dates clearly is much lower than what can be obtained today. Based on the other dates reported in 1972 (Crane and Griffin 1972), a standard deviation of ±100 years appears to be the best precision that could be obtained by that lab at that time. The Michigan lab did not report stable carbon-isotope ratios, so the conventional radiocarbon age (obtained by adjusting the measured age according to the $\delta^{13}C$ value) can only be estimated using an estimated $\delta^{13}C$ value of -25‰, which is typical for prehistoric wood. The Michigan dates were calculated using a half-life of 5,570 years, while the more recent bone date is based on a half-life of 5,568 years. The difference between the two half-lives is negligible when the dates are normalized. The dates were calibrated with Calib 6.0 (Stuiver et al. 2011). Perino (2006a) noted that the wood charcoal dates were closely clustered but felt that the oldest date (1180 BP, or about AD 800 in radiocarbon years) was most likely to be closest to the true age of the site based on the artifacts associated with the burials and a similar date from the nearby Klunk site that produced very similar artifacts from similar burial features.

We obtained three new radiocarbon dates (table 4.3). One (Beta-240983) was on charred bone from an adult femur from the Mound 6–7 tomb. Two others (Beta-311359 and Beta-311360) were on wood charcoal fragments. We sought retained wood samples from the Gilcrease Institute at the University of Tulsa (Perino's employer and the archive for the collections from the site) and from the Museum of Anthropology at the

Table 4.3. Radiocarbon dates from the Yokem phase tombs

Sample	Provenience[a]	Measured radiocarbon age (BP)	Radiocarbon years AD	Calibrated 2σ range
Beta-240983	Bone from Tomb 6–7	1340±40	610	AD 637–772
Beta-311359	Tomb 6–7, Sample 1	1270±30	680	AD 668–771
Beta-311360	Tomb 6–7, Sample 2	1200±30	750	AD 712–936
M-2188	Tomb 6–7	1040±120	910	AD 695–1222
M-2189	Mound 7, Tomb A	1080±120	870	AD 682–1183
M-2190	Mound 8 Tomb	1080±120	870	AD 682–1183
M-2191	Mound 9, Tomb A	1180±120	770	AD 637–1149

[a] Wood charcoal unless otherwise noted.

University of Michigan. However, neither the Gilcrease Institute (Eric Singleton, personal communication, April 5, 2011) nor the University of Michigan (Karen O'Brien, personal communication, August 25, 2011) appears to have retained charcoal samples. The wood charcoal radiocarbon dates were obtained from small fragments of charcoal found with the curated bones that were fortuitously retained when they were mistaken for fragments of charred bone. The charcoal was from the white oak group, an excellent firewood (Leslie Bush, personal communication, October 20, 2011). Figure 4.2 shows the probability distributions of the 2σ calibrated radiocarbon dates listed in table 4.3. The relatively large standard deviations of the Michigan wood dates produce broad distributions with a low probability for any specific date or narrow date range. The Michigan wood dates are relatively similar to each other, as are the Beta wood dates, and all appear to be slightly later than the 6–7 tomb bone date. There appears to be a systematic difference of about a century between the Michigan and Beta Analytic dates (we believe

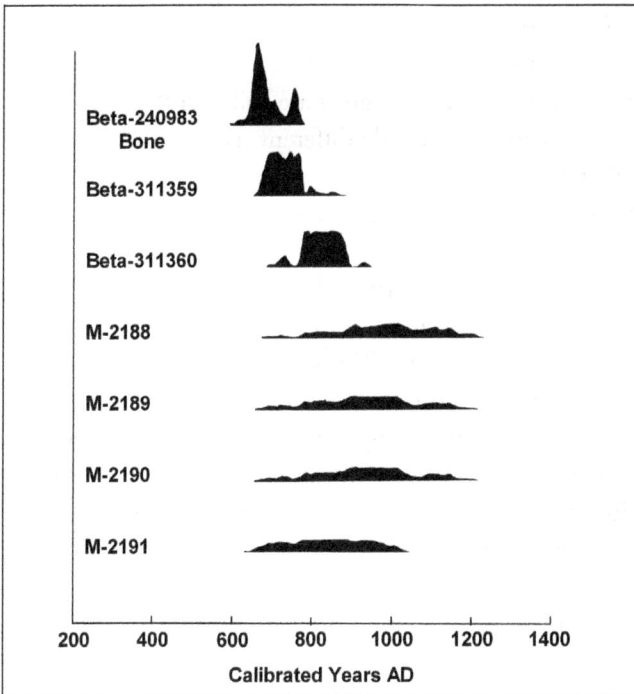

Figure 4.2. Calibrated probability distributions of radiocarbon dates from Yokem.

the Beta Analytic dates to be more accurate). However, the consistency within each set of dates suggests that all the burned wood was gathered at about the same time.

We would expect the wood dates from the 6–7 tomb to be earlier than the bone date because of the "old wood effect" of wooden timbers having fixed their carbon an unknown period of time before they were used. In this case, the Michigan dates just barely overlap with the bone date, with the wood date being later on the average than the bone date (table 4.3, figure 4.2). The bone date and the Michigan wood date are statistically different at a confidence level of α=.05 according to a t-test performed with Calib 6.0 (t=5.625, χ^2(df=1)=3.85). Similar results were obtained when the new wood charcoal dates with their much better precision were compared to the bone date, even though the mean calibrated dates for the wood charcoal samples recently dated by Beta Analytic are earlier than that of the Michigan sample. When only the dates from Beta Analytic are considered, the calibrated mean dates for the wood charcoal samples are still later than the bone sample. The three dates are significantly different ($t=8.10$, $\chi^2(df=2)=5.99$, $\alpha=.05$) among themselves, indicating that at least one of the dates is different from the others. The two charcoal samples are statistically identical ($t=2.72$, $\chi^2(df=1)=3.84$, $\alpha=.05$). The earliest charcoal date (Beta-311359) is not significantly different from the bone date ($t=1.96$, $\chi^2(df=1)=3.84$, $\alpha=.05$), but the later charcoal date is different from the bone date ($t=7.84$, $\chi^2(df=1)=3.84$, $\alpha=.05$). This suggests that the wood was probably formed later than the bone, but not much later, because we probably did not have the outermost ring of the timber. The internal consistency of the recently obtained radiocarbon dates, as well as the fact that their $\delta^{13}C$ values are what we expect for the dated materials, gives us a high level of confidence in the recently obtained dates.

Two explanations come to mind. The first is that the tomb roof was built (or rebuilt) after the burial that we dated was placed in the grave and was then burned. The second possibility is that the charcoal came from wood that was placed on the tomb to deliberately burn it before the tomb was covered with earth. If tombs were maintained in order to shelter their contents, roofing material and some structural supports would have required repair or replacement perhaps once a decade (Warrick 1988).

Discussion

A typical explanation for the pattern of burning seen at the Yokem site would be to conclude that partial cremation was a part of the mortuary ritual of the Yokem phase and that the differential use of cremation signaled some sort of difference between cremated and uncremated burials. For example, in their discussion of Late Archaic mortuary practices, Charles and Buikstra (1983) note that bluff-top burial sites in the lower Illinois Valley include a mix of uncremated and partially cremated burials that do not reflect two different corporate groups (one common explanation for bipartite mortuary patterns) but instead symbolize some other dichotomous aspect of Late Archaic society that is currently obscure (see Goldstein and Meyers, chap. 11, this volume).

As noted above, the cemeteries located at intervals along the bluff tops along the Illinois (and Mississippi) River valleys have been interpreted as evidence that lineages acting as corporate groups placed their dead in highly visible locations to signal their ownership of specific territories (Charles and Buikstra 1983). In the lower Illinois Valley, the earliest cemeteries were established closest to the bluff edge, and later groups successively added their burial sites farther away from the bluff edge (table 4.4). The Schild site in the lower Illinois Valley (Perino 1973b) provides a good illustration of the typical chronological arrangement of mounds in the region. At Schild, mounds and cemeteries follow the expected Illinois Valley pattern of earlier burials near the bluff edge and later ones farther from it. The mounds were distributed across three different bluff tops. On the northern bluff top, Mounds 4 through 8 dated to the Late Woodland, and Mound 3 (the farthest from the bluff edge) dated to the late Late Woodland. On the southern bluff top, middle Late Woodland mounds are located at the bluff edge, with a later Jersey Bluff burial area located on the ridge behind them (and interestingly enough, a historic cemetery is then located behind the Jersey Bluff mounds). A final Late Woodland mound (Mound 9) was located on a ridge above Dayton Hollow and is the most distant mound from the bluff edge. A Mississippian cemetery was located to the south of that mound even farther from the valley.

The opposite pattern is present at Yokem, where later burial sites are successively closer to the bluff edge, and consequently more visible from the valley floor. For Mounds 2 and 3, the final burial feature (a Mississippian-acculturated charnel house) was placed on a mound previously used as a cemetery by earlier Jersey Bluff phase people. In the lower Illinois Valley, it could be argued that the general pattern is one of continuity of title, where later groups incorporated earlier burial features into their own local burial landscapes. At Yokem, later groups could possibly have attempted to obliterate or obscure earlier burial features, perhaps as a statement about the presence of new corporate owners establishing title to the site. In this scenario, the burnt or collapsed and lightly mounded Yokem phase tombs at Yokem were damaged and buried by people wishing to destroy earlier titles to the landscape symbolized through mortuary ritual. The cremations at Yokem would therefore be incidental to the act of tomb destruction.

Table 4.4. Burial patterns over time in the region

Period	Dates	Burial patterns
Middle and Late Archaic	4000–2000 BC	Establishment of bluff-top cemeteries
Terminal Archaic	~ 1000 BC	Crematories at Klunk Mound 7
Early Woodland	1000–150 BC	Red Ocher burial ceremonialism
Middle Woodland	150 BC–AD 350	Hopewell burial ceremonialism
Middle Late Woodland	AD 600–800	Burned tombs at Yokem, Klunk, Joe Gay, Perrins Ledge
Late Late Woodland	AD 800–1000	Jersey Bluff—cremation of about 10 percent of burials, cremated burials mainly in group burials
Mississippian	Post–AD 1000	Charnel houses, burned

Nevertheless, cremation was clearly sometimes a part of the middle Late Woodland burial program, and we cannot absolutely rule out the possibility that incidental cremation was part of the Yokem mortuary program. For example, the Perrins Ledge Crematory site in the lower Illinois Valley is roughly contemporary with the Yokem phase tombs at the Yokem site, based on the types of artifacts found at each site, including pottery styles and clay pipes at each site (Buikstra and Goldstein 1973). The Perrins Ledge site contained two crematory features, only one of which was excavated. The excavated feature consisted of a circular ring of limestone slabs and pieces about 6.1 meters in diameter with a central area about 2.4 meters in diameter that contained less limestone. The central area was a crematory basin in which thirteen individuals were cremated in more than one episode over some period of time. The last two burials made at the site had been partially cremated while the body was still fleshed. Because of the fragmentary nature of the other remains, and the diverse burning patterns upon them, it was not possible to say whether those individuals had also been cremated in the flesh with additional burning of their fragments as later cremations occurred, or whether some of the cremated bones were from disarticulated burials (Buikstra and colleagues consider the former to be more likely). At this time, the Perrins Ledge Crematory seems to be a unique mortuary feature that probably served small middle Late Woodland groups that resided in the vicinity (Buikstra and Goldstein 1973; Goldstein and Meyers, chap. 11, this volume). The Perrins Ledge Crematory reflects a different set of cremation practices than at Yokem. The cremation of a few individuals at a time in a designated crematorium is very different from the pattern at Yokem, where many defleshed individuals were simultaneously cremated when their tomb was burned.

A limestone cremation feature was also found at the Joe Gay site (Perino 2006b), a Late Woodland bluff-top mound site that probably dated to the early Late Woodland White Hall phase that preceded the Yokem phase. Joe Gay is located about 13 kilometers to the north of Yokem along the Mississippi Valley. The feature is roughly similar to the circular ones at Yokem but was badly disturbed. Instead of containing burials cremated in situ, it apparently served as a cremation area for burials that were interred intrusively into a nearby mound (Cook and Palkovich 2006). The Homer Adams Mounds, the mound group nearest to Yokem, contained at least one mound (Mound 5) that was contemporary with the Yokem phase mounds at the Yokem site (Perino 2006c). Homer Adams Mound 5 contained a subfloor tomb and other burials. Our understanding of this site is limited by poor bone preservation, looting, and missing excavation plans. However, the site contained no cremations or limestone tombs, highlighting the substantial variation in mortuary activities during the Late Woodland even among closely contemporary sites. At this time, we believe that sites such as Yokem, Homer Adams, Joe Gay, and Perrins Ledge served as burial sites for nonsedentary hunter-collectors who lived in widely dispersed homesteads or hamlets. These inferences are based primarily on surface surveys and limited excavations of habitation sites (O'Gorman and Hassan 2000; Studenmund 2000), and the limitations of the existing data could mask additional variations in middle Late Woodland burial practices.

For an example of a burnt burial from a later period, Mallorie Hatch (2012) has called attention to burnt elements in a comingled, secondary burial of twelve persons at the Mississippian Larson site in the central Illinois Valley. A young adult vault with cut marks suggesting careful removal of the temporalis muscle is described as scorched, and seventeen other fragments range from scorched to calcined. Hatch considers scenarios ranging from accidental burning to cannibalism but favors captive sacrifice in her interpretation. She relies on Jesuit accounts of Iroquois ritual torture and consumption of captives, who were then "burned upon a pyre" (Hatch 2012:205). There happens to be archaeological confirmation of Iroquois practices (Tuck 1971a, 1971b), which, however, do not resemble the Larson site find in detail: the defleshed skeleton was burned in situ and thus recovered from a hearth deposit, and the bones were extensively and relatively uniformly burnt. Likewise, the practices documented at Larson do not resemble the Yokem Late Woodland examples, and the Mississippian component at Yokem produced little burnt bone.

The Pete Klunk site in the lower Illinois Valley also contained Late Woodland cremations (Perino 1973a). They included small crematory basins, burnt wooden structures within mounds, and two crematories constructed using limestone slabs. Perino added a postscript to his discussion of the seven Late Woodland crematories at the Pete Klunk site, indicating that he had concluded that the "crematories" at Pete Klunk were originally log tombs similar to the wooden Tomb C in Mound 6 at the Yokem site. They appeared to be crematories because the log structures were accidentally or deliberately burned. He concludes that although there were definite, deliberate cremations during the Late Archaic period, Late Woodland cremations may have been incidental when the tombs were burned. He asks several questions that still bedevil us today (Perino 1973a:89): "How does one define an intentional crematory from one created by other means such as the burning of wooden charnel structures or the roofs on stone tombs, charring the human remains inside[?] Can the burning of a charnel structure with human remains inside be considered a crematory? It is important to know if the human remains were intentionally burned in these structures; or were they burned in an effort to be rid of the dilapidated structures?"

There is no well-developed theoretical framework that can be used to determine whether the use of fire at Yokem was part of the mortuary program undertaken by those burying their ancestors, or by successors attempting to obliterate the monuments of their predecessors so the site could be repurposed for their own burials. In the former case, we could view the burnt tombs at Yokem as "ephemeral monuments" produced through cremation (Williams 2004a). In the latter case, cremation might have been used in a way analogous to the Norman destruction of Anglo-Saxon churches and monuments (D. O'Sullivan 2011). Although the origins of the Jersey Bluff phase are not well understood, it is generally accepted to have developed in the Illinois Valley (Studenmund 2000) and then expanded to appear intrusively in other areas such as the American Bottom to the south (J. Kelly 2000:172), and perhaps in the vicinity of the Yokem site as well. Jersey Bluff phase habitation sites are larger and more spatially structured and appear to represent longer-term occupations than those of the preceding phases (Studenmund 2000:326). Larger and more-permanent population concentrations supported by maize cultivation would likely have been associated with changes in the concept of land tenure. Those changes could have been symbolized by using fire to destroy or transform earlier burial markers. If all the tombs were burned simultaneously, it would have been a visually striking and memorable event. Bement (1994) has pointed out that semi-defleshed bones produce a bright light when burned, a property that lies at the root of the word *bonfire*.

Conclusion

The formal attributes of the tombs, associated artifacts, radiocarbon dates, and human stable carbon-isotope ratios indicate that the burnt Yokem phase tombs at the Yokem site, including the 6–7 tomb, were produced near the start of the middle Late Woodland period. Cremation was practiced in different ways at sites in the region over more than two millennia, but in general, cremation seems to have been a less popular mortuary treatment than unburnt inhumation, except at a few sites such as Perrins Ledge and Yokem. The differing uses of cremation through time suggest that there was no long-term continuity in the ways in which fire was employed in mortuary rituals in the region. If the radiocarbon dates from the site are correct, the Yokem cremated burials could have been placed in tombs built by middle Late Woodland Yokem phase people, and some of those tombs could have been burned or collapsed after about AD 890 by Jersey Bluff people who later co-opted the site for their own cemetery. The Yokem phase tombs may have been deliberately obliterated by the Jersey Bluff people to erase the land titles of their non-maize-growing predecessors. At least one such account of destruction and desecration of an ossuary during warfare is recorded in the narratives of the de Soto expedition in the mid-sixteenth century: "Then they threw to the floor each of the wooden chests which served as sepulchers, and for their own satisfaction and vengeance, as well as for an affront to their enemies, strewed upon the ground the very bones and bodies the chest enclosed. Afterward not content with having cast these remains to the ground, they trod upon them and kicked them with utter contempt and scorn" (Sabo 1993:201–2).

When cremated and noncremated burials are found in contemporary archaeological contexts, they are frequently interpreted as evidence for some form of social differentiation within a society. By closely examining the cultural and chronological contexts of the Yokem cremations, we have shown that one possible explanation for the presence of cremation at the Yokem site was not as a marker of intrasocial differentiation or unfortunate accidents but instead may have been the deliberate attempt by successor groups to obliterate physical markers of land title created by earlier occupants of the valley. This illustrates how close consideration of the timing of the burning episode is critical for understanding cremation in the past. The Yokem site provides a unique insight into the challenge of defining "cremation" and an incidental yet distinctive Native American contribution to the global conversation about the practices and social meanings of cremation in this volume.

5

A Well-Urned Rest

Cremation and Inhumation in
Early Anglo-Saxon England

Howard Williams

Cremation and inhumation practices in early medieval Europe are usually considered separately. This chapter considers the contemporaneous use of these two mortuary corporeal trajectories deployed in one area of early medieval Europe: early Anglo-Saxon England. Cremation and inhumation are theorized as related but distinct technologies of remembrance. They each operated to transform and rebuild the personhood of the deceased by selective social remembering and forgetting, albeit via contrasting tempos and materialities. Focusing on the similarities and differences between cremation and inhumation in the commemorative significance afforded to pottery vessels, the chapter addresses the single most-ubiquitous artifact type deployed in the burial of the cremated dead in early Anglo-Saxon England and one of a series of vessel types placed in inhumation graves. For the first time, the study explores how the use of pottery allows us to identify both contrasts and themes linking the burning and burial of the early Anglo-Saxon dead. Specifically, pots are argued to have mnemonically and metaphorically "rehydrated" and "nourished" inhumed cadavers and were placed on pyres with a similar motivation. The difference comes in the postcremation rites, in which cinerary urns had an additional significance by "storing" and perhaps even "fermenting" cremains in the grave, interpreted here as a means of corporeal regeneration and animation following death. Hence, the use of pots shows a distinction in how cremation and inhumation practices operated as commemorative mechanisms through their deployment of material culture, yet equally how these uses of pots in both disposal methods were closely connected to each other and to the pots' daily use. Therefore, I contend that the pots' varied mortuary significances as a commemorative medium were rooted in the habitus of early Anglo-Saxon daily life, especially in making and storing food and drink. In so doing, my approach resonates with a practice-oriented approach to understanding early medieval pottery (see Gosden 2011; Jervis 2011; Perry 2012a, 2012b) but extends and adapts this approach to consider the use of pots in the mortuary arena, particularly the use of vessels in the sequence and tempo of the funeral. This presents a different perspective on the relationship between cremation and inhumation in early Anglo-Saxon England by seeing them as related mortuary technologies operating dialectically with each other, the results of practical choices made by the survivors to negotiate their identities and social memories. This approach contrasts somewhat with previous attempts to regard cremation and inhumation as oppositional indices of specific cultural origins, religious cults, ethnic identities, or ideologies. Likewise, it confronts attempts to regard cremation and inhumation as arbitrary choices, by seeing them as either synonymous mechanisms for mortuary display or interchangeable fashions in corpse disposal (for critiques of previous work, see Williams 2002a, 2011a; for a recent view, see Hines 2011:979).

The focus of inquiry is a single burial site chosen because it has received extensive excavation and detailed osteological analysis and its grave catalogues have been published. The site in question is the large cemetery of Spong Hill, Norfolk (Hills 1977; Hills and Penn 1981; Hills et al. 1984, 1987, 1994; McKinley 1994b). The cemetery comprises approximately 2,500 cremation graves and a small group of 58 inhumation graves. The final chronological and social analysis of this cemetery was published only after this paper was composed (for interim discussions, see Hills 1980, 1993, 1994, 1998, 1999; McKinley 1994b); Lucy and Hills now suggest that the burial ground dated from the early fifth century through to the mid-sixth century, with the inhumations representing an element of the later part of the cemetery's use (Lucy and Hills 2013; see also Higham and Ryan 2013).

Introducing Cremation in Early Anglo-Saxon England

The term "early Anglo-Saxon England" refers to the lowland south and east of the island of Britain between the middle of the fifth century and the early seventh century AD (see Hamerow et al. 2011). Direct Roman control of their province of Britannia ceased by the second decade of the fifth century and was followed by socioeconomic and political fragmentation. Germanic settlers and political domination spread through southern and eastern Britain over the next century. Powerful kingdoms formed by the late sixth and early seventh centuries, subsuming both Germanic and British rival territories. Following conversion to Christianity, the early eighth-century monk, the Venerable Bede, tells us that the royal families of the kingdoms of his day—Kent, Essex, Sussex, Wessex, East Anglia, Mercia, and Northumbria—charted descent from three Continental tribes: the Angles, Saxons, and Jutes (Higham and Ryan 2013:70–126; Sims-Williams 1983).

Despite the simplicity of Bede's account, both the scale of Germanic immigration and the level of British survival in the fifth century remain hotly debated (e.g., Brugmann 2011; Härke 2011). The situation in all likelihood fluctuated considerably between localities and regions. As well as significant native British contributions, Germanic immigrants probably derived from many more groups than those historically recognized and may have come from Frankia, Frisia, and Norway as well as Saxony and the Jutland peninsula.

Furnished graves are pivotal to understanding the complex cultural and socioeconomic shifts under way in southern and eastern Britain during the so-called Migration Period. They were first described in the late seventeenth century by Thomas Browne and then by the mid-eighteenth-century barrow digger Bryan Faussett. However, they were first attributed to the Saxons by James Douglas, a late eighteenth-century barrow digger (Content and Williams 2010). The political climate of the early Victorian era saw an intense interest in the "pagan Anglo-Saxon" grave, reflecting contemporary pro-German nationalist and imperialist discourses (Content and Williams 2010; Williams 2006a, 2008b). The systematic compilation and culture-historical analysis of early Anglo-Saxon burial evidence had to wait until the extensive work on brooches by E. T. Leeds and pottery by J. N. L. Myres during the early to mid-twentieth century (Williams 2002a). Throughout these studies, cremation as a burial procedure received limited comment, but when it did, burning the dead was regarded as emblematic of pagan Germanic customs.

Over the past half century, early Anglo-Saxon burial archaeology has been the focus of intense debates and rapidly evolving archaeological theories and methods applied to an ever-expanding data set. Increasingly, studies have integrated archaeological and osteological approaches together with evidence for burial position, grave structures, monuments, cemetery organization, and landscape analyses (reviewed in Williams 2011a). Consequently, early Anglo-Saxon burial archaeology is important for scholars of early medieval history and archaeology interested in migration, social structure, ideology, and religious change, but it also contributes an important venue for testing and debating the social interpretation of mortuary data. Traditionally, furnished burial practice—including cremation and inhumation—has often been seen as reflecting Germanic settlement and/or influence (e.g., Hills 2003). Yet in the light of recent approaches and perspectives, death rituals might be more profitably regarded as one important arena in which identities and memories were negotiated and created from families and households of contrasting and diverse origins (Williams 1999a, 2006a). Death rituals were constitutive, not simply reflective, of new sociopolitical formations.

Exploring Cremation in Early Anglo-Saxon England

In the archaeological investigation of early Anglo-Saxon mortuary practice, cremation has received less attention from archaeologists in comparison with contemporary early Anglo-Saxon furnished inhumation graves. Yet cremation has been identified throughout southern and eastern England in this period and is found in varying proportions at different cemeteries.

In eastern England, we find a distinct category of large cremation cemeteries where inhumation is the minority rite. The principal large cremation cemeteries of eastern England excavated by modern methods and reaching publication include Cleatham, North Lincolnshire (Leahy 2007); Newark, Nottinghamshire (Kinsley 1989); Rayleigh, Essex (Ennis 2009); Sancton, East Yorkshire (Timby 1993); and Spong Hill, Norfolk (McKinley 1994b; see below). Elsewhere, cremation was utilized contemporaneously alongside inhumations within the same burial sites. Recently published examples of mixed-rite cemeteries of southern and central England include Alwalton, Cambridgeshire (Gibson 2007); Apple Down, Sussex (Down and Welch 1990); Great Chesterford, Essex (Evison 1994a); Mucking, Essex (Cemetery II: Hirst and Clark 2009); Springfield Lyons, Essex (Tyler and Major 2005); Wasperton, Warwickshire (Carver et al. 2009); and Worthy Park, Kingsworthy, Hampshire (Hawkes and Grainger 2003).

There are many more cemeteries in which cremation appears as a minority practice, for example, at Norton (Cleveland), where 117 inhumation graves were found but only three cremation pits (Sherlock and Welch 1992). Partly, this can be explained by cremation being rapidly abandoned in some areas during the late fifth and the sixth century. Yet it must be borne in mind that shallow cremation graves are likely to be underrepresented during most excavations, lost to the plow or machine truncation. Nevertheless, although cremation had become increasingly rare—and perhaps absent in many areas—by the seventh century, there are examples from southern England of late seventh-century cremation graves that serve to illustrate that cremation could be a tenacious or resurgent practice during and after Christian conversion (Stoodley 2005:76).

Early Anglo-Saxon cremation was a variable technology over time and space but clearly also in relation to the social identity of the deceased and the circumstances of the death (Ravn 2003; Richards 1987; Williams 2000). However, in general terms, it often involved the burning of one or more human bodies together with a range of materials, substances, and structures. There is evidence that the cadavers were dressed and wrapped when placed on the pyre, as indicated by copper-alloy dress accessories fused to cremated human bone (McKinley 1994b). Food and drink accompanied the dead, as evidenced by fragments of vessels, plant remains, and animal bones (most commonly sheep/goat and pig). Whole animals were sometimes placed on pyres with the cadaver, usually horses but sometimes also cattle and dogs (Bond 1996). The color of the cremated bone indicates that burning the dead in early Anglo-Saxon England was usually an efficient and complete process, particularly in the large cremation cemeteries of eastern England (McKinley 1994b).

Cremation pyres are rarely found, but there are some examples of possible pyre sites and pyre debris deposits on cemetery sites. This suggests that limited excavation and taphonomic factors (particularly medieval and postmedieval agriculture), rather than their absence, explain their rarity (e.g., Ennis 2009:55; Filmer-Sankey and Pestell 2001:252–55; C. Gibson 2007:250; see also Williams 2000:214–22).

We know more about the postcremation treatment of the cremains. This featured the collection and burial of a portion of the ashes in a cinerary urn. Sometimes this portion might be the whole body (or bodies), sometimes only a handful of cremains, but most often somewhere in between these extremes. Some of the ashes may have been left at the pyre or circulated among mourners. The urns used were often decorated with incisions, stamps, and/or bosses. Artifacts showing traces of having accompanied the cadaver on the pyre were often present, including items of dress such as glass beads and brooches. Unburnt artifacts were sometimes added to the contents of the urns, including fragments of bone and antler combs and toilet implements (tweezers, shears, razors, and ear scoops) of bronze and iron.

The urns were buried in shallow pits, sometimes containing multiple urns. The pits were sometimes protected with stones, flints, or reused Roman tiles (Williams 2000:223–26).

Cremation allowed cinerary urns to be placed within close proximity, itself a significant and distinctive aspect of the burial process. There is evidence that many had modest aboveground markers, either low mounds with or without ring ditches, lines of posts or fences, and single posts (Williams 2000:226–32; e.g., Carver et al. 2009:27–28). At some southern and central English sites, four- and five-post structures cover certain cremation burials, and indeed, cremated human remains could have been interred aboveground in these structures (Down and Welch 1990:25–26; C. Gibson 2007:250). Tentative evidence from undated tree-throws has led C. Gibson to suggest that cremation burials may have been placed in wooded glades (C. Gibson 2007:291). Cremation burials are found in rows or clusters and were interred in cemeteries of varying size and duration, together with inhumation graves in varying proportions.

My research has drawn upon the excavation results cited above and has been inspired by the work of Julian D. Richards (1987), who first addressed the mortuary variability of early Anglo-Saxon cremation practices in a systematic manner. Building on my doctoral studies, over the past decade I have considered the relationship between cremation and inhumation through the following arguments:

1. Victorian racial and religious ideas have had an enduring influence and have tended to stereotype and stylize early Anglo-Saxon cremation in normative terms as distinctively "Germanic," "pagan," and "primitive" in relation to inhumation (Williams 2002a, 2006b, 2008b). Despite the influential work of Hills (1980, 1993, 1998), Richards (1987), and Ravn (2003), this has continued to stifle our interpretations of mortuary variability within and between the cremation rite and its shifting relationships with inhumation graves.

2. Early Anglo-Saxon mortuary practices (both cremation and inhumation) remain susceptible to misinterpretations pervading how we reconstruct graves and funerals through text and images (Williams 2006a, 2007a, 2007b, 2009).

3. The distributions of cremation and inhumation suggest that both disposal methods were prevalent in varying proportions across most of southern and eastern England and operated to articulate social distinctions in different ways in different burial environments. Excavations in East Yorkshire, the eastern Midlands, and East Anglia (and perhaps also parts of Essex) have revealed a distinctive use of cremation in large cemeteries, possibly a strategy of distinction by certain groups who persisted over many generations with an overtly conservative burial tradition (Williams 2002a).

4. Cremation and inhumation involved contrasting uses of mortuary monumentality and cemetery space and place (Williams 2000). Early Anglo-Saxon cemeteries tend to reuse locally prominent ancient monuments (Williams 1997, 2006a), yet the large cremation cemeteries may have had a further and distinctive landscape context as elements of central places with sociopolitical and cultic functions (Williams 2002b, 2004c).

5. Cremation and inhumation were linked but contrasting technologies of remembrance in which the experience of the cadaver's transformation operated through distinctive forms and different tempos (Williams 2004b, 2006a).

6. Iron items—buckles, knives, and weapons—are underrepresented in cremation graves, suggesting their recycling and deliberate disassociation from the cremains. Rather than the male gender being negated or de-emphasized in cremation practices, the circulation patterns of material culture during the ritual process of cremation might have been significant in the commemoration of personhood in death. This avoidance of iron pyre goods stands in contrast to those in operation in inhumation graves, where weapon burials were commonplace as expressions of adult male identity (Williams 2005a).

7. The high proportion of animal remains, particularly horse and sheep/goat, suggests that domestic animals were more important in constructing the identity of the cremated dead (Williams 2001, 2005b), whereas animal remains found in inhumation graves are significant—varied with regard to both species and being found as whole animals, fragments, and artifacts—but relatively rare (e.g., Nugent 2011a).

8. Certain artifacts held a distinctive commemorative role in the cremation burial rite in contrast with the material culture found in inhumation graves. The cinerary urn provided a new metaphorical and mnemonic "skin" or "body" for the cremated person(s). Unburnt items were sometimes added to the cinerary urn after the cremation, suggesting a specific association between hair management and postcremation rituals. Combs and both full-sized and miniature tweezers, razors, shears, and ear scoops placed with the cremains can be seen as items polluted through close association with the mourning rituals and/or the cadaver. As such, they served in mnemonic and metaphorical body building, providing the cremains with a new corporeality by signaling practices and material culture linked to hair management (Williams 2003a, 2006a, 2007a).

Extending these arguments, the remainder of the chapter presents comparisons and contrasts between cremation and inhumation in early Anglo-Saxon England, focusing on hitherto underexplored similarities and differences in the use of pottery in the two methods of disposal. This allows us to better understand the significance of cremation practices in early Anglo-Saxon England, the relationship of cremation with contemporary inhumation practices, and the ultimate decline of cremation.

Pottery and the Relationship Between Cremation and Inhumation

The underlying arguments addressed by this case study are twofold. First, across many past cultures, humble pottery vessels can be readily available and convenient receptacles for cremains. Yet for the cremated dead, they can also serve as highly charged mnemonic media by which the dead are transported, interred, mourned, and commemorated (see Larsson 2009a; Williams 2004b). The pottery of early Anglo-Saxon England has been considered in terms of its economic and symbolic roles from both burial and settlement contexts (Haith 1997; Hamerow 1993; Richards 1987), but its comparative mortuary uses in both inhumation and cremation graves have escaped detailed investigation (although see Lee 2007).

Second, in the human past, cremation is almost always a ritual technological choice situated among other possibilities for the disposal of the dead. Past mortuary programs involving cremation in isolation are the exception. Therefore, interpreting cremation in past societies should focus on not only why groups cremate and what cremation meant per se but also how and why cremation was utilized in relation to other disposal strategies within the same societies and communities.

Many cemeteries dating to the early Anglo-Saxon period (circa AD 425–650) deployed at least two contrasting mortuary technologies: cremation and inhumation. There might have been other disposal choices, but these have not left a conclusive archaeological trace. Ceramic vessels were deployed in both burial traditions. Past explanations for this variability have been either simplistic or ill considered. For instance, seeing the distinction as resulting from cremation being more conservative, pagan, or Germanic and seeing the disposal methods as contrasting ideologies are misleading (Williams 2002a, 2011a; see also C. Gibson 2007). Likewise, regarding both as simply alternative ways of doing the same thing—displaying identity in a public ritual arena—overlooks the very different tempos and technologies employed in each disposal method, as well as the very different corporeal and material forms created by each process.

A more satisfactory approach is to regard early Anglo-Saxon cremation and inhumation as neither identical nor complete opposites. Instead, the two disposal strategies might be regarded as *relational technologies* employing different but related chains of techniques in corporeal transformation to construct strategies of distinction (Williams 2002a, 2011a). As such, each did not possess a single meaning or message. Sometimes either cremation or inhumation might have been employed to signal social and ideological distinctions between groups. In other instances, the choice mediated distinctions within communities. In other words, context seems to have defined the significance of the two technologies (see Hills 1999:21). The implications of this point are widely applicable in the study of past cremation practices. Archaeologists should be less worried about explaining *why* cremation and inhumation were used together. Indeed, multiple disposal methods should be seen as the norm for the mortuary programs of most societies past and present. Instead we should focus on *how* they were employed in relation to each other (see Williams 2002a, 2011a). If we accept this argument, then the similarities and contrasts in how pottery was deployed may have mediated the creation of distinctions and shared identities linking the living with the dead.

Pots from Cremation Graves at Spong Hill

Thanks to careful and extensive excavations and high-quality grave catalogues (Hills 1977; Hills and Penn 1981; Hills et al. 1987, 1994), together with the detailed osteological research of Jackie McKinley (1994b) and Julie Bond (1996), it is possible to regard cremation practices at Spong Hill as involving not only fiery transformation but also the building of a new ancestral "skin" or "body" for the cremains. A large portion of cremains were retrieved from the remnants of the pyre and placed in poorly fired, handmade cinerary urns, many with complex incised, plastic, and stamped decorative schemes on their upper surfaces (figure 5.1). Some pots had lids, and many were carefully packed around with flints. A minority of urns (approximately 10 percent) were "holed" through their walls and/or base before burial. This is often regarded as a ritual act using a tool or weapon, although Perry (2012a, 2012b) has proposed

Figure 5.1. A group of Spong Hill cinerary urns. (Reproduced by kind permission of Norfolk Museums Service.)

a convincing alternative suggestion that these were vessels used to make butter or beer. Certainly, some of the holes were plugged with lead prior to use as cinerary urns, which Perry (2012a) sees as a practical postfiring repair rather than a ritual act. Indeed, the inclusion of a selection of the cremains together with unburnt items added following cremation *within* an urn emphasizes the importance of transportation and containment within the postcremation rituals.

Pots were not only used to contain the human dead; often, animal remains were placed in the same pots (see Bond 1996; McKinley 1994b). In further instances, so-called animal accessory vessels were included, usually dominated by cremated horse remains (Fern 2007; Williams 2005b). The pots therefore contained an identity forged by fire that merged material culture, animals, and humans.

Urn size, shape, and decoration may have all had a bearing on the pot's role in communicating and constituting the deceased's identity in death (Richards 1987; see also Ravn 2003; Williams 2000). This argument is supported by the evidence that those artifacts preferentially placed with the cremains were items used in hair dressing, plucking, cutting, and shaving: combs and toilet implements (Williams 2003a,

2007a). Together this evidence indicates that the principal role of the cinerary urn was to protect and constitute an integrity and commemorative wholeness following the destruction and fragmentation of the cremation process—a form of corporeal regeneration.

While Richards (1992) noted that urn decoration, when viewed from above, displays a similar impression to contemporary annular brooches worn as an element of Anglian female costume, Hills has observed how both the motifs employed and the emphasis on the "framing" of animal and human cremated material by the decorated cinerary urns resemble the same relationship identified on the punch-marked surrounds encircling the representation of deities and monsters on southern Scandinavian gold bracteates of the sixth century (Hills 1999:23–24). These Migration Period Scandinavian renditions of Roman imperial coins are often seen as symbols of political and sacred authority depicting beasts, birds, and human figures, often appearing to merge and transform into each other. This imagery has often been linked to the psychopompic and shape-shifting attributes of shamans and the Norse god Odin in particular (e.g., Hedeager 1999). Indeed, the role of abstract decoration in adorning surfaces, thresholds, and liminal zones is widely found in late Antique and early medieval artifacts, art, and architecture (Hawkes 1997).

This argument has some specific implications for the significance afforded to the decoration of cinerary urns in the mortuary arena, for just as the pot physically contains the ashes, so too the decoration creates a symbolic boundary, "framing" the cremated remains of humans and animals. Indeed, this may have mirrored the "framing" of the cadaver as it was dressed and placed on the pyre surrounded by sacrificed animals. In this regard, the very act of selecting a decorated cinerary urn—even if the precise meaning of the decorative motifs may elude us—enhanced the commemoration and reconstitution of the cremated dead. Each pot cites its own life history of use to contain and store things, as well as simultaneously invoking memories of previous funerals in which pots were also interred as cinerary urns (see A. Jones 2001). Therefore, pot and artifacts did not symbolize a static social identity held by the deceased and constructed by survivors but instead created mnemonic citations linking the deceased with pot use as part of the habitus of early Anglo-Saxon settlements and the recollection of past funerals. Moreover, these artifacts were not merely only about citations to past events and practices; they were also prospective, creating a new identity for the grave and/or the afterlife. In this regard, pots can be considered to be catalytic converters of memory, articulating the regeneration of corporeality following fiery destruction (Williams 2013). Elsewhere I argue that the cinerary urns were afforded a further significance because of the ocular qualities of their decoration (Nugent and Williams 2012). The cremated dead were remade as sensing beings, inhabiting their graves, as indicated by the "ocular" character of many cinerary urns.

The life histories of the cinerary urns may have also been important to their commemorative significance as vessels for the cremated dead. Urns could have been either made for or selected for the funeral to fulfill the practical role of housing the cremains, both for an unknown duration following the collection of the cremains from the funeral pyre and for burial. Between collection and burial, cinerary urns may have been displayed, transported, and handled aboveground for days, weeks, months, or even years. For other cemeteries, such as Mucking (Essex), the settlement, cremation, and inhumation pottery were compared and found to be similar, although the larger urns and "finer" fabrics were selected for the cinerary urns (Hirst and Clark 2009:603, 610). This evidence suggests that vessels were not purpose-made, but instead the "best" available vessels were preferentially selected as cinerary containers for their size and perhaps for their shape and decorative schemes in relation to the social identity of the deceased. We can only speculate as to whether urns with a particular biography were considered predestined to operate as cinerary urns during their use-lives. These may have been possessions of the deceased, intimately connected to the person and hence polluted and requiring disposal, or else gifts brought by mourners to the funeral containing food or drink.

For the Lincolnshire cremation cemeteries of Cleatham and Elsham, recent research on internal and external use-alteration by Gareth Perry is providing evidence suggesting that decorated cinerary urns had previous use-lives that involved making and/or storing beer and dairy products. In contrast, undecorated pots are more commonly sooted and were therefore more likely to have been involved in cooking and heating activities (Perry 2012a, 2012b).

Therefore, decorated pots preferentially selected as cinerary urns were associated with food production and storage, the prelude to cooking, eating, and drinking. Indeed, this association with food and drink production and storage, rather than any links to fiery technologies of pot making and use, may have been the sought-after metaphors by which the cremated dead were conceptualized and commemorated. In the postcremation stages, urns served to "store" (or indeed "ferment") the cremains.

What is clear is that the cremated dead had already been transformed by fire, and the pots selected as cinerary urns were also products of a parallel fiery transformation. Yet their significance as vessels linked to storage and production is what may have rendered cinerary urns significant in terms of how the dead were mourned and remembered. Moreover, the process of beer or butter making, the former requiring the use of heat to malt the grain and both involving a heat-producing fermentation process, might have been seen by early Anglo-Saxon people as having closer parallels to the multistage cremation process involving the burning and subsequent inurnment of the cremains than pot making, metalworking, or food preparation (contra Williams 2005a; this point is also made by Perry 2012a). This affords us with an alternative view on the cremated dead in early Anglo-Saxon England, one by which the cinerary urn was not a final destination but a place where the dead were regenerated and lived on in, or travelled onward from, their graves.* More specifically, burying cremains in an urn created a future-memory of the deceased as planted, nourished, and growing, not simply stored, within the cemetery.

Yet ceramic vessels clearly were also employed in earlier stages of the cremation ceremonies. From ninety-one cremation graves at Spong Hill, reburnt Saxon potsherds were recovered (McKinley 1994b:91; see also Hirst and Clark 2009:620). Cereal grains and nutshells from a small number of urns might represent the traces of food offerings placed on the pyre (McKinley 1994b:91–92). Moreover, wooden vessels and boxes, iron-bound buckets, and glass vessels were also added to pyres (Evison 1994b; C. Morris 1994). Together with the zooarchaeological evidence

---

*I am indebted to Åsa Larsson for her superbly insightful observations on this issue and to Gareth Perry for discussions about his work on pottery from early Anglo-Saxon contexts.

that horses, cattle, and dogs, and more rarely foxes and raptors, were likely placed as whole animals, other animal species found are likely to reflect food remains placed on pyres. These include the frequent occurrence of sheep/goat and pig, augmented by the possibility that some of the cattle and horse remains reflect feasting. Rarer occurring species that may have formed part of funerary feasting shared between mourners and the dead include deer, domestic fowl, and fish (Bond 1994, 1996). Pyres may have been stacked with food and drink together with the bodies of people and animals, indicating that food and drink were integral to performance and significance, particularly those connected with consumption and destruction, in the early stages of the cremation ceremonies of early Anglo-Saxon England. In other words, the early Anglo-Saxon cremated dead were being nourished and hydrated during the cremation ceremonies from pyre to burial. Alcoholic drinks may have been shared by mourners and placed on the pyre but might also have been used to accelerate ignition, as might have butter. Likewise, beer might have been used to douse the smoldering pyre. We also do not know whether the cremains were submerged in food and liquids poured into the urn for burial.

Indeed, at a number of early Anglo-Saxon burial sites where both inhumation and cremation were practiced, there is now increasing evidence that feasting activities took place around graves; this is indicated at Cossington (Leicestershire) by two grave-shaped pits contained burnt stone (Jo. Thomas 2008:58, 63–65; see also Filmer-Sankey and Pestell 2001:259–61).

The implications of this evidence are fourfold. First, pottery drew its presence and significance from the importance of eating and drinking during the cremation ceremony itself, including cooking and consumption taking place at the burial site and perhaps also accelerating and fuelling ("feeding") the fire with food and drink. Second, the cinerary urns were the last of a succession of vessels and their contents involved in caring and catering for the dead through multiple stages of the funeral, perhaps connected to the widespread idea that the ghost of the deceased required nourishment and refreshment on its journey to the next world (Hertz 1960 [1907]). Third, vessels selected as cinerary urns were those decorated vessels used to make and store food and drink despite the presence of alternatives. Finally, these decorated urns lent to the postcremation inurnment of the dead the metaphor of storing, fermenting, and nourishing, facilitating the future-memory of an ongoing animate presence of the dead within the grave.

Pots from Inhumation Graves at Spong Hill

In early Anglo-Saxon inhumation graves, we find a wide range of vessels—wooden bowls, glass drinking cups, drinking horns, and metal-bound buckets, as well as ceramic vessels. Pots are usually seen as low status, because they were readily available (Lee 2007:76). Certainly, they are widespread grave goods in early Anglo-Saxon inhumation graves, found with both genders and all age groups (Stoodley 1999:33; see also Lee 2007:75; Penn and Brugmann 2007:40–41). These vessels tend to be smaller, and fewer are decorated when compared with those used as cinerary urns. Among the inhumation graves from Spong Hill and two other inhumation cemeteries from Norfolk—Morning Thorpe and Bergh Apton—three-quarters were undecorated (Penn and Brugmann 2007:40). Hirst and Clark make a similar observation for the mixed-rite Cemetery II from Mucking, Essex (Hirst and Clark 2009:603). Therefore, while some were likely used to make and store food and liquids (see Perry 2012a, 2012b), a larger proportion were cooking and drinking vessels.

Despite these differences in likely function and significance, the larger urns resemble cinerary urns, and those that are decorated bear comparable designs to those found among cinerary urns. This suggests that the vessels deployed in both cremation pits and inhumation graves were part of the same pot-making tradition regularly brought into the mortuary milieu. I contend that rather than being readily available containers of low status, they held a related but different role in commemorating the dead, perhaps comparable to the smaller vessels that may have accompanied the cremated dead on their pyres, containing food and drink for the deceased. Here again, pots relate to care for, and sustenance for, the dead. To explore this argument, we need to look at how the pots were placed within the inhumation graves at Spong Hill and put this into context by exploring other East Anglian and Essex inhumation graves.

Spong Hill is unique in the high frequency of pot deposition in its small group of inhumations: 44 pots found in 37 of the 58 graves (64 percent), including graves with both male- and female-gendered artifact assemblages (figure 5.2). This compares with 167 graves of a total of 365 (45 percent) with pottery from the Morning Thorpe inhumation cemetery, which is the closest parallel I have identified to Spong Hill in terms of urn frequency. Perhaps more typically, at Bergh Apton (Norfolk), 18 of 63 (29 percent) inhumation graves contained pottery (Green and Rogerson 1978), while at Westgarth Gardens (Suffolk) 14 of 69 (20 percent) contained pots.

Catherine Hills observed the importance of pots in the inhumation practice at Spong Hill and also observed that those graves without urns contained alternatives, including a bronze bowl and bronze-bound bucket (Hills et al. 1984:7). Christina Lee (2007:73) also noted that this frequency may have been influenced in some way by proximity with so many cinerary urns. Following Lee (2007:85), I suggest that this provision reveals acts of care for the dead, symbolically "feeding" the deceased after death. Moreover, because the deposition of pots is a practice shared between cremation and inhumation ceremonies, I suggest that the significance of pots in both disposal methods foregrounds their relational character as technologies for commemorating personhood and sustaining bonds with the deceased in which vessels held a particular significance (for catalogue, see Hills et al. 1984).

Even within the small sample, there appears to have been choreography to pot deposition, which Lee (2007:84) observes is negotiated individually at each burial site she studied. At Spong Hill, most pots were placed beside or above the skull, hinting at a close relationship with feeding the dead and perhaps between pot, head, and the senses (see also Lee 2007:84).

This pattern is found elsewhere in East Anglia and Essex. As noted above, the largest sample of inhumation graves from Norfolk comes from the inhumation cemetery of Morning Thorpe. Despite this cemetery's size, its lack of surviving skeletal remains complicates associating pots to body position precisely (this is a widespread issue in the acidic soils of East Anglia). However, in instances with skeletal fragments, weapons and dress accessories strongly imply the way the body was likely to have lain; hence we can estimate the likely position of the pot in relation to the body. In the vast majority of cases, pots were placed beside the head, as in female-gendered grave 208 (Green et al.

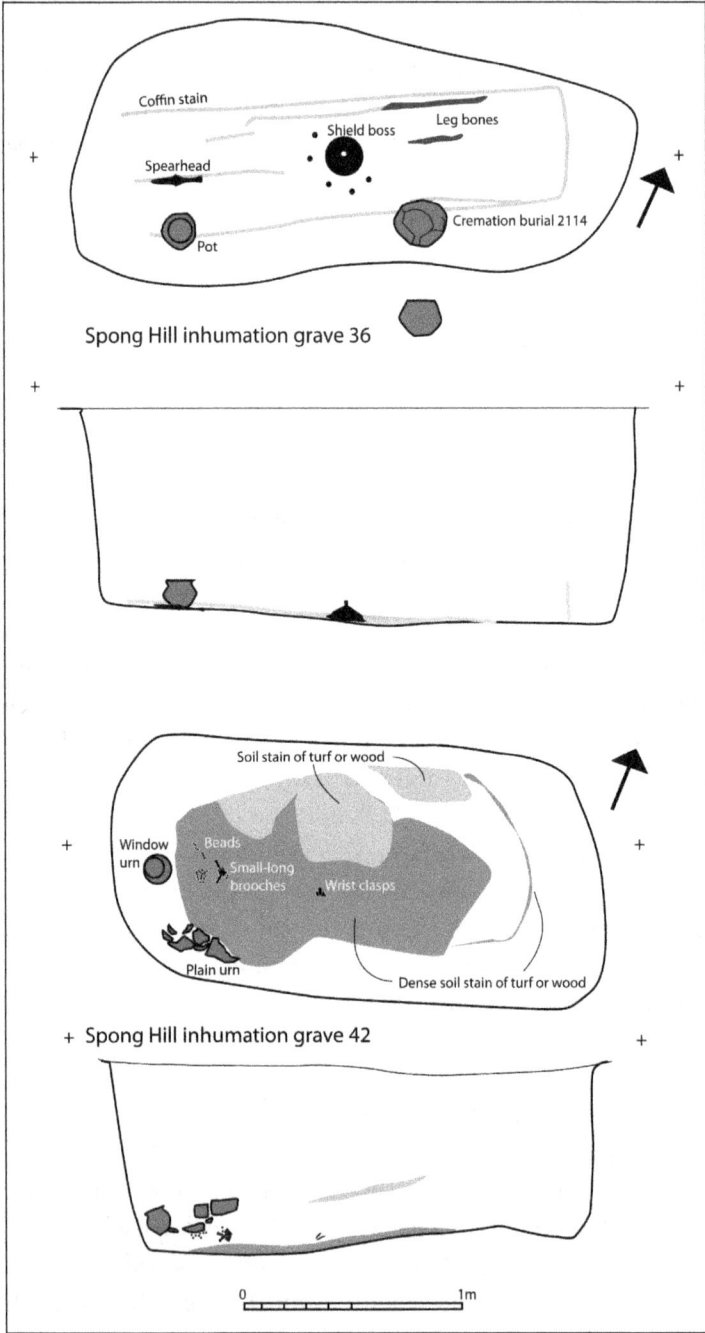

Coffin stain

Shield boss

Leg bones

Spearhead

Cremation burial 2114

Pot

Spong Hill inhumation grave 36

Soil stain of turf or wood

Window urn

Beads

Small-long brooches

Wrist clasps

Plain urn

Dense soil stain of turf or wood

Spong Hill inhumation grave 42

0   1m

Figure 5.2. Spong Hill inhumation graves 36 and 42, artifacts and grave plan. (Redrawn by the author after Hills et al. 1984:87, 96.)

1987:89). Likewise, seven out of the ten pots (70 percent) recorded on grave plans from Bergh Apton (Norfolk) are in this location. Similarly, at Westgarth Gardens (Suffolk), all the pots are right next to the skull of the cadaver, with one exception, a weapon grave where the pot is at the feet and beside the head is a glass cone beaker, its rim placed adjacent to the skull (West 1988:33). At Springfield Lyons (Essex), urns are all at the west (head) end of graves 4701, 4758, 4861, 4882, 4909, 4966, and 6280 (Tyler and Major 2005:54, 56–58, 62).

The same pattern can be identified at Mucking's Cemetery II for graves 260, 347, 351, 493, 534, 566, 585, 596, 691, 784, 851, 854, 860, 878, 915, 967, 970, 975, and 989 (Hirst and Clark 2009:559). In two cases where urns are farther away from the head, there is a clear logic to this. In grave 588, two pots were by the left arm and adjacent to each other, while a copper-alloy-bound wooden stave bucket was placed beside the cadaver's head (Hirst and Clark 2009:75–76). Another exception is an infant's grave containing a small Romano-British vessel placed on the lower body (Hirst and Clark 2009:87). Indeed, buckets and glass vessels share the choreography of pots and are placed beside the head (as in grave 843 [Hirst and Clark 2009:145]).

At Spong Hill, in most cases the pot was on the floor of the grave, but in other instances, as with inhumation grave 8, pots were added during the grave's backfilling as "closing" deposits. In two graves, inhumations 4 and 14, the pottery was situated on ledges far above the grave itself. This suggests that many more pots may have been placed in graves at shallow depths at the time of the funeral or afterwards during commemorative ceremonies and were subsequently destroyed by plowing or erosion prior to the excavation. If so, these pot depositions would mirror the shallow burial of cinerary urns at Spong Hill, suggesting a strong similarity between the act of situating some vessels in inhumation graves and the burial of the cremated dead.

As with cinerary urns, breaking pots could be a ritual act in the inhumation graves, perhaps comparable to placing or breaking pots on the pyre prior to conflagration. However, rather than the "holing" of cinerary urns (if indeed this had anything to do with rituals of fragmentation, as discussed above), pots in inhumation graves were in some cases subject to severe fragmentation. Indeed, only fifteen pots were complete or near-complete, and most were present only in the form of sherds or parts of bases. Similar practices have been found at other early Anglo-Saxon inhumation graves from East Anglia (e.g., Penn 1998). In grave 38, one pot was near-complete but the adjacent pot was incomplete, suggesting that this fragmentation is not evidence of grave disturbance. In grave 57, the pot at the head was intact, while in the middle of the grave half a pot was placed with the dead. The same pattern is found in grave 42, where a broken undecorated pot was placed at the head end of the female-gendered grave. Adjacent to it was an intact and decorated "window" urn—the hole had pierced its base and was filled with a sherd of vessel glass (figure 5.2). In this instance, a drinking glass fragment was afforded a new life within a pottery vessel, perhaps an heirloom even in a fragmented state. Conversely, Hills and colleagues (1984:7) suggest that some pots may have been deliberately smashed in the burial ritual; whether this was to destroy the vessel to articulate loss or to release the contents, this was likely a dramaturgical graveside act (figure 5.2).

The inclusion in the grave fill of individual potsherds is a further factor in the mortuary practice at Spong Hill, also observed at other early Anglo-Saxon cemeteries, notably at Snape (see also Filmer-Sankey and Pestell 2001:244–46). This is a more specific act than simply indirect evidence of funerary feasting at the cemetery (see above) or gift giving (cf. King 2004). Lee (2007:79) observes that sherds might symbolically stand for whole pots but that the act of breaking at the graveside or during the backfilling of the grave may have not articulated merely mourning and loss. As Åsa Larsson (2009a:348) notes for past funerals, breaking an object creates new bonds and relationships. Potsherds and vessel parts—when placed with the dead or in the grave fill—might allow material bonds between the living and the dead to be created as the pot is partly buried and partly retained among the living. A comparable practice has been identified in some cremation graves where snapped fragments of unburnt antler combs were placed in graves and presumably the other parts were kept by mourners as mementos of the deceased (see Crummy 2007:261–66; Williams 2003a).

Cremation and inhumation graves overlap in the northern sector of the cemetery at Spong Hill. In some cases, cremation burials in ceramic urns were themselves added to the fills of inhumation graves in this area. In some examples, as with inhumation graves 22 and 23, this appears to be a deliberate practice: in the former case, the cinerary urn was situated directly above the position of an accessory vessel placed below it on the base of the grave. Similar patterns were found at Snape (Suffolk), where a pair of cinerary urns were placed on a ledge at the west end of the grave of an adult male interred with a spear and knife (Filmer-Sankey and Pestell 2001:52–54). This example is instructive, since the commemoration of the fiery transformation seems to have been marked by placing burned oak logs on either side of the inhumation, the two lines of burned oaks mirroring the pairing of urns close by. Therefore, pots that contained food and drink, and pots that contained ashes, were equally potent commemorative material culture in inhumation graves at Spong Hill.

The Broader Context: Pots, People, and Place

In early Anglo-Saxon England, pots were clearly integral to the habitus of daily life—including the storage, production, preparation, and consumption of food and drink. Moreover, rituals involving the consumption of food and drink were likely important in pagan season festivals and gatherings, making them central to the construction of social and political relationships and identities. The giving and receiving of food, but also the handling and exchange of vessels, were likely to be integral to such acts (see Scull 2011). An illustration of the importance of the material culture used to prepare, store, and serve food and drink is the rich feasting gear in the early seventh-century chamber-in-ship grave beneath Mound 1 at Sutton Hoo (Scull 2011; Williams 2011a), yet this elite funeral unquestionably drew upon a broader repertoire of ideas about life and death shared in humbler graves from earlier centuries. Indeed, the association of vessels more generally with ritual practices of eating and drinking is revealed in the rare twelve miniature bucket pendants that may have formed part of a cloth-lined bag placed in an adult female inhumation grave with other distinctively amuletic artifacts from a cemetery at Bidford-upon-Avon, Warwickshire (Dickinson 1993). The dispensing and consumption of drink might have held cultic import for "cunning women" in early Anglo-Saxon England.

Therefore, pots in both cremation and inhumation practices can be seen as concerned with material exchanges and multisensory experiences in mortuary memory-making rituals. Yet the extent of the specific significance of pottery in both inhumation and cremation seems particularly pronounced at Spong Hill, where we see both disposal strategies closely linking ceramics with the cadaver in the grave. Pottery—presumably containing food and drink—was placed on the pyre and subsequently was used to contain, transport, and inter the cremains. Likewise, we have identified the breaking and placing of pots in inhumation graves, often beside the head, as well as the placing of pots, potsherds, and cinerary urns during the closing of graves.

I do not consider the different uses of pottery as explicable in terms of a simple division between "possessions" and "gifts" (contra King 2004): pots clearly contributed to successive stages of early Anglo-Saxon funerals involving both disposal methods. However, I would follow King (2004) and Lee (2007) in seeing these as evidence of the relationship between the living and the dead negotiated through gift giving and feasting. Yet we seem to be seeing a closer connection between the cadaver and ceramics than has hitherto been recognized.

A simple parallel between the making, life history, and deposition of pottery and the birth, life, and death of people as found in some cultures may be only part of the picture (e.g., David et al. 1988). What can be said with more confidence is that the breaking and remaking of the identities of the dead was mediated by pottery in both inhumation and cremation practices. Pots were *not* used to make bodies in inhumation graves, but they hydrated and nourished them and served to articulate the breaking and making of relationships between the living and the dead during the burial rituals. The distinction with cremation was that selected pots, rather than paralleling the fiery destruction of the body, while sometimes subject to deliberate breakage, *became* bodies or skins when used to contain the cremains.

Therefore, we have two disposal methods that involve linked but distinctive uses of pottery in relation to cadavers—pots to feed the dead operated in both strategies, but only in cremation did pots serve in body-building, that is, refleshing the cadaver. This particular emphasis might have been on creating a sensing, even animate, identity for the dead within their graves. Indeed, the provision of decorated pottery as cinerary urns is combined with clear evidence for the regular placing of whole animals on the pyre with the dead and the inclusion of toilet implements and combs in postcremation practices. All these correspond with an efficient cremation process and evidence that attention was often paid to separating and retrieving a substantial portion of the cremains from the pyre, as revealed by bone weight. These practices seem connected to a distinctive necrogeography, since they are associated with the large cremation cemeteries of "Anglian" eastern England. In southern and central England, we also find cremations placed in cinerary urns. Yet there, by contrast, less attention seems to be afforded to collecting and burying cremains. There is less evidence for pyre and grave goods, a higher proportion of undecorated urns, lower bone weights, a larger number of unurned cremation deposits, and less evidence for animal sacrifice (McKinley 2005; Powers 2009:48). Conversely, in some inhumation graves, pots are rarely found (e.g., Kinsley 1989).

We are dealing with a spectrum of mortuary practices, not a hard-and-fast distinction between "Anglian" and "Saxon" cremation practices. Still, there is clearly a constellation of ritual emphases associated with the larger cremation cemeteries of "Anglian" eastern England. Therefore, the emphasis on postcremation rituals corresponded to places of social aggregation for ritual purposes in the early Anglo-Saxon landscape in which mourning and disposing of the dead, and sharing food and drink, may have been integrated practices.

Elsewhere, I have contended that large cremation cemeteries were more than burial facilities and may have served as locales for ritual and political power—that is, localized cult and ceremonial sites (Williams 2002b, 2004d). While evidence for these other features is inconclusive, ritual specialists, or incipient elites in control of these sites, could possibly have mobilized cremation as a means of creating a distinctive but readily recognized strategy of distinction and inclusion, drawing on remembered traditions from Continental homelands and invented/contrived identities rooted in an imagined mythological past for fluid and ethnically diverse social groups. It may have also been a form of burial organization that took on power because these more opportunistic circumstances of social fragmentation rendered mortuary arenas spheres for asserting a hyperconservative identity in death. A question of scale meant that this form of burial worked appropriately for localized groups whose socioeconomic networks may have been extensive but whose power networks had a more limited geographical reach.

Certainly, by the late fifth century, those using large cremation cemeteries were interleaving with contemporary communities primarily using inhumation, and these cemeteries do not appear to have exclusively served a coherent "tribal" territory. What is clear, however, is a regionally focused constellation of ritual practices that may have constituted an "ideology of transformation" (see Williams 2001), creating and promoting a way of treating and perceiving the cadaver in death that may have linked to a coherent eschatology and cosmology of transformation and regeneration of the dead as animated and corporeal within the landscape in their pots. This was not exclusive of inhumation, as we have seen, and indeed, inhumation was a minority rite at many of these sites that display a comparable connection between pottery and nourishing and hydrating the dead. Yet if cremation was deployed in a climate of ethnogenesis at the local level, then mortuary practices might have been one arena where identities were linked to land, resources, and myths and memories of descent.

This in turn might provide a new perspective on these sites' abandonment. Rather than Christianity, the rise of larger regional powers during the sixth century could have been what rendered obsolete the power and significance of these localized cult sites where public ritual had been orchestrated through place, ritual technology, and acts of care and emotive engagement with the dead on a relatively small scale. The shift from cremation to inhumation, and the fragmentation of these early, large cremation cemeteries, may be seen in a context in which the increasing scale and extent of sociopolitical networks by elites rendered these traditional "tribal" places of power and memory, where mortuary and cultic practices took place, increasingly irrelevant.

Conclusion

Cremation and inhumation were both multistaged processes in early Anglo-Saxon England that facilitated unfolding commemorative engagements with the dead through corporeal transformations, staged closures, and body-building material cultures (Williams 2006a). At Spong Hill, we find a burial site dominated by cremation, with perhaps one household or segment of society adopting inhumation to define themselves apart from others in the later part of the site's use. Yet the treatment of pots was integral to both disposal methods found at the cemetery. The intimate commemorative association of pottery and cadavers is apparent through many generations of the dead who were interred in cinerary urns. Equally, the regular placing of pots—whole or in part—within and above inhumation graves meant they had a distinct but perhaps related significance in negotiating relationships between the living and the dead. This significance has been overlooked hitherto because studies of inhumation have not considered the contemporary cremation rite and have instead afforded attention to weaponry and dress accessories (e.g., Penn and Brugmann 2007).

In later, Christian, sources, it was only revenants (corporeal ghosts that followed bad deaths) that were animate and threatened to destroy the living (Blair 2009). In the pagan period, are we dealing with an understanding of death and the dead as both potentially harmful and beneficial to the living, inhabiting their graves even following the cremation process? Elsewhere, I have argued that "deviant burials" might be extreme responses with a spectrum of commemorative technologies creating dialogues with the dead to constitute their mnemonic transformation into ancestors. Whether because of the personality of the deceased, the manner of their death, or as a punishment, these individuals were still interred within communal cemeteries as part of the community of the dead (Williams 2007b; see also Nugent 2011b; Reynolds 2009).

At Spong Hill, the grave was perhaps only a staging post for afterlife destinations in which ceramic vessels—what they contained, what was spilled, and what was retained whole and what was broken—may have mediated and punctuated ritual practices and the staging of social remembering and forgetting. As Ing-Marie Back Danielsson puts it with regard to late Iron Age Scandinavian graves, burials can be considered engines of transformation that required feeding (Back Danielsson 2007:257–63). Cemeteries apparently were not mere repositories for cadavers. Instead, the pots suggest that the burial place was where the hungry and sensing ancestors were reincorporated into a community of the dead through the burial of cadavers and ashes. The attention afforded to the corporeal integrity of ashes within the urn may not have come from an equation of cremains with food and drink (cf. Back Danielsson 2007; Oestigaard 2000) but may well relate to a conceptualization of the dead as still living, still sensing within their graves; in particular, they appear to have required haptic and gustatory care and provision as well as distinctive topology provided by the urn (cf. Nugent 2011b; Nugent and Williams 2012; Williams 2011b). Bodies and pots were here not simply connected metaphorically but linked together in chains of operations from death to burial. Emotive acts of care within the funerary rituals, including those involving ceramics, were likely intended to feed and sustain the unburned cadaver in the grave or when placed on the pyre; hence, the shift toward inhumation led not to an abandonment but to an adaption of existing concerns with furnishing and "feeding" the dead. In cremation practices, the significance of pottery had been taken one stage further, serving to reflesh cremains within highly decorated urns. In these contrasting and changing ways, both the inhumed and the cremated early Anglo-Saxon dead were repeatedly made memorable by affording them a well-urned rest.

Acknowledgments

I wish to thank all those present at the Amerind Foundation seminar for their constructive comments on my paper. I am particularly grateful to Åsa Larsson for her comments on the significance of pottery and transformation. Special thanks go to Gareth Perry for letting me view two of his articles prior to publication based on his doctoral research investigating the preburial use of early Anglo-Saxon pottery. All errors remain my responsibility.

6

Cremation, Gender, and Concepts of the Self in the British Early Bronze Age

Joanna Brück

Recent work highlighting the variability of British Neolithic funerary rites has challenged arguments for an evolutionary trajectory from the communal mortuary monuments of the Neolithic to the single burials of the Bronze Age. Traditions of single burial are now well-known in certain regions during the Neolithic (Barclay 2011; Kinnes 1979), while the practices involved in the treatment and deposition of human remains in Neolithic megalithic monuments hint at complex processes of social categorization for both the living and the dead (Smith and Brickley 2009; Ju. Thomas 2000; see Cooney, chap. 10, and Larsson and Nilsson Stutz, chap. 3, this volume). Discussions of the British Bronze Age, in contrast, generally assume that single burials of complete individuals were the norm (e.g., Parker Pearson 1993:78–81; Renfrew 1974; but see A. Jones 2008; Petersen 1972). The presence of exotic grave goods—including objects of bronze, gold, amber, and faience—in some Bronze Age burials is widely interpreted as indicating an increase in social differentiation (e.g., Sheridan and Davis 1998). Our narratives of the period have, therefore, come to be dominated by social evolutionary perspectives that describe how Bronze Age chiefs engaged in strategies of competitive self-aggrandizement through the accumulation and exchange of personal wealth and the display of individual status in the mortuary context (e.g., Earle 2002; Kristiansen 1998a). In fact, this vision of Bronze Age personhood is uncannily similar to the competitive individualism characteristic of the modern Western world.

In this chapter, I examine evidence that calls this model into question, both for certain categories of people and for Bronze Age communities more generally. I focus on the treatment of the human body but also consider certain aspects of the role of objects in the mortuary rite. In particular, I explore the distinction between inhumation and cremation burial. Both forms of mortuary rite were practiced during the British Bronze Age (Needham 1996), with inhumation burial dominating the archaeological record during the first part of the period (from circa 2500 BC to 1700 BC). In contrast, cremation appeared circa 2100 BC and increased in prevalence to become the most common mode of mortuary treatment from circa 1700 BC to 1100 BC (Ellison 1980). Here, I consider the chronological overlap between inhumation and cremation burial during the Early Bronze Age and discuss what different forms of mortuary treatment might tell us about the constitution of the self.

Previous work has noted that cremation burials are often poorly furnished in comparison to inhumations (Braithwaite 1984; Pierpoint 1980:216). In addition, the primary interments in Early Bronze Age barrows were often inhumations, while cremations were usually placed in secondary or satellite positions (Burgess 1980:297–99; Mizoguchi 1993). The argument has therefore been made that the distinction between inhumation and cremation in the British Bronze Age provided a way of marking differences in social status (Bradley 1984:84; Braithwaite 1984:104–5; Rowlands 1980). Cremation—it has been suggested—acted as a means of destroying the body and of negating the individuality of the deceased, while inhumation facilitated the preservation of bodily integrity and the maintenance of personal identity after death. Osteoarchaeological studies indicate that men were often inhumed, whereas women tended to be cremated (Burgess 1980:297; Sofaer Derevenski 2002:201). In addition, the primary positions within barrows and grave pits were frequently reserved for males, while females were placed in secondary locations (Mizoguchi 1993; Pierpoint 1980:chap. 9). As such, it is widely accepted that women held lower social positions than men in British Early Bronze Age society (e.g., Mizoguchi 1993; Pierpoint 1980:238).

This way of explaining the apparent link between women and cremation echoes the distinctly androcentric tone of much research on the European Bronze Age (e.g., Kristiansen 1998a; Treherne 1995; for a critique of the androcentric tone, see M. Sørensen 1992). Artifacts such as elaborate bronze weaponry have formed a particular focus of interest among researchers working on the period. As a result, the competitive activities of male warriors, chiefs, and traders are thought to have been the key stimuli of social and economic change (e.g., Burgess and Shennan 1976), while the role of women has rarely been considered. In contrast, I would argue that our framing of gender roles and relationships during this period is a by-product of the uncritical imposition of contemporary norms and values onto the past. Women may have been cremated more frequently than men, but—as we shall see below—it is not clear that this indicates their status was lower.

Gender, Inhumation, and Cremation

This chapter reevaluates the evidence for gendered differences in the prevalence of inhumation and cremation burial during the British Early Bronze Age. By retaining a critical awareness of the impact of modern Western gender ideologies on the past, I suggest an alternative way of interpreting the distinction between cremation and inhumation and explore the implications of this for our understanding of the body and the self during the period (see also Cerezo-Román, chap. 8, Williams, chap. 5, and Sørensen, chap. 9, this volume).

Let us begin by reassessing the evidence for the sexing of cremation and inhumation burials during the Early Bronze Age. Although several thousand Early Bronze Age burials have been recorded, a significant number of these were excavated during the nineteenth and early twentieth centuries. The standard and level of detail of osteoarchaeological analysis and publication are highly variable for such older excavations, and often burials were sexed purely on the basis of their associated grave goods. Recent methodological improvements mean that only in the past few decades have cremated remains been routinely subject to analysis; prior to that, they were often discarded (McKinley 1997:129). For these reasons, the following analysis is restricted to burials that were published after 1960 (in the majority of cases, these were published in the 1980s and more recently) and that included a specialist osteoarchaeological report.

In total, 544 individuals were included in the analysis, of which 348 had been cremated and 196 had been inhumed. However, the sex of these individuals could be confidently identified in only 141 cases;

a further 80 individuals could be less confidently sexed, while the sex of the remainder could not be identified. This is the result of a variety of taphonomic processes. The bone itself is often highly fragmented so that sexing can be difficult if not impossible. Moreover, as we shall see below, most Bronze Age cremations contain only a portion of the body of the deceased, and sexually dimorphic elements may be missing. Soil conditions and postdepositional disturbance are clearly significant factors; many of the sites examined here were the focus of sequential episodes of mortuary activity over the Bronze Age, and graves were often reopened for the addition of further burials (Petersen 1972).

Despite these complications, this data set shows some interesting trends. First, let us examine mortuary practice by sex (table 6.1). Out of the 196 inhumations, 44 males and 21 females could be confidently identified. In other words, 68 percent of the sexed inhumations were male, and 32 percent were female. A further 10 probable/possible males and 12 probable/possible females were also identified, and if these are included, the total number of sexed burials rises to 54 males (62 percent) and 33 females (38 percent). Out of the 348 cremation burials, only 44 males and 32 females could be confidently identified. In other words, of the 76 cremations that could be sexed, 58 percent were male while 42 percent were female. A further 19 probable/possible males and 39 probable/possible females were also identified. If these are included, the total number of sexed cremation burials rises to 63 males (47 percent) and 71 females (53 percent).

A subtly different pattern emerges if we examine each sex group individually (table 6.2). Out of the 88 males that could be identified with a high degree of confidence, 44 (50 percent) were inhumed and 44 (50 percent) cremated. If we include probable/possible males, this brings the total number of individuals to 117, of which 54 (46 percent) were inhumed and 63 (54 percent) were cremated. In contrast, a total of 53 individuals could be confidently identified as female, of which 21 (40 percent) were inhumed while 32 (60 percent) were cremated. If we include probable/possible females, this brings the total number of individuals to 104, of which 33 (32 percent) were inhumed and 71 (68 percent) were cremated. Together, these numbers suggest that although the overall numbers of sexed burials is small and the pattern is not statistically significant, women were more likely than men to be cremated.

Table 6.1. Percentage (with actual number in parentheses) of male and female burials by mortuary treatment

	Inhumations (confident only)	Inhumations (incl. prob./poss.)	Cremations (confident only)	Cremations (incl. prob./poss.)
Males	68% (44)	62% (54)	58% (44)	47% (63)
Females	32% (21)	38% (33)	42% (32)	53% (71)

Table 6.2. Percentage (with actual number in parentheses) of inhumation and cremation burials by sex

	Males (confident only)	Males (incl. prob./poss.)	Females (confident only)	Females (incl. prob./poss.)
Inhumations	50% (44)	46% (54)	40% (21)	32% (33)
Cremations	50% (44)	54% (63)	60% (32)	68% (71)

Cremation and Social Status

I now turn to critically assessing previous interpretations that have viewed cremation as a mortuary rite reserved for those of low status. To begin with, it is clear that Early Bronze Age burials (both inhumation and cremation) were highly selective: only a small percentage of the population is likely to have been afforded formal burial (McLaren 2011). The tendency for cremation burials to be located in "satellite" positions—toward the edge rather than at the center of Early Bronze Age barrows—is likely to be at least in part the result of the shift over time from inhumation to cremation. However, primary cremation burials also occur—for example, the cremation burial of an adult female at the center of ring ditch 801 at Barrow Hills in Oxfordshire (Barclay and Halpin 1999:48–49).

Although grave goods are found less frequently in cremation than inhumation graves (e.g., Pierpoint 1980:216), there are certainly examples of "rich" cremation burials. The cremation burial of an adult female from barrow 16 at Barrow Hills was accompanied by a bronze awl, a knife-dagger, and a necklace of amber, faience, and jet beads (Barclay and Halpin 1999:162–65). Indeed, the relative lack of grave goods accompanying Early Bronze Age cremations need not indicate that this form of burial was reserved for low-status individuals. During the Middle Bronze Age, when inhumation burial was virtually unknown, cremation burials were rarely accompanied by grave goods (Ellison 1980), and it is widely accepted that social status may have been expressed in other ways, for example, by the deposition of fine bronze weaponry in rivers, lakes, and bogs (Bradley 1990:97–154).

The lack of grave goods could also be a product of the multistage character of cremation rites (Barrett 1991a:121–22). Objects may have been displayed on or around the body before it was cremated and may not have been deposited with the burnt remains in the grave: as we shall see below, there is evidence that heirlooms were sometimes passed down across the generations rather than being buried with the dead (e.g., Sheridan and Davis 2002; A. Woodward 2002). Likewise, artifacts placed on the pyre may not have survived the cremation process (McKinley 1997:132); finds such as the burnt bone whistle found with the cremation burial of a child at Eaglestone Flat, Derbyshire, indicate that objects accompanied the dead onto the pyre, while the green staining noted on the bones of this individual hints that small bronze items burned alongside the body may sometimes have been destroyed in the fire (Barnatt 1994:304). It must also be noted that most British Early Bronze Age cremation burials comprise collections of bone and other burnt material gathered from the pyre site for redeposition in a separate grave. It is therefore possible that objects burned on the pyre may not always have accompanied the cremated bone to its final resting place.

The suggestion that cremation was a low-ranking form of mortuary rite can be contested on other grounds. Those who were cremated during the Early Bronze Age were far from invisible (Downes 1999); cremations were visually striking events, while the smells and sounds of the pyre are likely to have made a profound impact on those who witnessed the spectacle (Williams 2004d:271–76; Sørensen, chap. 9, and Larsson and Nilsson Stutz, chap. 3, this volume). Moreover, cremation is a labor-intensive, time-consuming, and complex process (McKinley

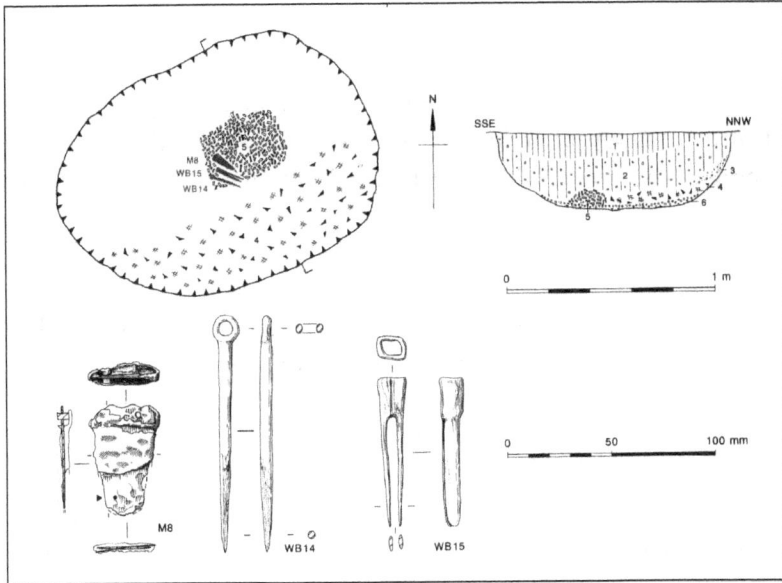

Figure 6.1. Cremation 11, Barrow Hills, showing the discrete central deposit of cremated bone and adjacent spread of pyre debris. A bronze knife-dagger (M8), bone pin (WB14), and tweezers (WB15) were carefully placed on top of the burial. (After Barclay and Halpin 1999:fig. 4.82, with kind permission from Oxford Archaeology.)

1997; Cerezo-Román, chap. 8, this volume); wood for the pyre must be collected, the pyre itself built and tended, and the cremated bone retrieved for burial. Postcremation processing of pyre materials is likely to have been time-consuming and indicates a concern at the (re)constitution of the "body" as it was placed in the grave (see also Williams, chap. 5, Cooney, chap. 10, and Sørensen, chap. 9, this volume). For example, the cremation burial from Findhorn, Moray (in eastern Scotland) comprised a deposit of clean cremated bone, suggesting that this was carefully separated from the rest of the pyre and possibly washed before it was buried (Shepherd and Shepherd 2001:105). At Barrow Hills in Oxfordshire, a tightly packed concentration of cremated bone was centrally placed in grave pit 11, while a more extensive spread of burnt soil, charcoal, and ash that can be interpreted as pyre debris lay in the southern half of the pit (figure 6.1; Barclay and Halpin 1999:141).

Cremation as Fragmentation

If the distinction between cremation and inhumation cannot be explained as a way of indicating differences in status, then we must consider other ways of interpreting gendered preferences in mortuary treatment. The appearance of cremation burial during the Bronze Age has often been suggested to indicate a change in religious beliefs (e.g., Alexander 1979). The rise of cremation in Western Europe over the past century provides a useful analogy here. Although this can be linked to a decline in Christianity in this region (Parker Pearson 1982:110), it also reflects changing concepts of the body and the self (e.g., Ariès 1974; but see Larsson and Nilsson Stutz, chap. 3, this volume), and this line of inquiry is the one I wish to pursue here.

An intriguing feature of Bronze Age cremation burials is that they usually contain only a portion of the remains of the deceased. Modern adult cremations produce on average approximately 1.6 kilograms of burnt bone (McKinley 1993), but Bronze Age cremations usually weigh much less (McKinley 1997:137). Taphonomic processes do not always appear to account for this pattern. At sites such as Eaglestone Flat, Derbyshire, the cremated bone was well preserved but the mean weight of bone recovered from the fourteen cremation burials was just 385.1 grams (McKinley 1994c:339), suggesting that this was not the result of soil conditions alone. At Llanilar in Dyfed, Wales, the cremated remains of a young adult female and child found in a Collared Urn weighed just 380 grams (Briggs 1997:27). Anatomical elements that usually survive the cremation process well (such as the petrous temporal bones) were not present. In comparison, three other cremations from this site deposited without the protection of a pot were heavier. Together, these observations suggest that factors such as soil acidity cannot account for the small size of this burial.

McKinley (1997:142) has argued that such "token" burials result from careless retrieval processes and represent individuals of low status. In comparison, larger deposits of cremated bone may indicate that more attention was paid to collecting the bone from the pyre, suggesting the presence of higher-status individuals. There are, however, hints that this may not always have been the case. At some sites, even small deposits of cremated bone provide evidence for complex postpyre processing.

The cremation of an adult female from cairn 3 at Stoneyburn Farm, Lanarkshire (Banks 1995:297), included small bones from the hands and feet, suggesting careful retrieval of the remains from the funerary pyre, but it weighed just 538 grams. The adult female from barrow 16 at Barrow Hills in Oxfordshire was represented by just 545 grams of bone but was buried with a bronze awl, a knife-dagger, and a bead necklace (Barclay and Halpin 1999:162–65)—items that would usually be seen as indicators of wealth. We need to consider other ways of explaining the "partial" nature of cremation burials at sites such as these.

The treatment of grave goods in Early Bronze Age burials provides some interesting and useful parallels. Artifacts such as jet spacer plate necklaces, for example, were rarely deposited complete: the cist at Abercairney, Fowlis Wester (Scotland), produced enough beads to form only a small portion of one such necklace (Rideout et al. 1987). Elsewhere, evidence for wear and for variation in raw material and decorative motifs indicates that assemblages of beads may have constituted objects with quite different histories. At Pen y Bonc on Anglesey in North Wales, two worn jet beads formed part of a larger assemblage consisting of other unworn beads and spacer plates made of a jet-like material (Sheridan and Davis 2002). The curation of old beads indicates that at least some of these artifacts were considered heirlooms (Sheridan and Davis 2002; A. Woodward 2002), while the deliberate fragmentation of spacer plate necklaces and the recombination of beads suggest that the circulation of such artifacts gave material form to interpersonal relationships (Barrett 1994:121–22; Brück 2004). Assemblages of beads may have been brought together and dispersed as part of the mortuary rite, as mourners gave gifts to the deceased or kept significant objects as remembrances.

Other objects were also subject to deliberate fragmentation during Early Bronze Age funerary rites (e.g., Brück 2004; A. Woodward 2002; see also Williams, chap. 5, this volume). For example, the bone pommel from burial H at Bedd Branwen on Anglesey had been carefully snapped in two; one half of this object was deposited in the grave but the other piece, along with the blade of the dagger to which it was once attached, is missing (figure 6.2; F. Lynch 1971). The entire rim had been removed from an urn found in barrow CCX at Kirk Whelpington, Northumberland (Greenwell 1877:433). The deliberate breaking of such

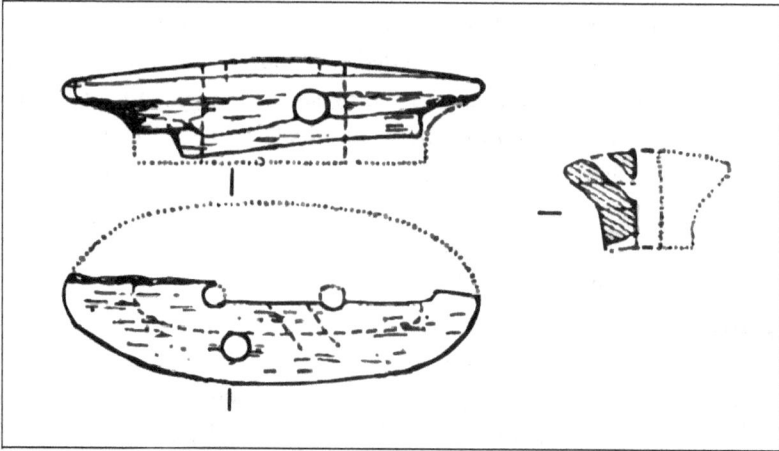

Figure 6.2. Snapped bone pommel from Bedd Branwen. (After F. Lynch 1971:fig. 10, with kind permission from *Archaeologia Cambrensis*.)

objects and—I would suggest—the retention of the missing pieces by the mourners worked to draw attention to the significance of particular relationships between the dead and the living.

Unburnt human remains sometimes appear to have been treated in similar ways. Five of the seven inhumations deposited sequentially in a deep grave pit at South Dumpton Down in Kent had had their skulls removed, presumably when the grave was reopened for the insertion of a new burial (Perkins n.d.). At Rockbourne Down in Hampshire, the inhumation of a young adult was accompanied by a pottery vessel containing the sacrum of an infant (Piggott and Piggott 1945). These examples suggest that unburnt bones may sometimes have circulated as ancestral relics for use outside of the mortuary context and that some of these were incorporated as fragments into later burials. Although traditional accounts of the British Bronze Age stress the predominance of complete single inhumation burials during the first few centuries of the period, it is now becoming clear that even bodies that were not burnt were often subject to complex forms of postmortem manipulation, with skeletal elements not only removed but also rearranged in the grave (A. Gibson 2004). This provided opportunities for the living to encounter, handle, and circulate the bones of the dead. Tracing the afterlives of fragments of objects or human bone that were retained by the mourners during Early Bronze Age funerary rites is difficult: few settlements of this date are known, and there is little evidence to suggest where the objects or bone were used or deposited. Tracing the postfunerary use of such fragments during later centuries is easier. For example, one of the pots from the Middle Bronze Age cremation cemetery at Itford Hill in Sussex was missing a portion of its upper body and rim (Ellison 1972:110). A contemporary settlement, some ninety meters to the south, produced a single rim sherd that matched the fabric of this vessel exactly, and Ellison (1972) argues that this is part of the same pot. Settlements of the Late Bronze Age produce occasional pieces of unburnt human bone, notably skull fragments; these were employed in depositional practices designed to mark the boundaries of these sites (Brück 1995). If fragments of artifacts and unburnt bodies were subject to processes of curation and circulation away from the mortuary site, it is surely possible that cremated bone might have been treated in a similar way (see also Schurr, chap. 12, and Larsson and Nilsson Stutz, chap. 3, this volume). If so (and contra McKinley 1997:142), smaller deposits of cremated bone may represent people of particular significance, over whose remains many others had claims (see also Cooney, chap. 10, and Cerezo-Román, chap. 8, this volume). As such, it is no surprise that fragments of burnt bone sometimes accompanied Early Bronze Age burials: for example, cist 6 at Sketewan, Perth and Kinross, contained the cremation burial of an adult male along with several pieces of burnt skull from an adult female (Mercer and Midgley 1997:294).

Cremation and Concepts of the Self

The dispersal of the remains of the dead and of significant objects associated with them during life hints at very different attitudes toward the body compared with those prevalent in modern Western society. In the contemporary Western world, individual burials are the norm, and care is taken to keep a person's bodily remains together for burial in a single location. Recent debates surrounding the unauthorized retention by hospitals of human organs or the use of animal organs for human transplants highlight the dominant ideal of the human body as a nonpartible entity. In a similar way, bodily matter out of place—blood, for example, or nail clippings—is usually viewed with disgust or even horror (Douglas 1966). Such attitudes are a product of post-Enlightenment philosophy, which is characterized by an ideology of individualism (e.g., Morris 1991): it is seen as morally, socially, and psychologically problematic to disaggregate the body, as this acts as a signifier of the individual. Contemporary concepts of personhood envisage the self as a bounded, stable, and homogeneous whole—an individual set apart from others and a key locus of agency.* This model of the self is, however, historically specific and can be linked into particular historical processes, notably, the rise of mercantile capitalism and European imperialism during the eighteenth and nineteenth centuries (e.g., Morris 1991; Ju. Thomas 2004): this concept of the individual facilitated the technologies of power (for example, the formation of disciplined armies and factory workplaces and the creation of institutions such as schools and prisons) that underpinned economic and social change during this period (Foucault 1977).

I would argue that the interpretation of cremation deposits as low status is a product of modern, Western ideologies of the body: the suggestion that cremation acted as a means of "destroying" the body and "negating" the self works only in a context where an idealized model of the person as a bounded and homogeneous individual is prioritized over other ways of constructing personal and social identity. Dominant accounts of the European Bronze Age have tended to uncritically impose contemporary concepts of the self onto the past. In Britain, the apparent rise of single burial at the beginning of the Bronze Age has long been considered to indicate the appearance of an ideology of the individual (e.g., Renfrew 1974; Shennan 1982). Although it has been critiqued (Barrett 1991b; A. Jones 2008), this model continues to underpin narratives of the period; these emphasize the emergence of social differentiation, the intensification of trade, and increasing levels of warfare (e.g., Earle 2002), so that imposing an ideology of competitive individualism onto the Bronze Age becomes all too easy. However, the dominance of cremation burial from circa 2000 BC calls this model into question, suggesting very different ideas surrounding the body

---

*Although dominant, other notions of the self are also present in a modern, Western context. This model, for example, is closely bound up with culturally specific concepts of masculinity; women's identities are constructed in rather different ways (Gero 2000).

and the self. Recent discussions of personhood in anthropology and archaeology provide alternative frameworks through which to understand the distinction between inhumation and cremation in the British Early Bronze Age. The modern, Western notion of the individual is not in fact universal (e.g., Battaglia 1990; B. Morris 1994; Strathern 1988). Many societies view the person in relational terms: links with other people, places, and things extending across time and space are central to the constitution of the self (e.g., Chapman 2000a; Fowler 2004; Heckenberger 2005; Skousen 2012). Here, the person comprises an unbounded amalgamation of substances and elements, brought together and reconstituted through exchange, intermarriage, and other interpersonal links. According to this "dividual" model of the self, personhood is fluid and dispersed and is not located solely within the confines of the human body.

Where the person is seen in this way, disaggregating the human body in the context of mortuary rites and other practices may not be considered problematic. Instead, just as the circulation of objects (both complete and partial) with significant histories is often central to the construction of identity, so too the fragmentation and dispersal of the human body may have been key to the successful reproduction of social relationships. In the British Bronze Age, the breaking of objects acted as a means of giving material form to relational concepts of identity, marking and mediating the links between the living and the dead and allowing distinctions between mourners to be affirmed and assessed (Barrett 1994:121–22; Brück 2004). The circulation of burnt bone functioned in a similar way (see also Cerezo-Román, chap. 8, this volume): the key distinction between inhumation and cremation was that the latter more easily facilitated the fragmentation of the human body on death (see also Cooney, chap. 10, this volume), and as we shall see below, this may have been what ultimately led to the shift from inhumation to cremation over the course of the period.

Gender and the Body

It is, as I argue above, problematic to assume that practices of single inhumation burial point to an ideology of the individual during the Bronze Age. As we have seen, inhumations are not always complete (and, as seen in other chapters in this volume, inhumations and cremations often co-occur). Graves may incorporate the remains of more than one individual, and these are often carefully arranged in relation to each other: for example, the seven sequential inhumations in the deep grave pit at South Dumpton Down in Kent each lay directly above but perpendicular to the body of the previous interment (Perkins n.d.), suggesting that interpersonal links were important to the constitution of identity in both forms of mortuary rite (Last 1998). Nonetheless, clearly cremation more easily facilitated the sorts of "dividual" or relational concepts of the self outlined above, and the contemporary use of both inhumation and cremation may indicate the existence of parallel but rather different understandings of personhood during the period.

Let us move now to explore the possible implications of this for the construction of gendered identity. We have already seen that women were more likely to be cremated than men. This is, however, a general trend rather than an absolute dichotomy. Inhumation was the dominant mortuary rite for both men and women during the first centuries of the Early Bronze Age, while by the end of the period, cremation was the normal mode of treatment of the dead—regardless of sex. This means that any relationship between women and cremation is likely to be obscured by more-general changes in mortuary rites over the period. The existence, noted above, of cremation burials (both male and female) in primary locations under barrows and accompanied by "rich" grave goods also challenges simplistic narratives in which binary oppositions such as male-female or high status–low status are mapped directly onto one another. Clearly, gendered identity was constructed and negotiated in contextually specific ways. It was not solely determined by biological sex but was instead shaped by other aspects of social identity, so that divergent and sometimes contradictory conceptions of gendered identity—influenced, for example, by age, family affiliation, or ethnicity—crosscut biological sex in complex and contingent ways (Sofaer Derevenski 2002). Some of the factors that may have informed this diversity in practice are considered below.

Notwithstanding these provisos, we need to consider why it was that women were more likely to be cremated than men. Even if the pattern is not hard and fast, it appears that women's bodies were more liable to processes of dispersal. This assertion is supported by an analysis of the

Table 6.3. Average weight of urned and unurned cremations by sex

	Average weight (urned)	Average weight (unurned)
Male	1,554 g	1,261 g
Female	905 g	730 g

weights of sexed cremation burials (table 6.3). Unfortunately, information on burial weights was available for only fifty-one of the sexed, cremated individuals included in this study. In general, only larger deposits of cremated bone can be sexed, so the following comments exclude the many "token" cremation burials that are known to have been deposited during the period. Nonetheless, some interesting trends emerge. For this analysis, cremations that were deposited in a pot were considered separately from those that were not, as the provision of a ceramic container is likely to have enhanced preservation. The average weight of urned male cremation burials (eight in total) was 1,554 grams, while the average weight of urned female cremation burials (seven in total) was 905 grams. Similarly, the average weight of unurned male cremation burials (thirteen in total) was 1,261 grams, while the average weight of unurned female cremation burials (twenty-three in total) was 730 grams. This marked disparity in weight between male and female cremations is unlikely to have been a result of sexual dimorphism alone.

We can therefore suggest that the bodies of women were more subject to fragmentation after death than those of men and that cremation was deliberately employed to facilitate this process (see also Chapman 2000a). I would argue that this may be the result of women's position and experience in Early Bronze Age systems of kinship and marriage. Although reconstructing kinship and marriage patterns is difficult, the primary burials in Early Bronze Age barrows are often male (Mizoguchi 1993), and the suggestion has been made that patrilineal forms of descent may have been common (Parker Pearson 1999a:90). In such a context, virilocal marriage would not be unusual. Indeed, in parts of north-central Europe where inhumations accompanied by regional styles of ornament were the norm during the early part of the Bronze Age, the movement of individual women, sometimes over distances of several hundred kilometers, can be traced through the presence of nonlocal objects in certain female burials (Jockenhövel 1991); it has been argued that these were foreign brides whose marriages cemented intergroup alliances (Kristiansen 1998a:398). Anthropological accounts of marriage patterns indicate that when women move away from their natal group to join their husband in marriage, their sense of self becomes fractured and they often experience a sense of dislocation and loss (e.g., Weiner 1992). At the same time, however, because marriage in many societies involves the strategic alliance of kin groups to facilitate access to particular economic, social, or political resources, women may have significant roles as intergroup mediators—creating and maintaining the networks of obligation between kin groups that are vital to social reproduction (Weiner 1992). In such contexts, women's location at the interstices means that they may come to be seen as partible persons—sometimes with a distinctly fractured and dividual sense of self.

These observations help explain the tendency for female burials to be placed in "peripheral" locations in Early Bronze Age barrows: this might have been a reflection not of perceived "status" but of the positioning of women within Bronze Age systems of kinship. A detailed regional study of burials in the upper Thames Valley (Sofaer Derevenski 2002) indicates that female burials were more varied in character than male burials (for example, in terms of the treatment of the body; type of accompanying pottery; and shape, size, location, and orientation of the grave), suggesting that the women's identities may have been more fluid than those of men in the same communities. Researchers have noted, too, that cremation burials located in primary positions within Bronze Age barrows tend to be heavier than those in secondary locations (McKinley 1997:142). Anthropological studies have observed that corporate groups may strive to keep hold of certain objects (notably, heirlooms) although their relationships with other groups mean that they are obliged to engage in reciprocal acts of gift exchange (Weiner 1992). In a similar way, it may have been considered important to preserve the bodily integrity of certain people after death—people whose bodies acted as symbols of the integrity of the descent group (see also Douglas 1973)—even while the remains of others were circulated as a means of maintaining important intergroup links. As such, the location of particular people in networks of kinship relations may have informed the treatment of their bodies. These points help us to make sense of the observed mortuary variability: clearly, for example, not all women were cremated, nor were all cremations located in secondary positions in mortuary monuments, suggesting that factors other than sex affected mortuary treatment. Likewise, recent strontium isotope analysis of Early Bronze Age burials indicates that at least some men were also highly mobile (e.g., Fitzpatrick 2011); this may have been one factor influencing variability in the spatial location of male burials in barrow cemeteries. People's diverse positions in the web of social relationships given material form in the mortuary context doubtless had an effect on what happened to their bodies after death.

Production, Reproduction, and Exchange

However, cremation was not simply a means of facilitating the circulation of the bones of important ancestors; it was also crucial to social, biological, and material reproduction. There are marked analogies between the treatment of bodies and objects on death: we have already seen how artifacts could be deliberately broken—and sometimes burned—prior to deposition in the grave (see also Cerezo-Román, chap. 8, this volume). Such practices extended outside of the funerary context. The abandonment of settlements during the Middle and Late Bronze Age, for example, was often marked by the deliberate destruction of objects central to the life of the household (Brück 2006a). Large dumps of unabraded ceramics in the upper fills of the enclosure ditches surrounding settlements such as Broomfield in Essex have been interpreted as "leave-taking deposits" (N. Brown 1995:14); the relatively high percentage of finewares in some of these contexts suggests that the abandonment of settlements may have involved ritualized acts of commensality.

We can suggest, therefore, that there were symbolic links between bodies and objects, so that for both, the end of the life cycle was marked in similar ways. However, there are also interesting parallels between cremation—a technology of the body—and the processes involved in the production of objects such as ceramics and metalwork (Brück 2006a). The manufacture of pottery required the grinding and sorting of clay and the firing of the pot. The addition of tempering agents such as grog (the broken fragments of older pots) and burnt flint (a waste product of cooking) meant that "dead" things were incorporated into new artifacts. The production of bronze objects involved the crushing and sorting of copper ores prior to smelting and casting. Recycling of bronze artifacts required the cutting, mixing, and remelting of broken objects to form new artifacts with new use-lives. As such, the activities of burning, breaking, and dispersing "dead" objects were closely associated with processes of transformation and rebirth. The similarities between cremation and other heat-mediated transformative activities hint that analogies may have been drawn between technologies of the self and other productive activities (see also Goldstein and Meyers, chap. 11, this volume). As such, the processes of burning, fragmentation, and dispersal did not simply symbolize death but facilitated the cyclical regeneration of life (see also Hingley 1997; Williams 2004d; see also Williams, chap. 5, this volume). Like pots and bronzes, the Bronze Age self was viewed as an amalgamation of substances and elements brought together through such processes as exchange, marriage, and other interpersonal contacts, so that the creative link between destruction and rebirth was central to the constitution of personhood.

It seems possible, therefore, that cremated bone was considered a powerful substance that itself had regenerative potential. The circulation of this material is likely to have played an important role in social, biological, and material reproduction. Anthropologists have long recognized that the exchange of objects and of marriage partners is crucial to the survival of kin groups in both practical and social terms: the circulation of objects, for example, creates an order of value for people and things, facilitating both the maintenance and the transformation of social categories (Gregory 1982; Weiner 1992). Yet exchange is an inherently ambivalent process, involving the transgression of boundaries and the loss of significant people and objects (Gregory 1982; Weiner 1992). This duality between loss and gain—between death and rebirth—is visible in the transformative technologies applied both to bodies and to objects during the Bronze Age. Processes of fragmentation and circulation were what facilitated the production of the self and the reproduction of society (see Battaglia 1990; Weiner 1992). In the mortuary context, the circulation of human bone ensured the cyclical flow of life by returning some of the "life force" or vitality of the deceased to the family who had originally given that person in marriage (see Battaglia 1990:171–79; De

Coppet 1981:185–89). It acted as a means of acknowledging the significant contribution of women to social reproduction by mapping out the intergroup relationships they had created and maintained during life. Such acts of exchange made productive the forces of death: through the releasing of objects and materials—including ancestral relics—to enter into new exchange relations, the regeneration of life could be ensured.

Cremation and Social Change

The shift from inhumation to cremation over the course of the Early Bronze Age heralded numerous other significant social, technological, and economic changes. A dramatic expansion in evidence for both the production and the recycling of bronze objects occurs around 1700 BC (P. Bray 2008): the idea that social and material reproduction was achieved through a cycle of fragmentation and reincorporation (see Chapman 2000a) may have provided people with the conceptual tools necessary for the increasing uptake of metallurgy (see also Goldstein and Meyers, chap. 11, this volume). Around the same time, there were significant changes in landscape organization and agricultural practice. Only at the end of the Early Bronze Age do field systems and settlements become archaeologically visible in most parts of Britain (Barrett 1994): prior to this, the archaeological record is dominated by ritual and funerary monuments, notably, barrows and various types of ceremonial enclosure, of which Stonehenge is the most famous. From circa 1700 BC on, however, the domestic/economic domain was what was given monumental form: substantial roundhouses set in embanked and ditched enclosures became some of the most visible features in the landscape (Barrett 1989). At the same time, the construction of field boundaries created a landscape that was increasingly subdivided (Yates 2007), so that access to resources depended on interpersonal and intergenerational links (Johnston 2005).

John Barrett (1989) has argued that this increasing concern with agricultural productivity is linked to changing modes of social reproduction: control over human and agricultural fertility became the key source of social power, such that the cyclical regeneration of life formed a major focus of ritual practice both within and outside of the mortuary context. Building on this, I would argue that the emergence of novel concepts of personhood may have facilitated significant economic and social change over the second millennium BC. From this period onward, the subdivision of land, people, and artifacts—and their subsequent mixing and recombination—was what ensured the continuity of life. The treatment of female bodies suggests that the role women played in the maintenance of relationships across space and time was central to this new mode of social reproduction.

What led to this change is unclear, however. There is an interesting tension in the Early Bronze Age between those aspects of funerary rites that emphasize the importance of place (notably, the construction of monumental barrows: e.g., Tilley 2010; see also Goldstein and Meyers, chap. 11, and Schurr and Cook, chap. 4, this volume) and those—such as the circulation of human bone—that crosscut and challenge spatially circumscribed formations of identity. Certainly, from the Middle Bronze Age onward, we see the development of very different concepts of place as settlements replaced barrows as key nodes in the social landscape. As groups became less mobile over the course of the second millennium (Barrett 1994), finding other ways of maintaining intercommunity relationships became increasingly important, and cremation may have provided one means of doing so.

Conclusion

Cremation has often been viewed as a practice geared toward the destruction of the human body—a means of socially controlling a biological process by deliberately removing the flesh from the body. In contrast, I suggest that cremation was a technology of the body whose primary significance—in the British Bronze Age, at least—lay in the fact that it facilitated the dispersal and circulation of the remains of the dead. Like other heat-mediated transformations, cremation enabled the regenerative potential of dead substances to be realized. The treatment of cremated bone—along with the objects the dead were associated with during life—challenges us to rethink the imposition of anachronistic models of the individual and normative assumptions regarding gendered identity onto the Bronze Age. At a more general level, cremation may indicate—in certain contexts—a very different conception of the body and the self from that indicated by inhumation. Of course, the case study considered in this chapter indicates that quite divergent models of the self can exist in parallel even within the same society, and evidence for the disarticulation of unburnt bodies suggests that these mortuary strategies may not have always been viewed as fundamentally opposed. Whatever the case, cremation provided a potent means of reflecting and transforming the link between bodily and social identity, as well as between the self and the wider social group; as such, its movement in and out of currency over the course of the British Bronze Age provides an important insight into wider social change during the period.

PART III

Social Impact of Cremation
Transformation, Movement, and the Body

7

Perspectives—Reflections on the Visibility of Cremation as a Physical Event

Liv Nilsson Stutz and Ian Kuijt

Cremation is a highly visual, sensual, and powerful process. As a destructive way, perhaps one of the most destructive ways, in which humans dispose of the dead, cremation produces physical by-products that are remarkably ephemeral and require researchers to think in inventive ways to identify and interpret their archaeological traces. To explore this, one must consider both the processes of how the dead were cremated in the past and the archaeological signatures of this social act. Surprisingly little research has addressed these questions. The systems of cremation would have varied with the cultural and geographical case study in question, and at this point researchers have yet to develop a clear sense of the diversity of cremation practices cross-culturally, let alone determining whether there are distinct archaeological signatures for different practices. But despite the obvious challenges of studying the discrete traces of cremation in the archaeological record, among the rewards of doing so is that a surprising amount of information can be retrieved to highlight many aspects of these complex practices in the past.

Where Were People Cremated?

From a methodological standpoint it is often extremely difficult to identify where people were cremated and how this was physically and socially linked to the eventual disposal of cremated remains. There are, of course, exceptions to this, such as, for example, Roman crematoria or bustum graves where the pyre is directly associated with the burial. Experimental research by McKinley (1993, 1997) and Marshall (1998, 2011) illustrates that effective cremation often involves building a crib of wood and other flammable materials (see McKinley 1995:fig. 4). Once ignited, this cribbing can burn at 800–1,000°C, igniting body fats. The cremation process can become surprisingly self-contained and require very little supervision. At the same time, cremation probably requires specific knowledge to obtain the ideal conditions of heat and oxygen flow for the combustion of the body. The research of McKinley and Marshall also demonstrates the complexities of successfully identifying the past presence, location, and/or intensity of cremation. One of the major methodological complications is that even intense cremation activity leaves a surprisingly light footprint in the archaeological record. Marshall (1998:173) notes, "Considering the intensity and duration of the burning for experimental pyres at Guiting Power, up to 800–1000°C for several hours, relatively little trace was left in the ground surface, and this as a relatively thick, friable crust, easily disrupted by trampling, weathering, or even careful clearance for extraction of cremated remains." Marshall's research, which is echoed by McKinley, illustrates that changes in soil coloration with cremation are usually restricted to the upper two centimeters (maximum). While these changes are potentially observable by archaeologists, interpreting them is complicated, as soil coloration changes can be produced by a range of human actions, including cooking fires. This, combined with the deliberate removal of cremated bone materials in many cultural contexts (see other contributions to this volume for expanded discussion), make it very difficult for even well-trained archaeologists and bioarchaeologists to identify the remains of the cremation pyre, let alone develop an interpretation based on physical data.

Many of the studies in this volume highlight the difficulties in identifying where people were cremated. For example, archaeological research at the Mound of the Hostages (County Meath, Ireland), occupied during the Neolithic and Bronze Age, highlights that in some cases, it is very difficult to determine whether people were cremated at the place their remains were interred, or whether cremation occurred at a totally different location. Despite the presence of at least two hundred prehistoric cremations (in this case based on counting individual bones from single individuals), as well as a long history of research (M. O'Sullivan 2005), whether people were originally cremated underneath what is now the physical area of the Mound of the Hostages tomb, around the mound, or somewhere off-site is unclear. This lack of archaeological visibility is not unique to the Mound of the Hostages, nor indeed to the Neolithic and Bronze Age periods. In fact, as the contributions to this book demonstrate, identifying the material act of human cremation is a challenge in almost all archaeological contexts regardless of place or time.

From Pyre to Interment: Invisibility of Cremation Pathways

Multiple lines of evidence in some cases do make clear that there were several stages and pathways between death and final deposition. In fact, this period of transition before the final deposition of the remains appears to have been both significant and incredibly varied. For example, many European Bronze and Iron Age urns are simply too small to contain the remains of an entire body. Several studies have shown that overall, for these periods, the remains in the urns correspond to 10–20 percent of the total mass of the burned bones of a body (Oestigaard 2013). This indicates that various other practices involving the burned human bones were possible. However, to identify these archaeologically is a huge challenge. We get a glimpse of the potential complexity in the archaeological identification of the presence of burnt human bones in property boundaries (Gansum 2004a) or in furnaces (Goldhahn and Oestigaard 2008), integrated into iron artifacts (Gansum 2004a, 2004b), or spread across the landscape in postholes and in cultivated fields (Kaliff and Oestigaard 2004). These finds hint at the wide variety of complex practices that may have been part of a socially meaningful web of significance in the treatment of the dead and their remains.

The process of selection of bones for deposition in the form that we archaeologically identify as a "cremation" today was probably complex and varying in the past. Archaeological studies have shown that besides the cremains, numerous other items were included in the final deposition, including, for example, unburned skeletal parts, unburned bone items, or even inhumations, as is shown at the Mound of the Hostages (Cooney 1992; Cooney and Grogan 1994; Kuijt and Quinn 2013; M. O'Sullivan 2005); animal bones (Larsson and Nilsson Stutz, chap. 3, this volume); artifacts burned or unburned (Sørensen, chap. 9, and Williams, chap. 5, this volume); and sometimes even other unburned human remains, such as the eyebrow hair from more than one individual in the Bronze Age cremation at Winterslow in Britain (Barrett 1994:123; see also Fahlander and Oestigaard 2008a:5), a find that may indicate a practice of shaving off the eyebrows of both the dead and the mourners before the cremation of the body (Gramsch 2013). Sørensen's contribution to this volume (chap. 9) further suggests that these archaeologically barely visible pathways to deposition were renegotiated in the past.

Conceptualization of the pathway of the body is a critical step in understanding the social, ritual, and cultural context of cremation. Brück (chap. 6, this volume) addresses the possible pathways of cremated bodies, with the body transformed through burning into divisible parts that were divided up and circulated among the living. This complexity of practices echoes that described in many of the chapters in this volume, and it is important to recognize that cremation and inhumation are not mutually exclusive practices. Rather, these are viewed as mutually compatible and integrated social systems that require us to reframe some of our traditional interpretive models.

Finally, we want to highlight how detailed study of the final deposit itself can provide insight into the cremation process. Careful microexcavation of deposits of cremated remains has long been practiced by French archaeologists and anthropologists (Giraud 1990; Grévin 1990) and has more recently been combined in an interesting way with computer tomography and X-ray technology in Denmark (Harvig et al. 2011). This time-consuming approach has the potential to reveal fundamental insights into age, sex, and health status of individuals, as well as important details about the social context of cremation. Attentive work has shown that microexcavation provides information about the mortuary practices, including details about the process of cremation (for example, whether several individuals were burned at once or on the same pyre) and the process of selection and deposition of the remains. One of the most striking examples of the rewards of such detailed studies is seen at the Lusatian Urnfield of Cottbus (Germany). There, microstratigraphic analysis of human remains from an urn revealed that the burned bones were deposited in anatomical order with the feet at the bottom and the cranial elements at the top. This stratigraphy could be understood as a practice of reconstituting the body in a transformed state or perhaps as the result of a standardized ritual practice of bone collection (Gramsch 2007).

Despite great interest, today researchers have only a limited understanding of the coexistence, frequency, and variation of cremation and inhumation practices at the regional and community scale. Despite the challenges, the increased attention to archaeological context and the development of new theoretical frameworks and methods (see Schurr, chap. 12, this volume) will lead to a better understanding of past cremation practices, and we are optimistic that researchers will be able to pull apart many of the complexities of past burial systems. In sum, the ways in which we perceive the remains may help us find new creative means to interpret the discrete traces of complex practices. From the broadest of perspectives, increased attention to the archaeological signatures of this dynamic phase between the act of cremation and the deposition of the remains has the potential to reveal exciting, and previously unrecognized, practices within human cultures.

8

Pathways to Personhood

Cremation as a Social Practice
Among the Tucson Basin Hohokam

Jessica I. Cerezo-Román

Personhood is constructed both in life and at death through multiple interactions of people with the deceased. In this chapter, by examining how bodies were treated at four Tucson Basin Hohokam archaeological sites, I explore how the Preclassic Hohokam of southern Arizona created different pathways to personhood for the dead; these are then compared with ethnographic accounts of Southwestern Native American funerary practices.

Mortuary practices have been viewed as proceeding through three stages associated with pre-death (preliminal), death (liminal), and post-death (postliminal) rituals (e.g., Hertz 1960 [1907]; van Gennep 1960). The entire sequence of death rituals, however, can be considered as dynamic transformative processes for personhood beginning with pre-death rituals and ending with the final mourning rituals. These processes are seen not as a series of unrelated separate stages (Bourdieu 1991:117–27; Brück 2006b) but as integrated and dependent upon the people involved. During the life-death transition, the personhoods of both the deceased and mourners are reconfigured through processes of dissolution, creation, negotiation, and transformation (e.g., Bloch and Parry 1982; Hertz 1960 [1907]; Metcalf 1982; Williams 2004d and chap. 5, this volume). Some researchers (e.g., McGuire 1992; Parker Pearson 1999b) suggest that mortuary rituals often mask or transform actual power or social relationships of the living. It is important to note that exclusively prioritizing the role of the living could diminish the role of the dead as an individual and a source of remembrance (e.g., Meskell 1996; Tarlow 1999). Furthermore, focusing only on the role of the living diminishes potential connections that the living may have had with the deceased (Williams 2004d).

The term *personhood* is employed in identity research and has been suggested for use particularly in the study of mortuary practices. Gillespie (2001), Fowler (2005), A. Jones (2005), and Brück (2006a), among others, study mortuary practices and identity through the lens of "personhood" and envision people as participating in mutually identifying community relationships and practices (Brück 2006a and chap. 6, this volume; Chapman 2000a; A. Jones 2005). Gillespie (2001:75), drawing from Marcel Mauss (1954, 1985), argues that personhood derives from the enactment of connections within a society including relationships between different individuals, individuals and groups, individuals and objects, and the living and dead. These connections shape social constructions that symbolize and refer to individuals.

In this chapter I use the concept of personhood to explore complex relationships between the dead, the living, and material culture among the Preclassic Hohokam from southern Arizona through the analysis of archaeological and osteological data from four sites in the Tucson Basin. I contrast these with ethnohistoric and ethnographic funerary accounts from different Southwestern Native American groups. Comparative data for this study derive from the archaeological sites of Honey Bee Village (Craig 1989), Sleeping Snake Village (Ezzo 2005), Fagan Ranch (Ezzo 2008), and Los Morteros (Wallace 1995a, 1995b). This research examines human remains from 415 burials, including cremations, inhumations, and burial deposits containing both burned and unburned bone. Most of these individuals were found in cemetery burials associated with courtyards. Courtyard groups are spatially patterned regions and facilities within sites (Fish and Fish 1991:159) and are generally believed by archaeologists studying the Hohokam to represent households and extended family households (e.g., Fish and Fish 1991; Wallace et al. 1995; Wilcox et al. 1981).

The Data Sets: Archaeological Assemblages and Historic Accounts

The Hohokam were farmers and artisans who lived mainly from AD 450 to 1450/1500 in the Sonoran Desert of the U.S. Southwest (Fish and Fish 2007). They were notable for their large-scale canal irrigation agriculture, red-on-buff ceramics, monumental architecture, and marine shell ornament production and circulation (Bayman 2001). They also have been described as consisting of different communities and settlements that expressed different levels of social organization,* interactions, and networks (e.g., Doelle and Wallace 1991; Fish 1996).

Historical accounts of cremation practices utilized here originate from the Pimas (Akimel O'odham), Tohono O'odham, and Yuman-speaking groups. Archaeological and linguistic evidence suggests that ancestors of these groups had contact with the Hohokam (Ezell 1963; Shaul and Andresen 1989; Shaul and Hill 1998).† The Pimas (Akimel O'odham) and the Tohono O'odham consider that the Hohokam were their ancestors, although the "Pima-Hohokam continuum" is a source of debate among Hohokam and Southwestern archaeologists (e.g., Bahr 1971; Ezell 1963; Jill 2001; Malhi et al. 2003).

In this chapter, I explore how ethnographies and oral traditions can be used for comparison and as a source of inspiration to evaluate social connections associated with cremation. I do not argue that the ethnographic practices had the same meaning to the prehistoric peoples or that there was direct cultural continuity between groups. Although some of these groups may believe that they have ancestral ties with the Hohokam, it is important to recognize that historic communities may live and interpret cultural domains very differently. The ethnographic and oral tradition accounts of mortuary practices also present several limitations intrinsic to the nature of these sources (see Vansina 1985 for expanded discussion). Regardless, they can provide insights that are of use in the interpretation of archaeological remains (e.g., Mason 2000; Wylie 1985). Descriptions of mortuary rituals in a written source

---

*Fish and Fish (1991) proposed different levels of social organization for the Hohokam: courtyard groups, suprahousehold units, site, and community. Suprahousehold units have been identified as social units that incorporate several courtyard groups. Site level incorporates different suprahousehold units. A community has been defined as bounded territorial units centered on pivotal sites. The community encompasses several multisite organizational units at the level of the ballcourt, platform mound community, or primary village.

† Shaul and Hill (1998) proposed that the Proto-Tepiman speech community incorporates attestation of language contact with the Proto-Yuman based on data from phonology, syntax, and lexicon. This suggests that the Hohokam were a multiethnic community who spoke both Proto-Tepiman and Proto-Yuman ca. 1,000 years ago.

provide analogs for some of the different types of social actions that individuals performed during mortuary rituals, as well as for possible material traces that these practices could have left behind.

Historic Accounts: Cremation Practices Among Southwestern Native American Groups

Southwestern Native Americans practiced different types of cremation throughout their histories. Archaeological evidence suggests that Puebloan groups, such as the Zunis of New Mexico, practiced cremation frequently (but not exclusively) in the past but no longer practiced cremation after the Spanish conquest (e.g., Howell 1994; Riley 1975). The nineteenth- and early twentieth-century Akimel O'odham and Tohono O'odham, located farther south in Arizona, also practiced cremation but only under special circumstances (such as death from warfare or in a violent encounter). They often, however, burned the houses and possessions of the deceased (Brew and Huckell 1987; Russell 1908; Underhill 1939, 1954; Velarde 1931).

Other groups in the Southwest, such as the Yuman-speaking peoples, regularly practiced cremation into recent history (for example, Colorado River Yumans such as the Halchidhomas, Maricopas, and Cocopas, and Southern California Yumans such as the Luiseños, Dieguños, Kumeyaay, and Quechans). Cremation mortuary rituals encompassed multiple activities practiced in sequence, and the activities are similar between groups. The mourning rituals, however, often varied (Spier 1933). For the Yumans, the cremation sequence began in the house of the moribund when the shaman and orator prepared the dying individual and family for the imminent death and departure (see table 8.1). Subsequent activities occurred once the individual died. The body was prepared at the house and taken to a funerary pyre to be cremated on the same day or the day after the individual died (W. Kelly 1949; Schaefer 2000). At the funerary pyre, a tribal orator, an official funeral orator, a fire tender (or *aumeʼva*), the relatives, people from the community, and guests from other tribes were assembled. Once the body arrived, it was placed in the pyre and burned (see table 8.1 for details). Among the Maricopa speakers, an orator, singers, and dancers performed and food was available for the guests while the body was

Table 8.1. Historic accounts of cremation rituals among Native Americans in the American Southwest

Process	Location	Actions
Individual is dying	House of the dead	Moribund individuals were assisted by a shaman, who sang several songs. After the shaman finished, an orator prepared the moribund and the relatives for death.
Individual dies	House of the dead	The body was washed and dressed in its best clothes, the hair combed, the body painted and decorated by the mourners. The body was then wrapped in a cloth by a person from outside the family.
After a day	Transportation of body	The body was taken outside to the pyre to be burned.
Burning pyre and burning of body	Pyre site	The body was placed on the pyre and laid with the head to the east and then turned on its right side. While the pyre was burning, a fire tender adjusted the body with a long pole, running it under the corpse to let in the air, and pushed the blazing logs over the corpse, so that it could not be seen by the relatives. Singers and dancers performed, and food was available for the guests. Objects and blankets were piled or thrown onto the fire by relatives or guests. People from the community and guests from other tribes were invited.
Body partially consumed		The speakers delivered an oration.
Body consumed/ cremated remains		The mourners and guests left the area, and the fire tender stayed with the body.
After fire		Most of the Yuman-speaking groups placed the remains in a secondary deposit: exceptions to this include the Luiseños, who buried the remains in the pyre site (other Yuman-speaking groups do this if an individual dies in enemy territory).

Table 8.1. (continued)

Process	Location	Actions
After fire	Rock piles away from village or elsewhere	The Diegueño Indians of southern California placed the remains in mortuary ceramic vessels after the cremation.
	Close to the pyre site	Maricopas and Halchidhomas divided the remains, once the body was burned, into four holes that were dug close to the heap of ashes: two on the south side, and two on the north after the fire had burned out. The fire tender, starting at the west end of the head, scraped the ashes alternately north and south of the centerline. He then divided the two piles to the west and to the east. Each pile was put in a hole and covered.
Post-death rituals	House of the deceased and adjacent space	O'odham, Apaches, and Navajos burned the houses and property of an individual at his/her death but did not practice cremation as a prevalent mode of interment (Mills et al. 2006). On some occasions, destruction of the property and house was not done by very poor families, or the dying person was removed from his/her house so destruction of the house could be avoided.
		Among Yuman-speaking groups, the destruction of the property and house of the dead was performed on a regular basis but varied in complexity and time. The Maricopas did it only for particular individuals, such as singers, warriors, and orators.
		Among the Quechans, the participants prepared a pyre, similar to the cremation pyre, and burned a memorial image of the deceased, personal belongings, and clothing. The participants might also throw in the pyre objects that belonged to them as an offering for the dead or as a contribution to the mourners, within four months to a year.
		Among the Cocopas, representations of the faces of the deceased were painted on the post of the houses and then the houses were burned with the associated objects. This practice was made for a particular deceased individual and for other relatives who had previously died. The properties of the other dead were included in the pyre.

burning. Objects and blankets were piled or thrown over the fire by relatives or guests (Schaefer 2000; Spier 1933).

Once the body was consumed by fire, most Yuman groups placed the remains in a different secondary depositional location. In this chapter, the term *secondary deposit* is used to describe a deposit where cremated human remains were placed after removal from the pyre, crematorium, or primary cremation locality. These deposits could consist of either urns or earth pits, or a combination of the two, containing cremated bone. Deposition of the remains after the fire, however, can vary between groups (Dubois 1907; McGuire 1992:45; Moriarty 1965:12; Schaefer 2000; Spier 1933). For example, among the Maricopas and Halchidhomas, the remains were divided into four piles and placed in four secondary deposits (see table 8.1; Spier 1933:302–3).

Additional rituals followed the final deposition of the body. These did not directly involve the deceased but involved the objects of the deceased, as well as the mourners. The O'odham, Apaches, and Navajos continued their mourning by burning the houses and property of an individual, but these groups do not practice cremation as the major funerary custom (Brew and Huckell 1987; Durivage 1937; Ezell 1961; Mills et al. 2006; Russell 1908). Yuman-speaking groups who practiced cremation also burned and destroyed the property of the dead and objects that belonged to them as an offering for the dead or as a contribution from the mourners (Dubois 1907; W. Kelly 1949:153; Moriarty 1965; Schaefer 2000; Spier 1933; Yarrow 1880). Mourning rituals varied in complexity and timing between groups (McGuire 1992; Spier 1933). In some instances the Pimas (Akimel O'odham) removed the main posts of the house prior to the fire and used them as construction material for a new house (see table 8.1 for exceptions). In cases when the dead were singers, orators, or warriors, the mourners also invited individuals from other tribes to be part of the mourning ceremony. Usually invited tribes had previously participated in other activities (such as going to war together) with the mourning tribe and/or were allies.

The practices of burning the body and destroying the property of the dead were done for several reasons, none of which are mutually exclusive (see table 8.1). Among Yuman-speaking accounts, individuals were cremated so that they could enter the "land of the dead" (Spier 1933), where, upon arrival, the dead performed similar activities and had similar life cycles as the living but with plenty to eat, and their life was "renewed." The aged became young, and old possessions burned in mortuary and mourning rituals were transported to the land of the dead as new (Spier 1933), thereby providing a rationale for the burning of property and possessions (W. Kelly 1949). Alternatively, mourners feared that the dead would return to the land of the living (Spier 1933; Underhill 1939:190). The accounts of Yuman speakers and the O'odham mention that cremation and mourning rituals would destroy enemy magic, the sickness of the deceased, and the polluted body (Hanlon 1972:106; Spier 1933; Underhill 1939:190).

Southwestern ethnographic accounts of cremation rituals help us interpret and understand the meanings of these practices. Ethnographic accounts can be utilized to evaluate the archaeological record and gain insight into past processes and practices. Although getting to the exact meanings of specific practices is difficult or almost impossible, comparison with historic groups that practiced cremation rituals allows us to explore the similar and/or multiple meanings represented by historic rituals and offer some reasonable hypotheses about what the Preclassic rituals may have meant to people in the past.

Archaeological Evidence

Cremation was practiced in southern Arizona since the beginning of the Early Agricultural period, circa 1600 BC–AD 200, albeit at low frequencies (Cerezo-Román 2013; Mabry 1998). The use of cremation slowly increased through time into the Preclassic period, AD 700–1150 (Fish and Fish 2007), when it became the prevalent mode of interment. For example, from the four archaeological sites in this research, 369 of 415 burials were cremations, 44 were inhumations, and 2 represented deposits that contained burned and unburned human bone. The overwhelming majority of inhumations were infants (newborn to two years at death) with the rare adult being inhumed. In this period the Proto-Yumans and Proto-Tepimans would have been living in close contact with one another (Shaul and Hill 1998). During the Classic period, AD 1150–1450/1500, cremation decreased as a mortuary practice. In the Phoenix Basin the decrease was earlier than in the Tucson Basin (Cerezo-Román and McClelland 2009).

Evidence for Burning Bodies

The Preclassic Hohokam practiced cremation as a primary mode of interment. Cremation was a multistage process in which several actions and activities were performed by the living prior to final disposal of the deceased. The first step was the burning of the body. Studies suggest that the body was first placed on a small wooden platform. Fuels may have included *Prosopis* sp. (mesquite), *Cercidium* sp. (paloverde), and *Olneya* sp. (ironwood), along with other desert legume-wood trees (Henry Wallace, personal communication, 2012). Personal adornment artifacts such as beads, shell, quartz crystals, bracelets, and pendants and activity-specific items such as hammerstones, polishing stones, quartzite saws, ground stone, and ceramic vessels were placed or thrown in the pyre. The majority of bodies were burned until the bones were white, indicating temperatures reaching 800°F (Holden et al. 1995a, 1995b). The homogeneity in color, high degree of incineration, and degree of fragmentation present in these cremations suggests that specialists were in charge of the technological and performance aspects of the burning. These specialists needed enough experience and knowledge to burn the bodies thoroughly.

The place where the body was burned—the crematory, pyre site, or primary cremation—was usually (sub)rectangular in shape and had an east-west orientation. The term *primary deposit of cremated bone* refers to a feature containing primary burned human remains and direct evidence of fire. The implication is that the complete body is placed and burned in situ, but this does not necessarily mean that the remains were found articulated. These primary deposits typically were used once by the Hohokam. Once the body was burned, the remains were collected from the pyre area and placed into a secondary deposit(s) of cremated bone (previously defined). The archaeological samples used in this study consist of 34 primary deposits of cremated bone, 258 secondary deposits of cremated bone, and 77 unspecified cremation deposits. Remains found in the secondary and unspecified cremation deposits could represent the same individuals found in the primary deposits of cremated bone or pyre sites. In fact, most cremated bone deposits analyzed in this study do not contain remains of complete individuals.

Recent research illustrates that bone weights can vary between males and females as well as between biological populations (e.g., Bass and Jantz 2004; May 2011; Van Deest et al. 2011). Nonetheless, the bones of a complete cremated individual usually weigh more than 1,500 grams. The mean weights of the cremations analyzed here (approximately 85 grams), however, were significantly lower. No significant differences in weight were found between males or females and a specific cremation burial practice. In contrast, infants were not found in any primary deposit of cremated bone but were found in five instances of secondary deposits of cremated bone. Primary deposits of cremated bone contain bones from all anatomical regions of the body (including cranial, axial, appendicular, and extremities). In 29 of the 34 primary cremations, the deposits did not present any major postburial disturbances and only one individual was present. Weights for these ranged from 1 to 1,091 grams, with a mean bone weight of approximately 204 grams (figure 8.1).

There were no major postburial disturbances and only one individual was present in 196 of the 258 secondary cremated bone deposits. No significant differences were found between sex or age at death in secondary deposits of cremated bone. The majority of these cremations were placed in a pit, although a few remains also were found in vessels or under vessels. Secondary deposits of cremated bone included bones from all anatomical areas of the body. The mean weight for these cremations was approximately 73 grams. The plotted distribution has a significant positive skewness with wide variation in bone weights (see figure 8.1). However, most primary and secondary deposits of cremated remains clearly do not contain complete individuals or bodies, and it is possible that the remains of a single individual could be spread between multiple deposits. Despite the use of high-recovery protocols, some bone, such as very small fragments, could have been lost during archaeological excavation. Regardless, the low bone weights in these cremation deposits cannot be explained by differential excavation and recovery techniques alone.

A total of 172 of the 415 deposits did not contain any associated objects. However, in the remaining deposits, different types of objects were found in primary and secondary cremation deposits (figure 8.2). Secondary cremation deposits have a greater variability in associated objects

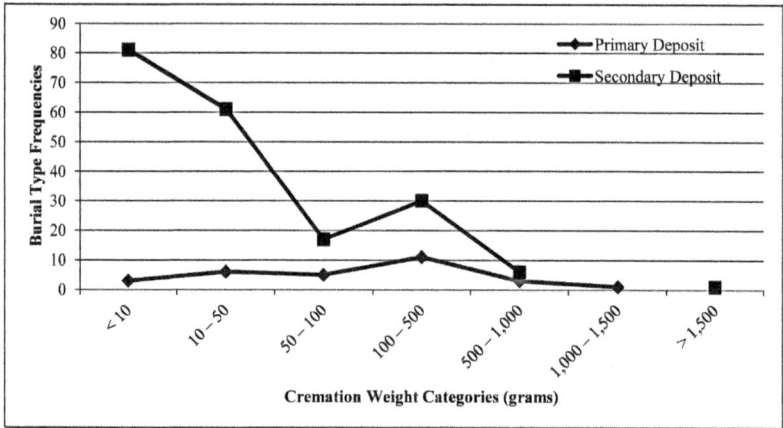

Figure 8.1. Classification of cremation weights (grams).

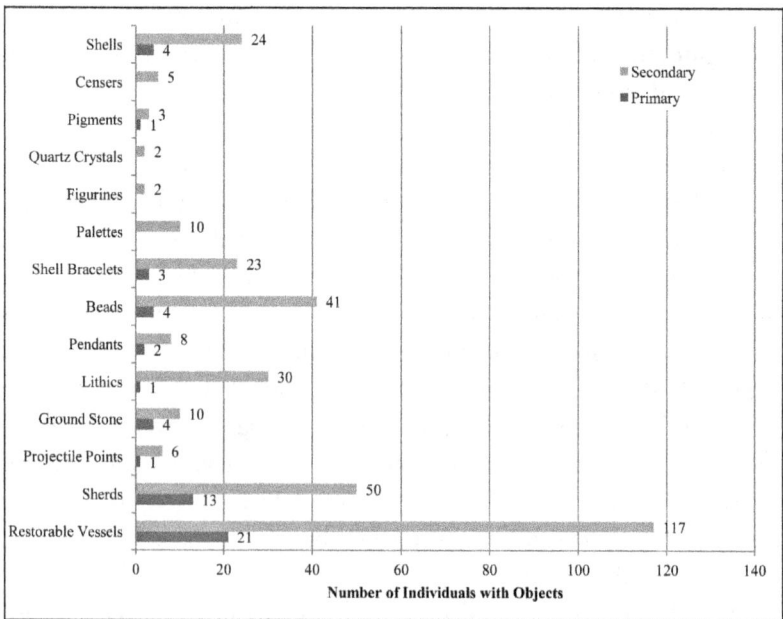

Figure 8.2. Frequencies of burial objects found in cremation deposits.

than primary deposits of cremated bone, and some objects may have been collected from the pyre area with the cremated bone. Many burned objects found in secondary cremation deposits may have accompanied or decorated the body during the burning on the pyre. In rare cases, objects (such as some vessels and hammerstones) did not exhibit evidence of fire, and thus they were added to the secondary deposits of cremated bone. There was no significant correlation between the quantity of objects, type of cremation, and age or sex of the individuals. However, Crown and Fish (1996), among others (McGuire 1992; Teague 1984), found that male adult cremations were usually buried with a variety of types of mortuary items, such as shell ornaments and ritual-related items. In contrast, women were more often buried with a higher mean number of ceramic vessels than males (Crown and Fish 1996).

Evidence for Postdepositional Practices

Burning structures and objects is a common occurrence in Hohokam sites. Some might be associated with rituals that occurred after final disposition of the dead. In a survey of more than thirty-four sites and eight hundred excavated Preclassic period pit houses, Mills and colleagues (2006) found that at least 35 percent and as many as 75 percent of the structures had evidence of burning, a frequency that was too high to be accidental or random. Two main theories have been proposed to explain these findings: (1) fires were caused by conflict or warfare (Oliver 2001; Rice 2001; Wallace and Doelle 2001), and (2) the houses were burned as part of a ritual related to the death of a member of the household or head of the family (Greenleaf 1975; Huntington 1986; Wallace 1995a, 1995b; Wallace and Doelle 2001). These theories are not mutually exclusive, and other models can explain the archaeological record. Therefore, each burned house should be evaluated independently. Mills and colleagues (2006), however, also mention that some of the houses were heavily burned, lacked large center posts, and contained minimal useable artifacts, and that recovered artifacts were usually broken. These findings are consistent with a funerary ceremony in which interiors of the houses were cleaned out prior to a burning ceremony, the center post was removed, and the structure mainly contained offerings or property of the deceased. Mills and colleagues (2006) argue that mortuary ritual, and not warfare, was the major factor in household burning.

Transformation of Personhood: Death of the Individual

Archaeologists have yet to develop the means of identifying pre-death mortuary rituals associated with the sick and dying. It is possible that in some cases transitional death rituals to the "afterlife" started when people were still alive. Once biological death occurred, however, rites began that potentially produced archaeological traces. At times the family acquired a situational personhood of mourners (Bird-David and Israeli 2010). The family prepared the body, including dressing the dead for the funeral ritual. When the body was ready, it was taken to the pyre to be cremated.

Archaeological evidence for body preparation can include particular objects found with the remains. Many objects found in primary and secondary cremation deposits appear to have been directly associated with the body and/or ritual during the cremation fire. Objects such as beads, shell, bracelets, pendants, and pigments decorated the bodies and were probably part of this initial stage of ritual preparation. Also, primary and secondary cremation deposits often contain figurines, quartz crystals, stone tools, and ceramic vessels that were burned with the body or placed after the burning of the body. These objects may have been possessions of the deceased or gifts from mourners. Likewise, palettes (Hawley 1947), censers, and pigments may have been utilized in the ritual performance. Some objects may also have been burned separately in a post-death/mourning ritual. Through their selection these objects acquire capacities to sustain memory relationships between the survivors and departed, as well as to represent multidimensional social networks among the deceased and mourners. It is, moreover, possible that the deceased's possessions were designated as aspects or extensions of the personhood of the individual, potentially creating object biographies that entangled the biographies of the person(s) and the objects (e.g., Brück 2006b:76; Gosden and Marshall 1999; Hallam and Hockey 2001; Hoskins 1989).

Differences in the deceased's personhood are potentially reflected through variation between burials and types of objects. These objects entered the archaeological record with the remains in at least three different ways: as decorative ornamentation as part of the clothing or accessories, as objects accompanying the body in the pyre, and/or as objects deposited with the body after burning. It is also possible, however, that the objects entered the archaeological record in later mourning rituals. In addition, burned houses and burned and fragmented objects found in caches could present similar characteristics and may have acquired an extension of personhood.

Cremation as a Physical Change: From Flesh to Bones

Cremation involves both physical and social transformation of the deceased (Cooney, chap. 10, and Goldstein and Meyers, chap. 11, this volume). In these transitions, the dead were closely connected with the living throughout the funeral rituals. Spier notes that among the Yumans the soul leaves the body during burning (1933:296). During cremation ceremonies, orators, dancers, and singers helped direct the soul of the deceased to the world of the dead (W. Kelly 1949). Very little archaeological evidence exists for these types of activities among the Hohokam. The presence of certain objects in cremation deposits, however, such as palettes, censers, and pigments illustrates that they may have been utilized in the ritual performance (see figure 8.2).

Roasting and feasting were often part of funerary events of many Southwestern Native American groups. At Honey Bee Village (Cerezo-Román and Wallace 2008), Fagan Ranch (Ezzo 2008), and Los Morteros (Wallace 1995b:252–53), *hornos* (furnaces or adobe outdoor ovens), roasting pits, and possible cooking pits were found in close proximity to cemetery areas. Thus, feasting and cremation may have occurred among the Hohokam. The number of people who participated in the transition may have been low even though cremations were visually more spectacular than inhumations and more people would have been aware of when they occurred. Archaeological data suggest that cremation rituals were performed in the cemeteries of courtyard groups (spatially distinct clusters of houses that represented extended families), and it is possible that the only participants in these ceremonies were members of the household and suprahousehold group, as well as individuals involved with ritual funeral performance.

As the center of ritual, the body of the dead possessed an agency that affected experiences, provoked memories, and altered decision making and the actions of mourners and the community (Chesson 2001;

Hallam and Hockey 2001; Tarlow 1999; Williams 2004d). One way in which the dead body may have had social agency was in the choice of mortuary treatment. It is, for example, common to find that only a few adults and the great majority of infants (newborn to two years at death) were inhumed. The reason for inhumation probably differed for adults and infants. In the case of adults, it was probably because of their particular identity or role in society (Cerezo-Román 2010; Cooney, chap. 10, this volume; McGuire 1992), while infants were not considered fully active members of the society. Tohono O'odham ethnographic evidence indicates that dead infants did not present any danger to the living because they were not full persons (Kozak 1991). Among the Hohokam, infants had fewer social networks than older individuals. Infant networks may have been oriented toward the household rather than toward a specific suprahousehold or other sectors of the community. It is common, for example, to find infants buried under the floors of pit houses. In sum, personhood was likely not yet established among infants, possibly because of high mortality rates.

Division of the Remains: Social Implications of Fragmentation of the Body

After burning, the body no longer resembled or had the physicality of a person and was converted into calcined bone. The personhood of the deceased was also transformed at that time. Few individuals were left in the place where they were burned. Some burned bone, varying from a small amount to the whole individual, was collected from the pyre site and moved to a secondary location. Relationships between the living and dead were transformed at this point. After burning, the cremated remains may have begun to be treated more like a "body-object" that could be fragmented, divided, distributed, and easily transported by the Hohokam, similar to what has been observed among other groups practicing cremation (see Brück, chap. 6, and Cooney, chap. 10, this volume). Interestingly, no significant age-specific differences are found between cremation groups (except infants, who usually were not cremated). Likewise, no differences are observed between sex and cremation type, although only forty-one individuals could be sexed by standard accepted protocols (Buikstra and Ubelaker 1994). The homogeneity in cremation types does not mean that the multiple inter-secting identities of the dead ceased to exist or were no longer a source of remembrance or personhood. Rather, identities were extended and transformed during these rituals.

Historic accounts of the Maricopas and Halchidhomas indicate that after burning, the bones were deposited into four different pits as sec-ondary cremation deposits. Archaeological evidence suggests a some-what similar practice, in which a single individual's bones were divided into one or more deposits (e.g., Birkby 1976; Minturn and Craig 2001). Beck (2000, 2005) examined ethnographic documents, bone weights of cremation deposits, degree of incineration, and fragmentation to ex-plore the low bone weights of Hohokam cremations. She suggested that after initial burning the remains were left in place, placed in a second-ary deposit, or reburned as part of a memorial ceremony. However, in the current research, no direct archaeological evidence for reburning episodes of secondary cremated deposits was found.

It is likely that no additional burning episodes of secondary crema-tion deposits occurred and that remains from primary cremation de-posits were dispersed into one or more pits. This practice would explain why bone weights are so low in Hohokam cremations. Most modern cremations have more than 1,500 grams of bone, while the mean weight of Hohokam cremations is much lower (see figure 8.1). Moreover, the osteological analysis suggests that not all the cremated remains of an individual were deposited in the same cemetery. The Hohokam often divided remains between communities and even within courtyards. For example, at the Fagan Ranch site, remains of a single individual were identified in two separate secondary cremation deposits in close prox-imity within the same courtyard group (Ezzo 2008). At Honey Bee Vil-lage, however, a refitting exercise was done between burials within the same courtyard, and no refitting skeletal elements were found between the deposits. It is possible that at all four sites low cremation weights indicate that remains were highly fragmented and divided between members of the same and/or different courtyards, and possibly between different communities, reflecting different social networks.

Rebay-Salisbury (2010) suggests that the practice of fragmenting and dispersing a body might indicate that the body was thought of as con-sisting of many parts rather than being an indivisible entity (e.g., Brück, chap. 6, this volume; Fowler 2010; LiPuma 1998). From this perspective, the deceased is transformed and treated as a "body-object." The body-objects may evoke the deceased person's life but also evoke the absence of the embodied person (Hallam and Hockey 2001). The concept of in-alienable possessions may provide insight into the Hohokam case study. Weiner (1992) discusses the concept of inalienable possessions, defined as "objects made to be kept (not exchanged), [that] have symbolic and economic power that cannot be transferred, and are often used to au-thenticate the ritual authority of corporate groups" (Mills 2004:238). These types of objects are broken and circulated but retain meaning de-rived from their original relationship(s), in which they became imbued with the intrinsic and ineffable identities of their owners. Inalienable possessions do not just control the dimension of giving; their historici-ties also are retained for the future and have memories from the past (Weiner 1992). Transformation of the original objects into fragments and distribution of these fragments suggest a different way to maintain, reinforce, or form new social relations. Mills (2004:239) suggests that the concept of inalienable possessions "provides an important alterna-tive for conceptualizing how objects are differentially valued and how that value is formed by social relationships that go beyond economic transactions." When applied to human remains, this transforms the personhood of the deceased from a complete bounded unit to that of part-object and part-person. With the Hohokam, after the body was burned it would have evoked the personhood of the deceased but was transformed into "body-objects" that could be divided and circulated as inalienable possessions. The differing levels of Hohokam organization consisted of different networks tied together by a source web of affilia-tions, including biological, civic, political, social, economic, religious, and ritual (Fish and Fish 1991, 2007). The remains could have been distributed among families and along specific social networks in which remains had symbolic power as sources of remembrance and created a material enactment of connections and networks.

From this perspective, value could be imparted through the distri-bution of the remains, with ritual and symbolic values imbued by par-ticipation in the event and possibly by placing the remains in a final deposition. While the number of people who could have participated in the distribution of the remains remains uncertain, it is possible that greater connections in life would be linked to increased fragmentation and distribution of the remains. Brück (2006b:88) suggests that gifts given at death (such as fragments of the deceased) "are a material manifestation of the substance of the dead person; they reconstitute the deceased in all his or her elements." Moreover, because people are constituted relationally, funeral mourners may feel that they have lost part of themselves. One way they avoid losing identity is to transform it into something else, to disaggregate the energy locked into the deceased and convert it into objects that can be used to form new social relationships (Battaglia 1990; Brück 2006b:88). Furthermore, circulating these body-objects in the rituals compensates all those who contributed to the life of the deceased (Brück 2006b:88) and authenticates particular connections.

Through the division of the remains, alliances could be reinforced by the distribution and partitioning of inalienable body/objects, and the process of division establishes a time when alliances could be created among participants in the ceremonies. At the same time, existing networks could be destroyed by the death of a person who functioned as the connection between other individuals, communities, and society as a whole. For example, in the case of a village, clan, or association, the duties of one member could be readily assumed by another, but this is not so easily accomplished within the family (W. Kelly 1949). Among the Yumans, when one spouse died the other spouse was no longer considered related to the deceased's family (Spier 1933:215). Accounts suggest that the length of the mourning period was not fixed. Some remarried within a few months, but people normally waited a year (Spier 1933:304), when new alliances could be formed.

Although determining precisely when the cremated remains were placed in the final secondary deposits is difficult, the final secondary disposition is likely to have occurred when the remains/inalienable possessions still held remembrance power and identity of the deceased, albeit in a transformed way. Historic accounts suggest that the final disposition could occur on the same day or a few days after the cremation ritual, and there is no archaeological evidence that points to the contrary. There is neither obvious weathering of the bone nor any other indication that the cremains remained unburied for a long time. The acts of redistribution and redeposition of cremated remains by the mourners within a courtyard cemetery serve as a symbolic reaffirmation of social memory and identity, as well as a reaffirmation of membership identity within a particular social network related to the deceased and the mourning family (Gillespie 2002, 2011; Hodder and Cessford 2004; Kuijt 2000, 2001, 2008; McAnany 1995).

Transformation of Personhood: Rituals After the Final Deposition

Rituals that occurred after the final disposition of the dead are difficult to reconstruct from archaeological evidence. It is possible, however, that burned Hohokam structures and objects are associated with post-death mortuary rites. Southwestern Native Americans' historical accounts mention that rituals occurred four months or more after an individual's death in a commemorative ritual (Davis 1921; Moriarty 1965; Schaefer 2000; Spier 1933). J. Woodward (1968) mentions that the ideological basis of the mourning anniversary is dual: it is the termination of mourning by the living and the final dismissal of the dead. Burned and fragmented objects have also been found in caches at Hohokam sites, often in the fill of pit houses (Birkby 1976:175). Burned and/or broken objects in caches are interpreted as "killed" objects (Mills and Field Murray 2008). These objects could possibly be possessions of the deceased, objects used in the mortuary rituals, or other ritual objects that needed to be terminated appropriately. Many caches of Hohokam objects, including concentrations of palettes and censers, were treated like cremated individuals. Censers in particular were burned, broken, and deposited, with fragments re-excavated, dispersed, and reaccumulated (Mills and Field Murray 2008). These practices may have symbolized the destruction of a particular social persona and the transformation of interpersonal relationships that such significant moments involved. In addition, the destruction of the objects is a powerful symbolic statement of the social impact of death. The objects could never be used again, and the relationships that they once sustained and signified come to an end (Brück 2004:320). Burning of objects and houses, then, was seen as the most appropriate means of ending these objects' lives.

Conclusions

The Preclassic Hohokam present an opportunity to examine the dynamic transitions of personhood that occurred at death. These transitions occurred for both the dead and the living. In these transitions, relationships and networks were reconfigured between different individuals, individuals and groups, individuals and objects, and the living and dead throughout the funerary rituals. Bodies were converted into "body-objects" but continued to evoke memories of the deceased person's life, objects became extensions of personhood, and mourners' relationships were reconfigured. Rather than being examined through a static stage-oriented approach, bodies can be viewed as part of different sets of interactions—interactions that defined the personhood of each individual who was involved.

Acknowledgments

I especially would like to thank my advisor, Barbara Mills, and my husband, Thomas Fenn, for their wonderful advice and support in the improvement of this paper, and my dissertation committee members, Jane Buikstra, Suzanne Fish, John McClelland, and Tom Sheridan, for their insightful comments and advice on the current and earlier drafts of this chapter. I also would like to thank Lynne Goldstein, Ian Kuijt, Gabriel Cooney, Joanna Brück, Howard Williams, Liv Nilsson Stutz, Åsa Larsson, Colin Quinn, Mark R. Schurr, David Hurst Thomas, and John Ware for their stimulating conversations and advice on how to improve this chapter. I would like to thank the Tohono O'odham Nation, Henry Wallace, Joe Ezzo, the staff from Desert Archaeology and SWCA Environmental Consultants, Lane Beck, Alan Ferg, the Arizona State Museum library, and finally the Bioarchaeology Laboratory at the Arizona State Museum for giving me access to the collections. The laboratory analysis was partially funded by the William Shirley Fulton Scholarship (School of Anthropology, University of Arizona), the Raymond H. Thompson Endowment Research Award (Arizona State Museum, University of Arizona), and a National Science Foundation Dissertation Improvement Grant (Grant no. 1132395).

9

Re/turn

Cremation, Movement, and Re-collection in the Early Bronze Age of Denmark

Tim Flohr Sørensen

This chapter takes its title from the Russian movie *The Return.** The movie is the story of two boys who are reunited with their father—of whom they have no memory—after his twelve-year-long absence. Upon his return, he takes the boys for a trip into the wilderness, leading to dramatic events, confusion, and conflict between the brothers and the father. The title of the film refers to the return of the father, yet the movie also closes with an act of return when the brothers revisit their journey in photographs, offering themselves a moment of reflection. Paradoxically, when the boys look at their photos from the trip, their father does not appear in any of them. By the end of the movie, the question remains whether the father had ever been with the boys on the trip, whether his presence was a product of their imagination, or whether he is in the process of being erased from their memory.

Inspired by the ending of *The Return*, this chapter explores the relationship between the act of returning and the negotiation of socially shared reality. The chapter focuses on the particular context of the secondary mortuary practices that follow cremation, and it explores the relationship between the act of returning to the cremated body of the deceased and the construction and reconstruction of socially shared experiences. Thus, I ask how revisiting a deceased individual in the transformed physical state after cremation influences social relations and affective memory.

---

* Directed by Andrey Zvyagintsev, 2003, Ren Film.

Theorizing Return

The aim of the chapter is to explore how returning may be triangulated with memory and forgetting, as well as to consider whether the instance of going back may represent a third perspective, reconciling memory and forgetting in the light of the materiality of the dead. The point of departure is the multiple anthropological and archaeological studies that show how people frequently go back to places of burial, sometimes touching—or rather re-touching—the bodies, bones, or cremated remains of the deceased (e.g., Bloch 1971; Borić et al. 2009; Harris 2010; Metcalf 1987; Metcalf and Huntingdon 1991; Williams 2004d). Developing on these perspectives, the chapter questions the often-stated understanding of grief work and rituals as ways of finding meaning (e.g., Boivin 2009; Davis and Nolen-Hoeksema 2001; Kobler et al. 2007; Metcalf 1981; Moules 1998) and instead appreciates the possibility that ambiguity and vagueness of meaning can be essential aspects of rituals (Bloch 1974; Engelke 2007; A. Jones 2010; Nilsson Stutz 2006; T. Sørensen 2012; Tomlinson and Engelke 2007; see also Gumbrecht 2004).

The handling of the dead, or the place of the dead, is frequently discussed in terms of social rites of passage, viewing funerals and burials as performances of social recomposition, constituting ritual instruments for negotiating communal relations in the absence of the deceased (e.g., Bloch 1982; J. Brown 1995:19–20; Chapman 2000b; Chesson 2001:4; Hallam and Hockey 2001; Metcalf 1981; Poyil 2009). Here I wish to propose that these insights can be supplemented by a perspective on these moments of return as instances of emotional displacement, or as ways of facilitating unelaborated, ambiguous, and socially heterogeneous ties to the deceased.

It is difficult to talk about cremation without talking about return, that is, the movement back to the burnt remains of the deceased. Archaeologically, we may not be able to observe the movement itself but only trace the inert vestiges of the movement. Thus, movement inherently constitutes an epistemological and methodological problem (Hewitt 2005; Sheets-Johnstone 1979; T. Sørensen 2010b, forthcoming), but archaeologically we can start out by inferring the movements that would have connected the remains in the past. This allows us to address what moved, what was moved, who moved, and who were moved. The question is, in turn, how can we characterize these movements between human beings and material culture? Socially, emotionally, and materially, returning may signify a number of qualities, but at the most immediate level, the prefix *re-* implies going "back" or doing something "again." This does not necessarily mean that there is a repetitive nature in the return; it may simply denote that an object is contemplated anew after some kind of disruption. *Return* thus means to turn toward something again, but it may also mean turning away, leaving or rejecting an object or place. Finally, *return* may also imply that something is reverted or reversed conceptually or physically.

Cremation in the Context of Inhumation

We may stipulate that returning after cremations revolves around the cremated body and about how to handle the burnt remains of the deceased. This chapter focuses on cremation burials in Denmark in Periods II and III of the Nordic Bronze Age (circa 1500–1100 BC), which were an exception more than a rule at that time. The archaeologically best known form of burial from this time is inhumations of whole bodies in oak-log coffins and in stone cists in large burial mounds (Boye 1896; Holst et al. 2001; Randsborg 2006). Monumental burial mounds constitute the most conspicuous form of burial at that time, being up to thirty meters in diameter and between five and ten meters high. There are more than forty thousand mounds nationwide (Johansen et al. 2004:34), and they have long been recognized for their iconographic and aesthetic characteristics in the landscapes of Denmark because of their form as well as content (Brøndsted 1939; Glob 1970; Kristiansen 1987, 1998b; Müller 1897).

In the case of inhumations, a complex series of layers or shells around the deceased was formed around the dead body at the center. The body was first clothed, then wrapped in hides and put in an oak-log coffin or stone cist. The coffin was then covered with smaller stones, which served to keep the coffin in place, upon which several successive layers of turf were built (Holst et al. 2001; Holst et al. 2004). These "wrappings" (Holst et al. 2008:6–7) essentially created an increasing sensory distance between the dead body and the mourner. The construction of the mounds followed a very complex and simultaneously very stringent organization of labor and interaction that involved large numbers of people (Holst and Rasmussen 2012, 2013).

This process of engulfing the dead in continuous shells resulted in a complex stratigraphy, protecting the dead body from decay (for further details see Breuning-Madsen et al. 2003) and in effect preserving a bodily cohesion. These layers around the dead body also imply a perceptual disappearance of the materiality of the dead body in favor of a gradually increasing interaction with living bodies, working the wood, stones, soil, and turf as the grave was being constructed. At the same time as the burial mound grew during the construction process, the immediacy of the deceased thus decreased gradually. As the building of the mound added layer upon layer on the dead, her or his proximity was being replaced—or mediated—by a nearness to construction materials. The layering of the burial mound may thus be seen as a way of embracing the deceased metonymically in the materiality of the landscape: in its fabrics, hides, wood, stones, soil, and turf, and the vibrancy of the mound-building community.

Cremation in the Early Bronze Age

Even though inhumation constituted the most common form of burial at this time, cremation also began to appear in Period II (circa 1500–1300 BC) and gradually became more widespread during Period III (circa 1300–1100 BC). Eventually, cremation became the exclusive mode of disposal with the beginning of the Late Bronze Age (circa 1100–500 BC), when cremated individuals were buried in urns. In the archaeological evidence from the Early Bronze Age, however, urns are rather rare (see Feveile and Bennike 2002; Olsen 1990), and the discourse on how to handle the cremated individual was less regulated, demonstrating great variation and seemingly little prescribed cultural dogma. This has particularly interesting perspectives for the notion of returning, as the variation of burial practices may indicate that modes of disposal were contingent on each individual burial event and that the act of returning played a crucial role in exploring or determining how things should be done.

Archaeological finds indicate that cremations in the Early Bronze Age were carried out on open-air pyres, and in some cases there is evidence for shallow pyre-pits, dug for the burning of the corpse. These pits have, so far, mainly been found in the region of Thy in northwestern Jutland (summarized in Olsen and Bech 1994:171–86). The excavation of a Period III burial mound at Damsgård (Aner and Kersten 2001:no. 5026; Olsen and Bech 1994) offers a particularly informative glimpse of the handling of body and cremated matter in relation to a pyre-pit (figure 9.1). The excavation showed that the body of a woman between twenty-five and thirty-five years of age had been cremated in a pyre-pit on a bed of branches and peat. After the cremation, some of the surviving skeletal remains, metal objects, charcoal, and ashes were collected from the pyre-pit and deposited in an adjacent stone cist. The pyre-pit was, however, not cleared out entirely and thus contained a bronze arm ring with a partially cremated piece of arm bone piercing it, among a few other artifacts. Also, one skull fragment was left in the pyre-pit, while a fitting piece of the skull was located in the stone cist. After the stone cist was completed, a burial mound was erected on top of it, covering the grave as well as the pyre-pit.

Traces of a pyre-pit were also found beneath a burial mound at Nørhågård (Aner and Kersten 2001:no. 5176; Olsen and Bech 1994:174, 176), not far from Damsgård and dating to roughly the same time. The pyre-pit was partly covered by a one-meter-long stone cist that contained burnt skeletal remains. A contemporary burial mound at Villerup, also in Thy, likewise produced a small stone cist, located at one end of an elongated pit containing remains from a pyre. The cist contained bone fragments from an infant (seven to thirteen months old) and fragments of woolen cloth (Olsen and Bech 1994:177–78). Subsequently, but no later than Period III, two more cremation burials were added to the same mound, and each was also placed at the end of a pyre-pit. These graves contained fragments from another cremated child (aged eight to twelve months) and an individual of unknown age (Olsen and Bech 1994:180). Furthermore, two pyre-pits of Early Bronze Age date have been confirmed on the northern German island of Sylt, at Keitum and Wenningstedt (Olsen and Bech 1994:183–85).

I have argued elsewhere (Sørensen 2010b; Sørensen and Bille 2008) that these particular forms of cremation burials draw our attention to

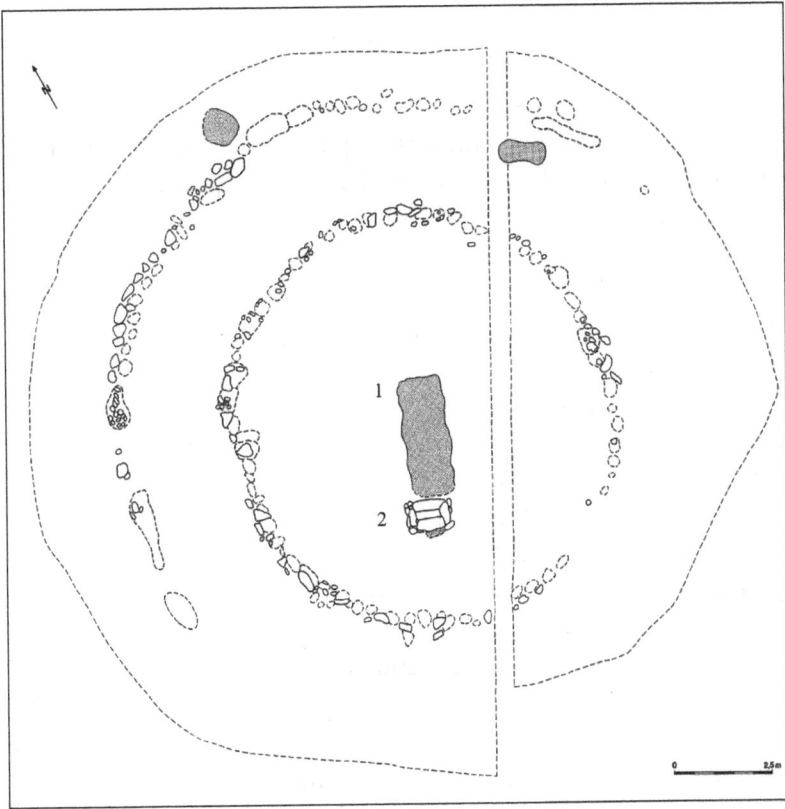

Figure 9.1. Period III burial mound at Damsgård in northwestern Denmark. 1 marks the elongated pyre-pit, and 2 marks the stone cist within which the majority of the burnt individual was buried (after Aner and Kersten 2001: no. 5026).

the sensuous effects that the burning of the corpse and the subsequent burial of the remains would have created. Moreover, excavations of burial sites with pyre-pits allow us to address themes that are centered on the dialogue between the actual cremation and the postcremation activities, that is, the movements revolving around the collection and relocation of the burnt remains after the burning of the dead body. At a fundamental level, the coexistence of pyre-pits and cremation graves shows that Early Bronze Age cremation involved the active movement of the cremated remains of the deceased from the pyre-pit to the stone cist. The observation may appear rather banal, but it highlights that this transfer of material involved an act of returning in the sense that the persons handling the deceased needed to go back to the pyre-pit after the cremation and engage in a bodily interaction with ashes, charcoal, bone fragments, and metal artifacts. Hypothetically, these remains from the cremation could have been abandoned in the pyre-pit and simply left to be covered by the burial mound, but people actively returned to pick up the cremated individual and move her or his remains. The act of returning to the pyre-pit and the cremated individual thus made the transformed format and substance of the body present to the senses for the bereaved.

The process of cremation on such open-air pyres entails a number of gradual changes in the materiality of the pyre. Igniting the pyre set ablaze the most immediately inflammable materials in the pyre, such as reeds and the clothes and hair of the deceased. With the gradual heating of the pyre, larger logs and the torso of the dead body would then be set afire, whereby the flames of the pyre would assume a more powerful form. The flames would embrace the entire pyre, engulfing the corpse in fire and smoke, increasing combustion of the pyre and the decomposition of the corpse. At this stage, the intensity of the fire would also increase, slowly giving the pyre a different color, sound, and smell, while the body of the dead also would burn, turning her or his skin black. The texture, consistency, and surface of the body would be reduced and skeletal parts and internal organs would become exposed. This burning and evaporation of the mass of the body would continue until the pyre and the corpse collapsed and the fire gradually died out. Embers would remain glowing amid the remains of the pyre and skeletal parts (Jonuks and Konsa 2005; Sørensen and Bille 2008; Williams 2004d).

In this connection it may also be stipulated that dead bodies are not inert (T. Sørensen 2009) and that the burning of a body has the capacity to animate it, making it move and thus potentially intensifying its affective agency on the mourners. This could imply that observing the behavior of the body on the pyre was one of the ways of deciding how to construct the grave, just as much as prescribed cultural expectations for the form of the proper grave (Sørensen and Bille 2008:255–56). This means that certain movements and contortions of the dead body could have been decisive in how it was treated after the cremation. This implies a change in the materiality of the corpse as well as the pyre, and the color, smoke, temperature, smell, sound, and form of the corpse and pyre would transform during the cremation, which could take up to ten hours (Williams 2004d:271). In certain parts of the process, change would be rapid and violent, while in other parts it would be gradual and slow. In the course of this process, the dead body would have transformed from one material format to another, and researchers have proposed that this changes the body from being "substantial" to being "substance" (Sørensen and Rebay 2008a). Observation of this transformation would have been of great importance to the significance of the cremation, and many ethnographical examples show how the ways in which the burning or charring corpse twists, contorts, bloats, explodes, implodes, or evaporates are crucial to the appreciation of the cremation as a staging of a transition (e.g., Hertz 1960 [1907]:42–43; Miller 2001; Oestigaard 2004:27).

The perception of qualities such as the temperature and smell of the burnt-out pyre are difficult to access archaeologically, but we may at least wonder whether the return to the pyre-pit was defined by the temperature of its contents. The incomplete clearing of the pyre-pit at Damsgård, for instance, may suggest that the embers were still so hot that only a hasty raking out of skeletal fragments and ashes would be conducted, after which the pyre-pit was not revisited, yet leaving some parts of the cremated remains behind in the pit may also have been deliberate, as discussed later.

Constructing Virtual Bodies

The examples above not only show how the deconstructed dead body was transferred from the pyre-pit to the grave but also imply that members of the community were engaging physically with the transfer. However, apart from one of the graves from Villerup, there seems to be no particular arrangement of the cremated remains in the abovementioned cremation burials. At Villerup, the ashes and bone fragments in the grave from Period II were placed as an elongated concentration in the central part of the stone cist and were accompanied by a bronze fibula (Olsen and Bech 1994:182). But in numerous other cases, there is evidence to suggest that this transfer involved an active, sensuous re-collection of the deceased. At Lækjær, another burial mound in northwestern Denmark, the remains of what was presumably a cremated woman were interred in a stone cist grave dating to Period II (Aner and Kersten 2001:no. 5085). The cremated remains are concentrated in the central part of the cist, and the personal items of the deceased—her dagger and belt plate—were placed in the grave in accordance with the organization of the conventional inhumation of the time, thereby mimicking the position on an uncremated body. The belt plate was located in the center of the grave, where the center of the body would have been in an inhumation, and thus over the stomach, and the dagger had been placed at the waist of the cremated, virtual body. In this way, the deposition of cremated bone represented the transformed material-ity of the dead body, while artifacts assumed the role of replicating the corporeal presence of the deceased. Organizing the remains in this way was a procedure that required certain individuals to collect the cremated bone from the pyre and give it a new form in the grave on which the artifacts were placed with the intention of constructing a virtual body.

Not only do these examples highlight the emulation of bodiness and corporeal intertextuality in the Early Bronze Age (Sørensen and Rebay 2008a, 2008b; T. Sørensen 2010a; Sørensen and Bille 2008), but they also raise further perspectives with regard to how the act of returning works as a moment of re-collection of the deceased. The return revolves around the confrontation with a body that has been deconstructed by the burning, which includes the disappearance of the organic dressing of the body. This means, of course, that it is not possible to say whether the body was clothed in the actual cremation, yet at least in some cases burnt and sometimes unburnt metal artifacts were associated with the cremated body. This question is not interesting solely in terms of re-constructing how the cremation would have taken place in the Early Bronze Age, but more so because it allows us to address the issue of what was transformed and transferred in the cremation event and in the act of returning after the cremation.

Burnt and Unburnt Matter

At Damsgård and Keitum, bronze objects would have been part of the body at the cremation event. As mentioned earlier, a bronze arm ring with a fragment of arm bone penetrating it was part of the Damsgård burial, and likewise a piece of a finger was left in a ring at the Keitum burial (Olsen and Bech 1994:162, 184). Elsewhere, organic material has been found among the buried ashes and bone fragments, such as in a burial mound from Period II at Nordenbro (Aner and Kersten 1977:no. 2060) on the island of Langeland, southern Denmark. This grave contained the remains of a cremated man buried with a sword in a wooden sheath, a fibula, and a double stud in the remnants of a wooden coffin. Adjacent to the grave was a burnt spot, which was located at roughly the same stratum as the bottom of the grave. Whether the burnt spot was that of a pyre is unclear, but one may surmise that the sheath, being made of wood, had not accompanied its owner on the pyre. The remains of the pyre could thus be combined with artifacts that had not been burned with the deceased, and certain objects appear to have been integral parts of the deceased body or person, while other things could be added to the cremated body later.

The question is, then, whether this suggests that artifacts and bodily remains were to maintain some form of integrity or even a corporeal authenticity upon being deposited in the final grave after the cremation. In short, there is no unequivocal uniformity in this regard in the Early Bronze Age, but the variations or heterogeneity might instead suggest that corporeal authenticity, divisibility, and extensions were negotiated, explored, or discovered through acts of returning to the cremated body and in the collection and composition of the final grave. A closer look at a few other burials may shed further light on this point.

At Egshvile (Aner and Kersten 2001:no. 5115; Olsen 1990) in northwestern Denmark, an elongated stone cist contained the remains of a cremated man and his personal artifacts, dating to Period III. The cremated remains were piled in the central part of the cist, shifted to one long side, while the artifacts—consisting of a sword, a chape, a fibula, double studs, a knife, and gold and bronze spirals—had been placed partly on the cremated remains and partly beside them. The metal artifacts were not organized in any way to resemble their location on a body but instead seem to have been grouped together and placed on top of the cremated body without any particular reference to bodily schema (Olsen 1990:148).

The Medium for Re-collection

The juxtaposition of burnt and unburnt material is further illuminated at the Hvidegård burial in eastern Denmark from Period III (Aner and Kersten 1973:no. 399; Herbst 1848). This contained the ashes and bone fragments of what has traditionally been presumed to be a cremated male individual that were placed in a piece of cloth resembling a cloak.* Ashes and numerous organic and inorganic artifacts were laid out to represent a dead body stretched out in the grave. The illustration in the original publication of the excavation (Herbst 1848:339, table II) suggests that the location of the deceased's sword may be mimicking its position at the waist of a unburnt corpse (figure 9.2).†

In terms of the re-collection of the deceased, other observations from Hvidegård are also relevant. The organic remains indicate that the cloak had been laid out in the grave first. Ashes, bone fragments, and other artifacts were placed on the cloak, which was then closed. This suggests that ashes and bone fragments might also have been enveloped in clothing at other burials of this period, where cremated remains are found pooled in a delimited area of the coffin or cist. Had the cremated remains been strewn more randomly within the confines of the grave, there would have been a more uneven scatter of bone fragments and artifacts in the graves. This suggests a construction of the cremated remains that resembles or retains the relative integrity of a body by imitating the format of an unburnt corpse (for a comparable case see Rævehøje, eastern Denmark [Aner and Kersten 1973:454]),‡ which has been described as a "technology of body coherence" (M. Sørensen 2010:60).

---

* However, a recent reinterpretation of the cremated bones suggests that the Hvidegård burial contains at least three individuals (Goldhahn 2012:245–46).

† Determining the exact position of swords in graves is not unproblematic, though, and may vary even in inhumations. Swords are sometimes located beside the deceased along his side (as at Muldbjerg [Aner and Kersten 1995:no. 4740]), at other times over the length of his chest (as at Tidselhøj, grave D [Aner and Kersten 2001:no. 5110]), at other times again across the upper body in an oblique angle, such as, for example, from the right shoulder to the left side of the hip (e.g., Aner and Kersten 1995: no. 4746).

‡ Such cremation burials may be compared to the organization of the well-preserved oak-log inhumations, for example, the Muldbjerg burial mound in western Jutland from Period II (Aner and Kersten 1995:no. 4740). It contained a man, who was

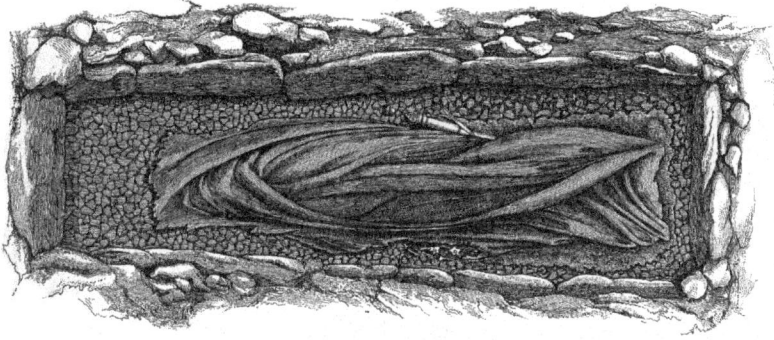

Figure 9.2. The Hvidegård burial in eastern Denmark from Period III (after Aner and Kersten 2001: no. 399).

What appears to have been placed in the grave at Hvidegård was clearly more than a cremated man and his personal accessories. The grave represents more than the transformation of a dead body through cremation; it also testifies to the transfer of objects and ontological positions across material forms. This transfer issued forth through the re-collection of the deceased: not simply the commemoration of the person but more significantly the integration of the physical and affective re-collection of the dead in different media. Some of these media had undergone cremation and some had not. It is precisely such an assemblage of material forms that captures the re-collection of the dead, being put together again from organic and inorganic, burnt and unburnt materials.

Beyond Bodiness

Other places, in turn, seem to represent a concern with placing the cremated material and artifacts in a nonrandom way, yet not citing a bodily presence. Just to mention one example, a mound at Stagstrup,

---

buried with a sword along his chest with his hand resting on the sheath of the sword. A cape and a blanket had been folded and placed on top of the sword, and the entire contents of the coffin were swaddled in an ox hide before it was closed.

dating to Period III, in northern Jutland contained a long (1.90 meters) and narrow (0.30 meters) stone cist in which were placed three distinct piles of cremated bones, possibly deriving from three individuals (Aner and Kersten 2001:no. 5022). Yet other places seem to represent the complete disintegration of the cremated body in the grave, where the ashes and bone fragments were strewn throughout the grave and not assembled in a delimited area. For example, at Himmark on the island of Als in southern Jutland (Aner and Kersten 1981:no. 3171; dated generally to the Early Bronze Age), the entire floor of the stone cist was covered with fragments of cremated bones. At a burial mound not too far south of Himmark at Augustenborg (Aner and Kersten 1981:no. 3181; dated to Period III), bone fragments appeared to have been scattered in random patches across the floor of the cist.

In some of the cases I have explored so far, it seems that cremated remains did not travel far but were simply moved from a pyre to a nearby grave a few meters from the pyre. This implies that the dead were less mobile compared to other cultural contexts, in which the cremated body is transferred to a mobile urn in which the cremated body stays (either buried in a cemetery or on display in a home) or from which a scattering in open space takes place (Kellaher et al. 2010; Mädler 2008; Prendergast et al. 2007; see also Williams, chap. 5, this volume). The cremated bodies that are found in contexts without evidence of nearby pyres may suggest that the burnt body was transferred to the place of burial in some form of container. In some burials there is evidence for the wrapping of cremated matter in what might have been a textile bag or sack, which may imply such a mode of transportation from pyre to grave (Aner and Kersten 2008:no. 5654), and a field of twenty-three burials from Period III in southern Jutland was characterized by a combination of ceramic urns and organic containers (Feveile and Bennike 2002:129, 132).

The Co-presence of Cremated and Carnal Bodies

In numerous cases, moreover, the archaeological evidence also points to instances of return, where the remains of a cremated individual were interred in the same grave as a whole carnal body. At Højsager (Aner and Kersten 2001:no. 5272), Period II, in northwestern Denmark, the remains of a cremated burial were revisited when a dead body was interred in the same grave at a later point. Similarly, a burial mound at Erslev (Aner and Kersten 2001:no. 5278), also Period II and in northwestern Jutland, contained an elongated stone cist with disturbed skeletal remains accompanied by a dagger blade, a pommel, and a fibula. At one end of the cist, where the feet of the buried body would have been, there was a small pile of cremated remains from another individual and fragments of an unburnt cranium belonging to a child.

In these particular cases, it is not clear how much time had passed between when the cremated remains were deposited and the bodies were buried, but the cremated remains were at least in place when the dead body was superimposed. Such coexistence of whole bodies and cremated bodies is sometimes found in graves that appear to have been established in the course of the very same event. Also in northwestern Denmark, the archaeological microstratigraphy at a burial mound near Nørhågård (grave A [Aner and Kersten 2001:no. 5176]) showed that the burial of a body and the deposition of another person's cremated remains were most likely carried out simultaneously. The body was buried in a rectangular stone cist, while the cremated remains were deposited in a smaller extension of the cist at the feet of the body.

The simultaneous burial of a cremated and a whole body is also found in the famous Egtved grave (Aner and Kersten 1990:no. 4357; Thomsen 1929) from eastern Jutland, dating to early Period III, where a young woman approximately sixteen to eighteen years of age was buried in an oak-log coffin with a cremated child enveloped in a bundle of cloth at her feet. A birch-bark box containing a form of brew was located next to the young woman's head, but parts of the cremated child, found at the feet of the young woman, were also located in the bark box. This containment of the cremated body is interesting in the sense that it serves a double function, which is somewhat contradictory. It allows for the integrity of the cremated body in its copresence with a whole body but also creates a material boundary between the two types of bodies. The fact that parts of the cremated child were contained in the bark box and other parts in the cloth wrapping thus represents a breakdown of a bodily cohesion.

So while we have seen before how the deceased were re-collected from the ashes of the pyre, these examples of an occasional copresence of inhumed bodies and cremated bodies show that the social relations of different deceased individuals may be re-collected by the juxtaposition of cremated and noncremated bodies (see Cooney, chap. 10, this volume). It suggests that there may have been numerous concurrent burial practices in the Early Bronze Age, which were not mutually exclusive but therefore also needed negotiation and authentication, which occurred through creative re-compositions of the physical remains of the dead. It may indicate that some persons were perceived as belonging together in death and were to be reunited regardless of the funerary customs that resulted in cremations and inhumations, respectively. So, while the earlier examples indicate the movements that took place in relation to individual acts of cremation, and the return people made to the cremated body, the corporeal copresences illustrate how people were also, occasionally, returning to older graves to reunite deceased individuals who had been separated by different times of dying or differing burial practices. It is interesting, moreover, to note that when cremated and carnal bodies are buried together, the cremated remains are never organized in ways that simulate carnal bodiness.

In the light of the cremated child, partly contained in the bark box at Egtved, it should be mentioned that urns do occur occasionally in the Early Bronze Age, such as in Graves 1 and 2 at Egshvile, both dating to Period II, containing the remains of a child and an adult woman, respectively (Aner and Kersten 2001:5115; Olsen 1990; see also Feveile and Bennike 2002). This kind of containment of the cremated remains adds yet another layer to what *collection* and *re-collection* mean, yet these cases are rare.

Community and Modes of Mourning

This wide variety in the treatment of cremated remains and in ways of collecting and re-collecting the dead points to a high degree of cultural heterogeneity and exploration of cultural forms in the Early Bronze Age. The evidence does not necessarily suggest a clear discourse on how to arrange the cremated body and other artifacts, which means that the return to the cremated matter offers a moment to explore how things are to be handled. This indicates that the burial form was not defined by prescribed dogma or strict, repetitive patterns. In the literature on the

Early Bronze Age, cremation often stands in the shadow of the famous and spectacular oak-log coffins and is treated as an epiphenomenon that can be ignored. Early Bronze Age cremation furthermore seems to be regarded as unimportant compared to cremation in the Late Bronze Age, where cremation and urn burial became the exclusive form of disposal. Unfortunately, this has meant that Early Bronze Age cremation practices have been seen as a transitional phenomenon, as an inferior practice among a smaller group of individuals that did not subscribe to the mainstream of society. It should be clear, however, that cremation and inhumation coexisted in Periods II and III, sometimes as independent burial practices and sometimes as overlapping modes of disposal. I contend that we should see this diversity of burial forms as a cultural paradigm in its own right, and not as the expression of a transitional cultural trait. The difference in burial forms was not a matter of changing customs over time, nor of variation between geographical areas with different traditions.

In the Early Bronze Age, the diversity of formulations of cremation burials, and the return to cremated bodies, potentially reflects the need to put some things back together, things that had otherwise been separated by different places or moments of dying and by differing disposal practices. Such "needs" for certain actions are frequently explained away in archaeology by the assumption that people in prehistory were stimulated by some kind of compulsory requirement to follow ideological schematics or ritual dogma. I would like to suggest, however, that these acts of return may point equally toward a need for social re-collection: not just re-collection of the dead as a memory trace but rather as an overlap between emotional and material re-collection, whereby affects and artifacts are collected, re-collected, and assembled in new ways.

This raises an important but rather difficult question: who were the people in charge of the cremation and who were the people that returned to and re-collected the dead body? It has been suggested elsewhere (e.g., Goldhahn and Østigård 2008) that the pyro-technological knowledge of cremation overlapped with that of metalwork, so that cremations may have been associated with specialists possessing a particular esoteric knowledge, enveloped in some form of socially powerful mystery (see also Goldstein and Meyers, chap. 11, and Brück, chap. 6, this volume). The evidence from Damsgård, however, with a dug-down pyre and a cremation occurring at rather low temperatures (approximately 400–600°C) and in an uneven burning process (Bennike 1994:189), suggests a relatively uncomplicated cremation event that would not require the most advanced pyro-technological skill yet would still serve the purpose of cremating a dead body. Of course, this does not exclude the possibility that the slow and irregular cremation process was intentional, but the knowledge necessary to perform the cremation would not have required a specialist. Separating cremation handlers and "spectators" may thus not be a convincing representation of how things took place in the Early Bronze Age.

Here, we may need to remind ourselves that inhumations as well as cremations were subsequently covered by large burial mounds and that the construction of these mounds followed similar trajectories, regardless of whether they contained a cremated body or an unburnt body. This calls for attention to the *place* of burial and to how it works as a locale for returning as a community; building the mound framed the social return in a different way compared to the return to the burnt-out pyre. This might suggest that the immediate return to the cremated body and the deposition of the remains in the grave was restricted to a limited number of mourners, while the construction of the burial mound would have included the wider community in the tactile engagement with the burial of the dead. The funeral, hence, changed from being a matter of the deceased to an engagement with the place of burial. This highlights a range of different levels of sensuous presence in the disposal practice. Inhumation and cremation would have offered different potentials for coming into contact with the reality of death in the course of these activities. In this regard, cremation would have offered a space for exploring the materiality of death, while mound building consolidated the communality of re-collection.

An interesting point is that the largely ephemeral traces of cremation stand in contrast to the monumentality, visibility, and durability of the monumental burial mound. The cremation of the human body may have been intended to signal the transience of individual human life, while the burial mound proclaims the perseverance of social relations in the face of bereavement. That said, we should, of course, keep in mind that cremated as well as whole bodies were deposited in monumental burial mounds in Periods II and III. There is currently nothing in the archaeological record to indicate that cremated bodies were deposited in different locales or under different circumstance than whole bodies, and the occasional mixture of the two disposal strategies also indicates that they were not set apart.

Re-collection and Passing

At the beginning of the chapter I describe how inhumation practice gradually decreased the immediacy of the deceased. Layer upon layer of materials engulfed her or him in the course of enclosing the body in a coffin and constructing the burial mound. In cremation, in contrast, mourners may have witnessed the changing materialities of the deceased during the cremation (to the extent that the body was not hidden in flames, branches, logs, and smoke) but would also have been confronted with the transformed body when returning to the burnt-out pyre. In this light, the mourning process is not simply a matter of emotionally feeling the passing of the deceased in cerebral terms but instead becomes a matter of physically feeling the passing of the deceased in a sensuously immediate way (see also Sørensen and Bille 2008).

So, cremation can be understood as the rapid transformation of the sensed body, producing an immediately perceptible change of bodiness. The re-collection and relocation of the burned remains after the cremation equally works as a transformer of the memory of the deceased by composing her or his emotional and social constitution into new forms. I suggest that the diversity in cremation burials indicates that differences in the mourners' memories of the deceased were played out in the grave. Returning to the cremated body offered an instance of negotiating what to recollect and what to abandon, materially as well as mnemonically. At the same time, the subsequent construction of a burial mound over the cremated remains in a grave could have united the practice of cremation with a wider notion of how a place of burial was to be integrated into the landscape.

We have seen how returning to the cremated body did not merely imply a confrontation with a burnt individual; returning to the deceased could sometimes also result in what appears to be a "refitting" of the dead, which allows us to expand on such instances of returning as a performance of "re-collection." This notion of re-collection goes beyond the mental evocation of an image or emotion of the deceased and implies the overlap of a bodily and cerebral exercise. Here, *re-collection* literally signifies a return to collect again, that is, to pick up and reassemble the deceased, whose physical and emotional constitution was deconstructed in the course of cremation. This draws on a literal understanding of re-collection as an act of gathering, or bringing things together that have been disrupted. Furthermore, it also suggests that the act can facilitate emotional re-collection, achieving composure or recovery from distraction (see Oxford English Dictionary, *s.v. recollection*).

In one sense, cremation needs re-collection, not just because of the physical disfiguration of the deceased but also because cremation in part creates a sensory vagueness of the deceased and her or his passing. When fire consumes the body of a dead person, it turns the fleshly body into various other transitory substances, such as vapor, smoke, ash, soot, charcoal, and calcified bone. The transformation of substance is only partially perceptible, as fire and smoke screen the visual details in the process, and only by returning to the burnt-out pyre are the bereaved confronted with the product of the transformation. Part of the transformation takes place at the periphery of what was perceptible to the senses, so the knowledge of the transformation builds on other faculties than the direct sensation of the actual, carnal cremation, and here I argue that the return to the cremated body is part of the re-collection of the dead and her/his physical, social, and emotive transfiguration.

Other scholars have argued that funerals and burial places can constitute instances of memory and commemoration and that they function as important instruments of establishing continuing bonds between the bereaved and the deceased (e.g., Hallam et al. 1999; Howarth 2007; Miller and Parrott 2007; Williams 2003b; see also T. Sørensen 2010b, 2011). This perspective may be supplemented by other approaches emphasizing the importance of forgetting and of being relieved of potentially traumatic memories and of the tyranny of emotional retrospection and introspection (e.g., Connerton 2008; Forty 1999; Lichtenthal and Cruess 2010; Rowlands 1999; see also T. Sørensen 2012).

In this light, we may contend that the disfiguration of the deceased in the cremation is not so much a matter of "destruction" or "fragmentation" but rather concerns how the very act of cremation stages a partial and vague perception of the deceased. Only in the return to the dead after the pyre has burned out is it possible to reconfigure the bodily reality of the dead. The transfer of substance from one material form to another (we may tentatively borrow the epithet *transubstantiation* from theology to capture this process; see Kemmler 1998) implies that the bereaved were confronted with the experience of a cremated individual, who would have no resemblance with how s/he appeared prior to the burning. Instead, the visual qualities of the deceased became inferior to other modes of sensing her or him, wherein touch clearly would have worked as a primary means of exploring the cremated remains. By taking hold of the cremated matter—whether directly by the hands or by some form of tool—the mourner would be in contact with and touched by the deceased in her or his new material format. Touch would thus have been a mode of authenticating and validating the passing, connecting re-collection as a cerebral and tactile action; we can only speculate whether the cremation produces an ontologically new person, but returning to the cremated remains and touching the ashes, charcoal, bone fragments, and objects would in any case have offered a way to evaluate her or his state of being (see also Paterson 2007).

Conclusion

This chapter tackles the often-overlooked social practice of returning. The Russian movie *The Return* implicitly suggests that the act of returning does not simply imply clarification and reassurance but may also stage a scene for negotiating heterogeneous experiences and ambiguous memories by re-collecting material and emotional traces of the past. Such traces can be characterized by an intrinsic vagueness; I would argue that acts of return can at the same time make things clear and unclear and that this ambiguity can function as a cultural resource (see also Engelke 2007; T. Sørensen 2012). In the light of the Early Bronze Age cases and especially taking their diversity into account, conceptual and perceptual vagueness can thus be seen as a subtext or even as an objective of these secondary mortuary practices. Returning to the cremated matter is thus a mode of reflection without definite conclusion and without a meaning-content made conscious.

In the title for the chapter, I try to capture the sense of a multidirectional movement in the act of returning by including a slash mark in the word *return*. This may read like a pretentious attempt to invoke a somewhat tiring philosophical jargon, but the ambition is slightly more pragmatic. I believe that the slash mark emphasizes the open-ended and nonconclusive nature of returning. "Re/turn" is not a linear motion, nor is it a solely geographic or corporeal journey, but rather it implies a movement that is at the same time about going back to something and about going over something again. "Re/turn" is also about *turning* toward something (attending to/keeping) or about turning *away* (leaving), and it can be about recontemplation or renewal by going back to, inverting, or abandoning the past.

In the particular context of the cremation burials discussed in this chapter, re/turning seems to constitute a movement that allows social heterogeneity, perceptual ambiguity, and mnemonic differences in relation to the dead. It is thus an alternative to the authoritarian and dogmatic narratives of personhood that can be found in the inhumation burials of the Early Bronze Age (but see also Brück 2006a and chap. 6, this volume). This means that re/turn and re-collection are means of simultaneous deconstruction and reconstruction and, in the context of cremation, about dismembering and remembering, if you will.

Acknowledgments

I would like to thank the editors for inviting me to contribute to this volume. I have benefitted from critique from them and the other contributors to the volume; Liv Nilsson Stutz and Howard Williams in particular have offered very extensive and valuable comments. I would also like to extend my thanks to Jo Appleby and Marie Louise Stig Sørensen for commenting on an earlier version of the chapter and to Lise Lock Harvig for directing my attention to literature I would otherwise have overlooked. All inadequacies and misunderstandings remain my own.

10

The Role of Cremation in Mortuary Practice in the Irish Neolithic

Gabriel Cooney

A key aspect of the archaeological evidence for Irish prehistory (8000 BC–AD 500) is a rich and diverse record of mortuary practice (e.g., Cooney and Grogan 1994). Cremation is the dominant documented burial rite in prehistoric Ireland, with over 63 percent of the burials being classified as cremations (Murphy et al. 2010). This is particularly the case for the Bronze Age (2500–600 cal. BC), and burials from Bronze Age cemeteries represent over 70 percent of the prehistoric burial record. But cremation has also been regarded as the main mortuary rite during the Neolithic (3800–2500 cal. BC; e.g., A. Jones 2008:190; Malone 2001), when early farming communities were established and developed, as part of a wider European transformation of society from hunter-gatherers to farmers (e.g., Finlayson and Warren 2010; Whittle and Cummings 2007).

For the earlier Neolithic (3800–3600 cal. BC), Bradley (2007a:60–61, 2007b) has argued that cremation was the dominant rite in burial monuments in Ireland and western Scotland, in contrast to southern Britain, where inhumed remains represent the primary mortuary rite in comparable mortuary monuments. These differences are seen as reflecting important contrasts in social practice and tradition, linked to the character of domestic life. A symbolic link is seen between the burning of contemporary houses in Ireland and the treatment of human corpses. The circulation of unburnt bone as relics or sacred objects in southern Britain is contrasted with practice in Ireland and western Scotland, where cremated bone was deposited in mortuary monuments. Cremation has also been regarded as the mortuary rite that characterizes practice in passage tombs, including spectacular examples such as Newgrange in the Boyne Valley, in the east of the island, in the later fourth millennium cal. BC (Bergh 1995; Eogan 1986; Herity 1974). This can be contrasted with practice in passage tombs such as Maes Howe in Orkney off the north coast of Scotland, which have many and specific points of similarity with developed Irish passage tombs (Sheridan 1986, 2004), suggesting deliberate and sustained contact. However, in Orkney the burial deposits predominantly consist of disarticulated human remains (see discussion in Schulting et al. 2010:5–11, 25–30).

These broad statements indicate strong linkages between the way we have as archaeologists constructed notions of the individual and society over the course of the Irish Neolithic and the character of mortuary rituals, with distinctions drawn between the use of inhumation and cremation. But they are also worth exploring further for a number of reasons. In reality there are significant variations within traditions of mortuary practice on the island that are perhaps inevitably glossed over in these general reviews (the term *tradition* as used here and below follows on Osborne's [2008] and Robb's [2008] discussion of the term to describe peoples' conscious engagement of current actions with a specifically discriminating view of the past, a historical process of creative continuity with rule-governed practice or knowledge). Excavation has demonstrated that people building and using megalithic tombs of the same type employed different mortuary rituals and rites, complementing a diversity of architectural expression and other activity (Davidsson 2003:326). The occurrence and significance of the evidence for the contemporaneity of the practice of inhumation and cremation also appear to have been underplayed. As one example, at the well-dated Mound of the Hostages passage tomb at Tara in the east of the island, the main phase of mortuary activity was in the range 3345–3095 cal. BC, and the dates for unburnt bone are comparable with those from cremated bone (Brindley et al. 2005). This implies that either the two rites were used in parallel and combined only at the stage of deposition, or, as in Balinese Hindu practice today (Downes 1999:24; Hobart et al. 1996:122), the rites were combined in a multistage mortuary rite, with cremation taking place a variable length of time after death and provision for the temporary burial of bodies.

Finally, it needs to be emphasized that Neolithic monuments containing human bone in most cases provide evidence not of burial practice as such but rather the selective, active use of human bone in ancestral rites (see Barrett 1988). Whitley (2002) argued that the term *ancestor* has been used in an uncritical way in Neolithic studies. However, its use is important in our understanding of the character of society in the Neolithic. Helms (1998:34–54) has shown that in nonindustrial, non-Western societies a distinction can be drawn between different types of ancestors, the kinds of people likely to become ancestors, and their significance in helping to create links with the past. Ancestors can refer either to distant beings who were involved in social origins or to specific, named dead who are remembered as having lived a socially successful life, as defined by contemporary custom and practice (Ingold's [2000:132–51] models of identity, genealogical and relational, and the recognition of memory as being either experiential or referential [Kuijt 2008:174] are also relevant here). These conditions may apply to a relatively small number or to the majority of the deceased adults. Helms (1998) notes that people often acknowledge and sometimes combine the two types of ancestors. Thus, the recently deceased may have a relatively short shelf life as ancestral beings, or over time they may become remembered collectively as creator ancestors.

In early agricultural groups, what Helms (1998:24-9) calls the "distinguished dead" would have been important in demonstrating the durability of the group and the link between the living and previous generations. For people living in Ireland during the Neolithic, the challenge was how to create ancestors who would continue to be present and "alive," although physically deceased, to help the living (Gell 1998:222; A. Jones 2008:177). The dichotomy between the decomposition of the body on death and the ancestors as an active, immortal presence who provided the critical basis for remembering the past, for looking back (Whittle 2003:107–32), had to be confronted.

An Overview of Mortuary Practice in the Irish Neolithic

Over nearly a millennium and a half, there is a rich and varied record of mortuary practice. This is documented in the archaeological record by the deposition of human remains in specific settings in a series of distinctive architectural traditions. Some of these traditions overlap geographically and chronologically, others are particular to a shorter time-span and to specific regions. In thinking about how people approached the challenge of creating ancestors through cremation in different ways over time and space, one may find it useful to refer to a key observation by Hertz (1960 [1907]:202). He suggested that the meaning of cremation was not to destroy the body of the deceased but to re-create it and make it capable of entering a new life, achieving the same result as multistage inhumation but more rapidly (but see nuanced discussion in Cerezo-Román and Williams, chap. 13, this volume). To examine the relevance of this perspective, I briefly outline the features of the range of mortuary practice that occurs during the Neolithic in Ireland and compare and contrast two traditions—court tombs and passage tombs—in more detail.

Megalithic tombs have tended to dominate narratives of the Irish Neolithic, given both their number, over 1,500 (Cody 2002), and place as part of a wave of monumentalization across western Europe from around 4,000 cal. BC (Joussaume 1988; Renfrew 1981; Scarre 2007). Documentation of settlement evidence from the large number of development-led excavation programs over the decade beginning in the mid-1990s has provided a more balanced view (e.g., Smyth 2011). There are four main types of megalithic tomb, each named after a distinctive architectural feature (de Valera and Ó Nualláin 1961). Court, portal, and passage tombs all date to the fourth millennium cal. BC (A. Jones 2008:table 8.1), with the most numerous type, wedge tombs, dating to the period 2450–2050 cal. BC (O'Brien 1999; Schulting et al. 2008), in the Final Neolithic/Early Bronze Age. Wedge tombs are not considered here, but they appear to represent a notable reinvention of the megalithic tradition at the end of the Neolithic (Carlin 2011), a period of notable diversity in mortuary practice (Schulting et al. 2008:10–13).

Schulting and colleagues (2012) have demonstrated that the range 3700–3570 cal. BC is currently the most probable time frame for the initial use of court tombs, with initial construction slightly earlier. Mortuary practice in these monuments incorporated the use of both inhumation and cremation (Herity 1987; Schulting et al. 2012), and this is discussed in more detail below. Portal tombs are related to court tombs as part of a long cairn and barrow tradition that occurs not just in Ireland and Britain but also across northwestern Europe (e.g., Midgley 2005). The most important and best-dated mortuary assemblage from a portal tomb comes from Poulnabrone in the southwest (A. Lynch 1988; Lynch and Ó Donnabháin 1994). Here the disarticulated remains of a minimum of twenty-two individuals were placed on and in the limestone pavement that formed the floor of the tomb chamber. The character of the mortuary deposit suggests that the bones are the result of successive inhumation and bone circulation (Beckett 2011; Ann Lynch, personal communication 2013). If this interpretation is correct, the remains of individuals from successive generations were placed in the tomb, as the oldest date from human bone is 4270–3715 cal. BC and the youngest is 3290–2530 cal. BC (see discussion in Cooney et al. 2011:604–5). Some of the bones appear to have been scorched or burned after the flesh had gone. Commenting on the few dates from other portal tombs in Ireland and southwestern Britain, Kytmannow (2008:110) suggested that cremation generally postdates inhumations in portal tombs.

In the second half of the fourth millennium cal. BC, mortuary practice became increasingly diverse. While there is ongoing debate about the date of the beginning of the passage tomb tradition (Whittle et al. 2011:848–53; Sheridan 2010), more-elaborate forms of passage tomb clearly date to the second half of the fourth millennium cal. BC (Brindley et al. 2005; Cooney et al. 2011; Schulting et al. 2015). Their use seems to have focused on the period 3495–3285 cal. BC (the third quarter of the fourth millennium BC), ending in 2860–2795 cal. BC. Passage tombs are discussed in detail below; here, other broadly contemporary practices are outlined. Linkardstown burials are characterized by the placement of one or more inhumed individuals (either articulated or disarticulated) in a central cist under a cairn covered by a mound and accompanied by a highly decorated round-based ceramic bowl. They are focused in a specific region in the central southern part of the island and have been interpreted as communal memorials to leading individuals (Cooney 2000:97), who in Helms's (1998) terms would have had socially successful lives. Dating of human bone suggest that they were in use from before 3600 to 3300 cal. BC (see Cooney et al. 2011:637). There are several points worth emphasizing in relation to Linkardstown burials. First, they are burials of specific individuals but often accompanied by the deposition of the bones of a child, as at Ashley Park (Manning 1985). Inhumation and multistage mortuary treatment is dominant, as at Poulawack, where the disarticulated bones of three adults (with the bones of a child in the deposit) could possibly have come from initial articulated burials, placed at intervals (Beckett 2011:411). While the dominant mortuary rite is inhumation, cremation was practiced; one of two adult burials in the cist at Jerpoint West had been cremated (Ryan 1973).

As Dowd (2008) has detailed, fourteen caves, all in areas of limestone geology, have produced human bone from the Neolithic period, with a marked concentration of dates in the period 3600–3400 cal. BC. The bone mostly occurs as isolated bones, but complete inhumation burials, as at Annagh (Ó Floinn 1992) and Kilgreany (Dowd 2002), are known. Dowd (2008:309–10) suggests that the repeated occurrence of small numbers of human bone in caves is reflective of two practices: excarnation and token deposition. She notes that cremated bone has to date been found in only one Irish cave, in the form of two discrete deposits of undated cremated human bone at Kilgreany cave. There are a few inhumed burials in what were apparently unmarked graves (e.g., Hartnett 1951; Ryan 1980), while placement in pits of both unburnt, disarticulated bone and cremated bone is also a feature of this period. The latter can be related to a wider and consistent appearance of burnt material in pits, suggesting that fire and burning had an important role in depositional activity (Smyth 2007). The mortuary record for the late Neolithic, 2900–2500 cal. BC, is not as well defined but includes instances of the deposition of both inhumed bone in court tombs (Schulting et al. 2011:35) and cremated bone in passage tombs (Schulting et al. 2015), as well as in pits and, more broadly, indications, at least in the east of the island, of both continuity with the passage tomb tradition and also shifting ceremonial foci (Cooney 2000:17–19).

Across this range of Neolithic mortuary practice, it is clear that the selected and deposited human remains, inhumed or cremated, can represent only a small proportion of the contemporary, living society at any time. Allowing for biasing factors, such as poor preservation of inhumed bone in the acidic soils that are common in northern and western Ireland, a contrast can be drawn, for example, between the number of people who would have been required to construct monuments; the long, if punctuated, history of use of some tombs; and the restricted amount of remains in tombs (see Burrow 2006:82–84). Human remains are dominated by adults (70 percent), with some suggestion of a greater representation of males, and subadults, particularly children, underrepresented (Cooney and Grogan 1994), compared to the proportion of the population they would represent in a living community (Chamberlain

2000). One of the few Neolithic human bone assemblages dominated by children is the burials found with the settlement site of Knockadoon, Lough Gur, in the southwest (Cleary 1995; Grogan and Eogan 1987), echoing the common practice of the burial of children close to the living (Borić and Stefanović 2004; Robb 2007). That communities and people made active choices about both who was to be represented in the "distinguished dead" and the type of monument in which they were placed is seen in the contemporary use of three different monument types—Parknabinnia (court tomb), Poulnabrone (portal tomb), and Poulawack (Linkardstown burial)—during the later part of the fourth millennium cal. BC within a few kilometers of each other on the limestone escarpment of the Burren in the southwest (Schulting et al. 2012:table 10).

Court tombs and passage tombs represent two of the major monumental and mortuary traditions in the Irish Neolithic. Some 390 sites are classified as court tombs and 230 as passage tombs. While these monumental traditions overlap in use and distribution, the construction and initial use of court tomb tradition was in the earlier Neolithic in Ireland and the main use of passage tombs was in the later part of the fourth millennium cal. BC. These two traditions have been seen as indicating significant wider changes in practices and processes in Irish Neolithic society over the course of that millennium. The more clustered distribution of passage tombs, allied to the large size and labor requirement of central tombs in passage tomb clusters, has been seen as reflecting a more differentiated, larger-scale society compared to the more locally based, smaller-scale social groupings reflected in and by court tombs (e.g., Bergh 1995; Cooney 2000; Darvill 1979). How do mortuary rites in these two major traditions of practice, particularly the use of cremation, inform these issues and the way in which the ancestral past was created and engaged with through the deposition of human remains?

Lining Up History—Mortuary Practice in Court Tombs

Numerous court tombs have been excavated, but in many cases this was in the earlier part of the twentieth century. Schulting and colleagues (2012:36–37), in a critical review of the dating of human bone from court tombs, suggest that with the current state of knowledge the question of the contemporaneous use of cremation and inhumation at particular sites in primary contexts has to remain open. However, both rites were certainly in use at different sites. Tully (Waterman 1978) in northwestern Ireland (figure 10.1) is an example of the dominant and most widespread form of court tomb, with a two-chambered gallery entered from an open, horseshoe-shaped court. In the front chamber the floor had been scorched red by burning, and a deposit of burnt soil, charcoal, and early Neolithic pottery covered most of the floor. This contained fragments of cremated bone from two children (Wells 1978). The bone has been dated to 3961–3718 cal. BC. Over the floor of the back chamber, a deposit of stone-free clay contained cremated bone of a young adult male (and a bone from a second person). A high proportion of the skeleton was represented; this has been dated to 3650–3532 cal. BC. A small stone structure or cist had been built against an outer side of the gallery, and this contained the fragmentary cremated remains of a child, scattered on the floor and sealed by small stone slabs. This has been dated to 3627–3374 cal. BC (see Schulting et al. 2012:table 5, 26–27 for comment on date from front chamber).

At Parknabinnia in the Burren (C. Jones 2004, 2007), a two-chamber gallery was fronted by a narrow "court" feature. In the chamber there were the fragmented remains of a MNI of at least twenty people (the majority were adults, but an adolescent and two young children were also represented). The character of the bone (mostly disarticulated) and the depositional patterns have been interpreted as reflecting primary inhumations disturbed in the course of successive interments (Beckett 2011). The piling up of bones in the front chamber against the blocking slabs separating it from the back chamber indicated that the back chamber had gone out of use first. In both chambers, the bottom layer of stone and bone seemed to stabilize the upright slabs and thus to have been part of the original construction (C. Jones 2004:48). A series of radiocarbon dates (see Schulting et al. 2012:table 5) supports the interpretation of successive interment, with the oldest bone dating to 3632–3168 cal. BC and the latest to 2905–2621 cal. BC.

At Tully and Parknabinnia, cremation and inhumation appear to have been used as alternative strategies to create the remembered dead, whose remains not only are deposited in the tombs but also appear to be

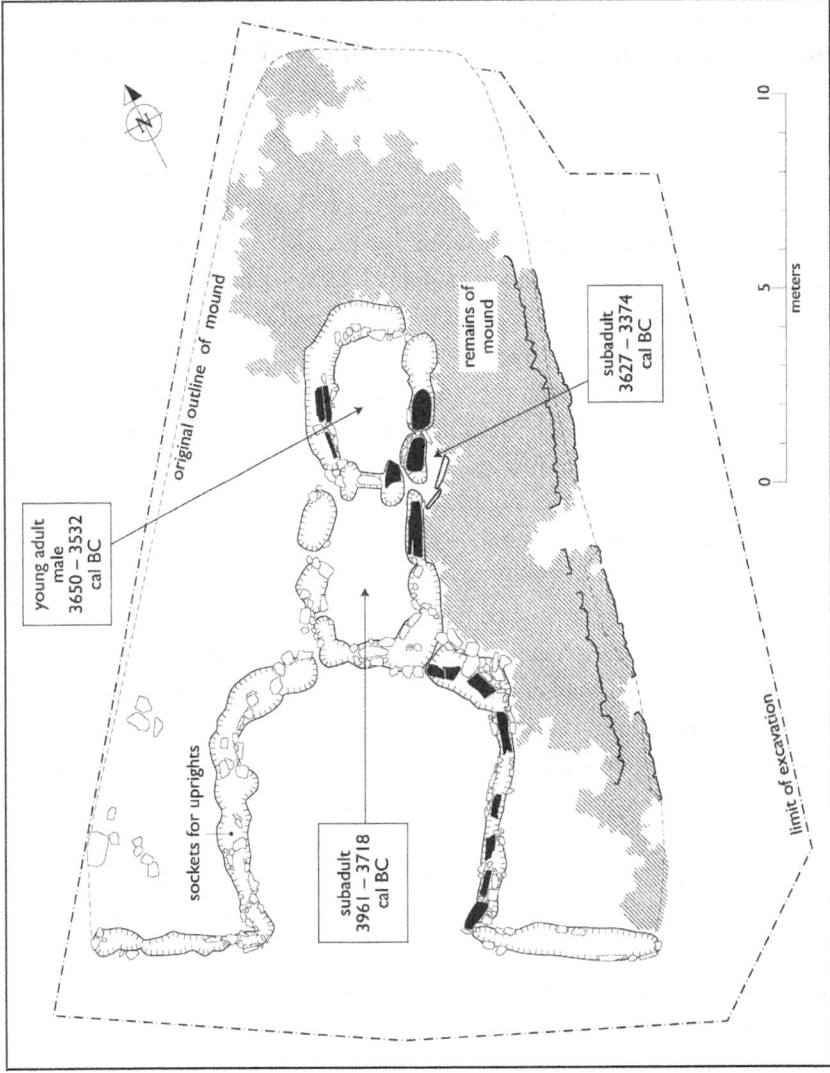

Figure 10.1. Plan of the Tully court tomb (based on Waterman 1978) with radiocarbon dates of bone deposits.

deliberately built into them. This supports Powell's (2005:22) argument that the architecture of the court tombs was combined with depositional practices to create a sense of social history that stressed lineage and descent. It is striking that the construction and initial use of court tombs corresponds so closely to the date range for early Neolithic timber-built rectangular houses in Ireland: 3730–3615 cal. BC (Cooney et al. 2011; Smyth 2011). The analogous form of these houses for the living and the dead has long been recognized (Cooney 2000:66). More widely, it is similar in date in the creation and initial use of many broadly related long cairns and barrows and the intensive period of construction of causewayed enclosures in southern Britain (Bayliss et al. 2011; Whittle et al. 2007), suggesting that this time was a period of considerable social dynamism across the two islands, both in settlement and in ceremonial spheres of life. What the evidence from Tully, Parknabinnia, and other court tombs suggests is that both inhumed and cremated bone could be used to link those spheres. Alongside the regional diversity model put forward by Bradley (2007a, 2007b), there appears to have been active divergence in mortuary practice at a local level. The cremated remains at Tully emphasize this point (Wells 1978). All the remains appear to represent the cremations of still-fleshed bodies, but the placement of most of the remains of the young adult in the back chamber can be contrasted with the more token representation of children in the front chamber and the cist: in the cist, the bones are formally placed and covered; in the chambers, the cremated bone forms part of spreads on the floor of the tomb. The latter appear to represent what Case (1969) referred to as settlement debris, reflecting the role of cremated bone in creating a performative connection between the house of the living and the dead. Memorably captured by the writer (and undertaker) Thomas Lynch (2010:16) is the point that cremation actually makes human bones and the body they represent *more* portable, divisible, and memorable.

Ballymacaldrack, or Dooey's Cairn (Collins 1976; Cooney 2000:99–102; Evans 1938), in the northeast adds another layer of complexity to the use of cremation. There a timber mortuary structure is succeeded by a stone one (Sheridan 2006). Three linear pits that held posts were the main components of a wooden or composite structure containing human bone, which may have been cremated by burning the structure, in a manner similar to a wider tradition known in Ireland and northern

Britain. At the site of Pencraig Hill in southeastern Scotland, a similar timber structure of early to mid-fourth millennium cal. BC date in its final phase appears to have been a pyre where the body parts had been disarticulated prior to cremation (Duffy and MacGregor 2008). At Dooey's Cairn, the inner pit contained the cremated remains of at least five adults. The structure was rebuilt with dry-stone walls (and supporting cairn) and a paved floor. Layers of charcoal and the fire-cracked character of the walls indicate further episodes of burning. Then a stone chamber and open court were added to the west end, and a covering cairn was constructed. There were no human deposits in the chamber, but a range of material was deposited at the front of the chamber. In turn, this activity ceased when the court was deliberately blocked with stone.

The ancestors were created and remembered in different ways by living communities using court tombs, but there appears to have been a similarity of intention despite the diversity of mortuary rites and individuality of practice at different sites. As Duffy and MacGregor (2008:72) put it, different transformative pathways were underpinned by similar structuring principles. The dynamic tempo of court tomb construction and initial use also has to be contextualized by the evidence from radiocarbon dating that many sites have long histories of deposition, stretching into the Bronze Age (Schulting et al. 2012), indicating that they continued to be seen as appropriate loci for contact with and creation of ancestors.

Creating a Spectacle—Cremation in Passage Tombs

In the passage tomb tradition, in contrast, the practice of cremation appears to have constituted the major treatment of the body after death. The deposits found in passage tombs are frequently described as communal deposits consisting of the cremated remains of several individuals. The number of people represented within tombs varies, with exceptions such as the Mound of the Hostages, Tara (M. O'Sullivan 2005), producing very large assemblages. A closer examination suggests that there was a complex sequence to the treatment of selected bodies at death and their transformation into ancestors (see Kuijt and Quinn 2013). Here I want to use the passage tomb complex at Fourknocks (Hartnett 1957, 1971) and one of the passage tombs at Knowth, part of the wider Boyne Valley passage tomb grouping (e.g., Eogan 1986), both in the east of the island, as foci in the discussion.

These communal deposits suggest the mingling together of the remains of different individuals, who were unlikely to have died at the same time. Were they were cremated at different times and/or locations and then brought together, or were they cremated communally? The frequent occurrence of unburnt bone, particularly skull and long bones, in these deposits suggests that there was a primary stage in the postmortem treatment of some bodies during which the soft tissue was allowed or facilitated to decompose (see Murphy 2003) and that at some point before cremation, selected bones were used for other purposes. While the excavation of the passage tomb at Fourknocks I predated the advent of detailed osteoarchaeological analysis, the excavator (Hartnett 1957:269) made a prescient observation on the character of the deposits: "The inhumed burials, in so far as these were separable from the cremations, consisted of groupings of skulls, whole or nearly so, and disarticulated long bones, suggesting that the bones were fleshless when placed in position. This and the absence of small trunk bones among the unburnt remains suggests previous burial elsewhere. . . . [T]he inhumed burials in the passage and side chambers were set in spreads of cremation in which were recognizable fragments of small bones of the trunk. This association provoked the suspicion in a number of cases that the cremation was part of the burial already represented by the unburnt skull and long bones."

Given the potency of the skull as a commemorative marker of both personal and collective identity (e.g., Kuijt 2008), finding it used in this way in passage tombs is not surprising. At the passage tomb at Fourknocks, there were series of bone deposits not just in the formal chamber but also in the passage. At the entrance on a paved floor, a human skull was set in a spread of cremated bone and partially protected by a setting of stones. At a higher level in the fill of the passage close to this location, two adult skulls were found side by side (each with a water-rolled pebble) facing outward, and there were long bones near the skulls with cremated bone. In turn, this deposit was covered in stone. At the passage tomb–related site at Ballynahatty, County Down, called Ballynahatty 1855 (MacAdam 1855), unburnt human skulls were placed on shelves in compartments with cremated human bone (and animal bone). At the Mound of the Hostages at Tara, several unburnt skulls clearly were associated with cremation deposits in the tomb (M. O'Sullivan 2005:113–18, table 11). Across a wide range of cultural contexts, the separation, through decapitation or postmortem removal, and display of skulls can be acts to either honor or dishonor the dead (Fry 1999:191; Thorpe 2003; Wait 1995:509; Whittle et al. 2011:880). The skulls in passage tomb contexts were part of the postmortem treatment of people, marking the shift from direct, experienced memory to referential, collective memory of ancestors (Talalay 2004).

Fourknocks provides very strong evidence that there, at least, the cremation process involved the burning of disarticulated bone. At Fourknocks II, 50 meters east of Fourknocks I, a trench measuring 10.6 meters long, 1.6 meters wide, and 1 meter deep showed signs of intense burning with large amounts of charcoal. There were four hollows or pits in the trench floor with cremated remains, three of which appeared to represent single adults burned in situ (Hartnett 1971:44), which could have been effective only if the remains were already disarticulated. The excavator suggested that this was a cremation trench and that bone from earlier episodes of cremation had been collected from the trench, cleaned of pyre material, and placed in the tomb. It is striking that in Fourknocks I, the formal deposition of the clean cremation deposits above stone flags and sealed by further stones in the burial chambers is complemented by a series of deposits in the entrance passage. These run from the construction of the site to its sealing off. Beside and at the base of one of the orthostats were the skeletal remains of a child, set in a pocket of cremated adult bone. Subsequent deposits in the passage appear to have been placed between rough stone sealing layers, creating a link to the character of the deposits in the chambers. This concern with creating history is echoed at Fourknocks II. The cremation trench was incorporated into what is best described as a pastiche passage tomb, which from the exterior would have provided a close visual match to Fourknocks I (Cooney 2000:103–12).

Site 16 at Knowth (figure 10.2) is one of a cluster of small passage tombs around the very large mound covering two passage tombs, Site 1 (Eogan 1984; Eogan and Cleary 2015; Eogan and Roche 1997). It is located immediately north of Site 1, predates it, and was partially remodelled to facilitate the construction of the large mound. The structure

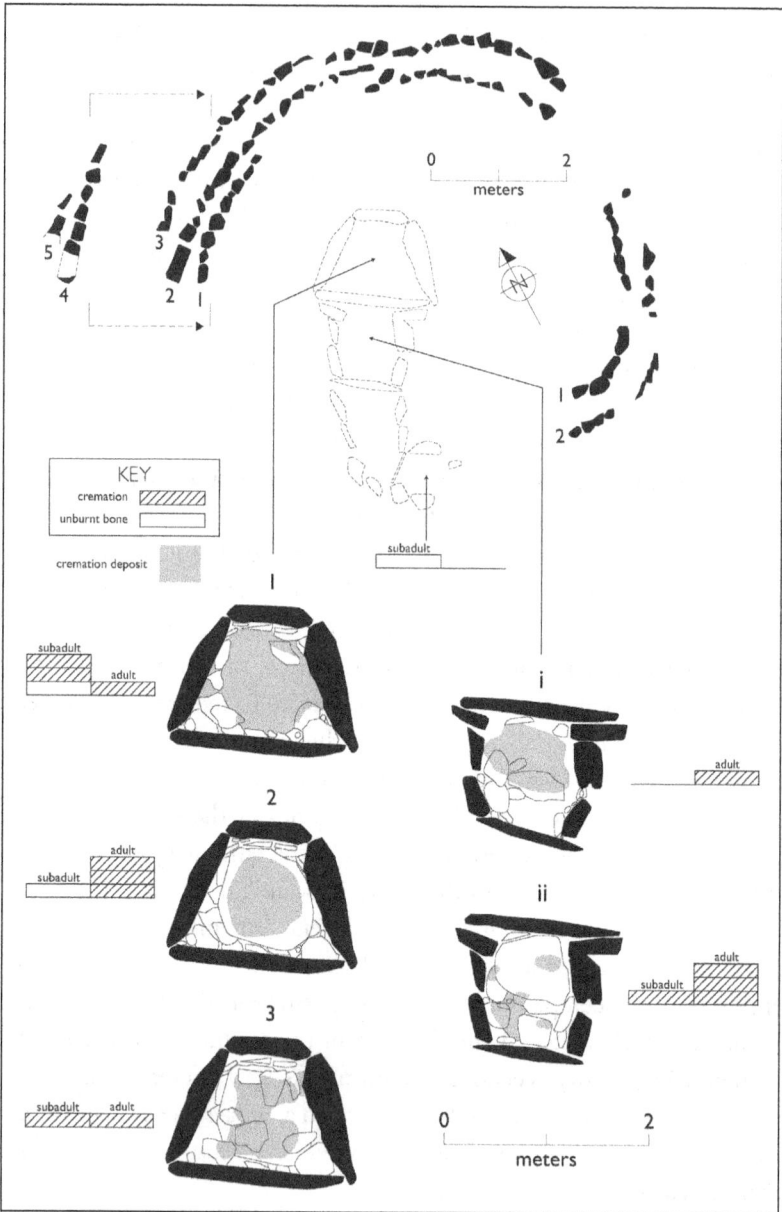

Figure 10.2. Plan of Knowth Passage Tomb 16, with details of bone deposits (based on Eogan 1984).

consisted of a passage divided by sills leading to an end chamber that is trapezoidal in form. There was a stone core outside and surrounding the chamber, and beyond that, mound material out to the kerb. Deposits of cremated bone and objects occurred in both the chamber and the passage.

All the stones of the passage and chamber are of nonlocal graywacke (see Corcoran and Sevastopulo 2015), a fine-grained sandstone. The working of the stone and the placement of cremated bone were integral to making the monument and to the actions that took place within it. In the chamber there were three cremation deposits. The primary deposit was placed on the old ground surface, and spalls of graywacke were placed around the edge of this to act as support for a slab that was placed on top. Eogan (1984:115) argues that this primary deposition and the placing of the flag happened before the roof of the chamber was put in place. A second deposit was placed on this flag and was covered by a paving of graywacke spalls. This sequence is matched in the inner segment of the passage; the stratigraphic sequence suggests that a period of time elapsed between the placement of the first and second deposit. The paving placed over the second deposit forming the floor of the passage was put in place only after the the passage was remodelled, that is, after the construction of Site 1 (Eogan 1984:123). There was subseqently a third deposit placed in the chamber. The deposits contained between one and four individuals, dominated by adults but with subadults present in most of the deposits (Buckley et al. 2015). Noncremated bone consisted of bone from a neonate and two infants. The cremation assemblages all weigh less than the minimum predicted weight that would be expected from the full cremation of this number of individuals.

This sense of interplay between the construction and use of Fourknocks and Site 16 at Knowth and the treatment and deposition of human remains is important to our understanding of the role of cremation and related mortuary rites in passage tomb contexts. Bone was not just placed within; it played a central role in how monuments were created and understood by the living. In this process, a complex series of pathways in the treatment of the dead was taken. Most children and many adults appear to have been forgotten, or at least buried in ways that are not visible in the archaeological record. For people of greater social concern, which could include children, their remains went through a series of stages that could involve disarticulation, retention of body parts (particularly skulls) for circulation and commemoration, and cremation. McQuillan and Logue (2008) have suggested that the final act may have involved comminuting cremated bone on basin stones with the tomb. Through depositional activity, a referential, collective memory of these people became wrapped up with the construction of the monument built to house them. The cremated remains are dominated by adults. Children are peripheral both in terms of their numbers and also, in cases like Fourknocks, in being differentiated by their location and mortuary treatment. Borić and Stefanović (2004) make the contrast between children, particularly newborn and small children, as being "boneless," and adults, whose bones on death are visible and socially meaningful. Fahlander (2008) emphasizes social distinction based on the achievement of the ability of procreation, while in Robb's (2007) terms this depositional history suggests a cultural judgement that they were less socially central than adults.

Cremation in the Irish Neolithic and the Passage Tomb Tradition

We can now place this striking evidence of the character of cremation deposits within passage tombs in the wider context of the Irish Neolithic. Cremation was practiced from early in the Neolithic as part of a range of funerary and mortuary rites to accomplish the transition from the living to the dead. Though we must acknowledge the paucity of the burial record for the Mesolithic period, this currently appears to be the first use of cremation in Ireland since the early Mesolithic and the cremations dating to before 7000 cal. BC from Hermitage in the southwest (Collins and Coyne 2003). Although cremation was practiced in Mesolithic Europe (Larsson and Nilsson Stutz, chap. 3, this volume), we should consider what role it had in changing modes of thought between the Mesolithic and the Neolithic and in the greater emphasis on genealogical memory in early farming communities (Barnard 2007).

The evidence suggests that inhumation was a more important rite in the earlier and Middle Neolithic across a range of burial and depositional contexts than has previously been recognized. This is despite the problem of the survival of inhumed bone in the acidic soil conditions that are typical of many regions of western and northern Ireland. Cremation was also practiced, and both rites were used within particular cultural traditions, such as court tombs, and by particular communities, such as those who placed the Linkardstown burials at Jerpoint West. It is also apparent that multistage mortuary rites, which could have involved different locations at different stages, were in widespread use and that there was a focus on selected individuals, particularly adults.

Some aspects of this summary picture also apply to the passage tomb tradition, but in other ways passage tomb mortuary practice is dramatically different from what had gone before. Mortuary practice creating the material embodiment of ancestor spirits (A. Jones 2008:194) had a focal role, and the distinction of the dead from the living is architecturally echoed in the passage of the tomb. Multistage postmortem treatment of particular people is seen in other traditions, but the mortuary pathways in the passage tomb tradition came to include retention of skulls for circulation and commemoration and cremation (of both bodies and disarticulated bones?) as central elements. Cremated and unburnt bone were deliberately and frequently deposited together. Specific depositional events or episodes involving a small number of individuals can be recognized and distinguished within the larger-scale cremation deposits that we tend to see as characterizing mortuary and memory practice in this tradition.

In the case of the Mound of the Hostages at Tara, the cremation deposits, most with stone settings, that are on the perimeter of the covering mound appear to have had a key role in defining the future monument (M. O'Sullivan 2005:29–39). These small acts in their form and location may have pointed the way to the construction of a much larger marker and monument. Within the monument itself in Cist III, which when closed formed part of the tomb structure, a pottery vessel containing cremated bone rested on a layer of cremated bone placed on a paved floor. The pot contained cremated bone from at least three adults, in addition to the unburnt portion of an adult rib and a child's long bone (M. O'Sullivan 2005:75–76). Placing this bone in a ceramic container looks like a deliberate act to define these remains as different. Was it important to remember and focus on particular people within a wider framework of practice that emphasized the role of cremated bone in literally creating the structure of the tomb and passage tomb

society? Are we seeing here in practice the two types of ancestors—
some recently deceased who have a shelf life as ancestral beings placed
alongside or above those who have become remembered collectively
as the creator ancestors—being combined as part of the process of
monumentalization?

The treatment of the body after death could be read in several ways:
as a representation of bodily ideology in the passage tomb tradition
(A. Jones 2008:194), as a reconstitution of the social community in death
(Chesson 2007), as a social elite demonstrating its control of the super-
natural through placement in the monument (J. Brown 2003:219), as an
expression of social cohesion between communities (Powell 2005:23), as
a route that took the deceased into and up from the monument to the
realm above where the dead were revivified (Lewis-Williams and Pearce
2005:243–44). What is stressed here is how the "portability" of cremated
bone facilitated the physical incorporation of human remains into the
structure of the monuments. In each stage of the twinned sequence of
events at Fourknocks, where a cremation area was transformed into a
quasi-passage tomb matching the traditional passage tomb beside it,
the deposition of human remains plays a critical role. The remains of
the remembered dead became etched into the very fabric of passage
tombs. Analogy with the meaning of cremation in other religious contexts facilitates an understanding of how this might have worked. In
Hindu belief, cremation is regarded as a transition from earthly existence to the world beyond, restoring the body to its different elements
(e.g., Olivelle 1987:389). Kaliff and Oestigaard (2008:55) discuss how in
Nepal cremated bone is perceived and believed to be the equivalent of
stone or sand. In a very different context, Lindgren (2008) teases out
the relationship between crushed quartz and cremated bone in graves
at a Migration period cemetery in Uppland, Sweden, arguing that a
transformation of meaning takes place between these materials in this
very special, spiritually charged context. If we add as a third element of
analogy, but one closer to the Irish Neolithic world, Needham's (2000)
description of monuments such as large passage tombs as "World Pil-
lars," connecting the current world to the other world of the ancestors,
then we might suggest that it was imperative to incorporate the elemental bones of the dead to ensure the permanency and continuity of such
a pillar.

11

Transformation and Metaphors

Thoughts on Cremation Practices in the Precontact Midwestern United States

Lynne Goldstein and Katy Meyers

In a chapter that examines and questions traditional interpretations of the power of mound building, J. A. Brown (2006:198) makes the following observations about previous analyses: "This time-honored inclination to seek some sort of hierarchical control behind every engineered construction, a coercive power behind every substantial pile of earth or stack of stone, and an economic pull behind every accumulation of exotic goods rests on old preconceptions that limit our ability to construct narratives about the past. These notions drive archaeological thinking along predictable lines of thought that have had the unfortunate effect of excluding legitimate alternatives."

This chapter (along with others in this volume) tries to accomplish two things: first, examine, present, and encourage focused research on cremation of human remains as representing one part of a mortuary process; and second, develop alternative explanations for mortuary practices that include cremation and that have often been categorized without careful analysis.

Cremation has been documented in a variety of cultures through time and around the world. In few places, however, has the practice been studied intensively, examined in detail as one portion of a larger mortuary program or procedure, or analyzed for the range of variation within the practice. The act of cremation can result in the creation and manipulation of a powerful set of symbols and actions for groups today and in the past, even as many Western societies see it more specifically as an efficient way to dispose of the dead. In non-Western cultures, cremation draws our attention as a mortuary treatment, usually represents one stage in a mortuary process, and intuitively suggests the co-occurrence of a meaningful and physical transformation of the body.

Transformation in this case is not only associated directly with fire (and is thus both literal and symbolic), but the result of that fire can signal the end of one phase and the beginning of another; the essence of a person as a transformation from one state to another; a community display; and/or the distribution of physical remains in ways that are difficult to accomplish with unburnt human bone.

As powerful and dramatic as cremation can be, it is also perhaps the least well studied and theorized mortuary treatment. Until the relatively recent work of Williams (2006a, 2008a, and chap. 5, this volume) and others (see contributions to Schmidt and Symes 2008; Fahlander and Oestigaard 2008b; and this volume), few scholars have attempted to either contextualize or theorize the practice. One early exception is Binford (1963a, 1963b, 1972), who analyzed several cremations from sites in Michigan, and Buikstra and Goldstein (1973) made another early attempt at cremation research, although aspects of meaning were not fully explored in either of these analyses. In the case of Buikstra and Goldstein (1973), emphasis was placed on the amount of information that can be gained from cremated remains.

Biological anthropologists have also turned their attention away from cremation. They often note that cremations are difficult to analyze because of the fragmentary nature of the remains and physical changes in the bone resulting from burning. If the analyst can study the bone, the time it takes to conduct the research may be considered prohibitive. Not surprisingly, the osteological details of cremains and their context are often not reported or are minimally reported and discussed. As an example of this pervasive view, Larsen (1997) does not even mention cremation or the analysis of burnt human remains in his influential *Bioarchaeology* volume; this is notable, since Larsen presents the book as "a comprehensive synthesis of the emerging field of bioarchaeology" (Larsen 1997:frontispiece).

One example of a more contextualized approach to the study of cremation is Brück's (2006a and chap. 6, this volume) research on the British Bronze Age, including changes in mortuary practices over time. Brück questions previous analyses and interpretations of cremations and uses potential links between people and objects, arguing that processes such as metallurgy represent metaphors for the construction of self and that this construction may be very different from our views of individualism. She notes (2006a:311) that "fragmentation, transformation and regeneration were central cultural metaphors through which people conceptualized the passage of time, the production of food and other categories of material culture, and the creation of social agents. . . . Metaphor was used to explicate the cultural universe of Bronze Age people in a way that linked together such different social practices as house construction, the manufacture of bronze and the treatment of the dead."

Brück (chap. 6, this volume) has extended her Bronze Age research, examining how cremation might have been influenced by gender. Because she has been able to put together a reasonable—if limited—sample of identified cremains, her analysis was possible. Brück's conclusion is relevant for the current discussion because she argues that cremation may reflect a different conception of the body and the self from inhumation and that different conceptions of self may actually exist at the same time within the same society. Having noted this, we must also observe that emphasizing an opposition between inhumation and cremation may be problematic, since they often also represent different stages in a single mortuary rite. Detailed analyses of context are critical.

Numerous archaeologists who have included cremations in their analyses have simply categorized them as a different form of mortuary practice (for example, extended or bundle or cremation) but otherwise treat them equally to inhumation. This approach may allow statements about relative status (although those statements may also be limited or wrong) but ignores the significant, visually notable transformation that the body has undergone, as well as the multistage mortuary process required. Further, this categorization ignores the possibility of examining change and the nature of conception of the body and the self.

The Use of Cremation Over Time: A Case Study of the U.S. Midwest

Keeping in mind the potential power of cremation as a transformation on several different levels, and trying to view cremation in the archaeological record from a different perspective, in this chapter we examine the presence and structure of cremation over time in the greater U.S.

Midwest. We include cremations from the Archaic (roughly 6000–
1500 BC) through the Mississippian (AD 1000–1200) periods, looking
specifically at those contexts in which cremation occurs.

Examining this long time span over several different cultures over a
wide geographic area is not an attempt to argue that all of these cultures
are related (although some surely are), but because cremation does appear in several contexts in the archaeological record over time and few
researchers have examined its structure, looking at the whole record
for both similarities and differences is useful. By necessity, this analysis
is also cursory, since in many cases, we do not have details on the cremains, so variables such as age and sex cannot be directly compared or
even discussed in some instances.

Questions guiding this examination include the following:

1. When and where does cremation occur in the U.S. Midwest? Is
   cremation limited to particular time periods/cultures/geographic
   areas?
2. What are the structure and context of cremation in each context
   or period?
3. What meanings have been assigned and/or could be assigned to
   the behavior?
4. Are there similarities between different instances of cremation
   within the greater region over time?
5. How does cremation fit within a larger mortuary program for the
   particular culture?

At this point, it is useful to define some of the terms used for different kinds of facilities and mortuary rites. In the eastern United States,
archaeologists generally use three terms in ways that may differ from
other places in the world: accretional mounds, crypts, and charnel
houses. A "burial" can be in any of these facilities, but the facility itself also holds meaning. The addition of cremation to this vocabulary
makes things more complex, and cremated remains have been found in
all of these contexts, as well as within simple inhumations in cemetery
settings.

The term *accretional mound* refers to the practice of adding individuals
and soil to a mound as people in the community die. Sometimes the

first stages of these mounds are on natural high points in the region's topography. The location of the mound is important, and members who qualify for burial in the mound—which may or may not include everyone in the group—are placed within the mound at death. Sometimes accretional mounds include cremations, but the important part of the definition is that the mound acquires its final shape over time and continued use; it is a work in progress until the ritual cycle for that mound is completed. When only the term *mound* is used, it often refers to mounds that appear to have been built all at once, or perhaps in specific stages, but with the overall shape and structure planned and determined from the beginning.

The other terms, *crypt* and *charnel house*, are often used in opposition to each other. These structures also are found within mounds, but they may have actually been used in the open, before the structure was enclosed or covered by the mound. A crypt is a box—sometimes made of stone—that holds the dead and associated items. Crypts are generally the size needed for one or two bodies and associated grave goods. It is rare that anything further is done to remains once they are placed in a crypt, although occasionally skeletonized remains within a crypt are later bundled and moved elsewhere. Archaeologists have suggested that the facility seems to be designed to serve a single corporate or family group. By contrast, a "charnel house" is larger in size, and the individuals placed within it were subject to extensive body preparation before they were later interred in special facilities. Finding evidence of a charnel house with few remains inside is not uncommon, and in some cases charnel houses were burned after remains had been processed. Charnel house processing is not usually accessible to everyone in the society, and the charnel structures may have been left open for extended periods of time so that people could see the ceremonies conducted. J. Brown (1979) discusses the details and differences between crypts and charnel houses in more detail, and his work is discussed later in this chapter.

Michigan State University graduate student Katy Meyers, a coauthor of this chapter, assisted in the collection and tabulation of data, as well as in the preparation of the figures. The set of sites included in this review is neither comprehensive nor exhaustive. For the purposes of this overview, we have focused on broad cultural periods, represented largely in Wisconsin, Illinois, Michigan, Indiana, and Ohio. Schurr and Cook (chap. 4, this volume) examine in detail cremation at one site in Illinois and note that that site is enigmatic for a variety of reasons. Similarly, there are other exceptions, differences, and distinctions we may have missed or glossed over, but the goal is to outline the general structures of the practice, as well as its specifics in some instances, and to suggest and examine patterns that may be present. It is a different way to examine cremation in the U.S. Midwest and may lead to new avenues of analysis and interpretation. Figure 11.1 indicates the location of the various sites and traditions mentioned in this chapter.

Archaic

The best-known cremations for the Archaic period occur in the so-called Old Copper (Ritzenthaler and Wittry 1957) and Red Ocher (Ritzenthaler and Quimby 1962) cultures of the upper Midwest. Today, Old Copper is chronologically seen as Middle Archaic, and Red Ocher is placed in a terminal Late Archaic/Early Woodland period (Pleger 2000, 2001). Many years ago, Binford (1963a, 1963b) analyzed and summarized several of these sites in Michigan, using his developing approach to mortuary analysis (Binford 1971) to make some new interpretations. Binford's conclusions (1963a:108–9) about Michigan's Archaic cremations include details on the process of cremation itself: all of the Archaic cremations that Binford examined were determined to have been burned as fresh bone; the bones had been incinerated on discrete, as opposed to communal, pyres; and the Michigan cremations suggest the burning of complete or partial bodies, although if partial, disarticulated parts were not burned together or were in some cases not burned.

More recently, Pleger (2000) completed an analysis that incorporates data from reanalyses of these and other Red Ocher and Old Copper mortuary sites. Pleger (2001) also ran additional radiocarbon dates to better outline and understand the chronology within and between Old Copper and Red Ocher cultures.

Current work sees the Old Copper complex as a Middle Archaic stage traditionally defined by the presence of heavy, socketed tools—especially projectile points—manufactured from upper Great Lakes native copper (figure 11.2). This preceramic technology is associated with chipped and ground stone assemblages, as well as animal bone artifacts. The temporal range is roughly 4000–1000 BC in the western and upper

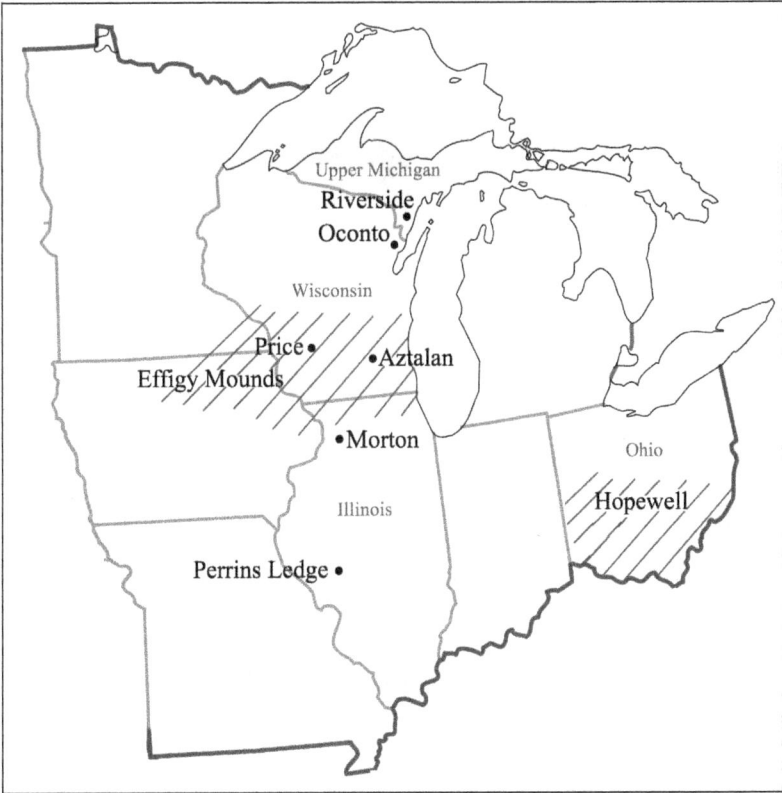

Figure 11.1. Map indicating the location of various sites and culture areas discussed in the text. Note that the outline given for various culture areas does not show the extent of the particular culture but rather the geographic area of that culture that is discussed here.

Great Lakes region. Data are limited, but among the sites Pleger (2000) discusses is the Oconto site, a complex Middle Archaic mortuary site in northeastern Wisconsin (see figure 11.1). Dates suggest an occupation between 4000 BC and 3000 BC. Although excavations yielded the remains of fewer than one hundred individuals, the original excavators estimated a total population of as many as two hundred before portions of the site were destroyed by quarrying. Individuals of both sexes and all age groups were represented. Burials were interred into a natural sand ridge, with primary flexed, bundle, and cremation burial present. Grave goods include copper beads and tools, as well as bone and stone

Period	Illustration	Size
Mississippian	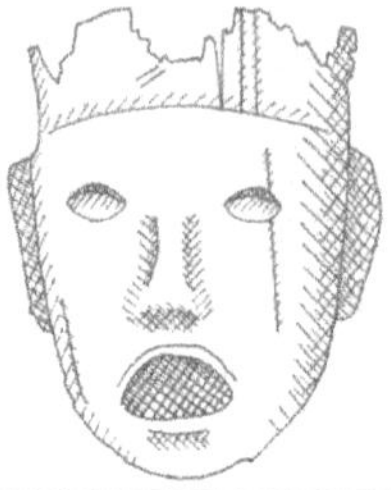	Mask: 11.9 × 9.9 cm
Late Woodland	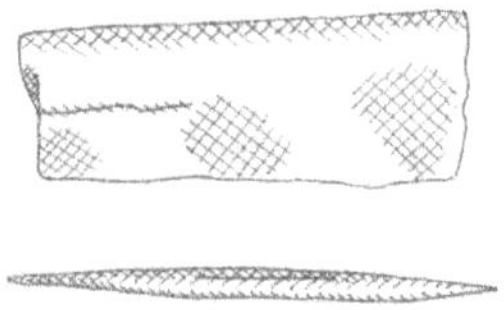	Celt: 9.5 × 3 cm Awl: 10 cm
Hopewell	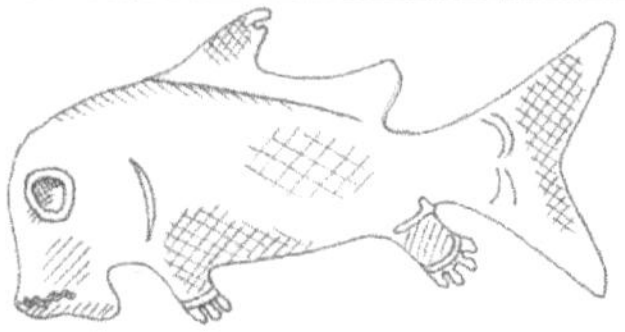	20 cm
Early Woodland	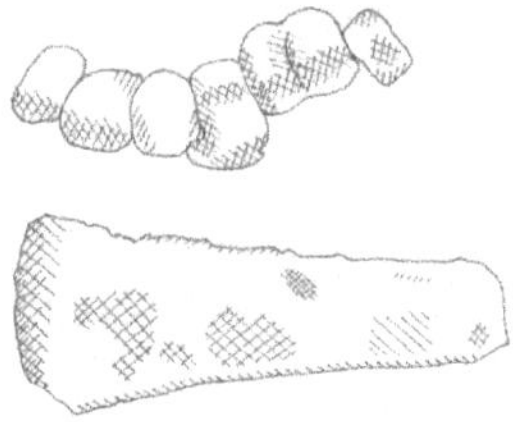	Beads: 0.6 – 1.6 cm Celt: 12 cm
Late Archaic	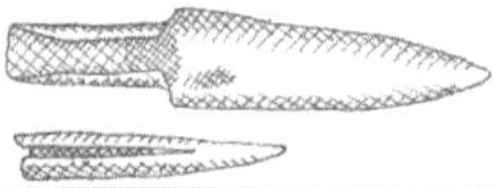	Socketed Blade: 6.6 cm Socketed Projectile: 14.2 cm

Figure 11.2. Outline of the major culture periods discussed in text (ordered chronologically with oldest at bottom), with one or two examples of copper artifacts found in mortuary contexts from each period. Note that these are not necessarily the most common artifact type recovered. (Drawn from original photos.)

artifacts, but only 23 percent of the individuals were buried with mortuary goods, and these included individuals of both sexes and all age categories.

The Riverside site is about twenty-five miles north of Oconto; it is in northern Michigan (adjacent to northern Wisconsin; see figure 11.1) and dates to the transitional Late Archaic to Early Woodland period (Pleger 2000). Although Riverside has been labeled as both an Old Copper and a Red Ocher cemetery, new dates put the site within the Red Ocher range of 1000–400 BC (Pleger 2001). Riverside (Pleger 2000) includes eight cremation pits, each containing remains of at least one individual. There is some evidence at Riverside—in at least two cremation burials—of in situ burning, although the majority of the cremations are thought to have taken place elsewhere, as indicated by the absence of smaller bones and lack of burnt soil surrounding the burials. Cremations show a wide variation of heat and duration of burning, and in some cases material objects included with the cremations were also burned. Within one cremation of two subadults, there was a cache of distinctive chipped stone turkey-tail points, some of which were broken because of heat exposure. In addition to the cremations, there were nine secondary bundle burials and seven primary inhumations at Riverside.

Burials at Riverside include flexed, bundle inhumations, and cremation (Binford examined the Riverside site as part of his 1963 study). In addition, red ocher staining was present throughout the cemetery. Unlike Oconto, Riverside includes only four adult males and no juvenile males (5 percent of the total). Females, in contrast, make up 22 percent of the sample. The rest of the individuals were adults of undetermined sex (28 percent), juveniles of undetermined sex (16 percent), infants (8 percent), and those of unknown age and sex (22 percent). Half of the seventy-six individuals were buried with grave goods, including copper, exotic lithics, local lithics, marine shell, and bone. Most artifacts were found with women and infants. Although the artifact distribution at Oconto appears to be skewed, researchers suggest that the patterns seen could be the result of excavation bias, since less than half of the original cemetery was recovered, and over a third of the adults that were excavated could not be sexed and/or aged.

In examining differences between Red Ocher burial sites, Binford (1972:388) outlines what he sees as pertinent facts:

1. Discrete burials of cremated remains thus far known are that a) there are multiple burials of several individuals previously cremated, and b) in all cases these individuals were adult females and adolescents or children.
2. At both the Andrews and Pomranky sites, it was observed that in all known cases where cremated human bone served as grave goods, such remains were of adolescents.

Binford (1972:388) then postulates that "the social function of cremation among the societies represented in our sample was to afford differential treatment to a recognized category of individuals. . . . [S]uch social distinctions are probably best understood as arising from the practice of exogamy and the consequent frequent lack of spatial congruence between the location of one's kin based 'membership unit' and one's local group (established as a result of marriage)."

Pleger (2000) argues that trade was limited at Oconto but that Riverside was part of a well-developed exchange network. In terms of quantity and diversity of trade items, Pleger suggests that the Riverside exotics rival those of the subsequent Hopewell Interaction Sphere. The Red Ocher trade system could be a regional variant of a larger interaction sphere, and/or the foundations for the later Hopewell exchange systems may have been established during Red Ocher times. Unfortunately, we know relatively little about associated habitation sites for either the Old Copper or Red Ocher complexes, since they have been documented almost exclusively from mortuary contexts.

Price Site III in Wisconsin (Price Sites I and II are nearby habitation sites) was excavated by Joan Freeman (1966) (see figure 11.1) and included twenty-one basin-shaped burial pits, with 1–7 individuals in each. Price has at least 111 cremated individuals, 63 bundle burials, and 8 flexed primary burials. Like other sites, there was great variability in burning and an absence of smaller bones, possibly because of transfer of the cremains from pyre to burial. Very few artifacts were present, but all burials had either red ocher and/or a limestone slab as markers. Over time at Price, Freeman notes an increase in the number of cremations and bundle burials and a decrease in grave goods.

At these Archaic sites, cremation is an important stage in the mortuary program, along with secondary bundle burial. Burning was highly variable at all sites, suggesting differences in timing and duration of burning, as well as differences in the disposition of the individual. Particular artifacts do not correlate with a specific burial type. The lack of cremation basins and minimal evidence for in situ burning suggests that the actual cremation and preparation of bundles likely occurred at different locations. Loss of skeletal elements is thought to suggest a period of curation and movement of individuals. Also interesting is the decrease over time in so-called practical copper artifacts (such as points) and an increase in decorative copper items or those for personal adornment (see figure 11.2). The specific stages of the mortuary rite are not clear—in part because of the way these sites were initially excavated—but it is interesting to speculate on these rites since some evidence suggests that pyres were for a single individual and that cremation was of fresh bone, whereas the cremation deposits appear to be mixed.

Archaic burial sites tend to be located on natural knolls or naturally higher ridges, with the possibility of some limited ground modification (see Schurr, chap. 12, this volume, for additional consideration of this technique). Most recent work suggests that although high spots were selected, in some cases people created low accretional mounds. In addition, there is often the presence of copper, and later of red ocher (spread across the top of the cremation or bundle burial), with more than one individual in a burial feature; groups or caches of turkey-tail points and other projectiles are also often included. Cremation and secondary burial are present at all sites.

Differing from this pattern are Archaic mortuary patterns farther south. Charles and Buikstra (1983, 2002), as well as Schurr and Cook (chap. 4, this volume), summarize the data for Archaic mortuary patterns in the lower Illinois and adjacent Mississippi Valleys, and while they note the development of formal cemeteries in the Middle Archaic, there is little evidence for cremation. Charles and Buikstra (1983:140) postulate a significant amount of competition for resources in a framework of relatively stable and sedentary settlements by 4000 BC, but the same pattern does not appear outside the major river valleys until about 2000 BC. As Charles and Buikstra (1983) note, there is little evidence for social ranking. However, at least some bluff-top cemeteries were restricted to the most productive members of the society; some old or disabled individuals were buried below the bluffs at the edges of habitation sites.

Across the U.S. Midwest, there are different mortuary programs during the Archaic, and the reason why cremation and bundle burial are common in the northern Midwest but largely absent in the south is not entirely clear. Copper is also absent in the southern portion of this region during the Archaic. It is possible that the geographic closeness of the upper Midwest to copper sources may be related to this difference, and/or that the upper Midwest was participating in a different kind of trade exchange or social system. In both areas, burial is often on high ridges or hills, adapted into accretional mounds, and in locations where later groups built mounds specifically for burial.

Early Woodland

The Early Woodland period in the U.S. Midwest is not well documented. Some now argue (as noted above) that numerous sites labeled as Red Ocher are likely Terminal Archaic–Early Woodland in age. The impressive 1986 volume on Early Woodland archaeology in the Midwest (edited by Farnsworth and Emerson) represents a compilation of information on what is known and documented for the period. Even though considerable information is brought together, including data on mortuary sites, the Early Woodland is still relatively little analyzed and documented.

More recently, Overstreet and colleagues (1996) and Haas (1996) have described the Henschel and Barnes Creek sites, providing more-detailed Early Woodland mortuary and habitation information. Overstreet and colleagues (1996) demonstrate that the Red Ocher complex components at Henschel and other similar sites are associated with large conical mound construction. This is significant, because prior to these studies there was little well-documented evidence of deliberate mound building in this period. This also means that both mound and non-mound mortuary contexts have been documented for Red Ocher. In the mounds, there are submound rock crypts or chambers (Overstreet et al. 1986:44–46). In her analysis of the human remains from Henschel and Barnes Creek, Haas (1996) documents both unburned and burned bone; there are also interments and bundle burials. The numbers of individuals are small, and Haas (1996:68, 70) indicates that the burned remains were too fragmentary to identify. Overstreet and colleagues (1996:44) note that a large copper vessel or dish was recovered from the central crypt area by amateur archaeologists who excavated much of the site. The relationship of the human remains to specific mound features is not entirely clear from the reports (Overstreet et al. 1996; Haas 1996).

In Illinois, Charles and colleagues (1986:472) summarized current knowledge: the Terminal Archaic–Early Woodland data suggest that increasing social and economic complexity occurred before the higher population levels of the Middle Woodland. They note that this higher population intensity in the main river valleys and changes in social organization developed in the absence of increasing population. Charles and colleagues (1986:472) conclude that Early Woodland is the setting for Middle Woodland, not only in terms of development of pottery and increasing use of starchy seeds but also socially. There are cremations associated with Early Woodland, most consisting of individual pits with multiple individuals represented. Grave goods are few but include chipped stone blades, some ceramics, and some copper beads and awls (see figure 11.2).

Hopewell and Middle Woodland

In contrast to the Early Woodland, there has been a considerable and extended amount of research conducted on Hopewell and other Middle Woodland mortuary sites (e.g., Baby 1954; J. Brown 1979; Carr 2006; Case and Carr 2008; Magrath 1945; Seeman 1979; Seeman and Soday 1980). While Hopewell is Middle Woodland in age, not all Middle Woodland sites or burials are Hopewell. Hopewell generally dates from 200 BC to AD 500. The Hopewell tradition was not a single culture or society but represents a widely dispersed set of related populations (see figure 11.1). Hopewell groups were connected via a common network of trade routes, known as the Hopewell Exchange System or Hopewell Interaction Sphere. At its greatest extent, the Hopewell system extended from the southeastern United States to the southeastern Canadian shores of Lake Ontario. Within this area, societies participated in extensive exchange, especially along major waterways (see Struever and Houart 1972). The objects created by the Hopewell system spread extensively and are seen in many burials outside the Midwest. Hopewell mounds tend to be conical and large and represent the burial location for most individuals. Elites are buried within central mound features (but see J. Brown 1979), and others are located elsewhere within the mound and also between mounds and at mound edges. Cremation does occur within Hopewell mounds (Baby 1954), especially in Ohio. Also associated with Ohio Hopewell are large, extensive geometric land features; the relationship of these features to specific mortuary patterning is unclear.

When Binford conducted his analysis of Archaic cremation sites in Michigan (1963a, 1963b, 1972), he noted that his replication of Baby's (1954) cremation experiments was consistent with Baby's results. Because of this confirmation, Binford used Baby's classification of the degree and extent of cremation of bones. However, when Binford analyzed the Michigan Archaic cremations, he found that the process of cremation was very different from the Ohio Hopewell results. Baby (1954) examined 128 Hopewell cremations and suggested that in Hopewell cremations, bodies were first dismembered in a systematic way before burning. This conclusion was based on the differential cremation of contiguous anatomical parts, Baby arguing that dismemberment is the only way that this pattern could logically happen. After burning, the remains were bundled and moved to a different location for burial.

In 1979, James A. Brown published a significant and influential paper about the structure and nature of Middle Woodland/Hopewell mounds (Brown 1979). Brown noted an important distinction among Middle Woodland burial facilities that help inform the facilities' social context. As he notes, the Hopewell dead "were subjected to a sequence of different treatment over a period of some duration—starting with the complete corpse and ending in various degrees of disarticulation and cremation" (Brown 1979:211). An important point of Brown's work is that the sequences constitute important links among physically different burial types.

Brown's focus is on both the presence of and differences between the charnel house and the mortuary crypt. Archaeologically, both features often appear within a mound (although not together), but each may have been aboveground and accessible during the time it was in use. A crypt is a large "box" for storage of the dead and accompanying grave goods. Once someone is placed in a crypt, nothing more is done unless skeletonized remains are later bundled or put outside. Minimal curation is done of the remains and items within the crypt once placed within it, and Brown (1979:211–12) suggests that crypts were "corporate facilities for a single resident community."

In contrast, the charnel house shelters both the dead and associated mortuary processing activities. Burials included in the charnel house were subject to "extensive body preparation and body reduction before final interment in specially prepared facilities" (Brown 1979:212). By arrangement within the facility, the status or social position of the charnel house burials was indicated to anyone who entered. Brown notes that charnel houses required more effort to maintain than crypts, because there was more extensive treatment of the individuals and the charnel house itself had to be maintained. The ceremonial and processing area in a crypt is unroofed and unprotected (sometimes activities do take place after placement, as when remains are bundled and removed), whereas it is both protected and roofed in the charnel structure, leading to activities that are more structured and bounded. Burial treatments and the social uses of each are different. They differ in size (both of the facility itself and of the sustaining population), as well as in the complexity of the societies; nonetheless, the two facility types appear to have been used contemporaneously for different parts of Middle Woodland society, although not usually within the same mound. Also in Hopewell, the trend toward decorated and elaborate copper artifacts (see figure 11.2) continues with the presence of cremation.

The majority of research on Hopewell and Middle Woodland mortuary practices has been done in Ohio and Illinois. In a summary of the Illinois Valley, Charles and Buikstra (2002) outline what they see as a shifting emphasis through time on mortuary ritual versus ancestor cult, and they indicate how this is manifested in form and location of burial mounds. For the Middle Woodland, they note that the community was the lineage, and by the later Middle Woodland, there was at least a dominant kin group with one or more subordinate lineages (Charles and Buikstra 2002:21). They suggest that these community- or lineage-based systems were related to risk management. Specifically, Charles and Buikstra (2002:21) note that local shortfalls related to resources as well as access to important rituals and religious ceremonies could be "ameliorated via the ritual and exchange ties among regional elite *males*" (emphasis in original). They suggest that by the end of the Middle Woodland period the male-dominated mounds and exchange networks disappeared and mounds became accretional cemeteries, more similar in form to those of the Late Archaic.

Charles (1992) argues that the Middle Woodland period, at least in the Illinois region, was an era of marked population redistribution. Hopewell exchange and mortuary ritual were used by elite segments of communities to create, sustain, and/or augment their social standing. The oft-labeled "less complex" Late Woodland culture is more a reflection of the stabilization of the social and demographic scene, setting the stage for Mississippian agriculture and social complexity. Although the structures of Middle Woodland and Hopewell mounds in Illinois are not as structurally complex as those in Ohio, some basic forms are notable.

The Hopewell, especially as seen in Ohio, produced artwork in a greater variety and with more exotic materials than their predecessors did. Grizzly bear teeth, freshwater pearls, seashells, sharks' teeth, copper, and even small quantities of silver were turned into well-crafted pieces. Hopewell artisans were expert carvers of pipestone, and many of the mortuary mounds are full of exquisitely carved statues and pipes. Many Hopewell dead are represented by cremation. Cremation also occurs in Illinois and elsewhere, but not with as great a frequency as in Ohio.

Thompson and Jakes (2005) conducted an interesting analysis of textiles in Ohio Hopewell burial practices, noting that cremation is a characteristic feature of Ohio Hopewell. Charred and uncharred remains of textiles have been recovered from a variety of Ohio Hopewell sites. Many of the textiles were apparently preserved because of their physical attachment to copper artifacts (Thompson and Jakes 2005:137). One of the most interesting things about Thompson and Jakes's (2005:138–40) analysis is the observation that because the textiles were preserved (whether charred or not), their presence indicates that they were associated with a burning event yet were not completely combusted. In other words, textiles were exposed to lower temperatures than would cause complete destruction or in some cases were not burned at all. Possible reasons for this preservation include the following:

1. The association with copper artifacts preserved them.
2. The textiles may have been associated with thicker areas of the body.
3. Distance from the heat source could protect them but would also result in incomplete burning of the body.
4. If the textiles were used in a final or closing ceremony, when the body was placed in the prepared grave, some charred specimens might remain. A first set of textiles might have been destroyed, but the charred set might have been exposed to lower temperatures or incomplete burning due to extinguishing the fire with a clay cap.
5. Partially burned fabric could be associated with secondary burials brought to the site for ritual burial.

As Thompson and Jakes (2005:140) conclude, "The charred or uncharred state of the textile fragments indicates the point at which they may have been introduced into the cremation and burial rituals and is an indication of the possibilities of how they were used, thus providing clues to the possible scenarios for these rituals."

Late Woodland

Late Woodland cultures broadly existed in the U.S. Midwest from about AD 400 to AD 1000 (refer to figure 11.1 for locations discussed here). There is far more variability in Late Woodland mortuary practices than in previous periods. The more local community focus of groups, due to a greater emphasis on food production, may relate to the presence of multiple mortuary types. Mounds are present, but so are other mortuary features.

One example of this diversity in practice is the Perrins Ledge Crematory (Illinois), which was a twenty-by-twenty-foot area in which a limestone basin was constructed; the basin contained the cremains of thirteen individuals, including ten adults, two children, and one infant, with both sexes represented (Buikstra and Goldstein 1973). Radiocarbon dating and similarity in artifacts suggest that Perrins Ledge likely dates from the early to middle Late Woodland, approximately AD 600–850. Two apparent episodes of burning took place, with the earlier remains pushed aside to make way for the second cremation event. Nonetheless, multiple lines of evidence suggest that the entire use of the site likely occurred over no longer than a decade. There were several artifacts found at the site, swept to the side with the remains, including ceramics, lithic debris, an abrader, and a knife. Perrins Ledge represents an anomalous mortuary site because in situ burning and burial have rarely been found in other Late Woodland mortuary sites in the region. Perrins Ledge may also represent the initial phase in the Late Woodland cremation process.

The Effigy Mound culture or complex represents another Late Wood-land tradition whose geographic distribution includes the area covered by present-day southern Wisconsin, southeastern Minnesota, eastern Iowa, and northern Illinois (see figure 11.1). Effigy Mound groups lived in villages, were possibly horticulturalists to some extent, and were much more locally/internally focused than the earlier Hopewell groups (see Birmingham and Eisenberg 2000; Goldstein 1995; Mallam 1976; Rowe 1956). The most distinctive characteristic of Effigy Mound sites is the presence of one or more low earthen mounds shaped in the form of animals; these mounds are usually part of a larger mound group that also includes oval and linear mounds. Mounds can be very long (some are about five hundred feet in length), but most are not more than three to four feet high. The published record indicates that burials are usu-ally placed in linear or oval mounds; finding burials (or more than one burial) in the mounds shaped like animals is rare.

Burials at Effigy Mound sites are primarily secondary burials (they may or may not be bundles). There are also quarter-flexed inhumations and a small percentage of cremation (Goldstein 1995). There is equal representation of ages and sexes in the mound burials, and grave goods are rarely found with burials themselves but are instead found in the mound fill or in features within the mound. Rowe (1956:57–58) notes that the most common types of copper tools found in Effigy Mound sites are the celt and the awl (see figure 11.2), but Hurley (1975:287–88) documents that copper beads and scrap copper flakes are also recovered. He does not discuss where within the mound these items are usually placed. The placement of burials in the mound, reuse over time, and multistage treatment suggest communal use. It is unlikely that *all* individuals had access to mound burial.

Although most Effigy Mound human remains have their final placement in conically shaped mounds, secondary burials and cremations are occasionally associated with so-called altars within mounds; the placement and treatment of these remains suggest that the initial mortuary program began elsewhere. An occasional bundle burial or set of human bones is sometimes buried with an altar (a large flat rock placed within the mound) and associated artifacts; in an animal-shaped mound the set is often placed where the "heart" of the animal would be (see Goldstein 1995). Occasionally, burned human bone is found in this context; whether it is a deliberate cremation or something done as part of the ritual associated with the placement and use of the altar is unclear. Unfortunately, few Effigy Mounds have been excavated in recent years, so our knowledge is based on earlier descriptions, which are often incomplete.

At Effigy Mound sites, there is a period of curation of remains between death and final burial. In contrast, Perrins Ledge contains only cremated remains, with the burning done in situ at this site. Perrins Ledge (or a similar type of site) may have been the crematory for a larger cemetery or set of cemeteries with several different disposal types, although there is no clear evidence that cremated remains were moved from Perrins Ledge to other sites. In all Late Woodland sites discussed here, there is a lack of individual identification with grave goods, and with the diversity of practices and so few individuals buried within a mound, it seems unlikely that everyone in the society was afforded the same mortuary treatment.

In the Illinois Valley, Late Woodland sites exhibit a return to the use of the accretional mound, having a resemblance to, but differing from, the Late Archaic pattern. Charles and Buikstra (2002:21) suggest that the patterns of the Late Woodland developed from earlier practices, but they also indicate that the simplification of Late Woodland funerary practices from the earlier Middle Woodland patterns represents a shift from exchange and funerary ties controlled by males "to kinship ties among women in what had become a geographically stable virilocal marriage system."

Mississippian

The Mississippian period represents the most complex prehistoric culture documented in the eastern United States.* Very large and complex towns with significant populations existed, and there was maize agriculture, as well as widespread trade and social stratification. The Cahokia site near St. Louis, Missouri, is probably the most well-known of these large Mississippian period sites. Although Mississippian cremation does not seem to have been the norm in mortuary practices, it does occur at several sites. For the purposes of this study, we use the Aztalan (Wisconsin) and Morton Mound 14 (Illinois) sites as examples of mortuary programs that include or may include cremation, and we also refer to the Schild cemetery in the Illinois Valley (Goldstein 1980, 1981; Perino 1971).

At Aztalan, a large palisaded village that represents one of the most northerly large Mississippian sites (see figure 11.1), there are several platform mounds, as well as some conical mounds. On the second level of the northwestern platform mound, ten extended individuals, as well as one secondary bundle burial, were found within a structure (Rowe 1958; Goldstein 2010). Although Rowe (1958), the original excavator, called this feature a "crematory" (because the structure had been burned, and thus some remains were burned), it was more likely a charnel house according to James Brown's (1979) definition (see earlier discussion plus Goldstein 2010 for detailed Aztalan discussion). The charnel house was burned, either accidentally or deliberately, and remains of the individuals within it at that time were also burned. The charnel house feature included a single pot and a woven bag that contained nuts and corn. Price and colleagues (2007) examined strontium isotopes from several individuals at Aztalan, including a sample from this charnel house. Their conclusions were that some of the individuals in the charnel house were nonlocal, relatively recent arrivals to Aztalan, and may have come from the Cahokia area. While copper was found at Aztalan, it is not consistently associated with the mortuary features.

---

*Note that this chapter does not include the Late Mississippian Oneota complex (primarily occurring after Middle Mississippian but co-occurrent in many places). While agriculture, cremation, and copper are also present on some of these sites, inclusion would have required an additional extensive discussion on the variation in Oneota practices (see O'Gorman 2001).

In many portions of the Aztalan site (Barrett 1933), there are numerous trash pits with disarticulated human remains, suggesting a form of secondary processing—whether or not this includes cannibalism, as has been traditionally argued (see Barrett 1933). Recent work suggests that there is little evidence for cannibalism, but there is extensive evidence for bone processing. However, few, if any, of these scattered disarticulated remains are burned. In one area near the northwest platform mound, there is evidence of a hierarchical set of deep pits through which bones and ceremonial objects were apparently processed (Goldstein 2010); the pits at a higher elevation (and closer to the platform mound) contain more disarticulated remains and objects such as ear spools, and those at a lower elevation contain increasingly more complete skeletons. This interesting mortuary practice representation is outside the current discussion but may provide important information on mortuary processing in this and other Mississippian contexts: at least some of the mortuary process appears to have required movement of bones and objects up the slope, from pit to pit, to the charnel house or elsewhere.

Morton Mound 14 in Illinois (see figure 11.1) was excavated in 1930 and reanalyzed by Strezewski (2003). The mound included mainly primary interments with few grave goods. The site is described as having a charnel house placed over the burials, and this charnel house was burned following use, but unlike that at Aztalan, the structure apparently contained no human remains at the time of burning. In addition to primary inhumations, there were three bundled individuals who were buried next to the charnel house with cut marks on the bone. This bundled group included more grave goods than the primary interments and was presumed by Strezewski to be of higher status.

In both sites, there were remnants of a charnel house that was burned, a higher number of primary interments in comparison with earlier time periods, and an overall lack of burned human remains. At the Mississippian Schild site in Illinois (Goldstein 1980), there is also evidence of two charnel houses, with bundled remains and some burned human bone. The burning of the charnel house might have been related to a closing ceremony for that portion of the cemetery (Goldstein 1980). An "offering" of animal bone, nuts, and corn was in a woven bag associated with the charnel structures. Grave offerings at Schild were more numerous than at Aztalan or Morton Mound 14, but there does not seem to be a co-occurrence of copper and human remains in pits or graves. Copper from Mississippian sites is often made into ritual objects, such as long-nosed god masks and repoussé copper tablets with scenes of warriors (see figure 11.2). These are often, but not consistently, found with burials.

Conclusions and Interpretations

Williams has noted that while archaeologists have focused on theory building associated with mortuary sites with unburnt human bone, few scholars have tried to develop explicit theoretical approaches to the phenomenon of cremation: "Certainly when cremated remains were interred, they were incorporated into a ritual space where a communal identity may have been more important than the celebration of the individual death" (Williams 2008a:263). Williams goes on to discuss the ideas of remembering and forgetting the social person through transformation, circulation, and burial of objects and bodies, and he makes several points that are useful for this discussion. Ashes represent both human remains and material culture. This facilitates diverse responses, treatments, and options for disposal. Williams, as did Rakita and Buikstra (2005) before him, questions Hertz's (1960 [1907]) notion of cremation as representing only an extreme form of secondary burial. Williams (2008a) notes that there has been a lack of appreciation of cremation as a ritual performance that requires theoretical consideration. Cremation is the result of a ritual sequence leading to transformation; it is much more than a formation process.

The technology of cremation can vary a lot within one period and between several periods. Significantly, there can be complex relationships with other means of disposing of the dead; as noted in these examples, it is either one among many options available at the same time in the same society, or one part of a process of mortuary rites. With the exception of the Perrins Ledge Crematory, finding cremation alone is rare, and whether the cremains at Perrins Ledge were destined to be moved to a cemetery is unclear. Cremation can also be deliberate or accidental. Cremation was sometimes a secondary rite that took place after other ritual practices and procedures. Because of this, there is considerable variability in what constitutes a cremation or cremation burial in the literature. As Beck (1995) has noted, sometimes cremation can include reburning of the ashes as a rite to end the mourning ceremonies.

In addition to being a means of memorialization and transformation, "cremation concerns not only the performance and agency of the living but also the mnemonic agency of the cadaver" (Williams 2008a:252). Williams suggests that the context of ashes might be best seen as a persistent arena for social interaction between the living and the dead, rather than as a final resting place.

How can we begin to see cremation in the U.S. Midwest differently? First, some of the cremains may have been incorporated into mounds and monuments—perhaps human cremains are incorporated into Effigy Mound sites and other kinds of sites and are not just symbolic of individuals, such that the place incorporates the actual individuals themselves (see Cooney, chap. 10, this volume). Extension of this idea correlates with theories that the mounds themselves are artifacts and memorializations (see Goldstein 1995 for example).

Second, the data presented here—which is by no means complete or exhaustive—show that there is a notable association between evidence of copper artifacts and copper working and cremation. This association is especially apparent in the Archaic and Hopewell contexts (although note that the association is by no means absolute, because there are copper artifacts without cremation and cremation without copper artifacts). There is certainly copper at Mississippian sites, but it is not directly correlated with cremation or burning aspects of mortuary ritual and may have developed a broader symbolic meaning (as in the copper long-nose god masks at numerous Mississippian sites). In a totally different context, Williams (2008a:248–49) notes that parallel ritualized transformation is often associated with both metalworking and cremation rituals. This association may be based on the idea that transformation by fire is a theme linking treatment of the dead to transformation of other forms of material culture. Perhaps the extensive presence of cremation in the Archaic is a kind of transformation that was associated with the first development of metalworking in copper. Indeed, the so-called Old Copper culture represents the first evidence of copper tools in the Midwest. Later, given the extraordinary skill demonstrated in Hopewell copper working, a link to cremation may also be related to development of that skill and related rituals (see especially the article by

Cooper on copper working in the U.S. Northwest, in which he notes a change of copper use from practical technology to prestige technology but also contends that copper had qualities of animacy and agency [Cooper 2011]). Similarly, red ocher may be linked to these practices as well and may take the place of copper in certain circumstances.

Williams (2008a) discusses connections between light, heat, and seasonality of the sun's interaction with a monument. Such associations may have been connected to the symbolism of cremation rituals conducted around and within these monuments. This idea could be applied to the presence of both ashes and cremains in mounds, as well as their presence in charnel structures, and links to copper working and red ocher, in addition to associations with "altars," such as are present in Effigy Mound sites.

Third, there is a strong link between cremation and secondary burial. Not all secondary burials are cremated, but many examples discussed here represent cremations that were part of a secondary burial process. On a practical level this is logical, because cremation that is not in situ is by definition secondary, but those cremains do not have to be buried. It is also the case that cremating someone who is at least partially decomposed may be easier, and bundling the cremains may make disposing of them, either ritually or practically, more convenient. There are circumstances in which bundled inhumations represent more than one individual or only one individual. Clearly, there are many different processes that have operated over time and across space, requiring far more detailed analysis. While all of these practical issues are reasonable, people were likely motivated by other factors. Cremation is a process and is often associated with other methods of transforming the body. Fire can be a primary rite of separation, or it can serve as a secondary rite following exposure, defleshing, temporary inhumation, or mummification.

The interaction of ritual, performance, and place must play a critical role, since none of these sites represent random appearances on the landscape. As Williams (2008a:248) also notes, "the potential afforded by cremation for the retrieval and circulation of the ashes means that many places and spaces from temples to houses can be incorporated into the mortuary process and subsequent commemorative and ancestral rites." Buildings and monuments can also be subject to deliberate ritualized fiery destruction. People may treat the building as symbolically equivalent to a dead human being. If this is the case, then the charnel houses that burned may not be accidental but instead a deliberate act of performance and memorialization.

In the Mississippian case, there is evidence of charnel houses burning or being closed with a ceremony or offering. At Aztalan (Goldstein 2010), Schild (Goldstein 1980), Yokem (Perino 1971), Kincaid (Muller 1978), and other sites, the burning or dismantling of the charnel structure may have been part of a closing ceremony (see Schurr, chap. 12, this volume, for the possibility that Yokem burning was linked to conflict and identity). Inside the structures are human remains, nuts, corn, animal bone, textiles, and ceramics, much of which was burned in the ceremony. This ceremony reflects the same sort of behavior that Cerezo-Román (chap. 8, this volume) discusses for closing or final ceremonies in the U.S. Southwest.

Such "ephemeral monuments" that were deliberately destroyed during funerary rituals may include houses of the living and mortuary structures built for preparation or display of the corpse prior to cremation. Cremation can then be connected to the life histories of monuments. Similarly, individual mounds and mound cemeteries may represent a changing performative space for cremation ceremonies and burial rites, with cremated remains integrated into communal monuments. None of these options are mutually exclusive.

In a wider sense, this research and brief survey confirms the value of looking at cremation as a transformation of the body, but in some instances the body (or what is left) becomes part of the monument, as well as part of a performance and ritual. In all of the cases presented here, there is a strong link between place, space, and the body.

All mortuary practices change the relationship between the living and the dead, but cremation may be especially powerful because of its association with fire, light, and place. One individual can be incorporated into multiple places and can represent or be associated with other transformations, such as technology. In the case of the sites examined here, that transformation often seems to link cremation to the technology of copper working (see Martin 1999 for details of the copper-working process). As copper working developed over time, the transformation of the copper ore into an artifact through heating, flames, pounding, and heating may have helped to stimulate a similar sort of transformation of the body.

Cremation can result in incorporation into the landscape, stand for the closing of a ritual or performative process, and represent technological transformations. In addition, cremation may physically and spatially represent one local family or a larger communal emphasis. There may be separate sets of transformations and rituals operating at the local and regional levels, each sending a separate set of messages. It is possible that what we find at a mortuary site could represent one or more portions or stages of rituals—the end ritual may be a cremation deposit or the burial of cremains, but because of a variety of circumstances, that end does not happen for everyone.

We see this chapter as a beginning. There are many other associations and links between cremation, mortuary processing, and ritual that can be examined and discovered for the prehistoric past of the U.S. Midwest. Many of the mortuary practices we see make sense only in relation to the practices that preceded them. However, changes in mortuary practices can relate to changing aspects of life, as practices are manipulated by the living. Our work is strengthened and informed by the work of other chapters in this volume. We have tried to highlight a few possibilities that link cremation and stages of mortuary processing and also link different portions of the past together.

PART IV

Reassembling the Pieces
Future Directions

12

Reflections—Techniques, Potential, and Challenges of Cremations

Mark R. Schurr

Studies of the social contexts of cremation have been hampered by a lack of knowledge about how prehistoric cremations were created and how best to study them. In many areas, the first archaeologists to discover cremations appeared to have relatively little interest in them, except to note their presence as traits that could be used to define prehistoric cultures. Baby (1954) noted that American archaeologists of the late nineteenth and early twentieth centuries confined their observations to noting very basic things such as differential burning and multiple individuals in some deposits. Cremations are relatively common in the sometimes spectacular Middle Woodland (circa 200 BC–AD 400) burial mounds built by the Ohio Hopewell and were also found in the mounds of their Adena (circa 1000–200 BC) predecessors. The first systematic discussion of Adena and Hopewell cremations (Webb and Snow 1974 [1945]:171–90) was primarily concerned with determining the depositional processes, including whether bodies were cremated in the flesh or not. Thus, not until after World War II did American archaeologists begin to wonder how cremations were formed and to investigate how they were produced. Since then, studies of cremations, and burnt bones in general, have increased in number over time.

A parallel situation occurred in Europe, with cremations being noted but largely ignored in the nineteenth and early twentieth centuries. Studies increased in frequency after 1950, when the research potential of cremated bone was still somewhat controversial but was becoming recognized as a profitable area for investigation (Gejvall 1969). The European approach to cremations appears to have been more frequent and more systematic than was the case for eastern North America. Along with the obvious studies of things such as how bone color changes with heating temperature, much attention was paid to basic osteological issues such as the number of individuals represented, age at death, sex, and pathologies, especially in regard to methods that could determine these characteristics using very fragmentary remains. Because of the frequency of cremation in some periods and places (most notably the Bronze and Early Iron Ages in some areas) and the large size of cemeteries, studies could employ very large samples of cremated burials (Wahl 2008). More recently, European scholars have produced an almost dizzying array of approaches for studying cremations (see below). Systematic or scientific approaches to determining how cremations were produced take one of three approaches. These include examining or analyzing archaeological specimens and inferring cremation processes from appearance or some other factor, using replicative experiments to try to reproduce cremations, and laboratory studies of burnt bone. The first of these is, of course, the earliest and still most widely used method. Differential burning patterns and surface appearance have long been used to infer whether bodies were cremated in the flesh or as disarticulated bones (Webb and Snow 1974 [1945]:187–89; e.g., Buikstra and Goldstein 1973). Visual indicators such as color, fracture patterns, and degree of fragmentation (Correia 1996) remain extremely important for the study of cremations, as shown by many of the chapters in this volume.

The first replication experiments appear to have been very ad hoc and exploratory in nature. One is left with the impression that they were conducted by people with absolutely no familiarity with cremation. For example, in perhaps the first North American replication experiment, the conditions of a cremated cadaver and "green" bones obtained by dissection were found to be similar to cremations from Ohio Hopewell mounds (Baby 1954), but no details about the cremation procedures are given. Early replication studies often used unrealistic conditions such as nonhuman bodies (Binford 1963a) or portions of formalin-embalmed corpses (Buikstra and Swegle 1989; Thurman and Willmore 1981).

Determining burning conditions in open-air cremations is difficult because of the multitude of variables, such as fuel type, amount, and placement and the size, condition, and posture of the body. Because replication experiments do not report on all possible variables and are often single one-off experiments, it is very hard to know how generalizable or even repeatable the results are. Even for a single configuration, attempting to monitor a basic variable such as temperature is very difficult because of variation within the pyre (McKinley 1994b). In addition, the temperature of the burning object will be several hundred degrees centigrade lower than the highly variable average temperature of the flame (DeHaan 2008). How and where to measure even a basic variable like temperature within the dynamic environment of a real cremation are not trivial questions.

Because of these difficulties, laboratory experiments have been conducted to characterize the response of tissues (mainly bone but sometimes teeth) to heat (some examples are cited below). Comparing one experiment to another is not always easy, because different variables have been used, including different heating times, different ranges of temperatures, the size of the bone and whether it was heated in air or buried in some medium such as soil, and even the type of burial medium. For example, bones heated within diatomaceous earth possessed different colors than bones heated in organic-rich topsoil at the same times and temperatures (Walker et al. 2008).

The color of the bone is an extremely important and accessible indicator of the burning conditions and has received much attention via laboratory studies of bones heated under controlled conditions (Correia 1996; Devlin and Herrmann 2008; McCutcheon 1992; Walker et al. 2008). Unfortunately, some studies use general terms, others use Munsell colors, and still others use color description systems such as RGB values, making the written discussions sometimes difficult to compare. Despite all these complexities, we now have a good understanding of the general range of changes that occur within a heated bone. Color is more dependent on heating temperature than on heating time. Bones heated below 200°C appear little altered, blackening occurs by 300°C, and bones heated above 450–600°C lose all organic content and are calcined. There is one prominent exception to this general picture and that is the sequence of changes described by Holck (1987:131–46), in which even moderate burning does not occur until temperatures of 1,000–1,100°C. Holck's results have been widely cited as evidence that many Bronze Age European cremations were produced in furnaces under conditions that rival those attainable by modern industrial crematoria and far exceed those found on an open pyre (Goldhahn and Oestigaard 2008). Given the number of laboratory experiments consistent with the lower temperature sequence outlined above (e.g., Buikstra and Swegle

1989; Walker et al. 2008; McCutcheon 1992; Schurr and Hayes 2008; Wahl 2008), the temperature ranges reported by Holck for the changes associated with them are clearly too high and the inferences drawn from them are therefore unlikely.

Many different analytical methods have been used to study cremations and to determine cremation conditions from the physical properties of bones and teeth. An impressive but incomplete list with just a few examples of each application includes several different methods for estimating the volume of cremated bone (Harvig and Lynnerup 2013), scanning electron microscopy (SEM) to examine small-scale surface appearance and texture (Correia 1996; McCutcheon 1992; Shipman and Schoeninger 1984), X-ray diffraction (XRD) to determine hydroxyapatite crystal morphology (Correia 1996; Munro et al. 2008; Pijoan et al. 2007; Shipman and Schoeninger 1984), and infrared spectrometry (IR), usually using Fourier transform IR (FTIR) spectroscopy to determine what chemical bonds are present and the degree of crystallinity (Munro et al. 2008; Thompson et al. 2011). More exotic techniques include electron spin resonance spectroscopy (ESR) to determine heating temperature (Schurr and Hayes 2008). AMS dating of bone carbonate (Lanting and Brindley 1998) has produced dates from cremations that can be used to create internal cemetery chronologies (De Mulder et al. 2009) and to date associated artifacts for improved chronologies of material culture (Brindley 2007).

Over the past half century, students of cremations have developed an impressive array of technical skills (as outlined above) and ever more sophisticated theoretical models (as shown by the chapters in this volume and the many influences they cite). It will be interesting to see whether some of the exciting new methods for studying unburned bone can be applied to cremations. The characterization of ancient DNA is still somewhat exploratory even when applied to unburned bone, and its application to cremations seems unpromising because of the effects of thermal alteration. In general, forensic scientists appear to be very skeptical about the potential for the preservation of useful DNA in cremated remains (Cattaneo et al. 1999), although DNA analysis appears to be theoretically possible for remains heated at very low temperatures (Harbeck et al. 2011). Some researchers have reported detecting human DNA in cremated remains (Pusch et al. 2000), but whether useful genetic comparisons between cremated people or populations will be possible is still unclear.

Stable isotope ratios—especially those of carbon, nitrogen, oxygen, and strontium—have been widely used for reconstructing diets and climates, and for tracing migrations using uncremated bones. Collagen stable nitrogen-isotope ratios are significantly altered by heating, but carbon-isotope ratios are not (Schurr and Hayes 2008). Limited data suggest that strontium-isotope ratios (Harbeck et al. 2011) and carbon-isotope ratios in bone carbonate (Munro et al. 2008) may be unaltered even at high temperatures. However, oxygen isotopes (used for climate reconstructions and determining place of origin) are altered by heating (Munro et al. 2008). The potential for using these techniques on cremations is therefore limited, and they must be applied with judgment. Other isotopes such as those of sulfur are yet to be explored. A final obstacle is the use of tooth enamel as the preferred tissue for oxygen- and strontium-isotope measurements. The tendency of teeth to fracture during cremation makes the recovery of suitable samples difficult in some cases.

There is clearly a large toolbox of techniques available for the characterization of burnt bones, although some of the most promising new approaches require additional evaluation. In most cases, multidisciplinary collaborations between archaeologists and physical scientists will be necessary to achieve the greatest level of success, and such collaborations need to be designed at the very start of the research project.

13

Future Directions for the Archaeology of Cremation

Jessica I. Cerezo-Román and Howard Williams

This chapter represents the results of, and responses to, discussion, dialogue, and deliberation before, during, and after the Fire and the Body workshop. "Cremation" is a complex set of funerary procedures in which the burning of the body is but one element. In effect, the term *cremation* is shorthand for various fiery ritual technologies in which the dead are mourned, transformed, and commemorated. Archaeologists have identified cremation practices in very different prehistoric and historic societies, operating within very different and changing social, religious, political, economic, and environmental conditions from early prehistory to the present day. Cremation, therefore, is a significant aspect of living and dying in the global human past.

Against this background, it is challenging to identify a set of narrow global questions for future archaeological research. Even in recent years, archaeologists have approached cremation with overlapping, but discrete, theoretical perspectives that broadly share social and interpretative approaches, including the archaeology of ideology and power, human and material agency, the senses and aesthetics, social identity and personhood, religion and cosmology, and social memory and the body. The archaeology of cremation is, therefore, a broad topic with many vested research interests in its future direction. Moreover, given the variability and changing deployment of cremation practices alongside other disposal methods, we contend that the most appropriate research questions are those sensitive to period- and region-specific research agendas, responsive to the quality and character of the archaeological data under scrutiny, and linked to the interests of local communities.

It remains, however, important to ask the big question: whither the study of cremation from a global perspective? Building on Williams's (2008a) argument for a wide theoretical and methodological scope for "the archaeology of cremation," in this chapter we explore research themes crucial for broadening and deepening the archaeological study of global cremation practices. A holistic and integrated "archaeology of cremation" must regard cremated human remains as mnemonic and emotive "abject" substances—once-humans and future-ancestors—that were affective on those handling and experiencing them (see also T. Sørensen 2009; Williams 2004d). This approach promotes a consideration of the complex ways in which material culture is involved in multistaged cremation practices. Cremation also includes the production, gathering, circulating, wrapping and containing, fuelling, igniting, burning, transforming, fragmenting, consuming, selecting, and depositing of artifacts, materials, and substances (Williams 2005a, 2007a). Past cremation involved diverse mortuary contexts and spaces (including settlements, pyres, and graves) through which the cadaver and mourners moved and engaged. Hence, cremation was distinctive from other mortuary procedures and opened up different possibilities for the storage, distribution, transportation, and placing of the dead. The storage possibilities of cremated remains, such as baskets, pouches, ceramic containers, and scatters throughout the landscape, are innumerable (e.g., Cooney 1992; McKinley 1994b; Rebay-Salisbury 2010; Willey and Scott 1999). Similarly, there is a substantial range of above- and belowground contexts, architectures, and monuments connected to different depositional locations of the cremation process. Cremation ceremonies and burials can involve settlement spaces and cemeteries, as well as ephemeral structures built for the funeral or those intended as lasting memorials to the dead (e.g., Potter et al. 2011; Williams 2004d). Pyres are themselves a kind of ephemeral monument, providing valuable information about the performance and complexity of burning the body (Nilsson Stutz and Kuijt, chap. 7, this volume). Finally, the locations and qualities of cemeteries within inhabited landscapes (including their topographic settings and relationships with vegetation, natural resources, settlements, and environments) can vary considerably and provide rich avenues for further research in their own right (e.g., Wickholm 2008).

Inspired by the discussions and debates raised by this book's chapters, we propose six avenues for future research in the archaeology of cremation.

Integrating Science and Theory in Cremation Research

Most scientific publications of cremated remains focus on evaluating methods and techniques to study cremated remains and/or have been fairly descriptive. While utilization of state-of-the-art archaeological science analytical methods in cremation studies may well be ground-breaking (see Agarwal and Glencross 2011), this kind of research has been criticized as lacking in the analytical and population-based focus of physical anthropology (e.g., Armelagos and Van Gerven 2003; Hens and Godde 2008). Still, these types of studies have advanced the scientific arsenal of methods available and opened up new areas of inquiry and avenues for answering broader, complex research questions.

Importantly, cremation studies require the skills of bioarchaeologists/osteoarchaeologists and other scientific researchers specialized in human skeletal remains (see Buikstra 1977). The integration of, and dialogue with, bioarchaeologists by archaeologists has been long been advocated (Buikstra 1977, 1991). An early American example in cremation research is the pioneering work at the Perrins Ledge Crematory, Illinois (Buikstra and Goldstein 1973). In this research, excavated cremated remains and the archaeological contexts where they were found were analyzed to provide in-depth understandings of individual life histories and rituals performed at the crematory. McKinley's (1994b) and Bond's (1996) work on early Anglo-Saxon cremation practices is a classic British example of integrative scientific analysis and archaeological interpretation. Today, numerous projects are beginning to integrate bioarchaeology with the archaeological analysis of mortuary contexts within both academic and public compliance-driven (or development-led) research (Fitzpatrick 1997; Gramsch 2007; MacGregor 2008; Ubelaker and Rife 2009). Seeing this applied in cremation analysis is less common, however.

To interpret thermal alteration of human remains, material culture, and archaeological features, one must have a clear understanding of what fire is, fire dynamics, combustion, and how the fire physically alters human tissue and material culture (Fairgrieve 2008). Specific attention to scientific methods that directly inform the quality of the excavated evidence also is required. Excavation and recovery strategies should consider budget, time constraints, available personnel, and, if possible, consultation with descendant communities. Accurate in situ archaeological field observations and visual documentation are essential in identifying deposits with cremated remains. Experienced researchers with a strong human osteology background should ideally excavate cremations.

To understand a cremation, one must understand the location and in situ anatomical position of the burned human remains. These will allow the reconstruction of the position of the body (e.g., Harvig et al. 2013), an understanding of how the fragments were deposited, and an inference of other ancient posthumous treatments and practices. The exact locations of all objects and substances—including material culture, charcoal, plant remains/residues, and animal remains—should be documented and the remains recovered. If objects and animal remains are discovered, their orientation within the deposits also should be documented. If objects and/or animal remains are deposited within a structure, then the relationship of the remains within the structure should be described (for example, the remains were placed under the roof, throughout the fill, or under the floor). Regardless of whether the remains are fully excavated or not (as sometimes burial agreements with descendant communities restrict removal), these types of details for in situ documentation should be standard practices. If detailed excavations cannot occur in the field, then removal of a block of deposits will facilitate later detailed excavations in the laboratory. For example, laboratory excavation of cinerary urns has long been practiced for small numbers of contexts (e.g., McKinley 1994b). However, the potential for the regular investigation of cremation burials in this manner is illustrated by Gramsch's (2007) discussion of the Late Bronze Age cremation cemetery of Cottbus (Brandenburg, Germany), where the urns were repeatedly found to contain cremated remains of all body parts and in anatomical order. Careful excavation and analysis consequently revealed an aspect of the mortuary ritual that had otherwise been overlooked, as well as the importance of "anthropomorphy" in postcremation rituals (Gramsch 2007:95; see also Rebay-Salisbury 2010; Williams 2007a). Likewise, recent work has foregrounded the importance of combining the excavation of cremation remains with computer tomography and radiography, not only for revealing artifacts and burial practices otherwise overlooked but also for challenging ritual interpretations based on retrieved bone weights (Harvig et al. 2011; Minozzi et al. 2010). The large-scale and systematic use of these techniques in the excavation of burial populations has considerable potential.

New scientific methods have enhanced what we can learn from cremated remains. Researchers have employed various methods to document age, sex, represented skeletal elements, pathologies, and nonmetric traits (e.g., Birkby 1976; Fink 1989). Others have successfully employed DNA analysis (Brown et al. 1995; Lutz et al. 1996). Still other researchers have explored thermal alterations and posthumous treatment of the body, or how the color of bone alterations derived from fire exposure (e.g., Buikstra and Swegle 1989; Gejvall 1969; Shipman et al. 1984; Ubelaker 1978; Van Vark 1975). Researchers (e.g., Bohnert et al. 2002; Gonçalves et al. 2011; Herrmann and Bennett 1999; Symes et al. 2008; Walker et al. 2008) debate the distinctions between different cremation conditions and resulting bone fracture types. Previous researchers also have examined bone weights (e.g., Bass and Jantz 2004; McKinley and Bond 2001; Sonek 1992; Trotter and Hixon 1974) and degree of fragmentation in cremated remains, to determine pyre technology or burial disturbance (McKinley 1989). However, further research needs to explore social variables that might cause differential burning rituals affecting cremated remains within specific sites and societies. Further work is needed to understand the intersections between differential burial treatments, biological information, gender, and social age (Brück, chap. 6, this volume).

The study of materials employed in the cremation process is a further avenue in which scientific analysis benefits archaeological interpretation: recent work has proven the use of seaweed in Bronze Age cremation practices in Orkney, moreoever speculating that its inclusion was more than a fuel. The creation of "cramp"—a glassy substance made up of sand, seaweed, and human bone—may have been a desired product of the cremation process linked to culturally specific understandings of burning the dead (Photo-Jones et al. 2007).

Many scientific cremation publications are descriptive or primarily evaluations of particular methods and techniques, but there are notable exceptions. Schurr and Cook (chap. 4, this volume), for example, explore a dietary study focused on stable carbon and nitrogen isotopes to illustrate the integration of scientific analysis using archaeometric techniques and archaeological interpretation at the intrasite level. This approach shows great potential for better understanding different consumption practices between and within populations.

There also is a need to explore more cohesively the relational networks between the material objects present in cremation funerary deposits and their relationships with the dead and living. There is significant knowledge to be gained from experimental replication of past funerary practices to determine the condition of remains prior to burning, pyre technology, and burial disturbance. Replication of past practices allows for more precise understanding of formation processes and posthumous treatments of bodies.

Different archaeometric techniques can be used to examine provenance, production, distribution, and use of objects. Critical application of these techniques and resulting data will produce a better understanding of life histories, agencies of objects, and different intersecting characteristics and attributes of the objects and remains. Such studies can reveal how objects actively become part of mortuary ritual practices.

Cremation in Theory and History

Understanding the fragmentary traces of past cremation funerary practices should be grounded in the archaeological record's complexity and variability. This is both helped and hindered by the application of analogies from accounts of cremation practices in the recent past recorded by ethnographers and/or historians (Beck 2005; Cerezo-Román, chap. 8, this volume; McKinley 1994b; Rakita and Buikstra 2005). Further critical appraisals of the merits of ethnographic and historic analogy are required, concerning not only the use of analogy but also the reliability of and biases inherent in the source material (e.g., Tonkin 1992; Vansina 1985). Descendant communities may be living very differently and could have very different beliefs and worldviews from those of their ancestors. Nevertheless, their histories may provide a source of insights and foils in the process of theory building, including the use of technology and the material, social, and religious contexts for cremation (e.g., Mason 2000; Wylie 1985). Ethnographic and historic accounts of mortuary practices also present several limitations due to the emotive tempos and intensities of mortuary events. Funeral rituals were usually performed within different spheres of social space and interactions. The cremation ritual, many aspects of which lack historical accounts, may have varied between private and public spaces, and only part of the funerary rituals may have been accessible to the ethnographer. The multiplicities of meaning in these types of practices, hidden mourning practices, and the variation of these events though space and time present significant challenges. Nonetheless, descriptions of mortuary rituals provide analogs of different types of social funerary practices and provide points of comparison for interpreting archaeological traces.

Hence, despite interpretative challenges, the ethnography of cremation should be considered in future research, particularly when investigating variability in how material cultures are deployed and cremains are collected, stored, circulated, and deposited (Williams 2000). Conversely, direct and uncritically evaluated ethnographic analogs should be avoided. Developing a more theorized ethnography of cremation, followed by its critical and cautious application to archaeological contexts, requires us to adopt new perspectives. In particular, we need to expand our use of ethnographies from Old World cremation ceremonies (for example, from the Ganges Valley, Nepal, and Bali) and also to explore ethnographies and historic documents from across the globe, including early eighteenth- through to twentieth-century accounts from Siberia, the American Northwest Coast, the American Southwest, Central and South America, and Southeast Asia. In addition, for the ethnography of cremations, we can explore insights and analogies gained from practices in industrialized nations where cremation is the dominant disposal method today. There are, moreover, few specifically designed ethnoarchaeological studies and sustained experimental archaeological programs investigating cremation in the contemporary world (see, however, Downes 1999; Oestigaard 2005).

Further research is needed to explore the historical process leading to the adoption of cremation, its coexistence alongside other disposal methods, and possible religious, ideological, and socioeconomic processes bringing about the abandonment of cremation. Researchers might explore the motives for the rise or fall of cremation in past societies, including the role of cremation in migrant communities and in identity strategies of colonization and resistance, as well as the use of cremation to mark social and cultural distinctions within communities.

It is important as well to explore the relationship of these practices with social memory—how uses of cremation can have enduring influences—particularly in areas where cremation is not the normative mode of burial and the rare and striking use of cremation might be long remembered.

Where cremation is regularly practiced, the organizational agents involved in cremation can be complex and diverse and affect how cremation operates and the destinations chosen for cremains. In modern societies, cremated remains from animals as well as humans are disposed of in different and creative ways, such as being incorporated into jewelry, placed in urns, and scattered in the landscape. The decision making of disposing of the remains might be dictated by state or federal laws but also shaped by practical factors such as ease of transportation, as well as emotional and religious belief systems. Future work must consider factors shaping the multiple pathways of cremation and deposition, as well as the entwined socioeconomic and ideological factors. For example, the spread of Hindu and Buddhist cremation practices and eschatology in Asia may provide insights into past comparable processes. Comparative work on the cessation of cremation in the Americas (particularly the Northwest Coast), India, Australia, and Siberia might provide insights into the how and why of cremation declines, providing insightful parallels into the end of cremation in past societies. For example, in the U.S. Southwest, archaeological and historical evidence suggests that in the past among the Zunis cremation was practiced on a regular basis, but once the Spanish missionaries entered the area this practice decreased (e.g., Howell 1994; Riley 1975). In contrast, archaeological evidence shows that cremation was already falling from favor before the historically attested conversion of the Anglo-Saxon kingdoms (Williams, chap. 5, this volume). Evaluating the rise and fall of cremation in the past and the present might create more enriched studies of cremation as a historically situated disposal method.

Cremation as *Rite de Passage*

Since the work of Hertz (1960 [1907]) and van Gennep (1960), researchers have often interpreted cremation as a ritual transition, not an event of burning a corpse. Numerous studies have sought to explore how cremation operated as a technology of remembrance: a chain of commemorative operations, not a single technique. As well as commemorating the dead, this sequence of acts and processes aimed to reproduce concepts of the person and cosmos by taking the survivors, the cadaver, and concepts of the soul on a parallel journey (e.g., Williams 2005b). This approach has done much to theorize cremation beyond an index of particular social attributes and its misunderstanding as "low status" or "destruction." Moreover, this approach envisions the selective and commemorative deployment of material cultures, architectures, and landscapes in the process of transforming the cadaver into cremated remains and their subsequent deposition (see also A. Jones 2003). It also foregrounds cremation as a ritual process that makes and remakes the identities of not only the deceased but also the living (Cerezo-Román, chap. 8, this volume; A. Jones 2003). Another value of this approach is the attention paid to the materialities of cremation—the many kinds of materials drawn into the cremation process and, at different stages, serving to transform the dead. For instance, Williams (2007a) explores the role of cosmetic and toilet implements and combs (some of them miniature items) and amulets as mnemonic catalysts in early medieval cremation practices. These were not items of great value or necessarily objects with significant "biographies" themselves; their miniature or diminutive form and their association with hair management made them appropriate for symbolizing and constituting the regeneration and reconstitution of the body in postcremation rituals. More recently, Williams (2013) has proposed that a range of other artifact types operated in comparable fashions at certain times and places within early medieval Europe.

Researchers need to explore the active roles of materials and substances in transforming the dead physically and conceptually in cremation processes, as well as thinking about funerary cremation rituals as a series of practices and a dynamic process that includes much more than just burning the body (Williams 2013). Fire produces a change in the body and objects that are placed with the deceased, but the entire funeral ritual could be the means of transition, particularly if consisting of several stages spread over time, with the act of burning the body as one or more stages in this ritual transition. New research is needed to explore the interrelationship between different objects, to investigate the point in time when objects enter cremation rituals, their ultimate disposition, and their relationship(s) to the transitional identities of the dead and living. The objects found in cremations could be part of the funerary ritual, possessions of the deceased, or belongings of the mourners. We should identify whether and where objects reflect intersecting identities of the individuals and mourners and their social networks (Barrett 1990, 1994; Chapman 2000a; Gillespie 2011; Joyce 2001). Gillespie (2011) suggests that this can be done by looking at burial characteristics that served as components of individual and multidimensional networks of reference. The networks become historical artifacts referenced by people in the community, and by doing this the objects acquired value and significance. This could be evaluated by having good chronological control, establishing biological data of the individual such as age and sex, and examining burials as referential chains, or citation of prior actions.

It is also important to examine the relationship between parts and wholes of cremated human remains as well as the objects deposited in the burial and/or related to the mortuary rituals (e.g., Chapman 2000a; Larsson and Nilsson Stutz, chap. 3, this volume; Rebay-Salisbury 2010). Human remains could be buried in place, redeposited into one or multiple deposits, or scattered. If redeposited into multiple pits/token burials, determining how and why the remains were divided and distributed throughout the landscape as well as how many individuals are represented will be a research challenge. Rebay-Salisbury's (2010) work focusing on Early and Late Bronze Age central Europe suggests that although cremation can be seen as a process of fragmentation, it does not necessarily destroy the sense of a body entity. Rebay-Salisbury (2010) interpreted the postburning treatment of the remains as reconstituting the fragments as a whole body, using the cinerary urn as a container for the bodily remains and creating a new form of corporeality (Rebay-Salisbury 2010). Likewise, the creation of "body-objects" or "inalienable possessions" could reinforce existing social networks through their distribution (see Cerezo-Román, chap. 8, this volume; Brück 2004, 2006a).

There is, however, a danger of re-creating normative explanations for cremation from this perspective without adequately considering mortuary variability—a regression to preprocessual archaeologies of cremation. Equally pernicious is the danger of equating mortuary process with the person per se, as well as only one aspect of the individual's and/or mourner's identity. This is a potential regression to a simplistic and heavily critiqued early New Archaeology equation of mortuary investment with social status (for further discussion see Goldstein 2001).

While the fragmentation and circulation of cremated remains might relate to concepts of personhood through strategies of remembering and forgetting, these practices need not be indexically linked to the ontological, social, and cosmological status of the deceased (for other views see Fowler 2004; Wickholm and Raninen 2006). Hence, the reading of both individuality and "dividuality" from the treatment of cremated remains should be cautiously considered. In this regard, the use of cremation in modernity challenges the idea that the fragmentation of the person is a sign of dividual personhood: emotional and social bonds and memories associated with the dead individual are clearly played out through the transformation of the cadaver and its scattering or disposal, sometimes in multiple locations, while the individuality and individual choices of the deceased are celebrated. Future work is needed to problematize personhood and memory in the treatment of cremated remains and to determine how the transhistorical constructions of personhood apply to past cremating societies. Studies might also explore and develop more sophisticated and contextual analyses of the transformations involved in cremation and how they may be utilized in the construction of ideals of the person in life and death. In addition, it is important to explore how this transformative process may be utilized in the construction of ideals of the society, social networks, and cosmology.

Cremation as Technology

A key issue for the archaeology of cremation is how the burning of the body drew technological knowledge, metaphors, symbolic significance, and social power from its similarities and associations with other fiery and elemental technologies (see Brück, chap. 6, Goldstein and Meyers, chap. 11, and Williams, chap. 5, this volume). On one level, cremation ritual can be seen as a spectacle; it is unique in its own sense but can be correlated to other forms of fire using performances to transform different types of material. Cremation rituals are performances that appeal to the senses of those who performed the ritual, participants and spectators alike. Fire transforms the body; when the body is burning, it generates odors, produces heat, and is visually and auditorily powerful.

The link between smelting and working metals and cremation is one avenue that has received some consideration (e.g., Gansum 2004a; Goldhahn and Oestigaard 2008). However, other fiery technologies—

including pottery production, glass production, food processing, and cooking—may have been regarded as analogous to cremation (Back Danielsson 2007; Oestigaard 1999; and see Brück, chap. 6, Larsson and Nilsson Stutz, chap. 3, and Williams, chap. 5, this volume). In addition, posthumous treatment of grinding cremains could be connected to food grinding; notions of fertility, transformation, and renewal; and the use of human cremated remains as temper in the production of pottery. Materials and processes perceived as luminous, heat producing, or regenerative may have been equally significant in certain cremation contexts. The association of stones that spark or glow, such as lead minerals (Hawley 1947), and materials used to start fires (flints, fire steels, and so forth) may have particular connections with cremation in certain past societies. Materials such as quartz crystal debris in the past could have been used as a metaphor for cremated human remains (Lindgren 2008), and ritually burned resin and incense could be related to the soul's journeys in the cremation fire. Heat-producing technologies in which fire plays only a limited role, such as the fermentation of beer (Larsson, personal communication 2011; see also Williams, chap. 5, this volume) and the sun baking of clay, need further consideration in appraising the metaphors and technological processes by which cremation was understood in past societies. Likewise, the metaphoric association of cinerary urns with homes, granaries, or bodies might have been more significant than the link with fire used to create both bodies and pots (e.g., Bradley 2002b). In short, further work is needed to differentiate superficial similarities from established and practiced metaphors deployed to conceptualize the cremated dead in past societies.

We also need to problematize relationships between the agency of people, animals, and objects participating in cremation ceremonies (Williams 2004d). Objects and animals could have mnemonic agencies in the funeral, and their life histories are relevant. Mills and Ferguson (2008:339) remind us that rather than seeing people as primary and objects and animals as secondary foci of rituals, things, plants, and animals might have, in some cases, been afforded primary status. In early Anglo-Saxon England, the underrepresentation in cremation graves of iron artifacts regularly found with contemporary inhumation graves—buckles, knives, and weapon blades—suggests recycling motivated by economy but perhaps also the desire to disassociate the dead from items, or the components of artifacts, that failed to be affected by the heat of the pyre (Williams 2005a). In other instances, several societies burned the property and gifts for the deceased and from mourners as part of mourning rituals for various reasons, and these relationships should be explored further.

Cremation Variability

How and why were cremation practices variable in the same period of time and geographical area? While simple monocausal explanations are unsatisfying, the need to explore cremation variability within and between cemeteries, as well as within and between sites, should be a research priority (see Larsson and Nilsson Stutz, chap. 3, and Williams, chap. 5, this volume). In instances where we find cremation avidly avoided or universally adopted, we should explore what powerful social, economic, ideological, or religious mechanisms created coherence and sustained traditions over time. We should, however, also consider the microarchaeology of diverse cremation practices within which traditions are performed and remembered within commemorative traditions (e.g., Gramsch 2007; see also Cerezo-Román, chap. 8, and Cooney, chap. 10, this volume). The role of cremation within the multistage funerary process may include temporary inhumation burials or the circulation and/or differential treatment of body parts, wherein only some bones are cremated. Researchers should also explore the social motivation for variable forms of cremation within a community or between communities, as well as the different triggers that caused change or social maintenance.

It is critical to explore instances of infrequent cremation: such instances throw into sharp relief the interpretation of noncremation practices within communities as well as the power of cremation in marking social and religious distinctions (Goldstein and Meyers, chap. 11, Larsson and Nilsson Stutz, chap. 3, and Schurr, chap. 12, this volume). Cremation can be socially efficacious even when it is reserved for a tiny minority or is rarely practiced.

Equal attention should be given to explore what were the relational networks as well as interconnections between ideology and power of these selected individuals in relation to the rest of the society. In late sixth- and early seventh-century England, cremation was waning, yet its use for the social elite in elaborate ceremonies ending in barrow burial projected wealth and status but also established territorial claims and ideological defiance (Williams 1999b).

Future research should give equal attention to communities that reserve cremation for exceptional circumstances. Such instances reveal the technological complications and ambivalent corporeal experiences of cremation. Indeed, early cremations in the American Midwest indicate a poorly instigated technology, although whether the degree of burning of remains was intentional or not is unclear (Schurr, personal communication 2011). In historic times, Native American groups in the American Southwest, such as the O'odham, cremated only individuals who died in violent encounters such as war and interpersonal conflict, to eliminate the enemy's magic and polluted body (Hanlon 1972:106; Underhill 1939:190). Another example includes some Pueblo groups, such as the Zunis of New Mexico, who maintained cemeteries at Hawikku and Kechiba:wa, where cremated burials were concentrated in only a few areas within each cemetery (see Howell 1994). Likewise, from late medieval and postmedieval Europe where cremation is a last resort to destroy revenant corpses, there are numerous accounts of botched conflagrations (Barber 1988).

The Archaeology of Modern Cremation

Our final proposition is that there is value in exploring the archaeology of cremation through the lens of the contemporary past and the rise of post-nineteenth-century cremation as an industrial and "modern" way of death. Modern furnace cremation is all too often misrepresented as the antithesis of traditional open-air cremation (e.g., Williams 2004d; and contributions to this volume). The study of modern cremation is a legitimate subject of archaeological research, for it connects to heritage conservation, in some cases the study of early nineteenth- and twentieth-century protected crematoria and their landscape cemeteries. There is also overlap with the study of the history of archaeology, as archaeologists and archaeology often have provided legitimacy for advocates of cremation and inspiration for cremation's material cultures, memorials, monuments, and landscapes (Back Danielsson 2011). The deposit type, ephemeralia, memorials, architectures, and landscapes of the cremated dead are a field ripe for future study from an archaeological perspective (Hockey et al. 2007; Prendergast et al. 2007; T. Sørensen 2009; Williams 2011a, 2011b). Studying cremation in the recent and contemporary pasts affords particular ethical and political challenges, including rights of respect for and sensitivity to survivors and the dead. This should not, however, prevent archaeologists from conducting non-invasive research in collaboration with individuals, communities, and organizations in which the traces, monuments, and landscapes of modern cremation are found.

The archaeological examination of both modern cremations in the recent and contemporary past *and* traditional open-air cremation practices in the more distant past may provide cross-fertilization of theories and ideas to the benefit of the study of both. Indeed, we suggest that all of the previously identified areas of future research will be enhanced by crossing this chronological and intellectual divide hitherto maintained between cremations past and present.

Conclusion

Why should we study cremation from a global perspective? To answer this question, we isolate some broad and overlapping archaeological research directions through the lens of different data and within contrasting intellectual and methodological traditions. Williams (2008a) proposes that the "archaeology of cremation" extends far beyond the examination of burned human and animal bone, conceptualizing cremated human remains as mnemonic and emotive "abject" substances that were affective on those involved in handling and experiencing them. It is important to consider the complexity of the entire mortuary ritual from the beginning to the end as well as the people, objects, things, spaces, and time associated with them. This requires the development and refinement of methods, as well as the creation and development of theories that are situated in cross-disciplinary dialogue that grows out of the research design and are expanded through fieldwork, analysis, publication, and exhibitions. The adoption of these methods and approaches could broaden our understanding of cremation in the past and present in new and innovative ways. These themes could be elaborated, adopted, and modified to period- and region-specific research agendas, and they should be responsive to the specific archaeological data under study and the interests of local communities. Inspired by the seminar and this book, we identify a range of rich future research directions to build on. The study of fire and the body in the human past and present promises to be a growing and exciting field of archaeological and interdisciplinary investigation.

REFERENCES CITED

Agarwal, S. C., and B. A. Glencross. 2011. Building a Social Bioarchaeology. In *Social Bioarchaeology*, edited by S. C. Agarwal and B. A. Glencross, 1–11. Wiley-Blackwell, Chichester, UK.

Alberthsen, S. E., and E. Brinch Petersen. 1977. Excavation of the Mesolithic Cemetery at Vedbæk. *Acta Achaeologica* 47 (1): 1–28.

Alexander, J. 1979. The Archaeological Recognition of Religion: The Examples of Islam in Africa and "Urnfields" in Europe. In *Space, Hierarchy and Society: Interdisciplinary Studies of Social Area Analysis*, edited by B. C. Burnham and J. Kingsbury, 215–28. BAR International Series 59. British Archaeological Reports, Oxford.

Anderson, D. G. 1996. Fluctuations Between Simple and Complex Chiefdoms: Cycling in the Late Prehistoric Southeast. In *Political Structure and Change in the Prehistoric Southeastern United States*, edited by J. F. Scarry, 231–52. University Press of Florida, Gainesville.

Andersson, H. 2004. Vart tog benen vägen? Återbesök i gropkeramiska gravar på Gotland. *Aktuell Arkeologi* 8:5–20.

Aner, E., and K. Kersten. 1973. *Die Funde der älteren Bronzezeit des nordischen Kreises in Dänemark, Schleswig-Holstein und Niedersachsen*. Vol. 1, *Frederiksborg und Københavns Amt*. Karl Wachholtz, Neumünster, Germany.

———. 1977. *Die Funde der älteren Bronzezeit des nordischen Kreises in Dänemark, Schleswig-Holstein und Niedersachsen*. Vol. 3, *Bornholms, Maribo, Odense und Svendborg Amter*. Karl Wachholtz, Neumünster, Germany.

———. 1981. *Die Funde der älteren Bronzezeit des nordischen Kreises in Dänemark, Schleswig-Holstein und Niedersachsen*. Vol. 6, *Nordsleswig—Syd / Tønder, Åbenrå und Sønderborg Amter*. Karl Wachholtz, Neumünster, Germany.

———. 1990. *Die Funde der älteren Bronzezeit des nordischen Kreises in Dänemark, Schleswig-Holstein und Niedersachsen*. Vol. 9, *Vejle Amt*. Karl Wachholtz, Neumünster, Germany.

———. 1995. *Die Funde der älteren Bronzezeit des nordischen Kreises in Dänemark, Schleswig-Holstein und Niedersachsen*. Vol. 10, *Ringkøbing Amt*. Karl Wachholtz, Neumünster, Germany.

———. 2001. *Die Funde der älteren Bronzezeit des nordischen Kreises in Dänemark, Schleswig-Holstein und Niedersachsen*. Vol. 11, *Thisted Amt*. Karl Wachholtz, Neumünster, Germany.

———. 2008. *Die Funde der älteren Bronzezeit des nordischen Kreises in Dänemark, Schleswig-Holstein und Niedersachsen*. Vol. 12, *Viborg Amt*. Karl Wachholtz, Neumünster, Germany.

Århem, K. 1988. Into the Realm of the Sacred: An Interpretation of Khasi Funerary Ritual. In *On the Meaning of Death: Essays on Mortuary Rituals and Eschatological Beliefs*, edited by S. Cederroth, C. Corlin, and J. Lindström, 257–99. Uppsala Studies in Cultural Anthropology 8. Almqvist and Wiksell, Uppsala, Sweden.

Ariès, P. 1974. *Western Attitudes Toward Death: From the Middle Ages to the Present.* Johns Hopkins University Press, Baltimore, MD.

Armelagos, G. J., and D. P. Van Gerven. 2003. A Century of Skeletal Biology and Paleopathology: Contrasts, Contradictions, and Conflicts. *American Anthropologist* 105 (1): 51–62.

Arnold, B. 1990. The Past as Propaganda: Totalitarian Archaeology in Nazi Germany. *Antiquity* 64:464–78.

Arnold, B., and H. Hassmann. 1995. Archaeology and Nazi Germany: The Legacy of the Faustian Bargain. In *Nationalism, Politics and the Practice of Archaeology*, edited by P. L. Kohl and C. Fawcett, 70–81. Cambridge University Press, Cambridge.

Arts, N., and M. Hoogland. 1987. A Mesolithic Settlement Area with a Human Cremation Grave at Oirschot V, Municipality of Best, The Netherlands. *Helinium* 27:172–89.

Artursson, M. (editor). 1996. *Bollbacken, en sen gropkeramisk boplats och ett gravfält från äldre järnålder. RAÄ 258, Tortuna sn, Västmanland.* Rapport no. 16. Arkeologikonsult, Upplands Väsby, Sweden.

Atkinson, J. A., I. Banks, and J. O'Sullivan (editors). 1996. *Nationalism and Archaeology.* Cruithne Press, Glasgow.

Baadsgaard, A., A. T. Boutin, and J. E. Buikstra (editors). 2011. *Breathing New Life into the Evidence of Death: Contemporary Approaches to Bioarchaeology.* School for Advanced Research Press, Santa Fe, NM.

Baby, R. S. 1954. *Hopewell Cremation Practices.* Papers in Archaeology no. 1. Ohio Historical Society, Columbus.

Back Danielsson, I.-M. 2007. *Masking Moments: The Transitions of Bodies and Beings in Late Iron Age Scandinavia.* Stockholm University, Stockholm.

———. 2011. Presenting the Past: On Archaeologists and Their Influence on Modern Burial Practices. *Mortality* 16 (2): 98–112.

Bahr, D. M. 1971. Who Were the Hohokam? The Evidence from Pima-Papago Myths. *Ethnohistory* 18 (3): 245–22.

Bahr, D. M., J. Smith, W. Smith Allison, and J. Hayden.1994. *The Short Swift Time of Gods on Earth: The Hohokam Chronicles.* University of California Press, Berkeley.

Banks, I. 1995. The Excavation of Three Cairns at Stoneyburn Farm, Crawford, Lanarkshire, 1991. *Proceedings of the Society of Antiquaries of Scotland* 125:289–343.

Barber, P. T. 1988. *Vampires, Burial and Death: Folklore and Reality.* Yale University Press, New Haven, CT.

————. 1990. Cremation. *Journal of Indo-European Studies* 18 (3–4): 379–88.

Barclay, A. 2011. Significant Individuals: Middle Neolithic Burials from the Thames Valley. Paper delivered at the Neolithic Studies Group, British Museum, London, 2011.

Barclay, A., and C. Halpin. 1999. *Excavations at Barrow Hills, Radley, Oxfordshire.* Vol. 1, *The Neolithic and Bronze Age Monument Complex.* Oxbow Books, Oxford, UK.

Barnard, A. 2007. From Mesolithic to Neolithic Modes of Thought. *Proceedings of the British Academy* 144:5–19.

Barnatt, J. 1994. Excavation of a Bronze Age Unenclosed Cemetery, Cairns, and Field Boundaries at Eaglestone Flat, Curbar, Derbyshire, 1984, 1989–1990. *Proceedings of the Prehistoric Society* 60:287–370.

Barrett, J. C. 1988. The Living, the Dead and the Ancestors: Neolithic and Early Bronze Age Mortuary Practice. In *The Archaeology of Context in the Neolithic and Early Bronze Age: Recent Trends,* edited by J. Barrett and I. Kinnes, 30–41. Department of Archaeology and Prehistory, University of Sheffield, Sheffield.

————. 1989. Time and Tradition: The Rituals of Everyday Life. In *Bronze Age Studies: Transactions of the British-Scandinavian Colloquium in Stockholm, May 10–11, 1985,* edited by H.-A. Nordström and A. Knape, 113–26. National Museum of Antiquities, Stockholm.

————. 1990. The Monumentality of Death: The Character of Early Bronze Age Mortuary Mounds in Southern Britain. *World Archaeology* 22:179–89.

————. 1991a. Introduction. In *Landscape, Monuments and Society: The Prehistory of Cranborne Chase,* edited by J. C. Barrett, R. Bradley, and M. Green, 120–22. Cambridge University Press, Cambridge.

————. 1991b. Early Bronze Age Mortuary Archaeology. In *Landscape, Monuments and Society: The Prehistory of Cranborne Chase,* edited by J. C. Barrett, R. Bradley, and M. Green, 124–28. Cambridge University Press, Cambridge.

————. 1994. *Fragments from Antiquity: An Archaeology of Social Life, 2900–1200 BC.* Blackwell, Oxford, UK.

Barrett, S. A. 1933. *Ancient Aztalan.* Bulletin of the Public Museum of the City of Milwaukee no. 13. Milwaukee, Wis.

Bass, W. M., and R. L. Jantz. 2004. Cremation Weights in East Tennessee. *Journal of Forensic Sciences* 49 (5): 901–4.

Battaglia, D. 1990. *On the Bones of the Serpent: Person, Memory and Mortality in Sabarl Island Society.* University of Chicago Press, Chicago.

Bayliss, A., F. Healy, A. Whittle, and G. Cooney. 2011. Neolithic Narratives: British and Irish Enclosures in Their Timescapes. In *Gathering Time: Dating the Early Neolithic Enclosures of Southern Britain and Ireland,* edited by A. Whittle, F. Healy, and A. Bayliss, 682–847. Oxbow Books, Oxford, UK.

Bayman, J. M. 2001. The Hohokam of Southwest North America. *Journal of World Prehistory* 15 (3): 257–311.

Beck, L. A. 1995. Regional Cults and Ethnic Boundaries in Southern Hopewell. In *Regional Approaches to Mortuary Analysis*, edited by L. A. Beck, 167–87. Plenum Press, New York.

———. 2000. Cremation Deposits from Sunset Mesa. In *Excavations at Sunset Mesa Ruin*, edited by M. W. Lindeman, 215–28. Desert Archaeology Research Series, Technical Report no. 2000-02. Desert Archaeology, Inc., Tucson, AZ.

———. 2005. Secondary Burial Practices in Hohokam Cremations. In *Interacting with the Dead: Perspectives on Mortuary Archaeology for the New Millennium*, edited by G. F. M. Rakita, J. E. Buikstra, L. A. Beck, and S. R. Williams, 150–54. University Press of Florida, Gainesville.

———. 2008. Human Remains. In *Craft Specialization in the Southern Tucson Basin: Archaeological Excavations at the Julian Wash Site, AZ BB:13:17 (ASM).* Part 1, *Introduction, Excavation Results, and Artifact Investigations*, edited by H. D. Wallace. Anthropological Papers no. 40. Center for Desert Archaeology, Tucson, AZ.

Beckett, J. 2011. Interactions with the Dead: A Taphonomic Analysis of Burial Practices in Three Megalithic Tombs in County Clare, Ireland. *European Journal of Archaeology* 14:394–418.

Bell, C. 1997. *Ritual Perspectives and Dimensions*. Oxford University Press, New York.

Bement, L. C. 1994. *Hunter-Gatherer Mortuary Practices During the Central Texas Archaic*. University of Texas Press, Austin.

Bender, M. M., D. A. Baerreis, and R. L. Steventon. 1981. Further Light on Carbon Isotopes and Hopewell Agriculture. *American Antiquity* 46:346–53.

Bennett, J. L. 1999. Thermal Alteration of Buried Bone. *Journal of Archaeological Science* 26:1–8.

Bennike, P. 1994. Antropologisk undersøgelse af brændte knogler fra THY 2959, Damsgård, Sønderhå sogn sb. nr. 52, Hassing Herred, Thisted Amt. *Journal of Danish Archaeology* 1993–1994:188–89.

Bergh, S. 1995. *Landscape of the Monuments*. Riksantikvarieambet Arkeologiska Undersoknigar, Stockholm.

Binford, L. R. 1963a. An Analysis of Cremations from Three Michigan Sites. *Wisconsin Archeologist* 44:98–110.

———. 1963b. The Pomranky Site: A Late Archaic Burial Station. In *Miscellaneous Studies in Typology and Classification*, edited by A. Montet-White and L. R. Binford, 151–92. Museum of Anthropology Anthropological Papers no. 19. University of Michigan Museum of Anthropology, Ann Arbor.

———. 1971. Mortuary Practices: Their Study and Their Potential. In *Approaches to the Social Dimensions of Mortuary Practices*, edited by J. Brown, 6–29. Society for American Archaeology Memoir 25. Washington, DC.

————. 1972. Analysis of a Cremated Burial from the Riverside Cemetery, Menominee County, Michigan. In *An Archaeological Perspective*, edited by L. R. Binford, 383–89. Seminar Press, New York.

Birbeck, V., R. J. C. Smith, P. Andrews, and N. Stoodley. 2005. *The Origins of Mid-Saxon Southampton: Excavations at the Friends Provident St. Mary's Stadium, 1998–2000.* Wessex Archaeology, Salisbury, UK.

Bird-David, N., and T. Israeli. 2010. A Moment Dead, A Moment Alive: How a Situational Personhood Emerges in the Vegetative State in an Israeli Hospital Unit. *American Anthropology* 112 (1): 54–65.

Birkby, W. H. 1976. Cremated Human Remains. In *The Hohokam: Desert Farmers and Craftsmen; Excavations at Snaketown, 1964–1965*, edited by E. W. Haury, 380–84. University of Arizona Press, Tucson.

Birmingham, R. A., and L. E. Eisenberg. 2000. *Indian Mounds of Wisconsin.* University of Wisconsin Press, Madison.

Blain, J., and R. J. Wallis. 2004. Sacred Sites, Contested Rites/Rights: Contemporary Pagan Engagements with the Past. *Journal of Material Culture* 9 (3): 237–61.

————. 2006. Past and Pagan Practices: Moving Beyond Stonehenge. *Public Archaeology* 5 (4): 3–16.

Blair, J. 2009. The Dangerous Dead in Early Medieval England. In *Early Medieval Studies in Memory of Patrick Wormald*, edited by S. Baxter, C. Karkov, J. T. Nelson, and D. Pelteret, 539–59. Ashgate, Farnham, UK.

Blakey, M. 2013. Profile of an Archaeologist. In *Archaeology*, edited by R. L. Kelly and D. H. Thomas, 342–43. Wadsworth Cengage Learning, Belmont, CA.

Bloch, M. 1971. *Placing the Dead: Tombs, Ancestral Villages, and Kinship Organization in Madagascar.* Seminar Press, London.

————. 1974. Symbols, Song, Dance and Features of Articulation. *Archives of European Sociology* 15 (1): 55–81.

————. 1982. Death, Women and Power. In *Death and the Regeneration of Life*, edited by M. Bloch and J. Parry, 211–30. Cambridge University Press, Cambridge.

————. 1988. Death and the Concept of Person. In *On the Meaning of Death: Essays on Mortuary Rituals and Eschatological Beliefs*, edited by S. Cederroth, C. Corlin, and J. Lindström, 11–29. Uppsala Studies in Cultural Anthropology 8. Almqvist and Wiksell, Uppsala, Sweden.

Bloch, M., and J. Parry (editors). 1982. *Death and the Regeneration of Life.* Cambridge University Press, Cambridge.

Bohnert, M., U. Schmidt, M. Grobe Perdekamp, and S. Pollack. 2002. Diagnosis of a Captive-Bolt Injury in a Skull Extremely Destroyed by Fire. *Forensic Science International* 127:192–97.

Boivin, N. 2009. Grasping the Elusive and Unknowable: Material Culture in Ritual Practice. *Material Religion* 5 (3): 266–87.

Bond, J. 1994. The Cremated Animal Bone. In *The Anglo-Saxon Cemetery at Spong Hill, North Elmham,* part 6, *The Cremations,* edited by J. I. McKinley, 121–35. East Anglian Archaeology 69. Norfolk Archaeological Unit, Dereham, UK.

———. 1996. Burnt Offerings: Animal Bone in Anglo-Saxon Cremations. *World Archaeology* 28 (1): 76–88.

Borić, D., J. Raičević, and S. Stefanović. 2009. Mesolithic Cremations as Elements of Secondary Mortuary Rites at Vlasac (Serbia). *Documenta Praehistorica* 36:247–82.

Borić, D., and S. Stefanović. 2004. Birth and Death: Infant Burials from Vlasac and Lepenski Vir. *Antiquity* 78:526–46.

Boroffka, N. 1994. *Die Wietenberg-Kultur.* Universitätsforschungen zur Prähistorischen Archäologie no. 19. Habelt, Bonn, Germany.

Bourdieu, P. 1991. *Language and Symbolic Power.* Cambridge University Press, Cambridge.

Bowler, J. M., R. Jones, H. Allen, and A. G. Thorne. 1970. Pleistocene Human Remains from Australia: A Living Site and Human Cremation from Lake Mungo, Western New South Wales. *World Archaeology* 2 (1): 39–60.

Boye, V. 1896. *Fund af Egekister fra Bronzealderen i Danmark: Et monografisk Bidrag til belysning af Bronzealderens Kultur.* Høst, Copenhagen.

Bradley, R. 1984. *The Social Foundations of Prehistoric Britain: Themes and Variations in the Archaeology of Power.* Longman, London.

———. 1990. *The Passage of Arms: An Archaeological Analysis of Prehistoric Hoard and Votive Deposits.* Cambridge University Press, Cambridge.

———. 2002a. *The Past in Prehistoric Societies.* Routledge Press, London.

———. 2002b. Death and the Regeneration of Life: A New Interpretation of House Urns in Northern Europe. *Antiquity* 76 (292): 372–77.

———. 2007a. *The Prehistory of Britain and Ireland.* Cambridge University Press, Cambridge.

———. 2007b. Houses, Bodies and Tombs. *Proceedings of the British Academy* 144:347–55.

Brain, C. K. 1993. The Occurrence of Burnt Bones at Swartkrans and Their Implications in the Control of Fire by Early Hominids. In *Swartkrans: A Cave's Chronicle of Early Man,* edited by C. K. Brain, 229–42. Transvaal Museum, Pretoria, South Africa.

Braithwaite, M. 1984. Ritual and Prestige in the Prehistory of Wessex, c. 2000–1400 BC: A New Dimension to the Archaeological Evidence. In *Ideology, Power and Prehistory,* edited by D. Miller and C. Tilley, 93–110. Cambridge University Press, Cambridge.

Bray, P. 2008. New Approaches to Analysing Jeannot's Knife and My Grandfather's Axe: Identifying, Quantifying and Explaining British and Irish Early Bronze Age Copper and Bronze Recycling. Paper delivered at the Bronze Age Forum, Sheffield, UK, November 2008.

Bray, T. (editor). 2001. *The Future of the Past: Archaeologists, Native Americans, and Repatriation.* Garland Publishing, London.

Breuning-Madsen, H., M. K. Holst, M. Rasmussen, and B. Elberling. 2003. Preservation Within Log Coffins Before and After Barrow Construction. *Journal of Archaeological Science* 30 (3): 343–50.

Brew, S. A., and B. B. Huckell. 1987. A Protohistoric Pima Burial and a Consideration of Pima Burial Practices. *Kiva* 52 (3): 163–91.

Briggs, C. S. 1997. A Neolithic and Early Bronze Age Settlement and Burial Complex at Llanilar, Ceredigion. *Archaeologia Cambrensis* 146:13–59.

Brinch Petersen, E., C. Christensen, P. Vang Petersen, and K. Aaris-Sørensen. 1976. Vedbæksprojektet: Udgravningerne i Vedbæk-området. *Sollerødbogen* 1976:97–122.

Brinch Petersen, E., and C. Meiklejohn. 2003. Three Cremations and a Funeral: Aspects of Burial Practice in Mesolithic Vedbæk. In *Mesolithic on the Move*, edited by L. Larsson, H. Kindgren, K. Knutsson, D. Loeffler, and A. Åkerlund, 485–93. Oxbow Books, Oxford, UK.

Brindley, A. L. 2007. *The Dating of Food Vessels and Urns in Ireland.* Bronze Age Studies 7. National University of Ireland, Galway.

Brindley, A. L., J. N. Lanting, and J. van der Plicht. 2005. Radiocarbon-Dated Samples from the Mound of the Hostages. In *Duma na nGiall: The Mound of the Hostages, Tara*, edited by M. O'Sullivan, 281–96. Wordwell, Dublin.

Brøndsted, J. 1939. *Danmarks Oldtid: Bronzealderen.* Nordisk, Copenhagen.

Brown, J. A. 1979. Charnel Houses and Mortuary Crypts: Disposal of the Dead in the Middle Woodland Period. In *Hopewell Archaeology: The Chillicothe Conference*, edited by D. S. Brose and N. Greber, 211–19. Kent State University Press, Kent, OH.

———. 1995. On Mortuary Analysis: With Special Reference to the Saxe-Binford Research Program. In *Regional Approaches to Mortuary Analysis*, edited by L. A. Beck, 3–26. Plenum Press, New York.

———. 2003. Collective Burial Practices Across the Agricultural Transition in the Eastern Woodlands. In *Stones and Bones: Formal Disposal of the Dead in Atlantic Europe During the Mesolithic-Neolithic Interface, 6000–3000 BC*, edited by G. Burenhult and S. Westergaard, 207–23. BAR International Series 1201. Archaeopress, Oxford, UK.

———. 2006. Where's the Power in Mound Building? An Eastern Woodlands Perspective. In *Leadership and Polity in Mississippian Society*, edited by B. M. Butler and P. D. Welch, 197–213. Occasional Paper no. 33. Center for Archaeological Investigations, Southern Illinois University, Carbondale.

———. 2010. Cosmological Layouts of Secondary Burials as Political Instruments. In *Mississippian Mortuary Practices*, edited by L. P. Sullivan and R. C. Mainfort, 30–53. University Press of Florida, Gainesville.

Brown, K. A., K. O'Donoghue, and T. A. Brown. 1995. DNA in Cremated Bones from an Early Bronze Age Cemetery Cairn. *International Journal of Osteoarchaeology* 5:181–87.

Brown, N. 1995. Prehistoric Pottery. In *A Late Bronze Age Enclosure at Broomfield, Chelmsford*, edited by M. Atkinson, 8–14. *Essex Archaeology and History* 26:1–24.

Brück, J. 1995. A Place for the Dead: The Role of Human Remains in Late Bronze Age Britain. *Proceedings of the Prehistoric Society* 61:245–77.

———. 2004. Material Metaphors: The Relational Construction of Identity in Early Bronze Age Burials in Ireland and Britain. *Journal of Social Archaeology* 4:7–33.

———. 2006a. Fragmentation, Personhood and the Social Construction of Technology in Middle and Late Bronze Age Britain. *Cambridge Archaeological Journal* 16 (2): 297–315.

———. 2006b. Death, Exchange and Reproduction in the British Bronze Age. *European Journal of Archaeology* 9 (1): 73–101.

Brugmann, B. 2011. Migration and Endogenous Change. In *The Oxford Handbook of Anglo-Saxon Archaeology*, edited by H. Hamerow, D. Hinton, and S. Crawford, 30–45. Oxford University Press, Oxford.

Buckley, L., C. Power, R. O'Sullivan, and H. Thakore. 2015. The Human Remains. In *Excavations at Knowth*, vol. 6, *The Archaeology of the Large Passage Tomb at Knowth, Co. Meath*, edited by G. Eogan and K. Cleary. Royal Irish Academy, Dublin.

Buikstra, J. E. 1977. Biocultural Dimensions of Archaeological Study: A Regional Perspective. In *Biocultural Adaptation in Prehistoric America*, edited by R. L. Blakely, 67–84. University of Georgia Press, Athens.

———. 1981. Mortuary Practices, Palaeodemography and Palaeopathology: A Case Study from the Koster Site (Illinois). In *The Archaeology of Death*, edited by R. Chapman, I. Kinnes, and K. Randsborg, 123–32. Cambridge University Press, Cambridge.

———. 1991. Out of the Appendix and into the Dirt: Comments on Thirteen Years of Bioarchaeological Research. In *What Mean These Bones?* edited by M. L. Powell, P. S. Bridges, and A. M. Wagner Mills, 172–220. University of Alabama Press, Tuscaloosa.

Buikstra, J. E., J. Bullington, D. K. Charles, D. C. Cook, S. R. Frankenburg, L. W. Konigsberg, J. B. Lambert, and L. Xue. 1987. Diet, Demography, and the Development of Horticulture. In *Emergent Horticultural Economies of the Eastern Woodlands*, edited by W. F. Keegan, 67–85. Occasional Papers no. 7. Center for Archaeological Investigations, Carbondale, IL.

Buikstra, J. E., and L. Goldstein. 1973. *The Perrins Ledge Crematory*. Illinois State Museum, Springfield.

Buikstra, J. E., J. C. Rose, and G. R. Milner. 1994. A Carbon Isotopic Perspective on Dietary Variation in Late Prehistoric Western Illinois. In *Agricultural*

Origins and Development in the Midcontinent, edited by W. Green, 155–70. Report no. 19. Office of the State Archaeologist, Iowa City, IA.

Buikstra, J. E., and M. Swegle. 1989. Bone Modification Due to Burning: Experimental Evidence. In *Bone Modification,* edited by R. Bonnichsen and M. H. Sorg, 247–58. Center for the Study of the First Americans, Orono, ME.

Buikstra, J. E., and D. Ubelaker. 1994. *Standards for Data Collection from Human Skeletal Remains: Proceedings of a Seminar at the Field Museum of Natural History Organized by Jonathan Haas.* Arkansas Archaeology Survey no. 44. Fayetteville.

Burgess, C. 1980. *The Age of Stonehenge.* J. M. Dent, London.

Burgess, C., and S. J. Shennan. 1976. The Beaker Phenomenon: Some Suggestions, 1: General Comments and the British Evidence, 2: Some Comments on the European Evidence. In *Settlement and Economy in the Third and Second Millennia BC,* edited by C. Burgess and R. Miket, 309–31. BAR British Series 33. British Archaeological Reports, Oxford.

Burke, H., C. Smith, D. Lippert, J. Watkins, and L. Zimmerman (editors). 2008. *Kennewick Man: Perspectives on the Ancient One.* Left Coast Press, Walnut Creek, CA.

Burrow, S. 2006. *The Tomb Builders in Wales, 4000–3000 BC.* National Museum of Wales, Cardiff.

Burström, M. 1999. Cultural Diversity in the Home Ground: How Archaeology Can Make the World a Better Place. *Current Swedish Archaeology* 7:21–26.

Burström, M., and J. Rönnby. 2006. *Arkeologi och Mångkultur: Rapport från Svenskt Arkeologmöte 2006.* Södertörn Archaeological Studies 4. Södertörn University, Flemingsberg, Sweden.

Carlin, N. 2011. A Proper Place for Everything: The Character and Context of Beaker Depositional Practice in Ireland. Unpublished Ph.D. thesis. University College Dublin, Dublin.

Carr, C. 2006. World View and the Dynamics of Change: The Beginning and the End of Scioto Hopewell Culture and Lifeways. In *The Scioto Hopewell and Their Neighbors,* edited by D. T. Case and C. Carr, 289–329. Springer, New York.

Carr, C., and D. T. Case. 2005. *Gathering Hopewell: Society, Ritual, and Ritual Interaction.* Kluwer Academic/Plenum, New York.

Carver, M., C. Hills, and J. Scheschkewitz. 2009. *Wasperton: A Roman, British and Anglo-Saxon Community in Central England.* Boydell, Woodbridge, UK.

Case, D. T., and C. Carr. 2008. *The Scioto Hopewell and Their Neighbors: Bioarchaeological Documentation and Cultural Understanding.* With contributions by C. A. Johnston, B. Goldstein, R. Weeks, M. Bahti, R. A. Zinser, and A. E. Evans. Springer, New York.

Case, H. 1969. Settlement Patterns in the North Irish Neolithic. *Ulster Journal of Archaeology* 32:3–27.

Cattaneo, C., S. DiMartino, S. Scali, O. E. Craig, M. Grandi, and R. J. Sokol. 1999. Determining the Human Origin of Fragments of Burnt Bone: A Comparative Study of Histological, Immunological and DNA Techniques. *Forensic Science International* 102 (2–3): 181–91.

Cauwe, N. 1998. Sépultures collectives du Mésolithique au Néolithique. In *Sépultures d'Occident et genèse des mégalithismes (9000–3000 avant notre ère)*, edited by J. Guilaine, 11–24. Éditions Errance, Paris.

————. 2001. Skeletons in Motion, Ancestors in Action: Early Mesolithic Collective Tombs in Southern Belgium. *Cambridge Archaeological Journal* 11:147–63.

Cerezo-Román, J. I. 2009. Fragmentation, Transformation, and Cremation Rituals Among the Hohokam of Southern Arizona. Paper presented at the Society for American Archaeology 74th Annual Meeting, Atlanta, GA.

————. 2010. Mortuary Practices and Personhood Among the Hohokam of Southern Arizona. Paper presented at the symposium "The Performance of Mortuary Ritual in the American Southwest" at the Society for American Archaeology 75th Annual Meeting, St. Louis, MO.

————. 2013. Unpacking Personhood and Identity in the Hohokam Area of Southern Arizona. Unpublished Ph.D. dissertation, University of Arizona.

Cerezo-Román, J. I., and J. McClelland. 2009. Mortuary Practices at Yuma Wash and the Hohokam Classic World. In *Archaeological Investigations at Five Sites West of the Santa Cruz River in Marana, Arizona*, vol. 1, edited by A. C. MacWilliams and A. Dart, 6.1–6.22. Old Pueblo Archaeology Center, Tucson, AZ.

Cerezo-Román, J. I., and H. D. Wallace. 2008. Mortuary Practices at Honey Bee Village. Paper presented at the symposium "Beyond Status, Meaning, Metaphor, and Identity in New World Mortuary Practices" at the Society for American Archaeology 73rd Annual Meeting, Vancouver, BC.

Chamberlain, A. 2000. Minor Concerns: A Demographic Perspective on Children in Past Societies. In *Children and Material Culture*, edited by J. Sofaer Derevenski, 206–12. Routledge, London.

Chapman, J. 2000a. *Fragmentation in Archaeology: People, Places and Broken Objects in the Prehistory of South-Eastern Europe*. Routledge, London.

————. 2000b. Tensions at Funerals: Social Practices and the Subversion of Community Structure in Later Hungarian Prehistory. In *Agency in Archaeology*, edited by M. A. Dobres and J. Robb, 169–95. Routledge, London.

Charles, D. K. 1992. Woodland Demographics and Social Dynamics in the American Midwest: Analysis of a Burial Mound Survey. *World Archaeology* 24:175–97.

Charles, D. K., and J. E. Buikstra. 1983. Archaic Mortuary Sites in the Central Mississippi Drainage: Distribution, Structure, and Behavioral Implications. In *Archaic Hunters and Gatherers in the American Midwest*, edited by J. L. Phillips and J. A. Brown, 117–46. Academic Press, New York.

————. 2002. Siting, Sighting, and Citing the Dead. In *The Space and Place of Death*, edited by H. Silverman and D. B. Small, 13–25. Archeological Papers of the American Anthropological Association no. 11. Fairfax, VA.

Charles, D. K., J. E. Buikstra, and L. W. Konigsberg. 1986. Behavioral Implications of Terminal Archaic and Early Woodland Mortuary Practices in the Lower Illinois River Valley. In *Early Woodland Archeology*, edited by K. B. Farnsworth and T. H. Emerson, 458–74. Center for American Archeology Press, Kampsville, IL.

Chesson, M. S. 1999. Libraries of the Dead: Early Bronze Age Charnel Houses and Social Identity at Urban Bab edh-Dhra', Jordan. *Journal of Anthropological Archaeology* 18:137–64.

———— (editor). 2001. *Social Memory, Identity, and Death: Anthropological Perspectives in Mortuary Rituals*. Papers of the American Anthropological Association no. 10. American Anthropological Association, Arlington, VA.

————. 2007. Remembering and Forgetting in Early Bronze Age Mortuary Practice on the Southeastern Dead Sea Plain, Jordan. In *Performing Death: Social Analyses of Funerary Traditions in the Ancient Near East and Mediterranean*, edited by N. Laneri, 109–40. Oriental Institute, University of Chicago, Chicago.

Citizens Information. 2013. Cremation. Electronic Document, http://www.citi zensinformation.ie/en/death/after_a_death/cremations.html. Accessed November 8, 2013.

Cleary, R. M. 1995. Later Bronze Age Settlement and Prehistoric Burials, Lough Gur, Co. Limerick. *Proceedings of the Royal Irish Academy* 95C:1–92.

Cody, E. 2002. *Survey of the Megalithic Tombs of Ireland*. Vol. 6, *County Donegal*. Stationery Office, Dublin.

Collins, A. E. P. 1976. Dooey's Cairn, Ballymacaldrick, Co. Antrim. *Ulster Journal of Archaeology* 39:1–7.

Collins, T., and F. Coyne. 2003. Fire and Water . . . Early Mesolithic Cremations at Castleconnell, Co. Limerick. *Archaeology Ireland* 64:24–27.

Colwell-Chanthaphonh, C., and T. J. Ferguson (editors). 2007. *Collaboration in Archaeological Practice: Engaging Descendant Communities*. AltaMira Press, Walnut Creek, CA.

Connerton, P. 2008. Seven Types of Forgetting. *Memory Studies* 1 (1): 59–71.

Content, S., and H. Williams. 2010. Creating the Pagan English. In *Signals of Belief in Early England: Anglo-Saxon Paganism Revisited*, edited by M. Carver, A. Sanmark, and S. Semple, 181–200. Oxbow Books, Oxford, UK.

Cook, D. C., and A. Palkovich. 2006. Appendix 13.1: Joe Gay Mound Group, Crematory A Excavations. In *Illinois Hopewell and Late Woodland Mounds: The Excavations of Gregory Perino, 1950–1975*, edited by K. B. Farnsworth and M. D. Wiant, 498–500. Illinois Transportation Archaeological Research Program, Urbana.

Cooney, G. 1992. Body Politics and Grave Messages: Irish Neolithic Mortuary Practices. In *Vessels for the Ancestors: Essays on the Neolithic of Britain and Ireland in Honour of Audrey Henshall*, edited by N. M. Sharples, A. Sheridan, and A. S. Henshall, 128–42. Edinburgh University Press, Edinburgh.

————. 2000. *Landscapes of Neolithic Ireland*. Routledge, London.

Cooney, G., A. Bayliss, F. Healy, A. Whittle, E. Danaher, C. Cagney, J. Mallory, J. Smyth, T. Kador, and M. O'Sullivan. 2011. Ireland. In *Gathering Time: Dating the Early Neolithic Enclosures of Southern Britain and Ireland*, edited by A. Whittle, F. Healy, and A. Bayliss, 562–669. Oxbow Books, Oxford, UK.

Cooney, G., and E. Grogan. 1994. *Irish Prehistory: A Social Perspective*. Wordwell, Dublin.

Cooper, K. H. 2011. The Life (Lives) and Times of Native Copper in Northwest North America. *World Archaeology* 43 (2): 252–70.

Corcoran, M., and G. Sevastopulo. 2015. The Provenance of the Stone Used in the Construction and Decoration of the Passage Tomb at Knowth. In *Excavations at Knowth*, vol. 6, *The Archaeology of the Large Passage Tomb at Knowth, Co. Meath*, edited by G. Eogan and K. Cleary. Royal Irish Academy, Dublin.

Correia, P. M. 1996. Fire Modification of Bone: A Review of the Literature. In *Forensic Taphonomy: The Postmortem Fate of Human Remains,* edited by W. D. Haglund and M. H. Sorg, 275–93. CRC Press, New York.

Craig, D. B.1989. *Archaeological Testing at Honey Bee Village (AZ: BB:9:88 ASM)*. Technical Report no. 89-6. Institute for American Research, Mesa, AZ.

Crane, H. R., and James B. Griffin. 1972. University of Michigan Radiocarbon Dates XV. *Radiocarbon* 14 (1): 195–222.

Cremation Society of Great Britain. 2013. International Cremation Statistics 2011. Electronic document, http://www.srgw.demon.co.uk/CremSoc5/Stats /Interntl/2011/StatsIF.html. Accessed November 8, 2013.

Crown, P. L., and S. K. Fish. 1996. Gender and Status in the Hohokam Pre-Classic to Classic Transition. *American Anthropologist* 98 (4): 803–17.

Crummy, N. 2007. Grave and Pyre Goods from the Cremation Burials. In C. Gibson, Minerva: An Early Anglo-Saxon Mixed-Rite Cemetery in Alwalton, Cambridgeshire, 261–74. In *Early Medieval Mortuary Practices*, edited by S. Semple and H. Williams, 238–95. Anglo-Saxon Studies in Archaeology and History 14. Oxbow Books, Oxford, UK.

Cullen, T. 1995. Mesolithic Mortuary Ritual at Franchti Cave, Greece. *Antiquity* 69:270–89.

Darvill, T. 1979. Court Cairns, Passage Graves and Social Change in Ireland. *Man* 14:311–27.

David, N., J. Sterner, and K. Gavua. 1988. Why Pots Are Decorated. *Current Anthropology* 29 (3): 365–89.

Davidsson, M. 2003. On the Anatomy of Megaliths: The Interrelation Between Physical Interment and Morphology in Irish Megalithic Tombs. In *Stones and Bones: Formal Disposal of the Dead in Atlantic Europe During the Mesolithic-Neolithic Interface, 6000–3000 BC*, edited by G. Burenhult and S. Westergaard, 235–41. BAR International Series 1201. British Archaeological Reports, Oxford.

Davies, D. J., and L. H. Mates (editors). 2005. *Encyclopedia of Cremation*. Ashgate, Farnham, UK.

Davis, C. G., and S. Nolen-Hoeksema. 2001. Loss and Meaning: How Do People Make Sense of Loss? *American Behavioral Scientist* 44 (5): 726–41.

Davis, E. H. 1921. *Early Cremation Ceremonies of the Luiseno and Diegueno Indians of Southern California*. Indian Notes and Monographs, vol. 7, no. 3. Museum of the American Indian, Heye Foundation, New York.

De Coppet, D. 1981. The Life-Giving Death. In *Mortality and Immortality: The Anthropology and Archaeology of Death*, edited by S. Humphreys and H. King, 175–204. Academic Press, London.

Dehaan, J. D. 2008. Fire and Bodies. In *The Analysis of Burned Human Remains*, edited by C. W. Schmidt and S. A. Symes, 1–13. Academic Press, London.

De Muldar, G., M. Van Strydonck, and M. Boudin. 2009. The Impact of Cremated Bone Dating on the Archaeological Chronology of the Low Countries. *Radiocarbon* 51:579–600.

de Valera, R., and S. Ó Nualláin. 1961. *Survey of the Megalithic Tombs of Ireland*. Vol. 1, *County Clare*. Stationery Office, Dublin.

Devlin, J. B., and N. P. Herrmann. 2008. Bone Color as an Interpretive Tool of the Depositional History of Archaeological Cremains. In *The Analysis of Burnt Human Remains*, edited by C. W. Schmidt and S. A. Symes, 109–28. Academic Press, London.

Diaz-Andreu, M., and T. Champion (editors). 1996. *Nationalism and Archaeology in Europe*. Westview Press, Boulder, CO.

Dickinson, T. 1993. An Anglo-Saxon "Cunning Woman" from Bidford-upon-Avon. In *In Search of Cult: Archaeological Investigations in Honour of Philip Rahtz*, edited by M. Carver, 45–54. Boydell, Woodbridge, UK.

Doelle, W. H., and H. D. Wallace. 1991. The Changing Role of the Tucson Basin in the Hohokam Regional System. In *Exploring the Hohokam: Prehistoric Desert Peoples of the American Southwest*, edited by G. J. Gumerman, 279–345. Amerind Foundation New World Studies Series. University of New Mexico Press, Albuquerque.

Douglas, M. 1966. *Purity and Danger: An Analysis of the Concepts of Pollution and Taboo*. Routledge, New York.

———. 1973. *Natural Symbols: Explorations in Cosmology*. Barrie and Jenkins, London.

Dowd, M. 2002. Kilgreany, Co. Waterford: Biography of a Cave. *Journal of Irish Archaeology* 11:77–97.

———. 2008. The Use of Caves for Funerary and Ritual Practices in Neolithic Ireland. *Antiquity* 82:305–17.

Down, A., and M. Welch. 1990. *Chichester Excavations VII.* Chichester District Council, Chichester, UK.

Downes, J. 1999. Cremation: A Spectacle and a Journey. In *The Loved Body's Corruption: Archaeological Contributions to the Study of Human Mortality*, edited by J. Downes and T. Pollard, 19–29. Cruithne Press, Glasgow.

Dubois, C. G. 1907. Diegueño Mortuary Ollas. *American Anthropologist*, n.s., 9 (3): 484–86.

Ducrocq, T. 1999. Le Mésolithique de la Somme (Nord-de-France). In *L'Europe des derniers chasseurs Épipaléolithique et Mésolithique: Peuplement et Paléoenvironment de l'Épipaléolithique et du Mésolithique*, edited by A. Thévenin and P. Bintz, 247–62. Documents Préhistoriques 12. Comité des Travaux Historiques et Scientifiques, Paris.

Duffy, P. R. J., and G. MacGregor. 2008. Cremations, Conjecture and Contextual Taphonomies: Material Strategies During the 4th to the 2nd Millennia in Scotland. In *The Materiality of Death: Bodies, Burials, Beliefs*, edited by F. Fahlander and T. Oestigaard, 71–77. BAR International Series 17687. British Archaeological Reports, Oxford.

Duncan, W. N., A. K. Balkansky, K. Crawford, H. A. Lapham, and N. J. Meissner. 2008. Human Cremation in Mexico 3,000 Years Ago. *Proceedings of the National Academy of Sciences* 105 (14): 5315–5320.

Durivage, J. E. 1937. Through Mexico to California: Letters and Journal of John E. Durivage. In *Southern Trails to California in 1849*, edited by R. P. Bieber, 159–258. Southwest Historical Series no. 5. Arthur H. Clark, Glendale, CA.

Earle, T. 2002. *Bronze Age Economics: The Beginnings of Political Economies.* Westview Press, Boulder, CO.

Eickhoff, M. 2005. German Archaeology and National Socialism: Some Historiographical Remarks. *Archaeological Dialogues* 12 (1): 73–90.

Ellison, A. 1972. The Bronze Age Pottery. In *A Bronze Age Cemetery-Barrow on Itford Hill, Beddingham*, edited by E. W. Holden, 104–13. Sussex Archaeological Collections 110. Sussex Archaeological Society, Lewes, UK.

———. 1980. Deverel-Rimbury Urn Cemeteries: The Evidence for Social Organisation. In *Settlement and Society in the British Later Bronze Age*, edited by J. C. Barrett and R. J. Bradley, 115–26. BAR British Series 83. British Archaeological Reports, Oxford.

Engelke, M. 2007. Clarity and Charisma: On the Uses of Ambiguity in Ritual Life. In *The Limits of Meaning: Case Studies in the Anthropology of Christianity*, edited by M. Engelke and M. Tomlinson, 63–83. Berghahn Books, Oxford, UK.

Ennis, T. 2009. *An Early Saxon Cemetery at Rayleigh, Essex.* East Anglian Archaeology 127. Essex County Council, Chelmsford, UK.

Eogan, G. 1984. *Excavations at Knowth, 1.* Royal Irish Academy, Dublin.

————. 1986. *Knowth and the Passage Tombs of Ireland.* Thames and Hudson, London.

Eogan, G., and K. Cleary (editors). 2015. *Excavations at Knowth,* vol. 6, *The Archaeology of the Large Passage Tomb at Knowth, Co. Meath.* Royal Irish Academy, Dublin.

Eogan, G., and H. Roche. 1997. *Excavations at Knowth,* vol. 2, *Settlement and Ritual Sites of the Fourth and Third Millennia BC.* Royal Irish Academy, Dublin.

Evans, E. E. 1938. Doey's Cairn, Dunloy, County Antrim. *Ulster Journal of Archaeology* 1:59–78.

Evison, V. 1994a. *An Anglo-Saxon Cemetery at Great Chesterford, Essex.* Council for British Archaeology Research Report 91. Council for British Archaeology, London.

————. 1994b. Anglo-Saxon Glass from Cremations. In *The Anglo-Saxon Cemetery at Spong Hill, North Elmham,* part 5, *Catalogue of Cremations,* edited by C. Hills, K. Penn, and R. Rickett, 23–30. East Anglian Archaeology 67. Norfolk Archaeological Unit, Dereham, UK.

Ezell, P. H. 1961. *The Hispanic Acculturation of the Gila River Pimas.* American Anthropological Association Memoir 90. American Anthropological Association, Menasha, WI.

————. 1963. Is There a Hohokam-Pima Cultural Continuum? *American Antiquity* 29 (1): 61–66.

Ezzo, J. (editor). 2005. *Ballcourt on the Bajada: Data Recovery at Sleeping Snake Village (AZ BB:9:104 [ASM]) and Los Venados (AZ BB:9:186 [ASM]), Oro Valley, Arizona.* SWCA Environmental Consultants, Tucson, AZ.

————. 2008. *Archaeological Data Recovery at Fagan Ranch, Corona de Tucson, Pima County, Arizona.* SWCA Environmental Consultants, Tucson, AZ.

Fahlander, F. 2008. Subadult or Subaltern? Children as Serial Categories. In *(Re) Thinking the Little Ancestor: New Perspectives on the Archaeology of Infancy and Childhood,* edited by M. Lally, 14–23. BAR International Series 2271. Archaeopress, Oxford, UK.

Fahlander, F., and T. Oestigaard. 2008a. The Materiality of Death: Bodies, Burials and Beliefs. In *The Materiality of Death: Bodies, Burials and Beliefs,* edited by F. Fahlander and T. Oestigaard, 1–16. BAR International Series 1768. Archaeopress, Oxford, UK.

———— (editors). 2008b. *The Materiality of Death: Bodies, Burials and Beliefs.* BAR International Series 1768. Archaeopress, Oxford, UK.

Fairgrieve, S. L. 2008. *Forensic Cremation: Recovery and Analysis.* CRC Press Taylor and Francis Group, Boca Raton, FL.

Farnsworth, K. B., and T. E. Emerson (editors). 1986. *Early Woodland Archeology.* Kampsville Seminars in Archeology no. 2. Center for American Archaeology, Kampsville, IL.

Farnsworth, K. B., and M. D. Wiant (editors). 2006. *Illinois Hopewell and Late Woodland Mounds: The Excavations of Gregory Perino, 1950–1975.* Illinois Transportation Archaeological Research Program, Urbana.

Fengming, L. 2005. China. In *The Encyclopedia of Cremation*, edited by D. J. Davies and L. H. Mates, 120–21. Ashgate, Aldershot, UK.

Fern, C. 2007. Early Anglo-Saxon Horse Burial of the Fifth to Seventh Centuries AD. In *Early Medieval Mortuary Practices*, edited by S. Semple and H. Williams, 92–109. Anglo-Saxon Studies in Archaeology and History 14. Oxford University School of Archaeology, Oxford.

Feveile, C., and P. Bennike. 2002. Lustrupholm—Et brandgravsfelt fra ældre bronzealder under flad mark. *Kuml* 2002:109–41.

Filmer-Sankey, W., and T. Pestell. 2001. *Snape Anglo-Saxon Cemetery: Excavations and Surveys, 1824–1992.* East Anglian Archaeology 95. Suffolk County Council, Bury St. Edmunds, UK.

Fine Dare, K. S. 2002. *Grave Injustice: The American Indian Repatriation Movement and NAGPRA.* University of Nebraska Press, Lincoln.

Fink, M. T. 1989. The Cremated Human Remains from Los Morteros. In *The 1979–1983 Testing at Los Morteros (AZ AA:12:57 ASM), A Large Hohokam Village Site in the Tucson Basin*, edited by R. C. Lange and W. L. Deaver, 277–84. Archaeological Series 177. Archaeology Section Research Division, Arizona State Museum, University of Arizona, Tucson.

Finlayson, B., and G. M. Warren. 2010. *Changing Natures: Hunter-Gatherers, First Farmers and the Modern World.* Duckworth, London.

Fish, P. R., and S. K. Fish. 1991. Hohokam Political and Social Organization. In *Exploring the Hohokam: Prehistoric Desert Peoples of the American Southwest*, edited by G. J. Gumerman, 151–75. Amerind Foundation New World Studies Series. University of New Mexico Press, Albuquerque.

———. 2006. Reorganization and Realignment: The Classic Period in the Tucson Basin. In *Hohokam Trajectories in Worldwide Perspective*, edited by P. R. Fish and S. K. Fish. Amerind Studies in Archaeology. University of Arizona Press, Tucson.

Fish, P. R., and S. K. Fish (editors). 2007. *The Hohokam Millennium.* School for Advanced Research Press, Santa Fe, NM.

Fish, S. K. 1996. Dynamics of Scale in the Southern Deserts. In *Interpreting Southwestern Diversity: Underlying Principles and Overarching Patterns*, edited by P. R. Fish, J. J. Reid, D. R. Abbott, and T. R. Roseck, 107–14. Anthropological Research Papers vol. 48. Department of Anthropology, Arizona State University, Tempe.

Fitzpatrick, A. 1997. *Archaeological Excavations on the Route of the A27 Westhampnett Bypass, West Sussex, 1992*. Wessex Archaeology Report no. 12. Wessex Archaeology, Salisbury, UK.

———. 2011. *The Amesbury Archer and the Boscombe Bowmen: Early Bell Beaker Burials at Boscombe Down, Amesbury, Wiltshire, Great Britain*. Vol. 1, *Excavations at Boscombe Down*. Wessex Archaeology, Salisbury, UK.

Fornander, E. 2011. *Consuming and Communicating Identities: Dietary Diversity and Interaction in Middle Neolithic Sweden*. Theses and Papers in Scientific Archaeology 12. Stockholm University, Stockholm.

Forty, A. 1999. Introduction to *The Art of Forgetting*, edited by A. Forty and S. Küchler, 1–18. Berg, Oxford, UK.

Foucault, M. 1977. *Discipline and Punish*. Vantage, New York.

Fowler, C. 2004. *The Archaeology of Personhood: An Anthropological Approach*. Themes in Archaeology. Routledge, London.

———. 2005. Identity Politics: Personhood, Kinship, Gender and Power in Neolithic and Early Bronze Age Britain. In *The Archaeology of Plural and Changing Identities: Beyond Identification*, edited by E. C. Casella and C. Fowler, 109–34. Kluwer Academic and Plenum, New York.

———. 2010. From Identity and Material Culture to Personhood and Materiality. In *The Oxford Handbook of Material Culture Studies*, edited by D. Hicks and M. D. Beaudry, 352–85. Oxford University Press, Oxford.

Freeman, J. E. 1966. Price Site III, RI 4, a Burial Ground in Richland County, Wisconsin. *Wisconsin Archeologist* 47:33–75.

Friedli, H., H. Lotscher, H. Oeschger, U. Siegenthaler, and B. Stauffer. 1986. Ice Core Record of the $^{13}C/^{12}C$ Ratio of Atmospheric CO_2 in the Past Two Centuries. *Nature* 324:237–38.

Fry, S. L. 1999. *Burial in Medieval Ireland, 900–1500: A Review of the Written Sources*. Four Courts Press, Dublin.

Gansum, T. 2004a. Role the Bones: From Iron to Steel. *Norwegian Archaeological Review* 37 (1): 41–57.

———. 2004b. Jernets fødles og dødens stål: Rituell bruk av bein. In *Minne och myt—konsten att skapa det förflutna*, edited by Å. Berggren, S. Arvidsson, and A.-M. Hållans, 121–55. Nordic Academic Press, Lund, Sweden.

Gathercole, P., and D. Lowenthal (editors). 1990. *The Politics of the Past*. Unwin Hyman, London.

Gejvall, N.-G. 1969. Cremations. In *Science in Archaeology*, edited by D. Brothwell and E. Higgs, 468–79. 2nd ed. Thames and Hudson, London.

Gell, A. 1998. *Art and Agency: An Anthropological Theory*. Clarendon Press, Oxford, UK.

Gero, J. 2000. Troubled Travels in Agency and Feminism. In *Agency and Archaeology*, edited by M. A. Dobres and J. Robb, 34–39. Routledge, London.

Gibson, A. 2004. Burials and Beakers: Seeing Beneath the Veneer in Late Neolithic Britain. In *Similar but Different: Bell Beakers in Europe*, edited by J. Czebrezuk, 173–92. Adam Mickiewicz University, Poznan, Poland.

Gibson, C. 2007. Minerva: An Early Anglo-Saxon Mixed-Rite Cemetery in Alwalton, Cambridgeshire. In *Early Medieval Mortuary Practices*, edited by S. Semple and H. Williams, 238–95. Anglo-Saxon Studies in Archaeology and History 14. Oxbow Books, Oxford, UK.

Gillespie, S. D. 2001. Personhood, Agency, and Mortuary Ritual: A Case Study from the Ancient Maya. *Journal of Anthropological Archaeology* 20:73–112.

———. 2002. Body and Soul Among the Maya: Keeping the Spirit in Place. In *The Space and Place of Death*, edited by H. Silverman and D. B. Small, 67–78. Archaeological Papers of the American Anthropological Association no. 11. American Anthropological Association, Arlington, VA.

———. 2011. Inside and Outside: Residential Burial at Formative Period Chalcatzingo, Mexico. In *Residential Burial: A Multiregional Exploration*, edited by R. L. Adams and S. M. King, 98–120. Archaeological Papers of the American Anthropological Association no. 20. American Anthropological Association, Hoboken, NJ.

Giraud, J. P. 1990. La fouille d'urnes funéraires: La nécropole à incenérations de Gourjade à Castres (Tarn). *Société d'Anthropologie de Paris* 20 (3–4): 75–76.

Glob, P. V. 1970. *Højfolket—Bronzealderens Mennesker bevaret i 3000 År*. Gyldendal, Copenhagen.

Goldhahn, J. 2012. On War and Memory and the Memory of War: The Middle Bronze Age Burial from Hvidegården on Zealand in Denmark Revisited. In *N-TAG Ten: Proceedings of the 10th Nordic TAG conference at Stiklestad, Norway, 2009*, edited by R. Berge, M. E. Jasinski, and K. Sognnes, 237–50. BAR International Series 2399. British Archaeological Reports, Oxford.

Goldhahn, J., and T. Oestigaard. 2008. Smith and Death: Cremations in Furnaces in Bronze and Iron Age Scandinavia. In *Facets of Archaeology: Essays in Honour of Lotte Hedeager on Her 60th Birthday*, edited by K. Chilidis, J. Lund, and C. Prescott, 215–42. OAS 10. Oslo Academic Press, Oslo.

Goldstein, L. G. 1980. *Mississippian Mortuary Practices: A Case Study of Two Cemeteries in the Lower Illinois Valley*. Northwestern University Archaeology Program Scientific Papers no. 4. Northwestern University, Evanston, IL.

———. 1981. One-Dimensional Archaeology and Multi-dimensional People: Spatial Organization and Mortuary Analysis. In *The Archaeology of Death*, edited by R. Chapman, I. Kinnes, and K. Randsborg, 53–69. Cambridge University Press, Cambridge.

———. 1995. Landscapes and Mortuary Practices: A Case for Regional Perspectives. In *Regional Approaches to Mortuary Analysis*, edited by L. A. Beck, 101–21. Plenum Press, New York.

————. 2001. Ancient Southwest Mortuary Practices: Perspectives from Outside the Southwest. In *Ancient Burial Practices in the American Southwest: Archaeology, Physical Anthropology, and Native American Perspectives*, edited by D. R. Mitchell and J. L. Brunson-Hadley, 249–56. University of New Mexico Press, Albuquerque.

————. 2010. Aztalan Mortuary Practices Revisited. In *Mississippian Mortuary Practices: Beyond Hierarchy and the Representationist Perspective*, edited by L. P. Sullivan and R. Mainfort, 90–112. University Press of Florida, Gainesville.

Gonçalves, D., T. J. U. Thompson, and E. Cunha. 2011. Implications of Heat-Induced Changes in Bone on the Interpretation of Funerary Behaviour and Practice. *Journal of Archaeological Science* 38:1308–13.

Gosden, C. 2011. Anthropology and Archaeology. In *The Oxford Handbook of Anglo-Saxon Archaeology*, edited by H. Hamerow, D. Hinton, and S. Crawford, 1003–21. Oxford University Press, Oxford.

Gosden, C., and Y. Marshall. 1999. The Cultural Biography of Objects. *World Archaeology* 31 (2): 169–78.

Götherström, A., N. Stenbäck, and J. Storå. 2002. The Jettböle Middle Neolithic Site on the Åland Islands: Human Remains, Ancient DNA and Pottery. *European Journal of Archaeology* 5:42–68.

Gramsch, A. 2007. A Microarchaeological Approach to the Social Significance of Late Bronze Age Burial Practices: Age and Gender at the Lusatian Urnfield of Cottbus Alvensleben-Kaserne (Germany). In *Encounters, Materialities, Confrontations: Archaeologies of Social Space and Interaction*, edited by P. Cornell and F. Fahlander, 83–99. Cambridge Scholars Press, Newcastle, UK.

————. 2013. Transformative and Communicative Practices. In *The Oxford University Press Handbook of the Archaeology of Death and Burial*, edited by L. Nilsson Stutz and S. Tarlow, 459–74. Oxford University Press, Oxford.

Gray Jones, A. 2010. The "Loose Human Bone" Phenomenon: Complexity in Mesolithic Mortuary Practice. Paper presented at the Mesolithic in Europe conference, Santander, Spain, September 2010.

————. 2011. Dealing with the Dead: Manipulation of the Body in the Mortuary Practices of Mesolithic North West Europe. Unpublished Ph.D. dissertation, University of Manchester, Manchester.

Green, B., and A. Rogerson. 1978. *The Anglo-Saxon Cemetery at Bergh Apton, Norfolk: Catalogue*. East Anglian Archaeology 7. Norfolk Archaeological Unit, Dereham, UK.

Green, B., A. Rogerson, and S. G. White. 1987. *The Anglo-Saxon Cemetery at Morning Thorpe, Norfolk*. East Anglian Archaeology 36. Norfolk Archaeological Unit, Dereham, UK.

Green, W., and D. J. Nolan. 2000. Late Woodland Peoples in West-Central Illinois. In *Late Woodland Societies: Tradition and Transformation Across the Midcontinent,* edited by T. E. Emerson, D. L. McElrath, and A. C. Fortier, 345–86. University of Nebraska Press, Lincoln.

Greenleaf, J. C. 1975. *Excavations at Punta de Agua in the Santa Cruz River Basin, Southeastern Arizona.* Anthropological Paper 26. University of Arizona Press, Tucson.

Greenlee, D. M. 1990. Environmental and Temporal Variability in $\delta^{13}C$ values in Late Prehistoric Subsistence Systems in the Upper Ohio Valley. Unpublished Ph.D. dissertation, University of Washington, Seattle.

Greenwell, W. 1877. *British Barrows: A Record of the Examination of Sepulchral Mounds in Various Parts of England.* Clarendon Press, Oxford, UK.

Gregory, C. 1982. *Gifts and Commodities.* Academic Press, London.

Grévin, G. 1990. La fouille en laboratoire des sepultures à incineration: Son apport à l'archéologie. In *Anthropologie et archéologie: Dialogue sur les ensembles funéraires,* edited by E. Crubézy, H. Duday, P. Sellier, and A.-M. Tillier, 67–74. Bulletins et Mémoires de la Société d'Anthropologie de Paris, vol. 2, nos. 3–4. Paris.

Grogan, E., and G. Eogan. 1987. Lough Gur Excavations by Séan P. Ó Ríordáin: Further Neolithic and Beaker Habitations on Knockadoon. *Proceedings of the Royal Irish Academy* 87C:299–506.

Gumbrecht, H. U. 2004. *Production of Presence: What Meaning Cannot Convey.* Stanford University Press, Stanford.

Haas, J. R. 1996. Human Skeletal Remains from Two Red Ocher Mortuary Contexts in Southeastern Wisconsin. *Wisconsin Archeologist* 77 (1): 63–72.

Haith, C. 1997. Pottery in Early Anglo-Saxon England. In *Pottery in the Making: World Ceramic Traditions,* edited by I. Freestone and D. Gaimister, 146–51. British Museum, London.

Håkansson, T. N. 1998. Rulers and Rainmakers in Precolonial South Pare, Tanzania: Exchange and Ritual Experts in Political Centralization. *Ethnology* 37 (3): 263–83.

Hall, R. L. 1979. In Search of the Ideology of the Adena-Hopewell Climax. In *Hopewell Archaeology: The Chillicothe Conference,* edited by D. S. Brose and N. Greber, 258–65. Kent State University Press, Kent, OH.

Hallam, E., and J. Hockey. 2001. *Death, Memory and Material Culture.* Berg, Oxford, UK.

Hallam, E., J. Hockey, and G. Howarth. 1999. *Beyond the Body: Death and Social Identity.* Routledge, London.

Halle, U. 2005. Archaeology in the Third Reich: Academic Scholarship and the Rise of the "Lunatic Fringe." *Archaeological Dialogues* 12 (1): 91–102.

Hallgren, F. 2008. *Identitet i praktik: Lokala, regionala och överregionala sociala sammanhang inom nordlig trattbägarkultur.* Coast to Coast Books no. 17.

Uppsala University, Department of Archaeology and Ancient History, Uppsala.

Hamerow, H. 1993. *Excavations at Mucking.* Vol. 2, *The Anglo-Saxon Settlement.* English Heritage, London.

Hamerow, H., S. Crawford, and D. Hinton (editors). 2011. *The Oxford Handbook of Anglo-Saxon Archaeology.* Oxford University Press, Oxford.

Hanlon, C. J. 1972. Papago Funeral Customs. *Kiva* 37 (2): 104–13.

Hanson, M., and C. R. Cain. 2007. Examining Histology to Identify Burned Bone. *Journal of Archaeological Science* 34:1902–13.

Harbeck, M., R. Schleuder, J. Schneider, I. Wiechmann, W. W. Schmahl, and G. Grupe. 2011. Research Potential and Limitations of Trace Element Analyses of Cremated Human Remains. *Forensic Science International* 204 (1–3): 191–200.

Härke, Heinrich. 2011. Anglo-Saxon Immigration and Ethnogenesis. *Medieval Archaeology* 55:1–28.

Harris, O. J. T. 2010. Emotional and Mnemonic Geographies at Hambledon Hill: Texturing Neolithic Places with Bodies and Bones. *Cambridge Archaeological Journal* 20 (3): 357–71.

Hartnett, P. J. 1951. A Neolithic Burial from Martinstown, Kiltale, Co. Meath. *Journal of the Royal Society of Antiquaries of Ireland* 81:19–23.

———. 1957. Excavation of a Passage Tomb at Fourknocks, Co. Meath. *Proceedings of the Royal Irish Academy* 58C:197–277.

———. 1971. The Excavation of Two Tumuli at Fourknocks (Sites II and III), Co. Meath. *Proceedings of the Royal Irish Academy* 71C:35–89.

Harvig, L., and N. Lynnerup. 2013. On the Volume of Cremated Remains—A Comparative Study of Archaeologically Recovered Cremated Bone Volume as Measured Manually and Assessed by Computed Tomography and Stereology. *Journal of Archaeological Science* 40:2713–22.

Harvig, L., N. Lynnerup, and J. Amsgaard Ebsen. 2011. Computed Tomography and Computed Radiography of Late Bronze Age Urns from Denmark: An Interdisciplinary Attempt to Develop Methods Applied to Bioarchaeological Cremation Research. *Archaeometry* 54 (2): 369–87.

Hatch, M. A. 2012. Meaning and the Bioarchaeology of Captivity, Sacrifice and Cannibalism. In *The Bioarchaeology of Violence*, edited by D. L. Martin, R. P. Harrod, and V. R. Perez, 201–25. University Press of Florida, Gainesville.

Hawkes, J. 1997. Symbolic Lives: The Visual Evidence. In *The Anglo-Saxons from the Migration Period to the Eighth Century*, edited by J. Hines, 311–44. Boydell, Woodbridge, UK.

Hawkes, S. C., and G. Grainger. 2003. *The Anglo-Saxon Cemetery at Worthy Park, Kingsworthy, near Winchester, Hampshire.* Oxford University School of Archaeology Monograph no. 59. Oxford University School of Archaeology, Oxford.

Hawley, F. G. 1947. The Use of Lead Mineral by the Hohokam in Cremation Ceremonials. *Southwestern Journal of Anthropology* 3 (1): 69–77.

Heckenberger, M. 2005. *Ecology of Power: Culture, Place and Personhood in the Southern Amazon, AD 1000–2000*. Routledge, London.

Hedeager, L. 1999. Myth and Art: A Passport to Political Authority in Scandinavia During the Migration Period. In *The Making of Kingdoms*, edited by T. Dickinson and D. Griffiths, 151–56. Anglo-Saxon Studies in Archaeology and History 10. Oxford University School of Archaeology, Oxford.

Helms, M. W. 1998. *Access to Origins: Affines, Ancestors and Aristocrats*. University of Texas Press, Austin.

Hens, S. M., and K. Godde. 2008. Skeletal Biology Past and Present: Are We Moving in the Right Direction? *American Journal of Physical Anthropology* 137 (2): 234–39.

Herbst, C. F. 1848. Hvidegaards Fundet. *Aarbøger for Nordisk Oldkyndighed* 1848:336–52.

Herity, M. 1974. *Irish Passage Graves*. Irish University Press, Dublin.

———. 1987. The Finds from Irish Court Tombs. *Proceedings of the Royal Irish Academy* 87C:103–281.

Herrmann, N. P., and J. L. Bennett. 1999. The Differentiation of Traumatic and Heat-Related Fractures in Burned Bone. *Journal of Forensic Science* 44 (3): 461–69.

Hertz, R. 1960 [1907]. *Death and the Right Hand: A Contribution to the Study of the Collective Representation of Death*. Free Press, Glencoe, IL; Cohen and West, London.

Hewitt, A. 2005. *Social Choreography: Ideology as Performance in Dance and Everyday Movement*. Duke University Press, Durham, NC.

Higham, N., and M. Ryan. 2013. *The Anglo-Saxon World*. Yale University Press, New Haven, CT.

Hills, C. 1977. *The Anglo-Saxon Cemetery at Spong Hill, North Elmham*. Part 1, *Catalogue of Cremations*. East Anglian Archaeology 6. Norfolk Museums Service, Dereham, UK.

———. 1980. Anglo-Saxon Cremation Cemeteries, with Particular Reference to Spong Hill, Norfolk. In *Anglo-Saxon Cemeteries 1979*, edited by P. Rahtz, T. Dickinson, and L. Watt, 197–208. BAR British Series 82. British Archaeological Reports, Oxford.

———. 1993. Who Were the East Anglians? In *Flatlands and Wetlands: Current Themes in East Anglian Archaeology*, edited by J. Gardiner, 14–23. East Anglian Archaeology 50. Norfolk Archaeology Unit, Dereham, UK.

———. 1994. The Chronology of the Anglo-Saxon Cemetery at Spong Hill, Norfolk. In *Prehistoric Graves as a Source of Information*, edited by B. Stjernquist, 41–49. Vitterhets Historie och Antikvitets Akademien, Konferenser 29. Almqvist and Wiksell, Stockholm.

————. 1998. Did the People of Spong Hill Come from Schleswig-Holstein? In *Studien zur Sachsenforchung 11*, edited by H.-J. Häßler, 145–54. Isensee, Oldenburg, Germany.

————. 1999. Spong Hill and the Adventus Saxonum. In *Spaces of the Living and the Dead: An Archaeological Dialogue*, edited by C. E. Karkov, K. M. Wickham-Crowley, and B. K. Young, 15–26. American Early Medieval Studies 3. Oxbow Books, Oxford, UK.

————. 2003. *The Origins of the English*. Duckworth, London.

Hills, C., and K. Penn. 1981. *The Anglo-Saxon Cemetery at Spong Hill, North Elmham*. Part 2, *Catalogue of Cremations*. East Anglian Archaeology 11. Norfolk Archaeological Unit, Dereham, UK.

Hills, C., K. Penn, and R. Rickett. 1984. *The Anglo-Saxon Cemetery at Spong Hill, North Elmham*. Part 3, *Catalogue of Inhumations*. East Anglian Archaeology 21. Norfolk Archaeological Unit, Dereham, UK.

————. 1987. *The Anglo-Saxon Cemetery at Spong Hill, North Elmham*. Part 4, *Catalogue of Cremations*. East Anglian Archaeology 34. Norfolk Archaeological Unit, Dereham, UK.

————. 1994. *The Anglo-Saxon Cemetery at Spong Hill, North Elmham*. Part 5, *Catalogue of Cremations*. East Anglian Archaeology 67. Norfolk Archaeological Unit, Dereham, UK.

Hines, J. 2011. Literary Sources and Archaeology. In *The Oxford Handbook of Anglo-Saxon Archaeology*, edited by H. Hamerow, D. Hinton, and S. Crawford, 968–85. Oxford University Press, Oxford.

Hingley, R. 1997. Iron, Ironworking and Regeneration: A Study of the Symbolic Meaning of Metalworking in Iron Age Britain. In *Reconstructing Iron Age Societies: New Approaches to the British Iron Age*, edited by A. Gwilt and C. Haselgrove, 9–18. Oxbow Books, Oxford, UK.

Hirst, S., and D. Clark. 2009. *Excavations at Mucking*. Vol. 3, *The Anglo-Saxon Cemeteries*. English Heritage, London.

Hobart, A., U. Ramseyer, and A. Leemann. 1996. *The People of Bali*. Blackwell, Oxford, UK.

Hockey, J., L. Kellaher, and D. Prendergast. 2007. Of Grief and Well-Being: Competing Conceptions of Restorative Ritualization. *Anthropology and Medicine* 14 (1): 1–14.

Hodder, I., and C. Cessford. 2004. Daily Practice and Social Memory at Çatalhöyük. *American Antiquity* 69:17–40.

Holck, P. 1987. *Cremated Bones: A Medical-Anthropological Study of an Archaeological Material on Cremation Burials*. Anthropologiske Skrifter no. 1. Anatomisk Institutt, University of Oslo, Oslo.

Holden, J. L., P. P. Phakey, and J. G. Clement. 1995a. Scanning Electron Microscope Observations of Incinerated Human Femoral Bone: A Case Study. *Forensic Science International* 74:17–28.

————. 1995b. Scanning Electron Microscope Observations of Heat-Treated Human Bone. *Forensic Science International* 74:29–45.

Holst, M. K., H. Breuning-Madsen, and M. Rasmussen. 2001. The South Scandinavian Barrows with Well-Preserved Oak-Log Coffins. *Antiquity* 75 (287): 126–37.

Holst, M. K., and M. Rasmussen. 2012. Combined Efforts: The Cooperation and Coordination of Barrow-Building in the Bronze Age. In *Excavating the Mind: Cross-Sections Through Culture, Cognition and Materiality*, edited by N. Johannsen, M. Jessen, and H. J. Jensen, 255–79. Aarhus University Press, Aarhus.

Holst, M. K., and M. Rasmussen (editors). 2013. *Skelhøj and the Bronze Age Barrows of Southern Scandinavia*. Vol. 1, *The Bronze Age Barrow Tradition and the Excavation of Skelhøj*. Jutland Archaeological Society, Højbjerg.

Holst, M. K., M. Rasmussen, and H. Breuning-Madsen. 2004. Skelhøj: Et bygningsværk fra den ældre bronzealder. *Nationalmuseets Arbejdsmark* 2004:11–23.

————. 2008. Cirkler, sfærer, hjulkors og høje. *By, Marsk og Geest* 20:5–14.

Holtorf, C. 2009. A European Perspective on Indigenous and Immigrant Archaeologies. *World Archaeology* 41 (4): 672–81.

Hoskins, J. 1989. *Biographical Objects: How Things Tell the Stories of People's Lives*. Routledge, London.

Howarth, G. 2007. The Rebirth of Death: Continuing Relationships with the Dead. In *Remember Me: Constructing Immortality—Beliefs on Immortality, Life, and Death*, edited by M. Mitchell, 19–34. Routledge, London.

Howell, T. L. 1994. Leadership at the Ancestral Zuni Village of Hawikku. Unpublished Ph.D. dissertation, Arizona State University, Tempe.

Hummel, S., and H. Schutkowski. 1986. Das Verhalten von Knochengewebe unter dem Einfluß höherer Temperaturen. *Zeitschrift für Morphologie und Anthropologie* 77 (1): 1–9.

Huntington, F. W. (editor). 1986. *Archaeological Investigations at the West Branch Site Early and Middle Rincon Occupation in the Southern Tucson Basin*, Anthropological Paper 5. Institute for American Research, Tucson.

Huntington, R., and P. Metcalf. 1979. *Celebrations of Death: The Anthropology of Mortuary Ritual*. Cambridge University Press, Cambridge.

Hurley, W. M. 1975. *An Analysis of Effigy Mound Complexes in Wisconsin*. Anthropological Papers no. 59. Museum of Anthropology, University of Michigan, Ann Arbor.

Ingold, T. 2000. *The Perception of the Environment*. Routledge, London.

Jacobs, K. 1995. Returning to Oleni'ostrov: Social, Economic, and Skeletal Dimensions of a Boreal Forest Mesolithic Cemetery. *Journal of Anthropological Anthropology* 14:359–403.

Jervis, B. 2011. Placing Pots: An Actor-Led Approach to the Use and Perceptions of Pottery in Medieval Southampton and Its Region (AD 700–1400). Unpublished Ph.D. dissertation, University of Southampton, Southampton.

Jill, J. H. 2001. Proto-Uto-Aztecan: A Community of Cultivators in Central Mexico? *American Anthropologist* 103 (4): 913–34.

Jockenhövel, A. 1991. Räumliche Mobilität von Personen in der mittleren Bronzezeit des westlichen Mitteleuropa. *Germania* 69:49–62.

Johansen, K. L., S. T. Laursen, and M. K. Holst. 2004. Spatial Patterns of Social Organization in the Early Bronze Age of South Scandinavia. *Journal of Anthropological Archaeology* 23:33–55.

Johnston, R. 2005. Pattern Without a Plan: Rethinking the Bronze Age Coaxial Field Systems on Dartmoor, South-West England. *Oxford Journal of Archaeology* 24 (1): 1–21.

Jones, A. 2001. Drawn from Memory: The Archaeology of Aesthetics and the Aesthetics of Archaeology in Earlier Bronze Age Britain and the Present. *World Archaeology* 33 (2): 334–56.

———. 2003. Technologies of Remembrance. In *Archaeologies of Remembrance: Death and Memory in Past Societies*, edited by H. William, 65–88. Kluwer/Plenum, New York.

———. 2005. Lives in Fragments? Personhood and the European Neolithic. *Journal of Social Archaeology* 5 (2): 193–224.

———. 2008. How the Dead Live: Mortuary Practices, Memory and the Ancestors in Neolithic and Early Bronze Age Britain and Ireland. In *Prehistoric Britain*, edited by J. Pollard, 177–201. Blackwell, Oxford, UK.

———. 2010. Layers of Meaning: Concealment, Containment, Memory and Secrecy in the British Early Bronze Age. In *Archaeology and Memory*, edited by D. Borić, 105–20. Oxbow Books, Oxford, UK.

Jones, C. 2004. *The Burren and the Aran Islands: Exploring the Archaeology*. Collins Press, Cork, Ireland.

———. 2007. *Temples of Stone: Exploring the Megalithic Tombs of Ireland*. Collins Press, Cork, Ireland.

Jonuks, T., and M. Konsa. 2005. The Revival of Prehistoric Burial Practices: Three Archaeological Experiments. *Folklore* 37:91–110.

Joussaume, R. 1988. *Dolmens for the Dead: Megalith Building Throughout the World*. Translated by A. Chippendale and C. Chippendale. Batsford, London.

Joyce, R. A. 2001. Burying the Dead at Tlatilco: Social Memory and Social Identities. In *Social Memory, Identity, and Death: Anthropological Perspectives on Mortuary Rituals*, edited by M. S. Chesson, 12–26. Papers of the American Anthropological Association no. 10. American Anthropological Association, Arlington, VA.

Kaliff, A. 1997. *Grav och kultplats: Eskatologiska föreställningar under yngre bronsålder och äldre järnålder i Östergötland*. Aun 24. Uppsala University, Department of Archaeology, Uppsala.

Kaliff, A., and T. Oestigaard. 2004. Cultivating Corpses: A Comparative Approach to Disembodied Mortuary Remains. *Current Swedish Archaeology* 12:83–104.

———. 2008. Excavating the Kings' Bones: The Materiality of Death in Practice and Ethics Today. In *The Materiality of Death: Bodies, Burials, Beliefs*, edited by F. Fahlander and T. Oestigaard, 47–57. BAR International Series 17687. Archaeopress, Oxford, UK.

Kan, S. 1989. *Symbolic Immortality*. Smithsonian Institution Press, Washington, DC.

Kay, M., and G. Sabo III. 2006. Mortuary Ritual and Winter Solstice Imagery of the Harlan-Style Charnel House. *Southeastern Archaeology* 25 (1): 29–47.

Kellaher, L., J. Hockey, and D. Prendergast. 2010. Wandering Lines and Cul-de-Sacs: Trajectories of Ashes in the United Kingdom. In *The Matter of Death: Space, Place and Materiality*, edited by J. Hockey, C. Komaromy, and K. Woodthorpe, 133–47. Palgrave Macmillan, Basingstoke, UK.

Kelly, J. E. 2000. The Nature and Context of Emergent Mississippian Cultural Dynamics in the Greater American Bottom. In *Late Woodland Societies: Tradition and Transformation across the Midcontinent*, edited by T. E. Emerson, D. L. McElrath, and A. C. Fortier, 163–75. University of Nebraska Press, Lincoln.

———. 2006. The Ritualization of Cahokia: The Structure and Organization of Early Cahokia Crafts. In *Leadership and Polity in Mississippian Society*, edited by B. M. Butler and P. D. Welch, 236–63. Occasional Paper no. 33. Center for Archaeological Investigations, Southern Illinois University, Carbondale.

Kelly, W. H. 1949. Cocopa Attitudes and Practices with Respect to Death and Mourning. *Southwestern Journal of Anthropology* 5 (2): 151–64.

Kemmler, F. 1998. Entrancing "Tra(un)ns/c": Some Metamorphoses of "Transformation, Translation, and Transubstantiation." In *Translation, Transformation, and Transubstantiation*, edited by C. Poster and R. J. Utz, 176–222. Northwestern University Press, Evanston, IL.

Kidd, K. E. 1953. The Excavation and Historical Identification of a Huron Ossuary. *American Antiquity* 18:359–79.

Killion, T. W. (editor). 2007. *Opening Archaeology: Repatriation's Impact on Contemporary Research and Practice*. School of American Research, Santa Fe, NM.

King, J. M. 2004. Grave-Goods as Gifts in Early Saxon Burials. *Journal of Social Archaeology* 4 (2): 1–38.

Kinnes, I. 1979. *Round Barrows and Ring-Ditches in the British Neolithic*. British Museum Press, London.

Kinsley, A. G. 1989. *The Anglo-Saxon Cemetery at Millgate, Newark-on-Trent, Nottinghamshire*. University of Nottingham, Nottingham.

Kobler, K., R. Limbo, and K. Kavanaugh. 2007. Meaningful Moments: The Use of Ritual in Perinatal and Pediatric Death. *MCN: The American Journal of Maternal/Child Nursing* 32 (5): 288–95.

Kohl, P. L., and C. Fawcett (editors). 1995. *Nationalism, Politics and the Practice of Archaeology*. Cambridge University Press, Cambridge.

Kohl, P. L., M. Kozelsky, and N. Ben-Yehuda (editors). 2007. *Selective Remembrances: Archaeology in the Construction, Commemoration and Consecration of National Pasts.* University of Chicago Press, Chicago.

Kozak, D. L. 1991. Dying Badly: Violent Death and Religious Change Among the Tohono O'odham. *Journal of Death and Dying* 23 (3): 207.

Kristiansen, K. 1987. Centre and Periphery in Bronze Age Scandinavia. In *Centre and Periphery in the Ancient World*, edited by M. Rowlands, M. T. Larsen, and K. Kristensen, 74–85. Cambridge University Press, Cambridge.

———. 1998a. *Europe Before History.* Cambridge University Press, Cambridge.

———. 1998b. The Construction of a Bronze Age Landscape: Cosmology, Economy and Social Organisation in Thy, Northwest Jutland. In *Mensch und Umwelt in der Bronzezeit Europas: Die Bronzezeit das erste goldene Zeitalter Europas*, edited by B. Hänsel, 281–91. Oetger-Voges, Kiel, Germany.

———. 2001. Borders of Ignorance: Research Communities and Language. In *Quo vadis archaeologia? Whither European Archaeology in the 21st Century?* edited by Z. Kobylinski, 38–46. Institute of Archaeology and Ethnology, Polish Academy of Sciences, Warsaw.

Kroeber, A. L. 1927. Disposal of the Dead. *American Anthropologist* 29 (3): 308–15.

Kroeber, C. B., and B. L. Fontana. 1992. *Massacre on the Gila: An Account of the Last Major Battle Between American Indians, with Reflection on the Origin of War.* University of Arizona Press, Tucson.

Kuijt, I. 1996. Negotiating Equality Through Ritual: A Consideration of Late Natufian and Pre-Pottery Neolithic A Period Mortuary Practices. *Journal of Anthropological Archaeology* 15:313–36.

———. 2000. Keeping the Peace: Ritual, Skull Caching, and Community Integration in the Levantine Neolithic. In *Life in Neolithic Farming Communities: Social Organization, Identity, and Differentiation*, edited by I. Kuijt, 137–64. Kluwer Academic, New York.

———. 2001. Place, Death, and the Transmission of Social Memory in Early Agricultural Communities of the Near Eastern Pre-Pottery Neolithic. In *Social Memory, Identity, and Death: Anthropological Perspectives on Mortuary Rituals*, edited by M. S. Chesson, 80–99. Papers of the American Anthropological Association no. 10. American Anthropological Association, Arlington, VA.

———. 2008. The Regeneration of Life: Neolithic Structures of Symbolic Remembering and Forgetting. *Current Anthropology* 49 (2): 171–97.

Kuijt, I., and C. P. Quinn. 2013. Biography of the Neolithic Body: Tracing Pathways to Cist II, Mound of the Hostages, Tara. In *Tara: From the Past to the Future*, edited by M. O'Sullivan, 130–43. Wordwell and University College Dublin School of Archaeology, Bray, Ireland.

Kytmannow, T. 2008. *Portal Tombs in the Landscape: The Chronology, Morphology and Landscape Setting of the Portal Tombs of Ireland, Wales and Cornwall.* BAR British Series 455. Archaeopress, Oxford, UK.

Lakoff, G., and M. Johnson. 1999. *Philosophy in the Flesh: The Embodied Mind and Its Challenge to Western Thought*. Basic Books, New York.

Lanting, J. N., A. T. Aerts-Bijma, and J. van der Plicht. 2001. Dating of Cremated Bone. *Radiocarbon* 43:249–54.

Lanting, J. N., and A. L. Brindley. 1998. Dating Cremated Bone: The Dawn of a New Era. *Journal of Irish Archaeology* 9:1–7.

Larsen, C. S. 1997. *Bioarchaeology: Interpreting Behavior from the Human Skeleton*. Cambridge University Press, Cambridge.

Larsson, Å. M. 2003. Secondary Burial Practices in the Middle Neolithic: Causes and Consequences. *Current Swedish Archaeology* 11:153–70.

———. 2009a. *Breaking and Making Bodies and Pots: Material and Ritual Practices in Sweden in the Third Millennium BC*. Aun 40. Department of Archaeology and Ancient History, Uppsala University, Uppsala.

———. 2009b. Organized Chaos: Defleshing, Cremation and Dispersal of the Dead in Pitted Ware Culture. In *Döda personers sällskap: Gravmaterialens identiteter och kulturella uttryck* [*On the Threshold: Burial Archaeology in the Twenty-First Century*], edited by I.-M. Back Danielsson, I. Gustin, Å. Larsson, N. Myrberg, and S. Thedéen, 109–30. Stockholm Studies in Archaeology. Stockholm University, Department of Archaeology, Stockholm.

Larsson, L. 1982. Skateholmsprojektet: Nya gravar och ett nytt gravfält. *Limhamniana* 1982:11–41.

——— (editor). 1988. *The Skateholm Project: Man and Environment*. Regiae Societatis Humaniorum Litterarum Lundensis 79. Almqvist and Wiksell, Stockholm.

Last, J. 1998. Books of Life: Biography and Memory in a Bronze Age Barrow. *Oxford Journal of Archaeology* 17 (1): 43–53.

Leahy, K. 2007. *"Interrupting the Pots": The Excavation of Cleatham Anglo-Saxon Cemetery*. Council for British Archaeology Research Report 155. Council for British Archaeology, York.

Lee, C. 2007. *Feasting the Dead: Food and Drink in Anglo-Saxon Burial Rituals*. Boydell and Brewer, Woodbridge, UK.

Lewis-Williams, D., and D. Pearce. 2005. *Inside the Neolithic Mind*. Thames and Hudson, London.

Lichtenthal, W. G., and D. G. Cruess. 2010. Effects of Directed Written Disclosure on Grief and Distress Symptoms Among Bereaved Individuals. *Death Studies* 34 (6): 475–99.

Liebmann, M. J. 2012. *Revolt: An Archaeological History of Pueblo Resistance and Revitalization in 17th Century New Mexico*. University of Arizona Press, Tucson.

Lindgren, C. 2008. Stones and Bones: The Myth of Ymer and Mortuary Practices with an Example from the Migration Period in Upland, Central Sweden. In *The Materiality of Death: Bodies, Burials, Beliefs*, edited by F. Fahlander and T. Oestigaard, 155–60. BAR International Series 1768. British Archaeological Reports, Oxford.

Lindqvist, C., and G. Possnert. 1999. The First Seal Hunter Families on Gotland: On the Mesolithic Occupation in the Stora Förvar Cave. *Current Swedish Archaeology* 7:65–87.

Lippert, D. 2013. Profile of an Archaeologist. In *Archaeology*, edited by R. L. Kelly and D. H. Thomas, 292–93. Wadsworth Cengage Learning, Belmont, CA.

LiPuma, E. 1998. Modernity and Forms of Personhood in Melanesia. In *Bodies and Persons: Comparative Perspectives from Africa and Melanesia*, edited by M. Lambek and A. Stratern, 53–79. Cambridge University Press, Cambridge.

Lucy, S., and C. Hills. 2013. *Spong Hill IX: Chronology and Synthesis*. McDonald Institute for Archaeological Research, Cambridge, UK.

Lutz, S., H. J. Weisser, J. Heizmann, and S. Pollak. 1996. MtDNA as a Tool for Identification of Human Remains. *International Journal of Legal Medicine* 109:205–9.

Lynch, A. 1988. Poulnabrone: A Stone in Time. *Archaeology Ireland* 5:105–7.

Lynch, A., and B. Ó Donnabháin. 1994. Poulnabrone, Co. Clare. *The Other Clare* 18:5–7.

Lynch, F. 1971. Report on the Re-excavation of Two Bronze Age Cairns in Anglesey: Bedd Branwen and Treiorwerth. *Archaeologia Cambrensis* 120:11–83.

Lynch, T. 2000. *Bodies in Motion and at Rest: On Metaphor and Mortality*. W. W. Norton, New York.

———. 2010. Catch and Release. In *Apparition and Late Fictions*, edited by T. Lynch, 9–34. Jonathan Cape, London.

Lynott, M. J., T. W. Boutton, J. E. Price, and D. E. Nelson. 1986. Stable Carbon Isotopic Evidence for Maize Agriculture in Southeast Missouri and Northeast Arkansas. *American Antiquity* 51:51–65.

Mabry, J. B. 1998. Mortuary Patterns. In *Archaeological Investigations of Early Village Sites in the Middle Santa Cruz Valley*, edited by J. B. Mabry, 697–737. Anthropological Paper no. 19. Center for Desert Archaeology, Tucson, AZ.

MacAdam, J. 1855. Discovery of an Ancient Sepulchral Chamber. *Ulster Journal of Archaeology* 3:358–65.

MacGregor, G. 2008. Elemental Bodies: The Nature of Transformative Practices During the Late Third and Second Millennium BC in Scotland. *World Archaeology* 40 (2): 268–80.

Mädler, I. 2008. Die Urne als "Mobilie": Überlegungen zur gegenwärtigen Bestattungskultur. In *Performanzen des Todes: Neue Bestattungskultur und kirchliche Wahrnehmung*, edited by Thomas Klie, 57–75. W. Kohlhammer, Stuttgart, Germany.

Magrath, W. H. 1945. The North Benton Mound: A Hopewell Site in Ohio. *American Antiquity* 11 (1): 40–46.

Malhi, R. S., H. M. Mortensen, J. A. Eshleman, B. M. Kemp, J. G. Lorenz, F. A. Kaestle, J. R. Johnson, C. Gorodezky, and D. G. Smith. 2003. Native American mtDNA Prehistory in the American Southwest. *American Journal of Physical Anthropology* 120:108–24.

Mallam, R. C. 1976. *The Iowa Effigy Mound Tradition: An Interpretive Model.* Report no. 9. Office of the State Archaeologist, Iowa City.

Malmer, M. 2002. *The Neolithic of South Sweden: TRB, GRK and STR.* Royal Swedish Academy of Letters, History and Antiquities, Stockholm.

Malone, C. 2001. *Neolithic Britain and Ireland.* Tempus, Stroud, UK.

Manning, M. 1985. A Neolithic Burial Mound at Ashleypark, Co. Tipperary. *Proceedings of the Royal Irish Academy* 85C:61–100.

Marciniak, M. 1993. Mesolithic Burial and Dwelling Structure from the Boreal Period Excavated at Mszano Site 14, Torun District, Poland: Preliminary Report. *Mesolithic Miscellany* 14:1–2, 7–11.

Marshall, A. 1998. Visualising Burnt Areas: Patterns of Magnetic Susceptibility at Guiting Power 1 Round Barrow (Glos., UK). *Archaeological Prospection* 5:159–77.

———. 2011. *Experimental Archaeology: 1. Early Bronze Age Cremation Pyres, 2. Iron Age Grain Storage.* BAR British Series 530. Archaeopress, Oxford.

Martin, S. R. 1999. *Wonderful Power: The Story of Ancient Copper Working in the Lake Superior Basin.* Wayne State University Press, Detroit, MI.

Mason, R. J. 2000. Archaeology and Native North American Oral Traditions. *American Antiquity* 65 (2): 239–72.

Mathissen, T. 1946. En boplads fra aeldre stenalder ved Vedbæk Boldbaner. *Sollerødbogen* 1946:19–35.

Mauss, M. 1954. *The Gift: Forms and Functions of Exchange in Archaic Societies.* Translated by I. Cunnison. Cohen and West, London.

———. 1985. A Category of Human Mind: The Notion of Person, the Notion of Self. In *The Category of the Person: Anthropology, Philosophy, History,* edited by M. Carrithers, S. Collins, and S. Lukes, 1–25. Cambridge University Press, Cambridge.

May, S. E. 2011. The Effects of Body Mass on Cremation Weight. *Journal of Forensic Sciences* 56 (1): 3–9.

McAnany, P. 1995. *Living with Ancestors: Kingship and Kinship in Ancient Maya Society.* University of Texas, Austin.

McCutcheon, P. T. 1992. Burned Archaeological Bone. In *Deciphering a Shell Midden,* edited by J. K. Stein, 347–68. Academic Press, New York.

McGuire, R. H. 1992. *Death, Society and Ideology in a Hohokam Community.* Investigations in American Archaeology. Westview Press, Boulder, CO.

McKinley, J. I. 1989. Cremations: Expectations, Methodologies and Realities. In *Burial Archaeology,* edited by I. C. A. Roberts, F. Lee, and J. Bintliff, 65–74. BAR British Series 211. British Archaeological Reports, Oxford.

———. 1993. Bone Fragment Size and Weights of Bone from Modern British Cremations and Its Implications for the Interpretation of Archaeological Cremations. *International Journal of Osteoarchaeology* 3:283–87.

———. 1994a. Bone Fragment Size in British Cremation Burials and Its Implications for Pyre Technology and Ritual. *Journal of Archaeological Science* 21:339–42.

———. 1994b. *The Anglo-Saxon Cemetery at Spong Hill, North Elmham.* Part 6, *The Cremations.* East Anglian Archaeology 69. Norfolk Archaeological Unit, Dereham, UK.

———. 1994c. Cremation Burials. In J. Barnett, Excavations of a Bronze Age Unenclosed Cemetery, Cairns and Field Boundaries at Eaglestone Flat, Curbar, Derbyshire, 1984, 1989–90. *Proceedings of the Prehistoric Society* 60:335–40.

———. 1997. Bronze Age "Barrows" and Funerary Rites and Rituals of Cremation. *Proceedings of the Prehistoric Society* 63:129–45.

———. 2005. The Cremated Human Remains. In *The Origins of Mid-Saxon Southampton: Excavations at the Friends Provident St. Mary's Stadium, 1998–2000,* by V. Birbeck, R. J. C. Smith, P. Andrews, and N. Stoodley, 17–23. Wessex Archaeology, Salisbury, UK.

McKinley, J. I., and J. M. Bond. 2001. Cremated Bone. In *Handbook of Archaeological Sciences,* edited by D. R. Brothwell and A. M. Pollard, 281–92. John Wiley and Sons, Chichester, UK.

McLaren, D. 2011. Funerary Rites Afforded to Children in the Earlier Bronze Age in Britain: Case Studies from Scotland, Yorkshire and Wessex. Unpublished Ph.D. dissertation, University of Edinburgh, Edinburgh.

McQuillan, L., and P. Logue. 2008. Funerary Querns: Rethinking the Role of the Basin in Irish Passage Tombs. *Ulster Journal of Archaeology* 67:14–21.

Mercer, R., and M. Midgley. 1997. The Early Bronze Age Cairn at Sketewan, Balnaguard, Perth and Kinross. *Proceedings of the Society of Antiquaries of Scotland* 127:281–338.

Meskell, L. 1996. The Somatisation of Archaeology: Institutions, Discourses, Corporeality. *Norwegian Archaeological Review* 29:1–16.

Metcalf, P. 1981. Meaning and Materialism: The Ritual Economy of Death. *Man* 16:563–78.

———. 1982. *A Borneo Journey into Death: Berawan Eschatology from Its Rituals.* University of Pennsylvania Press, Philadelphia.

———. 1987. Wine of the Corpse: Endocannibalism and the Great Feast of the Dead in Borneo. *Representations* 17 (1): 96–109.

Metcalf, P., and R. Huntingdon. 1991. *Celebrations of Death: The Anthropology of Mortuary Ritual.* Cambridge University Press, Cambridge.

Midgley, M. M. 2005. *The Monumental Cemeteries of Prehistoric Europe.* Tempus, Stroud, UK.

Mihesuah, D. A. (editor). 2000. *Repatriation Reader: Who Owns Native American Indian Remains?* University of Nebraska Press, Lincoln.

Miller, D., and F. R. Parrott. 2007. Death, Ritual and Material Culture in South London. In *Death Rites and Rights*, edited by B. Brooks-Gordon, F. Ebtehaj, J. Herring, M. Johnson, and M. Richards, 147–61. Hart Publishing, Oxford, UK.

Miller, J. 2001. Ashes Ethereal: Cremation in the Americas. *American Indian Culture and Research Journal* 25 (1): 121–37.

Mills, B. 2004. The Establishment and Defeat of Hierarchy: Inalienable Possessions and the History of Collective Prestige Structures in the Pueblo Southwest. *American Anthropologist* 106 (2): 238–51.

Mills, B. J., M. D. Elson, P. R. Fish, G. Rice, and H. D. Wallace. 2006. Ritual Practice and Hohokam Trajectories. Paper submitted for *Hohokam Trajectories in Worldwide Perspective*, edited by P. R. Fish and S. K. Fish. University of Arizona Press, Tucson.

Mills, B. J., and T. J. Ferguson. 2008. Animate Objects: Shell Trumpets and Ritual Networks in the Greater Southwest. *Journal of Archaeological Method and Theory* 15:338–61.

Mills, B. J., and W. Field Murray. 2008. Identity Communities and Material Practices: Logics of Ritual Deposition in the U.S. Southwest. *Proceedings of the World Archaeological Congress.* University College Dublin, Dublin.

Milner, G. R. 1998. *The Cahokia Chiefdom: The Archaeology of a Mississippian Society.* Smithsonian Institution Press, Washington, DC.

Minozzi, S., V. Giuffra, J. Bagnoli, E. Paribeni, D. Guistini, D. Caramella, and G. Fornaciari. 2010. An Investigation of Etruscan Cremations by Computed Tomography (CT). *Antiquity* 84:195–201.

Minturn, P. D., and D. B. Craig. 2001. Burials. In *The Grewe Archaeological Research Project*, vol. 1, *Project Background and Feature Descriptions*, edited by D. B. Craig, 137–45. Anthropological Papers no. 99-1. Northland Research, Flagstaff, AZ.

Mizoguchi, K. 1993. Time in the Reproduction of Mortuary Practices. *World Archaeology* 25 (2): 223–35.

Morgan, D. T. 1985. Late Woodland Ceramics from the Fall Creek Locality, Adams County, Illinois. *Wisconsin Archeologist* 66:265–81.

Moriarty, J. R. 1965. Cosmogony, Rituals, and Medical Practice Among the Diegueno Indians of Southern California. *Anthropological Journal of Canada* 3 (3): 2–16.

Morris, B. 1991. *Western Conceptions of the Individual.* Berg, Oxford, UK.

———. 1994. *Anthropology of the Self: The Individual in Cultural Perspective.* Pluto Press, London.

Morris, C. 1994. Finds Connected with Wooden Artefacts, Woodworking and Other Tools. In *The Anglo-Saxon Cemetery at Spong Hill, North Elmham*, part 5, *Catalogue of Cremations*, edited by C. Hills, K. Penn, and R. Rickett,

30–35. East Anglian Archaeology 67. Norfolk Archaeological Unit, Dereham, UK.

Moules, N. J. 1998. Legitimizing Grief: Challenging Beliefs That Constrain. *Journal of Family Nursing* 4 (2): 142–67.

Muller, J. 1978. The Kincaid System: Mississippian Settlement in the Environs of a Large Site. In *Mississippian Settlement Patterns*, edited by B. D. Smith, 269–92. Academic Press, New York.

Müller, S. 1897. *Vor Oldtid: Danmarks forhistoriske Archæologi almenfatteligt fremstillet*. Nyt Nordisk, Copenhagen.

Munro, L. E., F. J. Longstaffe, and C. D. White. 2008. Effects of Heating on the Carbon and Oxygen-Isotope Compositions of Structural Carbonate in Bioapatite from Modern Deer Bone. *Palaeogeography, Palaeoclimatology, Palaeoecology* 266 (3–4): 142–50.

Murphy, E. 2003. Funerary Processing of the Dead in Prehistoric Ireland. *Archaeology Ireland* 17:13–15.

Murphy, E., B. Ó Donnabháin, H. Welsh, M. Tesorieri, and C. McSparron. 2010. The People of Prehistoric Ireland: Progress Report on Phase 2, Synthesis of Osteological, Contextual and Chronological Data Relating to Irish Prehistoric Human Remains. Report prepared for the Heritage Council, Dublin.

National Funeral Directors Association. 2013. U.S. Cremation Statistics. Electronic document, www.nfda.org/consumer-resources-cremation/78-us-cremation-statistics.html. Accessed November 8, 2013.

Needham, S. 1996. Chronology and Periodisation in the British Bronze Age. In *Absolute Chronology: Archaeological Europe, 2500–500 BC*, edited by K. Randsborg, 121–40. Acta Archaeologica 67. Munksgaard, Copenhagen.

———. 2000. Power Pulses Across a Cultural Divide: Cosmologically Driven Acquisition Between Armorica and Wessex. *Proceedings of the Prehistoric Society* 66:151–207.

Nilsson Stutz, L. 2003. *Embodied Rituals and Ritualized Bodies: Tracing Ritual Practices in Late Mesolithic Burials*. Acta Archaeologica Lundensia Series 8, no. 46. Lund University Department of Archaeology and Ancient History, Lund.

———. 2006. Escaping the Allure of Meaning: Toward New Paradigms in the Study of Ritual in Prehistory. In *Old Norse Religion in Long Term Perspectives*, edited by A. Anders, K. Jennbert, and C. Raudvere, 89–92. Nordic Academic Press, Lund, Sweden.

———. 2008a. Archaeology, Identity, and the Right to Culture: Anthropological Perspectives on Repatriation. *Current Swedish Archaeology* 15–16:157–72.

———. 2008b. Capturing Mortuary Ritual: An Attempt to Harmonize Archaeological Method and Theory. In *Religion, Archaeology and the Material World*, edited by L. Fogelin, 159–78. Occasional Papers no. 36. Southern Illinois University, Carbondale.

————. 2010. The Way We Bury Our Dead: Reflections on Mortuary Ritual, Community and Identity at the Time of the Mesolithic-Neolithic Transition. *Documenta Praehistorica* 37:33–42.

Nugent, R. 2011a. Feathered Funerals: Birds in Early Anglo-Saxon Burial Rites. *Medieval Archaeology* 55:257–58.

————. 2011b. Heads and Tails: Corporeal Transformations in the Mortuary Arena. Unpublished M.Phil. thesis, University of Chester, Chester, UK.

Nugent, R., and H. Williams. 2012. Sighted Surfaces: Ocular Agency in Early Anglo-Saxon Cremation Burials. In *Encountering Images: Materialities, Perceptions, Relations*, edited by I.-M. Back Danielsson, F. Fahlander, and Y. Sjöstrand, 187–208. Stockholm Studies in Archaeology 57. Stockholm University, Stockholm.

Nuñez, M. 1990. On Subneolithic Pottery and Its Adoption in Late Mesolithic Finland. *Fennoscandia Archaeologica* 7:27–52.

O'Brien, W. 1999. *Sacred Ground: Megalithic Tombs in Coastal South-West Ireland.* Galway University Press, Galway.

Oestigaard, T. 1999. Cremations as Transformations: When the Dual Cultural Hypothesis Was Cremated and Carried Away in Urns. *European Journal of Archaeology* 2 (3): 345–64.

————. 2000. Sacrifices of Raw, Cooked and Burnt Humans. *Norwegian Archaeological Review* 33 (1): 41–58.

————. 2004. Death and Ambivalent Materiality: Human Flesh as Culture and Cosmology. In *Combining the Past and the Present: Archaeological Perspectives on Society*, edited by T. Oestigaard, N. Anfinset, and T. Saetersdal, 23–30. BAR International Series 1210. British Archaeological Reports, Oxford.

————. 2005. *Death and Life-Giving Waters: Cremation, Caste, and Cosmogony in Karmic Traditions.* BAR International Series 1353. British Archaeological Reports, Oxford.

————. 2013. Cremations in Culture and Cosmology. In *The Oxford University Press Handbook of the Archaeology of Death and Burial*, edited by L. Nilsson Stutz and S. Tarlow, 497–509. Oxford University Press, Oxford.

Ó Floinn, R. 1992. A Neolithic Cave Burial in Limerick. *Archaeology Ireland* 20:19–22.

O'Gorman, J. A. 2001. Life, Death, and the Longhouse: A Gendered View of Oneota Social Organization. In *Gender and the Archaeology of Death*, edited by B. Arnold and N. L. Wicker, 23–50. AltaMira Press, Walnut Creek, CA.

O'Gorman, J. A., and H. Hassan. 2000. Late Woodland in the Mississippi Valley of West-Central Illinois: The Sny Bottom. In *Late Woodland Societies: Tradition and Transformation Across the Midcontinent*, edited by T. E. Emerson, D. L. McElrath, and A. C. Fortier, 277–300. University of Nebraska Press, Lincoln.

Ojjala, C.-G. 2009. *Sami Prehistories: The Politics of Archaeology and Identity in Northernmost Europe.* Occasional Papers in Archaeology 47. Uppsala University, Uppsala.

O'Leary, M. 1988. Carbon Isotopes in Photosynthesis. *Bioscience* 38 (5): 328–36.

Olivelle, P. 1987. Rites of Passage: Hindu Rites. In *The Encyclopedia of Religion,* vol. 12, edited by M. Eliade, 387–92. Macmillan, New York.

Oliver, T. J. 2001. Warfare in Tonto Basin. In *Deadly Landscape: Case Studies in Prehistoric Southwestern Warfare,* edited by G. E. Rice and S. A. LeBlanc, 195–218. University of Utah, Salt Lake City.

Olsen, A.-L.H. 1990. Egshvile: A Bronze Age Barrow with Early Urn Graves from Thy. *Journal of Danish Archaeology* 9:133–52.

Olsen, A.-L.H., and J.-H. Bech. 1994. Damsgård: En overpløjet høj fra ældre bronzealder per. III med stenkiste og ligbrændingsgrube. *Kuml* 1993–1994: 155–98.

Olsson, E., G. Granath Zillén, and A. Mohr. 1994. *Korsnäs—en gropkeramisk grav- och boplats på Södertörn.* University of Stockholm Rapport 1994, no. 63. Riksantikvarieämbetet, Stockholm.

Ó Nualláin, S. 1972. A Neolithic House at Ballyglass near Ballycastle, Co. Mayo. *Royal Society of Antiquaries of Ireland* 102:49–57.

Osborne, R. 2008. Introduction: For Tradition as an Analytical Category. *World Archaeology* 40 (3): 281–94.

O'Shea, J. M. 1984. *Mortuary Variability: An Archaeological Investigation.* Studies in Archaeology. Academic Press, Orlando, FL.

———. 1988. Social Organization and Mortuary Behavior in the Late Woodland Period in Michigan. *Ohio State University Occasional Papers in Anthropology* 3:68–85.

———. 1995. Mortuary Custom in the Bronze Age of Southeastern Hungary: Diachronic and Synchronic Perspectives. In *Regional Approaches to Mortuary Analysis,* edited by L. A. Beck, 125–46. Plenum Press, New York.

O'Sullivan, D. 2011. Normanizing the North: The Evidence of Anglo-Saxon and Anglo-Scandinavian Sculpture. *Medieval Archaeology* 55:163–91.

O'Sullivan, M. 2005. *Duma Na Ngiall: The Mound of the Hostages, Tara.* Wordswell and University College Dublin School of Archaeology, Bray, Ireland.

Ousley, S. D., W. T. Billeck, and E. R. Hollinger. 2005. Federal Repatriation Legislation and the Role of Physical Anthropology in Repatriation. *Yearbook of Physical Anthropology* 48:2–32.

Overstreet, D. F., L. Doebert, G. W. Henschel, P. Sander, and D. Wasion. 1996. Two Red Ocher Mortuary Contexts from Southeastern Wisconsin: The Henschel Site (47Sb29), Sheboygan County and the Barnes Creek Site (47Kn41), Kenosha County. *Wisconsin Archeologist* 77 (1): 36–62.

Parker Pearson, M. 1982. Mortuary Practices, Society and Ideology: An Ethnoarchaeological Study. In *Symbolic and Structural Archaeology,* edited by I. Hodder, 99–113. Cambridge University Press, Cambridge.

———. 1993. *English Heritage Book of Bronze Age Britain*. B. T. Batsford/English Heritage, London.

———. 1999a. The Earlier Bronze Age. In *The Archaeology of Britain: An Introduction from the Upper Palaeolithic to the Industrial Revolution*, edited by J. R. Hunter and I. B. M. Ralston, 77–94. Routledge, London.

———. 1999b. The Politics of the Dead. In *The Archaeology of Death and Burial*, edited by M. Parker Pearson, 171–92. Texas A&M University Press, College Station.

Parry, J. P. 1994. *Death in Banaras*. Cambridge University Press, Cambridge.

Paterson, M. 2007. *The Senses of Touch: Haptics, Affects and Technologies*. Berg, Oxford, UK.

Pauketat, T. R. 1994. *The Ascent of Chiefs: Cahokia and Mississippian Politics in Native North America*. University of Alabama Press, Tuscaloosa.

Penn, K. 1998. *An Anglo-Saxon Cemetery at Oxborough, West Norfolk: Excavations in 1990*. East Anglian Archaeology Occasional Papers no. 5. Norfolk Museums Service, Dereham, UK.

Penn, K., and B. Brugmann (with K. H. Nielsen). 2007. *Aspects of Anglo-Saxon Inhumation Burial: Morning Thorpe, Spong Hill, Bergh Apton and Westgarth Gardens*. East Anglian Archaeology 119. Norfolk Museums and Archaeology Service, Norwich, UK.

Perino, G. 1967. Salvage and Research on the Provenience and Cultural Association of Certain Long Nosed God Masks in Pike County, Illinois. *Southeastern Archaeological Conference Newsletter* 11 (2): 10–11.

———. 1971. The Yokem Site, Pike County, Illinois. In *Mississippian Site Archaeology in Illinois I*, edited by J. A. Brown, 149–86. Illinois Archaeological Survey, Urbana.

———. 1973a. The Late Woodland Component at the Pete Klunk Site, Calhoun County, Illinois. In *Late Woodland Site Archaeology in Illinois I*, edited by J. A. Brown, 58–89. Illinois Archaeological Survey, Urbana.

———. 1973b. The Late Woodland Component at the Schild Sites, Calhoun County, Illinois. In *Late Woodland Site Archaeology in Illinois I*, edited by J. A. Brown, 90–140. Illinois Archaeological Survey, Urbana.

———. 2006a. The 1967–68 Excavations of the Yokem Site Late Woodland Mounds, Pike County, Illinois. In *Illinois Hopewell and Late Woodland Mounds: The Excavations of Gregory Perino, 1950–1975*, edited by K. B. Farnsworth and M. D. Wiant, 347–90. Illinois Transportation Archaeological Research Program, Urbana.

———. 2006b. The 1970 Joe Gay Mounds Excavations, Pike County, Illinois. In *Illinois Hopewell and Late Woodland Mounds: The Excavations of Gregory Perino, 1950–1975*, edited by K. B. Farnsworth and M. D. Wiant, 471–97. Illinois Transportation Archaeological Research Program, Urbana.

———. 2006c. The 1970 Homer Adams Mounds Excavations, Pike County, Illinois. In *Illinois Hopewell and Late Woodland Mounds: The Excavations of*

Gregory Perino, 1950–1975, edited by K. B. Farnsworth and M. D. Wiant, 455–70. Illinois Transportation Archaeological Research Program, Urbana.

Perkins, D. n.d. An Assessment/Research Design: South Dumpton Down, Broadstairs. Unpublished report, Trust for Thanet Archaeology, Thanet, UK.

Perry, G. 2012a. A Hole for the Soul? Possible Functions of Post-firing Perforations and Lead Plugs in Early Anglo-Saxon Cremation Urns. In *Make-Do and Mend: Archaeologies of Compromise, Repair and Re-use*, edited by B. Jervis and A. Kyle, 9–21. British Archaeological Reports, Oxford.

———. 2012b. Beer, Butter and Burial: The Pre-burial Origins of Cremation Urns from the Early Anglo-Saxon Cemetery of Cleatham, North Lincolnshire. *Medieval Ceramics* 32:9–21.

Persson, O., and E. Persson. 1984. *Anthropological Report on the Mesolithic Graves from Skateholm, Southern Sweden: Excavation Seasons 1980–1982*. University of Lund, Institute of Archaeology, Lund.

———. 1988. Anthropological Report Concerning the Interred Mesolithic Populations from Skateholm, Southern Sweden: Excavation Seasons 1983–1984. In *The Skateholm Project*, vol. 1, *Man and Environment*, edited by L. Larsson, 89–105. Regiae Societatis Humaniorum Litterarum Lundensis 79. Almqvist and Wiksell, Stockholm.

Petersen, P. F. 1972. Traditions of Multiple Burial in Later Neolithic and Early Bronze Age Britain. *Archaeological Journal* 129:22–55.

Photo-Jones, E., B. Ballin Smith, A. J. Hall, and R. E. Jones. 2007. On the Intent to Make Cramp: An Interpretation of Vitreous Seaweed Cremation "Waste" from Prehistoric Burial Sites in Orkney, Scotland. *Oxford Journal of Archaeology* 26 (1): 1–23.

Pierpoint, S. 1980. *Social Patterns in Yorkshire Prehistory, 3500–750 BC*. BAR British Series 74. British Archaeological Reports, Oxford.

Piggott, S., and C. M. Piggott. 1945. The Excavation of a Barrow on Rockbourne Down. *Proceedings of the Hampshire Field Club and Archaeological Society* 16:156–62.

Pijoan, C. M., J. Mansilla, I. Leboreiro, V. H. Lara, and P. Bosch. 2007. Thermal Alterations in Archaeological Bones. *Archaeometry* 49:713–27.

Pleger, T. C. 2000. Old Copper and Red Ocher Social Complexity. *Midcontinental Journal of Archaeology* 25 (2): 169–90.

———. 2001. New Dates for the Oconto Old Copper Culture Cemetery. In *Papers in Honor of Carol I. Mason*, edited by T. C. Pleger, R. A. Birmingham, and C. I. Mason. *Wisconsin Archeologist* 82 (1–2): 87–100.

Pope, E. J., and O. B. C. Smith. 2004. Identification of Traumatic Injury in Burned Cranial Bone: An Experimental Approach. *Journal of Forensic Sciences* 49 (3): 431–40.

Potter, B. A., J. D. Irish, J. D. Reuther, C. Gelvin-Reymiller, and V. T. Holliday. 2011. A Terminal Pleistocene Child Cremation and Residential Structure from Eastern Beringia. *Science* 331 (6020): 1058–62.

Powell, A. 2005. The Language of Lineage: Irish Court Tomb Design. *European Journal of Archaeology* 8:9–28.

Powers, N. 2008. Cremated Human Remains. In *An Early Saxon Cemetery at Rayleigh, Essex*, by T. Ennis, 46–48. East Anglian Archaeology 127. Essex County Council, Chelmsford, UK.

Poyil, M. 2009. Farewell Ritual and Transmigrating Souls: Secondary Funeral of the Attappadi Kurumbas. *Anthropologist* 11 (1): 31–38.

Prendergast, D., J. Hockey, and L. Kellaher. 2007. Blowing in the Wind? Identity, Materiality, and the Destinations of Human Ashes. *Journal of the Royal Anthropological Institute*, n.s., 12 (4): 881–98.

Price, T. D., J. H. Burton, and J. B. Stoltman. 2007. Place of Origin of Prehistoric Inhabitants of Aztalan, Jefferson County, Wisconsin. *American Antiquity* 72 (3): 524–38.

Pusch, C. M., M. Broghammer, and M. Scholz. 2000. Cremation Practices and the Survival of Ancient DNA: Burnt Bone Analyses via RAPD-mediated PCR. *Anthropologischer Anzeiger* 58:237–51.

Quinn, C. P., and I. Kuijt. 2013. The Tempo of Life and Death During the Early Bronze Age at the Mound of the Hostages, Tara. In *Tara: From the Past to the Future*, edited by M. O'Sullivan, 154–64. Wordwell and University College Dublin School of Archaeology, Bray, Ireland.

Rakita, G. F. M., and J. E. Buikstra. 2005. Corrupting Flesh: Reexamining Hertz's Perspective on Mummification and Cremation. In *Interacting with the Dead: Perspectives on Mortuary Archaeology for the New Millennium*, edited by G. F. M. Rakita, J. E. Buikstra, L. A. Beck, and S. R. Williams, 97–106. University Press of Florida, Gainesville.

Randsborg, K. 2006. Opening the Oak-Coffins: New Dates—New Perspectives. *Acta Archaeologica* 77 (1): 3–162.

Ravn, M. 2003. *Death Ritual and Germanic Social Structure (c. 200–600)*. BAR International Series 1164. British Archaeological Reports, Oxford.

Rebay-Salisbury, K. 2010. Cremations: Fragmented Bodies in the Bronze and Iron Ages. In *Body Parts and Bodies Whole: Changing Relations and Meanings*, edited by K. Rebay-Salisbury, M. L. S. Sørensen, and J. Hughes, 64–71. Oxbow Books, Oxford, UK.

Reinhard, K. J., and T. M. Fink. 1994. Cremation in Southwestern North America: Aspects of Taphonomy That Affect Pathological Analysis. *Journal of Archaeological Science* 21:597–605.

Renfrew, C. 1974. Beyond a Subsistence Economy: The Evolution of Prehistoric Europe. In *Reconstructing Complex Societies*, edited by C. B. Moore, 69–95. Bulletin of the American Schools of Oriental Research 20. American Schools of Oriental Research, Boston.

——— (editor). 1981. *The Megalithic Monuments of Western Europe*. Thames and Hudson, London.

Reynolds, A. 2009. *Anglo-Saxon Deviant Burial Customs*. Oxford University Press, Oxford.

Rice, G. E. 2001. Warfare and Massing in the Salt and Gila Basins of Central Arizona. In *Deadly Landscape: Case Studies in Prehistoric Southern Southwest Warfare*, edited by G. E. Rice and S. A. LeBlanc, 289–330. University of Utah Press, Salt Lake City.

Richards, J. D. 1987. *The Significance of Form and Decoration of Anglo-Saxon Cremation Urns*. BAR British Series 166. British Archaeological Reports, Oxford.

———. 1992. Anglo-Saxon Symbolism. In *The Age of Sutton Hoo*, edited by M. Carver, 131–48. Boydell, Woodbridge, UK.

Rideout, J. S., J. Comrie, A. Barlow, E. Halpin, S. Stevenson, and A. M. Gibson. 1987. A Cist at Abercairny, Perthshire. *Glasgow Archaeological Journal* 14:39–47.

Riley, C. L. 1975. The Road to Hawikuh: Trade and Trade Routes to Cibola-Zuni During Late Prehistoric and Early Historic Times. *Kiva* 41 (2): 137–59.

Ritzenthaler, R. E., and G. I. Quimby. 1962. The Red Ocher Culture of the Upper Great Lakes and Adjacent Areas. *Fieldiana Anthropology* 36 (11): 243–375.

Ritzenthaler, R. E., and W. Wittry. 1957. The Oconto Site—An Old Copper Manifestation. *Wisconsin Archeologist* 38(4):222–43.

Robb, J. 2007. Burial Treatment as Transformations of Bodily Ideology. In *Performing Death: Social Analyses of Funerary Traditions in the Ancient Near East and Mediterranean*, edited by N. Laneri, 287–97. Oriental Institute, University of Chicago, Chicago.

———. 2008. Tradition and Agency: Human Body Representations in Later Prehistoric Europe. *World Archaeology* 40 (3): 332–53.

Rose, F. 2008. Intra-community Variation in Diet During the Adoption of a New Staple Crop in the Eastern Woodlands. *American Antiquity* 73:413–40.

Rosen, F. 2004. *Cremation in America*. Prometheus Books, Amherst, NY.

Rowe, C. W. 1956. *The Effigy Mound Culture of Wisconsin*. Milwaukee Public Museum, Publications in Anthropology no. 3. Greenwood Press, Westport, CT.

———. 1958. A Crematorium at Aztalan. *Wisconsin Archeologist* 39 (1): 101–10.

Rowlands, M. 1980. Kinship, Alliance and Exchange in the European Bronze Age. In *Settlement and Society in the British Later Bronze Age*, edited by J. C. Barrett and R. J. Bradley, 59–72. BAR British Series 83. British Archaeological Reports, Oxford.

———. 1999. Remembering to Forget: Sublimation as Sacrifice to War Memorials. In *The Art of Forgetting*, edited by A. Forty and S. Küchler, 129–45. Berg, Oxford, UK.

Russell, F. 1908. *The Pima Indians*. Annual Report of the Bureau of American Ethnology. Government Printing Office, Washington, DC.

Ryan, M. 1973. The Excavation of a Neolithic Burial Mound at Jerpoint West, Co. Kilkenny. *Proceedings of the Royal Irish Academy* 73C:107–27.

————. 1980. Prehistoric Burials at Clane, Co. Kildare. *Journal of the County Kildare Archaeological Society* 16:108–14.

Sabo, G., III. 1993. Indians and Spaniards in Arkansas: Symbolic Action in the Sixteenth Century. In *The Expedition of Hernando de Soto West of the Mississippi, 1541–1543: Proceedings of the de Soto Symposia, 1988 and 1990*, edited by G. A. Young and M. P. Hoffman, 192–209. University of Arkansas Press, Fayetteville.

Sayer, D. 2010. *Ethics and Burial Archaeology.* Duckworth, London.

Scarre, C. 2007. *The Megalithic Monuments of Britain and Ireland.* Thames and Hudson, London.

Schaefer, J. 2000. Now Dead I Begin to Sing: A Protohistoric Clothes-Burning Ceremonial Feature in the Colorado Desert. *Journal of California and Great Basin Anthropology* 22 (2): 186–211.

Schanche, A. 2002. Sami Skulls, Anthropological Race Research and the Repatriation Question in Norway. In *The Dead and Their Possessions: Repatriation in Principle, Policy and Practice*, edited by C. Fforde, J. Hubert, and P. Turnbull, 47–58. Routledge, London.

Schmidt, C. W., and S. A. Symes (editors). 2008. *The Analysis of Burnt Human Remains.* Academic Press, London.

Schoeber, T. M. 1998. Reinvestigation of Maize Introduction in West-Central Illinois. Unpublished manuscript in lieu of thesis, Department of Anthropology, University of Illinois, Urbana-Champaign.

Schoeninger, M. J., and M. R. Schurr. 1994. Interpreting Carbon Stable Isotope Ratios. In *Corn and Culture in the Prehistoric New World*, edited by S. Johannessen and C. Hastorf, 55–66. Westview Press, Boulder, CO.

Schulting, R. J., C. Bronk Ramsey, P. J. Reimer, G. Eogan, K. Cleary, G. Cooney, and A. Sheridan. 2015. Dating the Human Remains from Knowth. In *Excavations at Knowth*, vol. 6, *The Archaeology of the Large Passage Tomb at Knowth, Co. Meath*, edited by G. Eogan and K. Cleary. Royal Irish Academy, Dublin.

Schulting, R. J., E. Murphy, C. Jones, and G. Warren. 2012. New Dates from the North and a Proposed Chronology for Irish Court Tombs. *Proceedings of the Royal Irish Academy* 112C:1–60.

Schulting, R. J., A. Sheridan, S. R. Clarke, and C. Bronk Ramsey. 2008. Largantea and the Dating of Irish Wedge Tombs. *Journal of Irish Archaeology* 17:1–17.

Schulting, R. J., A. Sheridan, R. Crozier, and E. Murphy. 2010. Revisiting Quanterness: New AMS Dates and Staple Isotope Data from an Orcadian Chamber Tomb. *Proceedings of the Society of Antiquaries of Scotland* 140:1–50.

Schultz, J. J., M. W. Warren, and J. S. Krigbaum. 2008. Analysis of Human Cremains: Gross and Chemical Methods. In *The Analysis of Burned Human Remains*, edited by C. W. Schmidt and S. A. Symes, 75–94. Academic Press, London.

Schurr, M. R., and R. G. Hayes. 2008. Stable Carbon- and Nitrogen-Isotope Ratios and Electron Spin Resonance (ESR) g-Values of Charred Bones: Changes with Heating and a Critical Evaluation of the Utility of g-Values for Reconstructing Thermal History and Original Isotope Ratios. *Journal of Archaeological Science* 35:2017–31.

Schurr, M. R., R. G. Hayes, and D. C. Cook. 2008. Thermally Induced Changes in the Stable Carbon- and Nitrogen-Isotope Ratios of Charred Bones. In *The Analysis of Burned Human Remains,* edited by C. W. Schmidt and S. A. Symes, 95–108. Academic Press, London.

Schwarcz, H. P., J. Melbye, M. A. Katzenberg, and M. Knyf. 1985. Stable Isotopes in Human Skeletons of Southern Ontario: Reconstructing Paleodiet. *Journal of Archaeological Science* 12:187–206.

Scott, R. M., H. R. Buckley, M. Spriggs, F. Valentin, and S. Bedford. 2010. Identification of the First Reported Lapita Cremation in the Pacific Islands Using Archaeological, Forensic and Contemporary Burning Evidence. *Journal of Archaeological Sciences* 37:901–9.

Scull, C. 2011. Social Transactions, Gift Exchange, and Power in the Archaeology of the Fifth to Seventh Centuries. In *The Oxford Handbook of Anglo-Saxon Archaeology,* edited by H. Hamerow, D. Hinton, and S. Crawford, 848–64. Oxford University Press, Oxford.

Seeman, M. F. 1979. Feasting with the Dead: Ohio Hopewell Charnel House Ritual as a Context for Redistribution. In *Hopewell Archaeology: The Chillicothe Conference,* edited by D. S. Brose and N. Greber, 39–46. Kent State University Press, Kent, OH.

Seeman, M. F., and F. Soday. 1980. The Russell Brown Mounds: Three Hopewell Mounds in Ross County, Ohio. *Midcontinental Journal of Archaeology* 5 (1): 73–116.

Sellevold, B. J. 2002. Skeletal Remains of the Norwegian Saami. In *The Dead and Their Possessions: Repatriation in Principle, Policy and Practice,* edited by C. Fforde, J. Hubert, and P. Turnbull, 59–62. Routledge, London.

Service, R. W. 1907. The Cremation of Sam McGee. In *The Spell of the Yukon, and Other Verses,* 50–54. Barse and Hopkins, New York.

Shaul, D. L., and J. M. Andresen. 1989. A Case for Yuman Participation in the Hohokam Regional System. *Kiva* 54 (2): 105–26.

Shaul, D. L., and J. H. Hill. 1998. Tepimans, Yumans, and Other Hohokam. *American Antiquity* 63 (3): 375–96.

Sheets-Johnstone, M. 1979. *The Phenomenology of Dance.* 2nd ed. Dance Books, London.

Shennan, S. 1982. Ideology, Change and the European Bronze Age. In *Symbolic and Structural Archaeology,* edited by I. Hodder, 155–61. Cambridge University Press, Cambridge.

Shepherd, I., and A. Shepherd. 2001. A Cordoned Urn Burial with Faience from 102 Findhorn, Moray. *Proceedings of the Society of Antiquaries of Scotland* 131:101–28.

Sheridan, A. 1986. Megaliths and Megalomania: An Account, and Interpretation, of the Development of Passage Tombs in Ireland. *Journal of Irish Archaeology* 3:17–30.

———. 2004. Going Round in Circles? Understanding the Irish Grooved Ware Complex in Its Wider Context. In *From Megaliths to Metals: Essays in Honour of George Eogan*, edited by H. Roche, E. Grogan, J. Bradley, J. Coles, and B. Raftery, 26–37. Oxbow Books, Oxford, UK.

———. 2006. A Non-megalithic Funerary Tradition in Early Neolithic Ireland. In *The Modern Traveller to Our Past*, edited by M. Meek, 24–31. DPK Publishing, Newtownards, Northern Ireland.

———. 2010. The Neolithization of Britain and Ireland: The "Big Picture." In *Landscapes in Transition*, edited by B. Finlayson and G. Warren, 89–105. Oxbow Books, Oxford; Council for British Research in the Levant, London.

Sheridan, J. A., and M. Davis. 1998. The Welsh "Jet Set" in Prehistory: A Case of Keeping Up with the Joneses? In *Prehistoric Ritual and Religion*, edited by A. M. Gibson and D. D. A. Simpson, 148–62. Sutton, Stroud, UK.

———. 2002. Investigating Jet and Jet-like Artefacts from Prehistoric Scotland: The National Museums of Scotland Project. *Antiquity* 76:812–25.

Sherlock, S. J., and M. G. Welch. 1992. *An Anglo-Saxon Cemetery at Norton, Cleveland.* Council for British Archaeology Research Report 82. Council for British Archaeology, London.

Shipman, P., G. Foster, and M. Schoeninger. 1984. Burnt Bones and Teeth: An Experimental Study of Color, Morphology, Crystal Structure and Shrinkage. *Journal of Archaeological Science* 11 (4): 307–25.

Silliman, S. W. 2008. *Collaborating at the Trowel's Edge: Teaching and Learning in Indigenous Archaeology.* Amerind Studies in Archaeology. University of Arizona Press, Tucson.

Simon, M. L. 2000. Regional Variations in Plant Use Strategies in the Midwest During the Late Woodland. In *Late Woodland Societies: Tradition and Transformation Across the Midcontinent*, edited by T. E. Emerson, D. L. McElrath, and A. C. Fortier, 37–76. University of Nebraska Press, Lincoln.

Sims-Williams, P. 1983. The Settlement of England in Bede and the Chronicle. *Anglo-Saxon England* 12:1–41.

Skousen, B. 2012. Posts, Places, Ancestors and Worlds: Dividual Personhood in the American Bottom Region. *Southeastern Archaeology* 31:57–69.

Smith, M., and M. Brickley. 2009. *People of the Long Barrows: Life, Death and Burial in the Earlier Neolithic.* History Press, Stroud, UK.

Smyth, J. 2007. Neolithic Settlement in Ireland: New Theories and Approaches. Unpublished Ph.D. dissertation, University College Dublin, Dublin.

———. 2011. The House and Group Identity in the Irish Neolithic. *Proceedings of the Royal Irish Academy* 111C:1–31.

Sofaer Derevenski, J. 2002. Engendering Context: Context as Gendered Practice in the Early Bronze Age of the Upper Thames Valley, UK. *European Journal of Archaeology* 5 (2): 191–211.

Sonek, A. 1992. The Weight(s) of Cremated Remains. *Proceedings of the 44th Annual Meeting of the American Academy of Forensic Sciences.* New Orleans.

Sørensen, M. L. S. 1992. Gender Archaeology and Scandinavian Bronze Age Studies. *Norwegian Archaeological Review* 25:31–49.

———. 2010. Bronze Age Bodiness: Maps and Coordinates. In *Body Parts and Wholes: Changing Relations and Meanings,* edited by K. C. Rebay, M. L. S. Sørensen, and J. Hughes, 54–63. Oxbow Books, Oxford, UK.

Sørensen, M. L. S., and K. C. Rebay. 2008a. From Substantial Bodies to the Substance of Bodies: Analysis of the Transition from Inhumation to Cremation During the Middle Bronze Age in Europe. In *Past Bodies: Body-Centered Research in Archaeology,* edited by J. Robb and D. Borić, 59–68. Oxbow Books, Oxford, UK.

———. 2008b. Interpreting the Body: Burial Practices at the Middle Bronze Age Cemetery at Pitten, Austria. *Archaeologia Austriaca* 85:153–75.

Sørensen, T. F. 2009. The Presence of the Dead: Cemeteries, Cremation and the Staging of Non-place. *Journal of Social Archaeology* 9 (1): 110–35.

———. 2010a. An Archaeology of Movement: Materiality, Affects and Cemeteries in Prehistoric and Contemporary Odsherred, Denmark. Unpublished Ph.D. dissertation, Aarhus University, Aarhus.

———. 2010b. A Saturated Void: Anticipating and Preparing Presence in Contemporary Danish Cemetery Culture. In *An Anthropology of Absence: Materializations of Transcendence and Loss,* edited by M. Bille, F. Hastrup, and T. F. Sørensen, 115–30. Springer, New York.

———. 2011. Sweet Dreams: Biographical Blanks and the Commemoration of Children. *Mortality* 16 (2): 161–75.

———. 2012. Delusion and Disclosure: Human Disposal and the Aesthetics of Vagueness. In *Embodied Knowledge: Historical Perspectives on Technology and Belief,* edited by M. L. S. Sørensen and K. Rebay-Salisbury, 27–39. Oxbow Books, Oxford, UK.

———. Forthcoming. Meaningless Movements: A Critique of the Bronze Age Mobility Paradigm. In *Mobility of Culture in Bronze Age Europe: Proceedings of an International Conference and the Marie Curie ITN "Forging Identities" at Aarhus University, June 2012.* Edited by P. Suchowska-Ducke and H. Vandkilde. Archaeopress, Oxford, UK.

Sørensen, T. F., and M. Bille. 2008. Flames of Transformation: The Role of Fire in Cremation Practices. *World Archaeology* 40 (2): 253–67.

Spier, L. 1933. *Yuman Tribes of the Gila River.* Ethnological Series. University of Chicago Press, Chicago.

Stoodley, N. 1999. *The Spindle and the Spear: A Critical Enquiry into the Construction and Meaning of Gender in the Early Anglo-Saxon Burial Rite.* BAR British Series 288. British Archaeological Reports, Oxford.

———. 2005. Discussion: The Early Cemetery and Its Place Within Southern England. In *The Origins of Mid-Saxon Southampton: Excavations at the Friends Provident St. Mary's Stadium, 1998–2000,* by V. Birbeck, R. J. C. Smith, P. Andrews, and N. Stoodley, 75–81. Wessex Archaeology, Salisbury, UK.

Stothers, D. M., and S. K. Bechtel. 1987. Stable Carbon Isotope Analysis: An Interregional Perspective. *Archaeology of Eastern North America* 15:137–54.

Strathern, M. 1988. *The Gender of the Gift.* University of California Press, Berkeley.

Strezewski, M. 2003. Morton Mounds 14 and Mortuary Ceremonialism in the Central Illinois River Valley. *Midcontinental Journal of Archaeology* 28 (1): 7–31.

Struever, S., and G. L. Houart. 1972. An Analysis of the Hopewell Interaction Sphere. In *Social Change and Interaction,* edited by E. Wilmsen, 47–80. Anthropological Papers no. 46. Museum of Anthropology, University of Michigan, Ann Arbor.

Studenmund, S. 2000. Late Woodland Occupations in the Lower Illinois Valley: Research Questions and Data Sets. In *Late Woodland Societies: Tradition and Transformation Across the Midcontinent,* edited by T. E. Emerson, D. L. McElrath, and A. C. Fortier, 301–44. University of Nebraska Press, Lincoln.

Stuiver, M., P. J. Reimer, and R. Reimer. 2011. *Calib Manual.* Electronic document, http://calib.qub.ac.uk/calib/manual/. Accessed October 20, 2011.

Svanberg, F., and K. H. Wahlgren. 2007. *Publik arkeologi.* Nordic Academic Press and Statens Historiska Museum, Lund, Sweden.

Symes, S. A., C. W. Rainwater, E. N. Chapman, D. R. Gipson, and A. L. Piper. 2008. Patterned Thermal Destruction of Human Remains in a Forensic Setting. In *The Analysis of Burned Human Remains,* edited by C. W. Schmidt and S. A. Symes, 15–54. Academic Press, London.

Talalay, L. E. 2004. Heady Business: Skulls, Heads and Decapitation in Neolithic Anatolia and Greece. *Journal of Mediterranean Archaeology* 17:139–63.

Tarlow, S. 1999. *Bereavement and Commemoration: An Archaeology of Mortality.* Blackwell, Oxford, UK.

Teague, L. S. 1984. Role and Ritual in Hohokam Society. In *Archaeology Along the Salt-Gila Aqueduct, Central Arizona Project,* vol. 9, *Synthesis and Conclusions,* edited by L. S. Teague and P. L. Crown, 155–86. Arizona State Museum Archaeological Series. University of Arizona Press, Tucson.

Thomas, D. H. 2000. *Skull Wars: Kennewick Man, Archaeology, and the Battle for Native American Identity.* Basic Books, New York.

———. 2006. Finders Keepers and Deep American History. In *Imperialism, Art and Restitution*, edited by J. H. Merryman, 218–55. Cambridge University Press, Cambridge.

Thomas, Jo. 2008. *Monument, Memory, and Myth: Use and Re-use of Three Bronze Age Round Barrows at Cossington, Leicestershire*. Leicester Archaeology Monograph 14. University of Leicester Archaeological Services, Leicester.

Thomas, Ju. 2000. Death, Identity and the Body in Neolithic Britain. *Journal of the Royal Anthropological Institute* 6 (4): 653–68.

———. 2004. *Archaeology and Modernity*. Routledge, London.

Thompson, A. J., and K. A. Jakes. 2005. Textile Evidence for Ohio Hopewell Burial Practices. *Southeastern Archaeology* 24 (2): 137–41.

Thompson, T. J. U., M. Islam, K. Piduru, and A. Marcel. 2011. An Investigation into the Internal and External Variables Acting on Crystallinity Index Using Fourier Transform Infrared Spectroscopy on Unaltered and Burned Bone. *Palaeogeography, Palaeoclimatology, Palaeoecology* 299:168–74.

Thomsen, T. 1929. *Egekistefundet fra Egtved, fra den ældre Bronzealder*. Gyldendal, Copenhagen.

Thorpe, I. J. N. 2003. Anthropology, Archaeology and the Origin of Warfare. *World Archaeology* 35 (1): 145–65.

Thurman, M. D., and L. J. Willmore. 1981. A Replicative Cremation Experiment. *North American Archaeologist* 24:275–83.

Tieszen, L. T., and T. Fagre. 1993. Carbon Isotope Variability in Modern and Archaeological Maize. *Journal of Archaeological Science* 20:25–40.

Tilley, C. 2010. *Interpreting Landscapes: Geologies, Topographies, Identities*. Left Coast Press, Walnut Creek, CA.

Timby, J. 1993. Sancton I Anglo-Saxon Cemetery: Excavations Carried Out Between 1976 and 1980. *Archaeological Journal* 150:243–365.

Tomlinson, M., and M. Engelke. 2007. Meaning, Anthropology, Christianity. In *The Limits of Meaning: Case Studies in the Anthropology of Christianity*, edited by M. Engelke and M. Tomlinson, 1–37. Berghahn Books, Oxford, UK.

Tonkin, E. 1992. *Narrating Our Pasts: The Social Construction of Oral History*. Cambridge University Press, Cambridge.

Treherne, P. 1995. The Warrior's Beauty: The Masculine Body and Self-Identity in Bronze Age Europe. *Journal of European Archaeology* 3 (1): 105–44.

Trigger, B. G. 2006. *A History of Archaeological Thought*. Cambridge University Press, Cambridge.

Trotter, M., and B. B. Hixon. 1974. Sequential Changes in Weight, Density, and Percentage Ash Weight of Human Skeletons from an Early Fetal Period Through Old Age. *Anatomical Record* 179:1–18.

Tuck, J. A. 1971a. The Iroquois Confederacy. *Scientific American* 224 (2): 32–49.

————. 1971b. *Onandaga Prehistory: A Study in Settlement Archaeology.* Syracuse University Press, Syracuse.

Turner, V. W. 1972 [1964]. Betwixt and Between: The Liminal Period in Rites de Passage. In *Reader in Comparative Religion: An Anthropological Approach,* edited by W. A. Lessa and E. Z. Vogt, 338–47. 3rd ed. Harper and Row, New York.

Tyler, S., and H. Major. 2005. *The Early Anglo-Saxon Cemetery and Later Saxon Settlement at Springfield Lyons, Essex.* East Anglian Archaeology 111. Essex County Council, Chelmsford, UK.

Ubelaker, D. H. 1978. *Human Skeletal Remains: Excavations, Analysis, Interpretation.* 3rd ed. Manuals on Archaeology. Taraxacum, Smithsonian Institution, Washington, DC.

Ubelaker, D. H., and J. L. Rife. 2009. Skeletal Analysis and Mortuary Practice in an Early Roman Chamber Tomb at Kenchreai, Greece. *International Journal of Osteoarchaeology* 21 (1): 1–18.

Underhill, R. 1939. *Social Organization of the Papago Indian.* Columbia University Press, New York.

————. 1954. Intercultural Relations in the Greater Southwest. *American Anthropologist* 56 (4): 645–56.

Van Deest, T. L., T. A. Murad, and E. J. Bartelink. 2011. A Re-examination of Cremains Weight: Sex and Age Variation in a Northern California Sample. *Journal of Forensic Sciences* 56 (2): 344–48.

van Gennep, A. 1960. *The Rites of Passage.* Routledge and Kegan Paul, London.

Vansina, J. 1985. *Oral Tradition as History.* University of Wisconsin Press, Madison.

Van Vark, G. N. 1975. The Investigation of Human Cremated Skeletal Material by Multivariable Statistical Methods, II. Measures. *Ossa* 2:47–68.

Varela, F. J., E. Thompson, and E. Rosch. 1991. *The Embodied Mind.* MIT Press, Cambridge, MA.

Velarde, P. L. 1931. Padre Luis Velarde's Relacion of the Pimeria Alta, 1716. *New Mexico Historical Review* 6 (2): 111–57.

Verlinde, A. D. 1974. A Mesolithic Settlement with Cremation at Dalfsen. *Berichten van der Rijkdienst voor het Oudheidkundig Bodemonderzoek* 24:113–17.

Viklund, K., A. Olofsson, and T. Larsson (editors). 2011. *Archaeology of Indigenous Peoples in the North.* Umeå University, Umeå, Sweden.

Wahl, J. 2008. Investigations on Pre-Roman and Roman Cremation Remains from Southwestern Germany: Results, Potentialities and Limits. In *The Analysis of Burnt Human Remains,* edited by C. W. Schmidt and S. A. Symes, 145–61. Academic Press, London.

Wait, G. 1995. Burial and the Otherworld. In *The Celtic World,* edited by M. J. Green, 489–511. Routledge, London.

Walker, P. L., K. W. Miller, and R. Richman. 2008. Time, Temperature, and Oxygen Availability: An Experimental Study of the Effects of Environmental Conditions on the Color and Organic Content of Cremated Bone. In *The*

Analysis of Burnt Human Remains, edited by C. W. Schmidt and S. A. Symes, 129–35. Academic Press, London.

Walker, W. H. 2008. Practice and Nonhuman Social Actors: The Afterlife Histories of Witches and Dogs in the American Southwest. In *Memory Work: Archaeologies of Material Practices,* edited by B. J. Mills and W. H. Walker, 137–58. School for Advanced Research Press, Santa Fe, NM.

Wallace, H. D. (editor). 1995a. *Archaeological Investigations at Los Morteros, a Prehistoric Settlement in the Northern Tucson Basin, Part 1.* Center for Desert Archaeology, Tucson, AZ.

——— (editor). 1995b. *Archaeological Investigations at Los Morteros, a Prehistoric Settlement in the Northern Tucson Basin, Part 2.* Center for Desert Archaeology, Tucson, AZ.

Wallace, H. D., and W. Doelle. 2001. Classic Period Warfare in Southern Arizona. In *Deadly Landscapes: Case Studies in Prehistoric Southwestern Warfare,* edited by G. E. Rice and S. A. LeBlanc, 239–88. University of Utah Press, Salt Lake City.

Wallace, H. D., J. M. Heidke, and W. H. Doelle. 1995. Hohokam Origins. *Kiva* 60 (4): 575–618.

Wallis, R. J., and J. Blain. 2006. The Sanctity of Burial: Pagan Views, Ancient and Modern. Paper delivered at the conference Respect for Ancient British Human Remains: Philosophy and Practice, Manchester Museum, November 2006.

Warrick, G. A. 1988. Estimating Ontario Iroquoian Village Duration. *Man in the Northeast* 36:21–60.

Waterman, D. M. 1978. The Excavation of a Court Cairn at Tully, Co. Fermanagh. *Ulster Journal of Archaeology* 41:3–14.

Webb, W. S., and C. E. Snow. 1974 [1945]. *The Adena People.* University of Tennessee Press, Knoxville.

Weiner, A. 1992. *Inalienable Possessions: The Paradox of Keeping-While-Giving.* University of California Press, Berkeley.

Wells, C. 1978. Notes on Cremated Bones from Tully Court Cairn. *Ulster Journal of Archaeology* 41:13–14.

West, Stanley. 1988. *Westgarth Gardens Anglo-Saxon Cemetery, Suffolk: Catalogue.* East Anglian Archaeology 38. Suffolk County Planning Department, Bury St. Edmunds, UK.

Whitley, J. 2002. Too Many Ancestors. *Antiquity* 76:119–26.

Whittle, A. 2003. *The Archaeology of People: Dimensions of Neolithic Life.* Routledge, London.

Whittle, A., A. Barclay, A. Bayliss, R. Schulting, and M. Wysocki. 2007. Building for the Dead: Events, Processes and Changing Worldviews from the 38th to the 34th Centuries cal BC in Southern Britain. *Cambridge Archaeological Journal* 17:123–47.

Whittle, A., A. Bayliss, and F. Healy. 2011. Gathering Time: The Social Dynamics of Change. In *Gathering Time: Dating the Early Neolithic Enclosures of Southern Britain and Ireland*, edited by A. Whittle, F. Healy, and A. Bayliss, 848–914. Oxbow Books, Oxford, UK.

Whittle, A., and V. Cummings. 2007. *The Mesolithic-Neolithic Transition in North-West Europe*. Oxford University Press/British Academy, Oxford.

Wickholm, A. 2008. Reuse in the Finnish Cremation Cemeteries Under Level Ground: Examples of Collective Memory. In *Materiality of Death: Bodies, Burials, Beliefs*, edited by F. Fahlander and T. Oestigaard, 89–97. BAR International Series 1768. British Archaeological Reports, Oxford.

Wickholm, A., and S. Raninen. 2006. The Broken People: Deconstruction of Personhood in Iron Age Finland. *Estonian Journal of Archaeology* 10 (2): 150–66.

Wiessner, P., and A. Tumu. 1998. *Historical Vines: Enga Networks of Exchange, Ritual, and Warfare in Papua New Guinea*. Smithsonian Institution Press, Washington, DC.

Wilcox, D. R., T. R. McGuire, and C. Sternberg. 1981. *Snaketown Revisited: A Partial Cultural Resource Survey, Analysis of Site Structure and an Ethnohistoric Study of the Proposed Hohokam-Pima National Monument*. Arizona State Museum Archaeological Series. Arizona State Museum, University of Arizona, Tucson.

Wilcox, M. V. 2009. *The Pueblo Revolt and the Mythology of Conquest: An Indigenous Archaeology of Contact*. University of California Press, Berkeley.

Wilkins, B. 2008. N6 Galway to Ballinasloe Scheme, Contract 2: Final Report on Archaeological Investigations at Site E2437, a Bronze Age Cremation Pyre and Burnt Mound in the Townland of Newford, Co. Galway. Unpublished report, Headland Archaeology, UK.

Willey, P., and D. D. Scott. 1999. Clinkers on the Little Bighorn Battlefield: In Situ Investigations of Scattered Recent Cremains. In *Forensic Osteological Analysis: A Book of Case Studies*, edited by S. I. Fairgrieve, 129–40. Charles C. Thomas, Springfield, IL.

Williams, H. 1997. Ancient Landscapes and the Dead: The Reuse of Prehistoric and Roman Monuments as Early Anglo-Saxon Burial Sites. *Medieval Archaeology* 41:1–31.

———. 1999a. Identities and Cemeteries in Roman and Early Medieval Archaeology. In *TRAC 98 Proceedings of the Eighth Annual Theoretical Roman Archaeology Conference*, edited by P. Baker, C. Forcey, S. Jundi, and R. Witcher, 96–108. Oxbow Books, Oxford, UK.

———. 1999b. Placing the Dead: Investigating the Location of Wealthy Barrow Burials in Seventh Century England. In *Grave Matters: Eight Studies of Burial Data from the First Millennium AD from Crimea, Scandinavia and England*, edited by M. Rundkvist, 57–86. BAR International Series 781. British Archaeological Reports, Oxford.

———. 2000. "The Burnt Germans of the Age of Iron": An Analysis of Early Anglo-Saxon Cremation Practices. Unpublished Ph.D. dissertation, University of Reading, Reading.

———. 2001. An Ideology of Transformation: Cremation Rites and Animal Sacrifice in Early Anglo-Saxon England. In *The Archaeology of Shamanism*, edited by N. Price, 193–212. Routledge, London.

———. 2002a. "The Remains of Pagan Saxondom"? Studying Anglo-Saxon Cremation Practices. In *Burial in Early Medieval England and Wales*, edited by S. Lucy and A. Reynolds, 47–71. Society of Medieval Archaeology Monograph Series 17. Maney, Leeds, UK.

———. 2002b. Cemeteries as Central Places: Landscape and Identity in Early Anglo-Saxon England. In *Central Places in the Migration and Merovingian Periods: Papers from the 52nd Sachsensymposium*, edited by B. Hårdh and L. Larsson, 341–62. Almqvist, Lund, Sweden.

———. 2003a. Material Culture as Memory: Combs and Cremation in Early Medieval Britain. *Early Medieval Europe* 12 (2): 89–128.

———. 2003b. Remembering and Forgetting the Dead: Exploring Death, Memory and Material Culture in Monastic Archaeology. In *Archaeologies of Remembrance: Death and Memory in Past Societies*, edited by H. Williams, 227–54. Plenum, London.

———. 2004a. Ephemeral Monuments and Social Memory in Early Roman Britain. In *TRAC 2003: Proceedings of the Thirteenth Annual Theoretical Roman Archaeology Conference*, edited by B. Croxford, H. Eckardt, J. Meade, and J. Weekes, 51–61. Oxbow Books, Oxford, UK.

———. 2004b. Potted Histories—Cremation, Ceramics and Social Memory in Early Roman Britain. *Oxford Journal of Archaeology* 23 (4): 417–27.

———. 2004c. Assembling the Dead. In *Assembly Places and Practices in Medieval Europe*, edited by A. Pantos and S. Semple, 109–34. Four Courts Press, Dublin.

———. 2004d. Death Warmed Up: The Agency of Bodies and Bones in Early Anglo-Saxon Cremation Rites. *Journal of Material Culture* 9 (3): 263–91.

———. 2005a. Keeping the Dead at Arm's Length: Memory, Weaponry and Early Medieval Mortuary Technologies. *Journal of Social Archaeology* 5 (2): 253–75.

———. 2005b. Animals, Ashes and Ancestors. In *Beyond Skin and Bones? New Perspectives on Human-Animal Relations in the Historical Past*, edited by A. Pluskowski, 19–40. BAR International Series 1410. British Archaeological Reports, Oxford.

———. 2006a. *Death and Memory in Early Medieval Britain*. Cambridge University Press, Cambridge.

———. 2006b. Heathen Graves and Victorian Anglo-Saxonism: Assessing the Archaeology of John Mitchell Kemble. In *Anglo-Saxon Studies in Archaeology and History 13*, edited by S. Semple, 1–18. Oxford University School of Archaeology, Oxford.

———. 2007a. Transforming Body and Soul: Toilet Implements in Early Anglo-Saxon Graves. In *Early Medieval Mortuary Practices: Anglo-Saxon Studies in Archaeology and History 14*, edited by S. Semple and H. Williams, 66–91. Oxford University School of Archaeology, Oxford.

———. 2007b. The Emotive Force of Early Medieval Mortuary Practices. *Archaeological Review from Cambridge* 22 (1): 107–23.

———. 2008a. Towards an Archaeology of Cremation. In *The Analysis of Burned Human Remains*, edited by C. W. Schmidt and S. Symes, 239–69. Elsevier, London.

———. 2008b. Anglo-Saxonism and Victorian Archaeology: William Wylie's Fairford Graves. *Early Medieval Europe* 16 (1): 49–88.

———. 2009. On Display: Envisioning the Early Anglo-Saxon Dead. In *Mortuary Practices and Social Identities in the Middle Ages: Essays in Burial Archaeology in Honour of Heinrich Härke*, edited by D. Sayer and H. Williams, 170–206. University of Exeter Press, Exeter.

———. 2010. At the Funeral. In *Signals of Belief in Early England: Anglo-Saxon Paganism Revisited*, edited by M. Carver, A. Sanmark, and S. Semple, 67–83. Oxbow Books, Oxford, UK.

———. 2011a. Mortuary Practices in Early Anglo-Saxon England. In *The Oxford Handbook of Anglo-Saxon Archaeology*, edited by H. Hamerow, D. Hinton, and S. Crawford, 238–59. Oxford University Press, Oxford.

———. 2011b. The Sense of Being Seen: Ocular Effects at Sutton Hoo. *Journal of Social Archaeology* 11 (1): 99–121.

———. 2011c. Ashes to Asses: An Archaeological Perspective on Death and Donkeys. *Journal of Material Culture* 16 (2): 219–39.

———. 2011d. Cremation and Present Pasts: A Contemporary Archaeology of Swedish Memory Groves. *Mortality* 16 (2): 113–30.

———. 2013. Death, Memory and Material Culture: Catalytic Commemoration and the Cremated Dead. In *The Oxford Handbook of the Archaeology of Death and Burial*, edited by L. Nilsson Stutz and S. Tarlow, 195–208. Oxford University Press, Oxford.

Woodward, A. 2002. Beads and Beakers: Heirlooms and Relics in the British Early Bronze Age. *Antiquity* 76:1040–47.

Woodward, J. A. 1968. The Anniversary: A Contemporary Diegueño Complex. *Ethnology* 7 (1): 86–94.

Wylie, A. 1985. The Reaction Against Analogy. In *Advances in Archaeological Method and Theory*, vol. 8, edited by M. B. Schiffer, 63–111. Academic Press, New York.

Yarrow, H. C. 1880. *Introduction to the Study of Mortuary Customs Among the North American Indians*. Contributions to North American Ethnology, Smithsonian Institution. U.S. Government Printing Office, Washington, DC.

Yates, D. 2007. *Land, Power and Prestige: Bronze Age Field Systems in Southern England*. Oxbow Books, Oxford, UK.

Zachrisson, I. 2002. "Den samiska samlingen" på statens historiska museum. *Douddaris* 20:83–85.

———. 2004. Archaeology and Ethics: The South Sámi Example. In *Swedish Archaeologists on Ethics*, edited by H. Karlsson, 117–34. Bricoleur Press, Lindome, Sweden.

Zvelebil, M. 2008. Innovating Hunter-Gatherers: The Mesolithic in the Baltic. In *Mesolithic Europe,* edited by G. Bailey and P. Spikins, 18–59. Cambridge University Press, Cambridge.

Joanna Brück, Ph.D. (University of Cambridge), is a reader in archaeology in the Department of Archaeology and Anthropology, University of Bristol, UK. Her primary area of research is the archaeology of the British Bronze Age. She is particularly interested in the treatment of the human body and concepts of the self, depositional practices, and the relationship between space and society.

Jessica I. Cerezo-Román, Ph.D. (University of Arizona), is a visiting scholar at the School of Anthropology, University of Arizona, and a Forensic Anthropology Postdoctoral Fellow at the Pima County Office of the Medical Examiner—Forensic Science Center, Tucson, Arizona, USA. Her research focuses on bioarchaeology, forensic anthropology, and mortuary practice.

Della Collins Cook, Ph.D. (University of Chicago), is a professor of anthropology at Indiana University, Bloomington, Indiana, USA. Her primary area of research is human osteology, paleopathology, and mortuary practices in the Americas and the Aegean.

Gabriel Cooney, Ph.D. (National University of Ireland), is the Professor of Celtic Archaeology at the School of Archaeology, University College Dublin, Ireland. His research interests focus on Ireland in its wider European context and include early farming societies, the use of stone (object and monument), and mortuary practices in prehistory.

Lynne Goldstein, Ph.D. (Northwestern University), is a professor of anthropology at Michigan State University, East Lansing, USA. Her interests include mortuary analysis, landscape use and change, and public archaeology. Most of her research has been focused in the United States on late prehistoric cultures of the Eastern Woodlands and nineteenth-century historic archaeology.

Ian Kuijt, Ph.D. (Harvard University), is a professor of anthropology and director of graduate studies at the University of Notre Dame, Notre Dame, Indiana, USA. His interests include mortuary analysis, the forager-farmer transition, and the ancient Near East. His most recent research focuses on post-1800s archaeology and history along coastal western Ireland.

Åsa M. Larsson, Ph.D. (Uppsala University), is the managing director of SAU (Societas Archaeologica Upsaliensis), a foundation carrying out surveys, rescue excavations, and osteological analyses in Sweden. She is an archaeologist and osteoarchaeologist. Her published Ph.D. dissertation (2009) is entitled *Breaking and Making Bodies and Pots: Material and Ritual Practices in Sweden in the Third Millennium BC.*

Katy Meyers is a Ph.D. candidate in the Department of Anthropology at Michigan State University, East Lansing, USA. Her research interests focus on mortuary archaeology, bioarchaeology, digital archaeology, and public archaeology. Her current research focuses on the examination of co-occurrence of cremation and inhumation in Anglo-Saxon England using GIS.

Liv Nilsson Stutz, Ph.D. (Lund University), is a senior lecturer in the Department of Anthropology, Emory University, Atlanta, Georgia, USA. She is an archaeologist and biological anthropologist interested in implementing social theory in archaeology, focused on burial archaeology. Her published Ph.D. dissertation (2004) is entitled *Embodied Rituals and Ritualized Bodies: Tracing Ritual Practice in Late Mesolithic Burials.*

Colin P. Quinn is a Ph.D. candidate at the Museum of Anthropology, University of Michigan, Ann Arbor, USA. His research interests include increasing social complexity and material culture use in a global perspective. His current research focuses on monitoring long-term dynamics in the articulation of mortuary practices, settlement patterns, and metal procurement in Bronze Age Transylvania.

Mark R. Schurr, Ph.D. (Indiana University), is a professor in the Department of Anthropology, University of Notre Dame, Notre Dame, Indiana, USA. He is editor of the *Midcontinental Journal of Archaeology*, and his research focuses on the archaeology of eastern North America. His work creatively blends isotopic analysis and archaeology, and he directs the Fluoride Dating Service Center.

Tim Flohr Sørensen, Ph.D. (Aarhus University), is an assistant professor at the SAXO Institute, University of Copenhagen, Denmark. He was an assistant professor at Aarhus University, 2012–2014, and a Marie Curie Fellow (postdoctoral researcher) at the McDonald Institute for Archaeological Research, University of Cambridge, 2010–2012. He is an archaeologist, interested in materiality, affect, space, and movement with reference to mortuary practice in the past and present.

David Hurst Thomas, Ph.D. (University of California–Davis), is the curator of North American archaeology at the American Museum of Natural History, New York, New York, USA, and a professor at the Richard Gilder Graduate School. His research includes redefining the relationship between Native American and anthropological communities, as explored in the book *Skull Wars*. He has directed a large number of projects, including a long-term project on St. Catherine's Island, Georgia.

Howard Williams, Ph.D. (University of Reading), is the Professor of Archaeology in the Department of History and Archaeology, University of Chester, Chester, UK. His research interests focus on death, burial, and commemoration, with special reference to the early Middle Ages. He is honorary editor of the *Archaeological Journal*. His book *Death and Memory in Early Medieval Britain* (2006) was published by Cambridge University Press.

Amerind Studies in Anthropology

Series Editor JOHN WARE